W9-CUH-418

PETERSON'S 1999

SCHOLARSHIPS FOR STUDY IN THE USA & CANADA

THE MONEY YOU NEED FOR THE EDUCATION YOU WANT

Peterson's
Princeton, New Jersey

2ND EDITION

About Peterson's

Peterson's is the country's largest educational information/communications company, providing the academic, consumer, and professional communities with books, software, and online services in support of lifelong education access and career choice. Well-known references include Peterson's annual guides to private schools, summer programs, colleges and universities, graduate and professional programs, financial aid, international study, adult learning, and career guidance. Peterson's Web site at petersons.com is the only comprehensive—and most heavily traveled—education resource on the Internet. The site carries all of Peterson's fully searchable major databases and includes financial aid sources, test-prep help, job postings, direct inquiry and application features, and specially created Virtual Campuses for every accredited academic institution and summer program in the U.S. and Canada that offers in-depth narratives, announcements, and multimedia features.

Visit Peterson's on the Internet (World Wide Web) at www.petersons.com

Editorial inquiries concerning this book should be addressed to: Editor, Peterson's, P.O. Box 2123, Princeton, New Jersey 08543-2123, U.S.A.

Copyright © 1998 by Peterson's

Previous edition © 1997

ISSN 1099-1972

ISBN 0-7689-0142-1

Composition and design by Peterson's

Printed in the United States of America

10   9   8   7   6   5   4   3   2   1

CONTENTS

▲

INTRODUCTION

▲

In the U.S. and Canada, foundations, fraternal and ethnic organizations, corporations and industry organizations, community service organizations, veterans groups, churches, and other religious groups have organized programs to provide money to students to help pay for tuition and fees and, sometimes, other college-related expenses. Most of these programs are restricted to U.S. or Canadian citizens. However, a number of these programs are either open to international students or specifically organized for the benefit of international students. *Peterson's Scholarships for Study in the USA & Canada* is compiled with the hope that it will introduce to the student who hopes to attend an American or Canadian college or university opportunities to support their studies that otherwise might be overlooked.

Essential Information for International Students on Financing an Education in the U.S., by Janet Irons, Associate Director of Financial Aid at Harvard and Radcliffe Colleges in Cambridge, Massachusetts, provides basic advice and information for the international student on how to estimate and meet the costs of an American education. The Fulbright Scholarship Program provides basic information about the international students' program within this largest U.S. government international student aid program. What International Students Need to Know About Loans in Financing an American Education, by Dwight Peterson, President of the International Education Finance Corporation, reviews the options available to students who need to supplement the money from their own

or scholarship sources. Scholarship Frauds: Advice for International Students, by Mark Kantrowitz, President of *FinAid: The Financial Information Page*, provides advice and tips for international students about fraudulent operations in the scholarship world. A Glossary of Special Terminology explains terms that may be unfamiliar to international students.

The largest section of *Peterson's Scholarships for Study in the USA & Canada* is a listing that provides complete profiles of 552 award programs, scholarships, fellowships, grants, prizes, and other gift aid, worth in aggregate more than $80 million, that are specifically available to individual international students. This listing is broken down into two sections: Undergraduate Awards and Graduate Awards.

Twenty-four indexes, twelve for undergraduate awards and twelve for graduate awards, conclude the book and include an Award Name Index, an Index to Academic/Career Areas, an Association Affiliation Index, a Corporate Affiliation Index, an Impairment Index, a Military Service Index, a National or Ethnic Background Index, a Religious Affiliation Index, a State of Residence Index, and a Talent Index.

HOW TO USE THIS GUIDE

The 552 scholarships described in this book are organized into ten broad categories that represent the major factors used to determine eligibility for scholarship awards and prizes. To find a basic list of scholarships available to you, look under the broad category or categories that fit your particular academic goals, skills, personal characteristics, or background. The ten categories are:

- Academic/Career Areas
- Association Affiliation
- Corporate Affiliation
- Employment Experience
- Impairment
- Military Service
- National or Ethnic Background
- Religious Affiliation
- State of Residence
- Talent

The Academic/Career Areas category is subdivided into individual subject areas that are organized alphabetically.

Full descriptive profiles of scholarship awards are sequentially numbered from 1 through 592. Although there are 552 awards profiled, about forty are open to both undergraduate and graduate students and have full profiles in both the undergraduate and the graduate sections; therefore, there are 592 full profiles. This number appears with a bullet in front of it in the upper right-hand corner of the profile. These profiles are broken down into two main sections, Undergraduate Awards and Graduate Awards. The Undergraduate Awards section profiles those awards that are available to undergraduate students. The Graduate Awards section profiles those awards that are available to graduate students. Each section is broken down into three categories: Academic/Career Areas, Nonacademic/Noncareer Criteria, and Miscellaneous Criteria. If an award is open to both undergraduate and graduate students, the award is profiled in both sections. You will find that most awards have more than one criterion that needs to be met before a student can be eligible. Cross-references by name and sequential

number within each section are made to the main description from locations under the other relevant categories where the award might also be listed. The full description appears in the first relevant location, cross-references in the later ones.

Because your major academic field of study and/or career goal has central importance in college planning, we give this factor precedence over others. This means that the Academic/Career Areas category appears first in each section, followed by the Nonacademic/Noncareer and Miscellaneous Criteria categories, and that if an academic major or career goal is a criterion for an award, the description of this award will appear within this category rather than in the later sections under other criteria. Within the appropriate categories, descriptive profiles are organized alphabetically by the name of the sponsoring organization. If more than one scholarship from the same organization appears in a particular section, the awards are then listed alphabetically by the name of the award under the name of the sponsor.

USING THE PRINTED INDEXES

The A-to-Z indexes are designed to aid your search. The indexes are also broken down into two sections: Undergraduate Indexes and Graduate Indexes. There are twelve indexes for each section. For each set of twelve indexes, two indexes are name indexes and ten indexes supply access by eligibility criteria. The indexes give you the sequence number of the descriptions of relevant awards. Except in the Sponsor Index, if an award is open to both undergraduate and graduate students, that award reference has an indication of the level of study to which the award is applicable: (G/UG) means that the award can be used at either the undergraduate or the graduate level of study.

These are the indexes:

Name Indexes
—Award Name Index
—Sponsor Index

Indexes to Eligibility Criteria
—Academic/Career Areas Index
—Association Affiliation Index
—Corporate Affiliation Index
—Employment Experience Index
—Impairment Index
—Military Service Index
—National or Ethnic Background Index
—Religious Affiliation Index
—State of Residence Index
—Talent Index

HOW THE DESCRIPTIVE PROFILES ARE ORGANIZED

Here are the elements of a full descriptive profile:

I. Name of Sponsoring Organization
This appears alphabetically under the appropriate category. In most instances acronyms are given as full names. However, occasionally a sponsor will refer to itself throughout the material that it publishes by acronym, and in deference to this seeming preference, we present its name as an acronym.

II. Award Name and Sequence Number

III. Brief Textual Description of the Award

IV. Academic/Career Areas (only in the Academic/Career Areas categories of the book)
This is a list of all academic or career subject terms that are assigned to this award.

V. Award Descriptors
Is it a scholarship? A prize for winning a competition? A loan? An internship? What years of college can it be used for? Is it renewable or is it for only one year?

VI. Eligibility Requirements

VII. Application Requirements
What do you need to supply in order to be considered? What are the deadlines?

VIII. E-mail Address

IX. Telephone and Fax Numbers
Some sponsors prefer that the first contact with applicants be by mail and have requested that their telephone numbers not be published. Peterson's honors this request. Most scholarship sponsors are willing to provide their telephone numbers to serious applicants after an initial screening.

X. World Wide Web Address

XI. Contact Name and Address

ESSENTIAL INFORMATION FOR INTERNATIONAL STUDENTS ON FINANCING AN EDUCATION IN THE U.S.

▲

by Janet Irons, Associate Director of Financial Aid, Harvard and Radcliffe Colleges

INTRODUCTION

According to the Institute of International Education, which annually compiles data on international educational exchange, more than 221,000 international students were studying toward undergraduate degrees in the United States in 1994–95. Their data also indicate that for a very large portion of those students (81 percent) most of the cost of that education was borne by the students and their families, with only a small amount of funding available from other sources. Only 7 percent of students receive funding from their U.S. colleges, about 5 percent from their home governments, and only about 5 percent from private sponsors or organizations.*

If you are considering pursuing your education in the U.S., you need to plan ahead, armed with the knowledge that nonfamily resources are few, but well informed enough to make your best attempt to obtain those limited resources that may be available. You will want to give careful thought to these critical questions:

- How much will an education in the U.S. really cost me?
- How much can my family realistically afford to help me?
- How can I apply for assistance from other sources?

By searching out the necessary information and pondering these issues with your family, relatives, friends, and other advisers, you will be able to make a well-informed decision about the affordability of an education in the U.S.

Do Your Background Research

You first must ask yourself some basic questions about the kind of education you wish to receive and the kind of college or university you are looking for. Costs for an average year of college in the U.S. range from about $8000 to $18,000, but many selective colleges can cost up to $30,000 or more a year. Using college guidebooks such as this one and other sources of information, you can explore all the various college options and select a realistic group of colleges to meet your educational needs and to which you might apply.

Gather as much information as you can about U.S. colleges and costs in general from all available sources. Some likely possibilities are your school's college adviser, headmaster, or

---

*Open Doors 1994/95: Report on International Educational Exchange, 1995. Todd M. Davis, ed. New York: Institute of International Education, pp. 2, 105.

librarian; the U.S. Embassy, U.S. Information Agency, Fulbright Commission, or Peace Corps office in your country; philanthropic organizations such as the Soros Foundation; publications of the colleges themselves; friends or relatives who already have children studying in the U.S.; and the World Wide Web. A good general Web site is www.finaid.org, which has a subsection on aid to international students, including a listing of U.S. colleges that offer significant aid to international students, a brief bibliography of useful books, and links to other possible sites of interest to you. Many colleges also have their own Web sites with information, including application forms, equivalent to what you would receive from them by mail. This guide is an excellent source for gathering information about financial aid that can be obtained from organizations that desire to help international students pay their college expenses.

Make a chart for yourself that has the names of all your possible college choices across the top and then rows for estimated expenses and resources below each college. After reading through the following pages and doing your background research, you will be able to analyze in a quantifiable way the financial differences among the various colleges and start to make decisions about where you will apply.

Estimating the Real Costs

Some of these expense items will be readily found in the literature provided by each college, but some others you may need to research further on your own. In many cases, you may want to use a range of figures (e.g., under room and board you might decide your cost at a certain college might range from $4000 if you share living accommodations with others to $7000 if you decide to live in a single room on campus and pay for a boarding plan).

Tuition and Fees: These figures should be clearly stated in the college's literature. These tend to be inflexible charges, not allowing much room for cost saving on your part.

Room and Board: Do you have an option for on- or off-campus housing and/or meals? Will one be clearly less expensive than the other? On the one hand, if you are off campus, you may need to pay for utilities such as electricity or heat in addition to rent and may have additional transportation costs to campus. You may also need to pay a security deposit on your apartment before you arrive that the landlord will hold until you leave the apartment in good condition at the end of the year. You may also miss out on much of the collegiate atmosphere if

> **TIP:** *Once you get to college, if you keep careful records of your actual expenditures, you can use that information for better future-year planning. If possible, talk to current international students in the U.S. and get figures for what they really spend on college.*

most students live in the dorms and you are off campus. On the other hand, if you can share an apartment with several other students and prepare your own meals together, you may well be able to realize significant cost savings over a standard room and board contract on campus.

Health insurance: Is this cost included in your tuition or is it an additional charge?

Deposit: If you accept an offer of admission, you must usually pay a deposit of several hundred dollars to hold your place at the college. This amount is not normally in addition to the charges above but, because it usually must be paid well before you arrive on campus, it is something for which you must prepare. Some colleges will waive the deposit fee for very needy or international students.

In addition to these standard "billed" expenses, you should expect to incur additional "unbilled" expenses associated with your college education. This is the area where you have more control over your spending, but you must plan ahead for at least modest amounts in each category.

Books and supplies: Depending on how many courses you take, whether you can purchase used books once you arrive, and whether you can share books with a roommate or use reserve books at the library, your book costs may vary widely. However, don't be surprised if you end up spending $700 or more per year for your books and school supplies.

Other personal expenses: Items like shampoo, medical supplies, late-night pizza or other snack foods, telephone bills, and entertainment all add up very quickly. Once you've finished constructing your budget at the end of this section, you can decide how much you realistically should limit yourself to in this area.

Local transportation: If you are commuting from off campus, be sure to factor in the cost of your transportation. Even if you are on campus, you may need to use the local bus or subway occasionally.

Living expenses during vacations and other times when classes are not in session: Will you be able to stay on campus at little or no cost? Can you stay with friends or relatives nearby? Do you plan to return to your home country? Depending on your choices here, your expenses could vary widely.

Start-up costs: During your first year at college, you may have some additional one-time expenses that you need to plan for. For example, if you are from a warm climate and are attending college in New England, you will need to purchase a good winter coat, boots, mittens, and sweaters. You may need to buy or rent linens (sheets, blankets, towels). Your room, whether on or off campus, may need some additional furnishings such as curtains, posters for the walls, a rug, or a sofa. This last area can be handled any way from total denial to total luxury, so your costs in this area are completely up to you.

Computer: Will you need to purchase a personal computer in order to do your course work on a par with other students? Or will the university facilities and sharing with roommates be all you need? If you need to make such a purchase, additional funding of at least $1000 to $4000, depending on your choices, will need to be found.

Taxation of scholarships: Current U.S. tax law mandates that students' scholarships over the amount of tuition, fees, and supplies be considered as taxable income. For international students, colleges are required to withhold from the student's scholarship the amount estimated as the tax liability (approximately 14 percent of the excess scholarship above the amount of tuition, fees, and supplies). Thus, for some students, less than the full amount of scholarship aid will be available to pay the college bill, although in most cases the IRS will refund the amount in the spring if your actual liability is less than what was withheld. The international adviser at your college will be able to give you more details about this regulation, but you should at least be aware of that possibility in advance if you do obtain a large scholarship.

Payment options: Some colleges will require payment for the whole year's or whole semester's charges at once or will charge a fee for monthly or quarterly or extended payment plans, so you may need to factor in some financing charges.

> **TIP:** *For all of these family resources, be sure that the figures you end up with are realistic and not wild guesses or wishful thinking. If admitted to a college, you and your sponsors will need to file affidavits of support, so don't promise any funding that you cannot reasonably provide.*

If you add up all of the above expenses, as well as any other costs or charges you find mentioned in your research, you can determine a fairly realistic assessment of costs for each college.

Estimating Family Resources

Since your family is likely to be the primary source of funding for college, you should sit down for a family meeting and have a frank discussion of how much will be available to help you. If you are planning on a four-year degree, you should plan ahead realistically for four years of college costs, using your estimates for the first year above, but increasing the cost by a modest percentage (perhaps 4 to 7 percent) per year to account for the inevitable inflation factor. If you will be applying for financial aid, first gathering all the financial data about the family will help you with these discussions and in completing the necessary aid application forms.

Here are some possible family resources for you to think about as potential ways to finance your education:

Parent income: If your parents will be providing you with some financial assistance, it may be helpful for them to write down a monthly or yearly cash flow statement to analyze what amount of their income might be available. By first listing all their sources of income (wages, business profits, rent from properties, interest or dividend earnings) and then listing all their expenses (rent or mortgage, groceries, utilities, car or other transportation expenses, medical costs, schooling for other family members, clothing and other household expenses, etc.), they will have a solid idea of their net monthly or annual cash surplus (or deficit) and thus, how much might be available to help pay your college costs.

Parent financing: If your parents have only a small amount per month they feel they can afford, they may be able to leverage that amount into a larger contribution for you by using a loan that will be paid back over several years. If such loans are not available in your country, they may be available in some cases through a U.S. financing source.

Parent assets: Do they have cash, stocks, rental properties, farmland, or other assets that might be partially available to you?

Your own assets: Do you have any savings or other assets that could be used for college costs?

> **TIP:** *If you are willing to work a few extra hours during holidays and vacation periods (when other student workers may have left), you can often earn some additional money.*

Other relatives' contributions: Are there any other family members who would be willing to give or lend you some funding for college?

Student work: In most cases you will have an opportunity (and in fact an expectation) of a student job to help cover some of your costs at college. To estimate how much you are likely to earn at a specific college, take the average job pay at that college multiplied by the hours per week you expect to work to find your likely net weekly paycheck. (Depending on the kind of tax treaty your country has with the U.S., you may have a small amount of taxes withheld from your wages so your net paycheck may be slightly less than that full amount). Multiply that figure by the number of weeks in your academic year to obtain your best estimate of total earnings. For example, if you will earn $6 per hour and work 12 hours per week, your weekly paycheck will be about $72. If the school year is thirty-two weeks long, you can expect to earn about $2300 during the year. Remember that you will most likely be on an F-1 (student) or J-1 (exchange visitor) visa and will have some limitations on the number of hours you may work each week and must normally work only in on-campus jobs. You will receive more information about these technical visa issues from the college you will be attending.

Aid from Colleges and Universities

The amount of aid available from U.S. colleges and universities varies from zero at some institutions to several million dollars at others. The cold, hard reality is that most colleges do not have enough financial aid to meet the needs of all their students, even if they only give aid to U.S. citizens. In most cases, the aid available to international students will be quite limited or nonexistent. Here is the area where it will pay for you to do a bit of research into the aid policies of the schools you are considering. Some questions to research for each college:

- *Is the admissions process need blind?* At most colleges, if you don't need financial aid, your chances for admission may be improved. However, if you really will need aid in order to attend, you should apply for it. At colleges that are need blind, aid and nonaid applicants are considered on an equal basis for admission.

- *Is there merit- as well as need-based aid?* Many colleges have special academic, athletic, music, or other merit-based scholarships for which you may qualify. Read the literature from the college carefully to find out if non-U.S. citizens may apply for this aid.

- *If aid is offered, will it meet my full need?* Since there is not enough aid to go around to all students, many colleges will leave a "gap" in the aid award that must be filled by the family or student.

- *What are the renewal policies for aid?* Do you need to maintain a certain grade point average or other qualification to keep the aid after the first year?

- *Is there a possibility if I am denied aid the first year that some aid would be available in subsequent years?* If this is the case, perhaps your family can struggle to pay for the first year.

How to Apply for College and University Aid

Check for the requirements of each individual college to which you are applying, but in general you can expect that some combination of the following forms will be needed:

College Scholarship Service Foreign Student Financial Statement: Since colleges that give out need-based aid want to make an accurate assessment of your family's relative financial strength, this form asks for information about family income, taxes paid, assets, debts owed, size of family, living expenses, and other available resources.

Institutional aid application: Some colleges will use their own form in lieu of or in addition to the CSS form. If you are also applying for merit-based aid, this application may ask you questions about your planned area of study, special talents, or other academic credentials.

Documentation: You may be asked to provide a photocopy of your family's most recent tax

> **TIP:** *If your family resources are very modest, such that the cost of the admission application will be a financial hardship for you, many colleges will waive that fee upon request.*

return or other financial accounting as used by your country's government. If tax forms are not used in your country, statements from a bank or employer may be required. You should provide English translations of any forms that are in other languages.

Affidavits of support: As mentioned above, you may be asked to provide proof of the availability of support from family, relatives, or sponsors. Some colleges ask for this as part of the admission or aid application process, while others will need it before issuing the I-20 form to allow you to obtain an entry visa into the U.S.

Be honest and thorough on your aid application forms. As best you can, think about what an American needs to understand about your family's finances and your country's financial situation to arrive at a reasonable assessment of your ability to afford college costs. Explain any pertinent cultural differences. For example, if your family is obligated to provide support for 10 other relatives in a neighboring village who are not listed on your aid application, give an estimate of the amount of support provided. If your family has formal or informal debts to other people, list the amounts and reasons for the debt. If the taxation rate is unusually high in your country, be sure to mention that fact. If inflation or currency devaluations are threatening the stability of your local economy and family income, include that information as well. Don't write more than a page or two, but this kind of useful detail can help the aid officer have a better understanding of your individual situation.

Aid from Other Sources

About 10 percent of international undergraduates receive some aid from their home government or a private sponsor. It is worth your time to do a bit of investigation to see what might be available to you locally. Some governments and corporations offer competitive scholarships for undergraduate study in the U.S. but may require you to work for them after graduation for several years in return for that sponsorship.

Peterson's Scholarships for Study in the USA & Canada is a complete resource to the more than 550 award programs, scholarships, fellowships, grants, prizes, and other gift aid from noninstitutional sources that are specifically available to international students. Scholarship money can help a great deal in financing higher education. However, most scholarship programs have more applicants than they have scholarships to give out. Scholarship money should not be a component in your university financial planning until you are notified in writing by the sponsor that you will receive it. Should you receive an award, be aware of the award's termination date. You will have to plan either to reapply for the scholarship or to search for alternative funding at the end of the award's period of coverage.

Aid from the U.S. Government

As you might expect, the U.S. government's primary responsibility is to its own citizens; therefore, not much financial assistance to international students can be expected from this source. However, since you will see these programs mentioned in the literature you read from colleges, to avoid confusion it might be useful for you to know the federal aid programs for which you are *not* eligible because of your international citizenship status: Federal Pell Grant, Federal Supplemental Educational Opportunity (FSEOG), Federal Stafford Loan or Federal Direct Stafford Loan, Federal Perkins Loan, Federal PLUS Loan, and Federal Work-Study Programs.

Figure Out the Bottom Line

Now go back to your chart of expenses and resources at each college and fill in your best estimates for family, student, college, and other sources of aid that might be available. You may need to use a range from the best-case scenario in which you win an academic scholarship to the worst-case scenario in which no aid is available from the college and your family can only provide a modest sum toward your costs.

The bottom line on each college is the difference between the total estimated costs and the total estimated resources. This analysis may help you determine the financial reasonableness of an application to each of your preliminary college choices. At this initial point in the process, the bottom line may be a range since some of the items above it are ranges. For example, for College A you may have estimated that your total costs could range from $15,000 to $18,000 (depending on what dormitory you live in), and you have also estimated that the total resources available to you could range from $5000 to $20,000 (depending on whether you obtain a scholarship from the college). Thus, for College A the worst-case scenario is the highest cost and the lowest resources, leaving you a gap of $13,000, while the best-case scenario is the lowest cost and the highest resources, in which case all your costs would be met. So, depending on the outcome of your scholarship application, attendance at College A might be a financial possibility. Do the same assessment for each of the colleges you have selected in this first round and analyze the results. If even in the best case you still couldn't afford to attend a college on your chart, you may decide to eliminate it from your group of applications.

When you have finally finished all your research on the academic, financial, and other aspects of a U.S. college education, you will be ready to complete your applications, and then wait, patiently or impatiently, for the results.

How to Choose Your College

If you end up in the fortunate position of having been admitted to several colleges, you can then compare the financial realities and any aid offers that have been made and make corrections to your earlier best estimates of costs and resources. As an admitted student, you will likely receive much more detailed information about housing and meal options, general campus costs, and specific financial aid award amounts. Based on this more final information, you can determine which of the colleges to which you have been admitted are affordable based on your family's actual resources. If more than one of your colleges is affordable on this basis, you may decide which one has the better aid offer (i.e., higher total percent of costs covered with aid and also higher percentage of grant versus loan or job); or you could decide on a nonfinancial basis, such as which academic program or physical location you prefer. Congratulations!

However, if after analyzing the cost-minus-resources situation at the colleges to which you have been admitted, you find that none of the colleges is affordable, what can you do? You should first reassess the amount that your family has committed itself to provide. If they felt they could contribute $5000 per year and a contribution of $6000 per year will allow you to attend, perhaps they will make that sacrifice on your behalf. You can also make one final attempt to plead your case at the college or colleges whose aid offer comes closest to meeting your need. Think again about what special circumstances might not have been considered and contact the financial aid office by telephone, fax, or e-mail to find out whether a letter of appeal might allow them to increase their aid offer. Sometimes other students may turn down their aid offers so that additional funding becomes available that could fill your gap. If the college knows that you are eager to attend the institution, it may be able to find some small additional resources to help make that possible.

CONCLUSION

It is important to be realistic about college costs in the U.S. and your ability to find the necessary resources to cover them. You certainly would not want to end up stranded at your college in the middle of the year with no money to pay your rent or be forced to interrupt your schooling after a year's study because of insufficient funds. If you invest time and thought into research about college costs and your own potential resources, as outlined above, you should be well informed enough to make a realistic decision about financing your college education in the United States.

THE FULBRIGHT SCHOLARSHIP PROGRAM

▲

The Fulbright Scholarship Program is the U.S. government's premier scholarship program that is available to international students. The Fulbright program sponsors study, research, or teaching by American scholars in host countries and by graduate-level students, teachers, or researchers from more than 125 countries at universities in the United States. In its fifty-one years of operation, the Fulbright program has sponsored nearly 200,000 scholars. Almost 5,000 Fulbright grants are awarded each year. The program was established in 1946 to foster mutual understanding through educational and cultural exchanges of people, knowledge, and skills between the United States and other countries. It is named for Senator J. William Fulbright, who sponsored the legislation in the United States Senate as a step toward constructing alternatives to armed conflict. The program's primary source of funding is the United States Information Agency (USIA).

Grants are made to citizens of participating countries, primarily for university teaching, advanced research, graduate study, and teaching in elementary and secondary schools. The Fulbright program does not cover medical studies. In fifty countries that have executive agreements with the United States, the Fulbright program is administered by a binational commission that annually decides the numbers and categories of grants. Some countries, for example, may emphasize the sponsorship of teachers in their programs. In approximately seventy-five other countries, the United States Information Service (USIS), the foreign service arm of the USIA, administers the program.

All prospective applicants must inquire about the application procedure through their home country's Fulbright Commission, if there is one, or the USIS post or section of the U.S. embassy that is concerned with cultural activities, education exchanges, libraries, press relations, or other public affairs. The application process usually takes about twelve months.

As a general rule, applicants are required to take the Test of English as a Foreign Language (TOEFL) and the Graduate Record Examination (GRE), although there may be exceptions. The Graduate Management Admissions Test (GMAT) is required for admission to business administration programs. Check with the Fulbright Commission or USIS post to ascertain which tests are required for a specific field of study. For the duration of their financial sponsorship and related travel, all non-U.S. student Fulbright grantees are required by the U.S. Information Agency and the Fulbright Scholarship Board to be on "J" visas, under Exchange-Visitor Program No. G-1-1.

COUNTRY CONTACT FOR INFORMATION REGARDING FULBRIGHT GRADUATE STUDY IN THE UNITED STATES

ALBANIA
Public Affairs Officer, United States Information Service Cultural Center, Rruga Ismail Qemali, Tirana. Telephone: 42-33-246; Fax: 42-32-222.

Student Advising Center: Open Society Fund, International Cultural Center, Room 28, Bulevardi Deshmoret e Kombit, Tirana. Telephone: 42-34-223, 34-621; Fax: 42-34-223, 34-621.

ALGERIA
Under a cooperative agreement with USIA, America-Mideast Educational and Training Services, Inc. (AMIDEAST) administers the Fulbright Program for students from the Middle East and North Africa. AMIDEAST has offices in Algeria, Bahrain, Egypt, Jordan, Kuwait, Lebanon, Morocco, Syria, Tunisia, the United Arab Emirates, the West Bank/Gaza Strip, and Yemen. For further information including field office addresses, please consult the AMIDEAST Web site. AMIDEAST has headquarters at 1730 M Street NW, suite 1100, Washington, D.C. 20036-4505. Telephone: 202-776-9600; Fax: 202-776-7000.

ARGENTINA
Executive Director, Commission for Educational Exchange Between the United States of America and the Argentine Republic, Viamonte 1653, Piso 2 1055, Buenos Aires. Telephone: 1-814-3561 or 814-3562; Fax: 1-814-1377; Cable: CEEBUSA; Telex: 39018156. E-mail: ng@fulb-ba.satlink.net/ or gc@fulb-ba.satlink.net/ Office Hours: 10 a.m–5 p.m. (Monday–Friday).

AUSTRALIA
Selection of awards is handled by the Foundation in Australia. Each year, approximately 15 travel grants are awarded for graduate study fields such as mathematics, journalism, economics, engineering, business, English, law, international relations, music and performance. For more information about the grant selection process and deadlines for submission of materials, please contact the Grant and Administration Officer, Australian-American Education Foundation, GPO Box 1559, Canberra, ACT 2601. Telephone: 61-62-270-5873; Cable: Beltz/Fulbright/Canberra; Fax: 61-62-476-554. E-mail: fulbrt@aaef.anu.edu.au/

AUSTRIA
Student Adviser, Österreichisch-Amerikanischen Erziehungskommission, Austrian-American Educational Commission, Schmidgasse, 14 A-1082, Vienna. Telephone: 313-3973 Ext. 2685; Fax: 408-7765 (USIS); Cable: USEDUCOM WIEN; Telex: 847-116082-USREX-Attn: Fruhwirth.

BAHAMAS
Public Affairs Officer, American Embassy, Queen Street, New Providence. Telephone: 322-4268 or 322-4269; Fax: 326-5579.

BAHRAIN
Under a cooperative agreement with USIA, America-Mideast Educational and Training Services, Inc. (AMIDEAST) administers the Fulbright Program for students from the Middle East and North Africa. AMIDEAST has offices in Algeria, Bahrain, Egypt, Jordan, Kuwait, Lebanon, Morocco, Syria, Tunisia, the United Arab Emirates, the West Bank/Gaza Strip, and Yemen. For further information including field office addresses, please consult the AMIDEAST Web site. AMIDEAST has headquarters at 1730 M Street NW, suite 1100, Washington, D.C. 20036-4505. Telephone: 202-776-9600; Fax: 202-776-7000.

BANGLADESH
Selection of awards is handled by the USIS post in Bangladesh. Each year, approximately three fully-funded grants are awarded for graduate study in a variety of fields. For more information about the grant selection process and deadlines for submission of materials, please contact the Assistant Public Affairs Officer, American Embassy, Jiban Bima Bhaban, Fifth Floor, 10 Dilkusha C.A., Dhaka. Telephone: 2-862-550/4; Fax: 2-833-987; Telex: 950-642319.

BARBADOS
Cultural Affairs Officer, American Embassy, Chelston Park, Building 2, Culloden Road, St. Michael, Bridgetown. Telephone: 436-6300 or 436-9732; Fax: 429-5316.

BELGIUM/LUXEMBOURG
Executive Director, Commission for Educational Exchange Between the United States of America, Belgium and Luxembourg, Royal Library Albert IER, Boulevard de l'Empereur 4, B-1000 Brussels, Belgium. Telephone: 32-02-519-5770 or 32-02-519-5772; Fax: 32-02-519-5773. E-mail: fulbrightadvising@kbr.be/

BELIZE
Cultural Affairs Officer, American Embassy, Gabourel Lane and Hutson Street, Belize City. Telephone: 2-77-161, 77-162, 77-163; Fax: 2-30-802.

BENIN
Public Affairs Officer, American Embassy, Centre Culturel Américain, Boulevard de France, Cotonou, Republique Populaire du Benin. Telephone: 30-03-12 or 30-14-77; Fax: 30-03-84.

BHUTAN
Selection of awards for the Bhutan program is handled by the USIS post in New Delhi, India. For more information about the grant selection process and deadlines for submission of materials, please contact

the Deputy Cultural Affairs Officer, American Embassy, 24 Kasturba Gandhi Marg, New Delhi 110001, India. Telephone: 11-331-6841; Fax: 11-332-9499. E-mail: aol@usisdel.ernet.in/

BOLIVIA
Cultural Affairs Officer, American Embassy, Avenida Arce 2780, P.O. Box 425, La Paz. Telephone: 2-431-838; Fax: 2-433-006.

BOTSWANA
Public Affairs Officer, American Embassy, Embassy Drive, Gaborone. Telephone: 357-326; Fax: 306-129.

BRAZIL
Executive Director, Commission for Educational Exchange Between the United States of America and Brazil, Edificio Casa Thomas Jefferson, SHIS Q109—CONJ. 17—Lote L, Lago Sul, 71625 Brasilia, D.F. Telephone: 61-248-7405, 248-7412, 248-7422; Fax: 61-248-7359; Cable: Fulbright Brasilia. E-mail: fulbright@brnet.com/ Office Hours: 8 a.m.–5 p.m. (Monday–Friday).

BULGARIA
Executive Director, Bulgarian-American Commission for Educational Exchange, 17 Stamboliiski Boulevard, Sofia 1000. Telephone: 359-2-981-8567 or 980-8211; Fax: 359-2-988-4517. E-mail: fulbrsof@sf.cit.bg/

BURKINA FASO
Public Affairs Officer, American Embassy, Centre Culturel Américain, Avenue du President John Kennedy, Ouagadougou. Telephone: 31 16 54 or 30 70 13, ext. 2144; Fax: 31 52 73.

BURUNDI
Public Affairs Officer, American Embassy, Centre Culturel Américain, 20-22 Chaussée Prince Louis Rwagasoreasore, Bujumbura. Telephone: 2-25646; Fax: 2-24561.

CAMBODIA
Selection of awards is handled by the USIS Post in Cambodia. Each year, approximately five fully funded grants are awarded for graduate study in professional and natural science fields. For more information about the grant selection process and deadlines for submission of materials, please contact the Public Affairs Officer, American Embassy, No. 20, Mongkol Lem Street (Street 228), Phnom Penh. Telephone: 23-426-436; Fax: 23-427-637.

CAMEROON
Public Affairs Officer, American Embassy, Calafatas Building, Rue Nachtigal, Boîte Postale 817, Yaound. Telephone: 230-416; Fax: 226-765.

CANADA
Executive Director, Foundation for Educational Exchange Between Canada and the United States of America, 350 Albert Street, Suite 2015, Ottawa, Ontario K1R 1A4. Telephone: 613-237-5366; Fax: 613-237-2029. E-mail: av551@fulbright.ca

CENTRAL AFRICAN REPUBLIC
Public Affairs Officer, American Embassy, Martin Luther King Center, Avenue David Dacko, Bangui. Telephone: 612-578; Fax: 614-494.

CHAD
Public Affairs Officer, American Embassy, Avenue Felix Eboue, Boîte Postale 413, N'djamena, Republic of Chad. Telephone: 519-233; Fax: 515-654.

CHILE
Executive Secretary, Fulbright Commission for Educational Exchange Between the United States of America and Chile, Casilla 2121, Victoria Subercaseaux 41, Piso 4, Santiago. Telephone: 562-633-0379; Fax: 562-638-0580; Telex: USIS Santiago. E-mail: fulcomm@reuna.cl/ Office Hours: 9 a.m–3 p.m. (Monday–Friday).

CHINA (PEOPLE'S REPUBLIC OF)
Assistant Cultural Affairs Officer (EDU), American Center for Educational Exchange, Jingguang Center, Suite 2801, Box 84, Hu Jia Lou, Chaoyang District, Beijing 100020. Telephone: 10-6501-5242/6; Fax: 10-6501-5247. E-mail: igosnell@usia.gov/ Telex: 716-22701 AMEMB CN.

COLOMBIA
Executive Director, Commission for Educational Exchange Between the United States of America and Colombia (Comision Para Intercambio Educativo), Calle 38, #13-37, Piso 11, Apartado Aereo 034240, Bogota, D.E. Telephone: 287-7831 or 232-4326; Fax: 287-3520; Cable: Fulcolombia, Bogota. E-mail: fulbrigh@anditel.andinet.lat.net/ Office Hours: 8 a.m–5 p.m. (Monday–Friday).

CONGO
Public Affairs Officer, American Embassy, Avenue Amilcar Cabral, Boîte Postale 1015, Brazzaville. Telephone: 83-2642; Fax: 83-4690.

COSTA RICA
Cultural Affairs Officer, American Embassy, Avenida 3 and Calle 1, San Jose. Telephone: 2-20-3939, ext. 2211; Fax: 2-32-7944.

COTE D'IVOIRE
Public Affairs Officer, American Embassy, American Cultural Center, 5 Rue Jesse Owens, 01 Boîte Postale 1866, Abidjan. Telephone: 440-597; Fax: 446-396.

CROATIA
Public Affairs Officer, American Embassy, Ulica Andrije Hebranga 2, 41000 Zagreb. Telephone: 41-444-800; Fax: 41-450-270.

CYPRUS
Program Officer, Commission for Educational Exchange Between the United States of America and Cyprus, 2 Egypt Avenue, Nicosia. Telephone: 357-245-3605 or 245-9757; Fax: 357-236-9151; Cable: Fulbright Nicosia Cyprus; Telex: 8262024 FULCOM CY Attn: Hadjittofi. E-mail: 100564.3332@compuserve.com/

CZECH REPUBLIC
Program Coordinator, J. William Fulbright Commission for Educational Exchange in the Czech Republic, Taboritska 23, 4th Floor, 130 87, Prague 3. Telephone: 420-2-277-155; Fax: 420-2-697-5600. E-mail: fulb@earn. mbox.cesnet.cz

Student Advising Centers: International Research and Exchanges Board (IREX), 3 Narodni Trida, 111 42 Prague 1. Telephone: 2-2424-0541; Fax: 2-2424-0516.

DENMARK
Executive Director, Denmark-American Foundation/ Fulbright Commission, Fiolstrade 24, 3 sal, DK-1171 Copenhagen K. Telephone: 3-312-8223; Fax: 3-332-5323; Cable: USEFDAN, Copenhagen. E-mail: fulbdk@ unidhp.uni-c.dk/

DOMINICAN REPUBLIC
Cultural Affairs Officer, American Embassy, Prolongacion Avenida Mexico No. 71, Santo Domingo, Republica Dominicana. Telephone: 541-3030; Fax: 541-1828.

ECUADOR
Executive Director, Commission for Educational Exchange Between the United States of America and Ecuador, PO Box 17-079081, Avenida Diegode Almagro 961 y Avenida Colon, Quito. Telephone: 593-2-22-103 or 104; Fax: 593-2-509-149 or 509-523; Cable: FULECUADOR. E-mail: scdevaca@fulbright.org; Office Hours: 9 a.m–3 p.m.

EGYPT
Executive Director, Commission for Educational and Cultural Exchange Between the United States of America and the Arab Republic of Egypt, 20 Gamal El Din Abou El Mahasin Street, Garden City, Cairo. Telephone: 2-354-8679, 354-4799, 357-2216, or 357-2258; Fax: 2-355-7893 or 354-8004. E-mail: bfceexec@ frcueun.eg/

EL SALVADOR
Cultural Affairs Officer, American Embassy, Final Boulevard, Station Antigua Cuscatlan, San Salvador. Telephone: 278-4444; Fax: 278-6015.

ERITREA
Public Affairs Officer, American Embassy, 34 Zera Yakob Street, Asmara. Telephone: 1-120-738; Fax: 1-120-685.

ESTONIA
Public Affairs Officer, American Embassy, Kentmanni 20, Tallinn EE0001. Telephone: 6-312-210; Fax: 6-312-026.

ETHIOPIA
Public Affairs Officer, American Embassy, Entoto Street, P.O. Box 1014, Addis Ababa. Telephone: 1-550-007; Fax: 1-551-748.

FINLAND
Executive Director, Finland-United States Educational Exchange Commission, Liisankatu 6 A 1, SF-00170 Helsinki. Telephone: 5-494-7400; Fax: 5-494-7474; Cable: FUSEEC; Telex: 857121644 Attn: Fulbright Mustanoja. E-mail: office@fulbright.fi.

FRANCE
Executive Director, Franco-American Commission for Educational Exchange, 9 Rue Chardin, 75016 Paris. Telephone: 1-4414-5360; Fax: 1-4288-0479; Telex: 842650319 Attn: Collombert; Cable: FRACOM-Paris. E-mail: cfa@fulbright.worldnet.fr.

GAMBIA
Acting Public Affairs Officer, American Embassy, Fajara Kairaba Avenue, P.M.B. No.19, Banjul, The Gambia. Telephone: 392-858; Fax: 392-475.

GAZA STRIP
Under a cooperative agreement with USIA, America-Mideast Educational and Training Services, Inc. (AMIDEAST) administers the Fulbright Program for students from the Middle East and North Africa. AMIDEAST has offices in Algeria, Bahrain, Egypt, Jordan, Kuwait, Lebanon, Morocco, Syria, Tunisia, the United Arab Emirates, the West Bank/Gaza Strip, and Yemen. For further information including field office addresses, please consult the AMIDEAST Web site. AMIDEAST has headquarters at 1730 M Street NW, suite 1100, Washington, D.C. 20036-4505. Telephone: 202-776-9600; Fax: 202-776-7000.

GERMANY
Executive Director, Commission for Educational Exchange Between the United States of America and the Federal Republic of Germany, Theaterplatz 1A, D-53177 Bonn. Telephone: 228-935-690; Fax: 228-363-130; Cable: FULKOM; Telex: 841885432 or 841885494 Attn: Ischinger. E-mail: fulkom@uni-bonn.de/

GHANA
Public Affairs Officer, American Embassy, Ring Road East, East of Danquah Circle, P.O. Box 2288, Accra. Telephone: 21-229-179; Fax: 21-229-882.

GREECE
Executive Director, United States Educational Foundation in Greece, 6 Vassilissis Sofias Avenue, Athens 106-74. Telephone: 72-41-811 or 812; Fax: 72-26-510; Cable: Fulbright Athens; Telex: 863218428 Fulbright Attn: Ammerman. E-mail: fbright@compulink.gr

GUATEMALA
Cultural Affairs Officer, American Embassy, Avenida de la Reforma 7-01, Zone 10, Guatemala City. Telephone: 2-311-541, ext. 250 or 251; Fax: 2-321-549.

GUINEA
Public Affairs Officer, American Embassy, 2nd Boulevard and 9th Avenue, Boîte Postale 603, Conakry. Telephone: 411-424; Fax: 411-522.

GUYANA
Pam Roberts, CAS, American Embassy, 99-100 Young and Duke Streets, P.O. Box 10507, Georgetown, Guyana. Telephone: 2-54900; Fax: 2-63636.

HAITI
Cultural Affairs Officer, American Embassy, Harry Truman Boulevard, P.O. Box 1761, Port au Prince. Telephone: 2-2-1504; Fax: 2-23-8324.

HONDURAS
Cultural Affairs Officer, American Embassy, Avenida La Paz, Tegucigalpa. Telephone: 36-9320; Fax: 36-9309.

HONG KONG
Public Affairs Office, American Consulate-General, 26 Garden Road, Hong Kong. Telephone: 2841-2225; Fax: 2845-0735. E-mail: pjchong@usia.gov/

HUNGARY
Executive Director, Hungarian-American Commission for Educational Exchange, Ajtosi Durer Sor 19-21, H-1146 Budapest. Telephone: 1-183-7777 or 183-6580; Fax: 1-252-0266. E-mail: fulbright@afki.huninet.hu/

Student Advising Centers: Szabo Ervin Library, 1 Szabo Ervin Sq., 1088 Budapest. Telephone: 1-138-4933; Fax: 1-118-5914.

ICELAND
Executive Director, Iceland-United States Educational Commission (Menntastofnun Islands og Bandarijanna), Laugavegir 59, 101 Reykjavik. Telephone: 552-0830; Fax: 552-0886 (USIS); Telex: 8583044 USEMB IS, (Attn: FULBRIGHT); Cable: Amembassy, Reykjavik USEFI. E-mail: fulb@ismennt.is/ Office Hours: 1 p.m–5 p.m. (Monday–Friday).

INDIA
Executive Director, United States Educational Foundation in India, Fulbright House, 12 Hailey Road, New Delhi 110001. Telephone: 11-332-6043 or 48; Cable: USEFI; Fax: 11-332-9718. E-mail: fulbright@usefid.ernet.in

INDONESIA
Executive Director, American-Indonesian Exchange Foundation (AMINEF), Gedung Balai Pustaka, 6th floor, Jalan Gunung Sahari Raya 4, Jakarta, 10720. Telephone: 21-345-2016 or 345-2018; Fax: 21-345-2050. E-mail: adnjkt@usia.gov/

IRELAND
Executive Director, The Ireland-United States Commission for Educational Exchange, 79 St. Stephen's Green, Dublin 2. Telephone: 478-0822; Fax: 676-0471; Cable: Amembassy PAO Pass Fulbright Commission; Telex: 85293684 Attn: PAO/Amemb EI Pass Fulbright Commission; E-mail: alumni@ucd.ie

ISRAEL
Executive Director, United States-Israel Educational Foundation, 1 Ben Yehuda Street, Tel Aviv 63801. Telephone: 3-517-2131; Fax: 3-516-2016. E-mail: sarbel@fulbright.org.il; Office Hours: 7 a.m–3 p.m. (Monday–Friday).

ITALY
Executive Director, Commission for Educational and Cultural Exchange Between Italy and the United States of America, Via Castelfidardo, 8, Rome 00185. Telephone: 481-8211 or 2126; Cable: Amcultural Roma; Telex: 843625847 USISRM 1; Fax: 06-481-5680; E-mail: fulbright.usis.it.

JAMAICA
Cultural Affairs Officer, American Embassy, 2 Oxford Road, 1st Floor, Kingston 5. Telephone: 929-4850; Fax: 929-3637.

JAPAN
Program Section, Japan-U.S. Educational Commission (JUSEC), #206, Sanno Grand Building, 2-14-2 Nagata-cho, Chiyoda-Ku, Tokyo 100, Japan. Telephone: 03-3580-3233; Fax: 03-3580-1217; Cable: Fulbright Tokyo. E-mail: fulgrant@jusec.go.jp/

JORDAN
Under a cooperative agreement with USIA, America-Mideast Educational and Training Services, Inc.

(AMIDEAST) administers the Fulbright Program for students from the Middle East and North Africa. AMIDEAST has offices in Algeria, Bahrain, Egypt, Jordan, Kuwait, Lebanon, Morocco, Syria, Tunisia, the United Arab Emirates, the West Bank/Gaza Strip, and Yemen. For further information including field office addresses, please consult the AMIDEAST Web site. AMIDEAST has headquarters at 1730 M Street NW, suite 1100, Washington, D.C. 20036-4505. Telephone: 202-776-9600; Fax: 202-776-7000.

KENYA
Public Affairs Officer, American Embassy, National Bank of Kenya Building, P.O. Box 30143, Nairobi. Telephone: 2-334141; Fax: 2-216511.

KOREA (REPUBLIC OF)
Korean-American Educational Commission, Kohap Building, Suite 403, 89-4 Kyongun-dong, Chongno-gu. Seoul 110-310. Telephone: 82-2-732-7922; Fax: 82-2-736-2718; Cable: Fulbrightcom, Seoul; Telex: Kaecsel K29554. E-mail: admin@fulbright.or.kr

KUWAIT
Under a cooperative agreement with USIA, America-Mideast Educational and Training Services, Inc. (AMIDEAST) administers the Fulbright Program for students from the Middle East and North Africa. AMIDEAST has offices in Algeria, Bahrain, Egypt, Jordan, Kuwait, Lebanon, Morocco, Syria, Tunisia, the United Arab Emirates, the West Bank/Gaza Strip, and Yemen. For further information including field office addresses, please consult the AMIDEAST Web site. AMIDEAST has headquarters at 1730 M Street NW, suite 1100, Washington, D.C. 20036-4505. Telephone: 202-776-9600; Fax: 202-776-7000.

LAOS
Public Affairs Officer, American Embassy, Rue Bartholonie, P.O. Box 114, Vientiane, Lao People's Democratic Republic. Telephone: 21-212582; Fax: 21-213045.

LATVIA
Public Affairs Officer, American Embassy, Smilsu Iela 7, Riga, LV-1050. Telephone: 2-216-565; Fax: 2-214-478.

Student Advising Center: University of Latvia, Educational Advising Center, Raina Bulvaris 19, Room 243, Riga, LV-1098. Tel &; Fax: 2-228-656.

LEBANON
Under a cooperative agreement with USIA, America-Mideast Educational and Training Services, Inc. (AMIDEAST) administers the Fulbright Program for

students from the Middle East and North Africa. AMIDEAST has offices in Algeria, Bahrain, Egypt, Jordan, Kuwait, Lebanon, Morocco, Syria, Tunisia, the United Arab Emirates, the West Bank/Gaza Strip, and Yemen. For further information including field office addresses, please consult the AMIDEAST Web site. AMIDEAST has headquarters at 1730 M Street NW, suite 1100, Washington, D.C. 20036-4505. Telephone: 202-776-9600; Fax: 202-776-7000.

LITHUANIA
Public Affairs Officer, American Embassy, Akmenu 6, 2600 Vilnius. Telephone: 2-22-04-81; Fax: 2-22-04-45.

Student Advising Centers: University of Vilnius, Universiteto 3, Room 40, 2734 Vilnius. Telephone: 2-62-50-53; Fax: 2-61-05-59.

LUXEMBOURG
Executive Director, Commission for Educational Exchange Between the United States of America, Belgium and Luxembourg, Royal Library, Albert I, Sixth Floor, Boulevard de l'Empereur, 4 (Keizerslaan) B-1000 Brussels, Belgium. Telephone: [32 02)] 519-5770, 519-5771, 519-5772; Fax: [32 02)] 519-5773. E-mail: fulbright@kbr.be/

MADAGASCAR
Public Affairs Officer, American Embassy, 4 Lalana Drive, Razafindratandra Ambohidahy, Antananarivo. Telephone: 2-20596; Fax: 2-21397.

MALAWI
Public Affairs Officer, American Embassy, City Center, Old Mutual Building, P.O. Box 30373, Lilongwe 3. Telephone: 782678; Fax: 781142.

MALI
Public Affairs Officer, U.S. Information Service, Centre Culturel Américain, Rue Mohamed V, Boîte Postale 34, Bamako. Telephone: 225834; Fax: 222025.

MAURITIUS
Public Affairs Officer, American Embassy, Rogers Building, 4th Floor, President Kennedy Street, Port Louis. Telephone: 212-2802; Fax: 212-2808.

MEXICO
Executive Director, U.S.-Mexico Commission for Educational and Cultural Exchange, Bibioteca Benjamin Franklin, Londres 16, Mexico City, D.F. Telephone: 5-211-0042 Ext. 3478; Fax: 5-208-8943. E-mail: comexus@servidor.unam.mx/

MONGOLIA
Public Affairs Officer, American Embassy, PSC 461, BOX 300 FPO AP 96521; Street address for express

mail: Big Ring Road, Microdistrict #11, Ulaanbaatar, Mongolia. Telephone: 1-329-095; Fax: 1-320-776.

MOROCCO
Under a cooperative agreement with USIA, America-Mideast Educational and Training Services, Inc. (AMIDEAST) administers the Fulbright Program for students from the Middle East and North Africa. AMIDEAST has offices in Algeria, Bahrain, Egypt, Jordan, Kuwait, Lebanon, Morocco, Syria, Tunisia, the United Arab Emirates, the West Bank/Gaza Strip, and Yemen. For further information including field office addresses, please consult the AMIDEAST Web site. AMIDEAST has headquarters at 1730 M Street NW, suite 1100, Washington, D.C. 20036-4505. Telephone: 202-776-9600; Fax: 202-776-7000.

MOZAMBIQUE
Public Affairs Officer, American Embassy, Mao Tse Tung, No. 542, Maputo, Republica Popular de Mocambique. Telephone: 1-491116; Fax: 1-491918.

NAMIBIA
Public Affairs Officer, American Embassy, Austlan Building, 14 Lossen Street, Private Bag 12029 Auftann Platz, Windhoek, 2540. Telephone: 61-229801; Fax: 61-232476.

NEPAL
Executive Director, United States Educational Foundation in Nepal Thamel (behind Hotel Malla), P.O. Box 380, Kathmandu. Telephone: 1-414-845; Fax: 1-410-881.

NETHERLANDS
Executive Director, Netherlands-America Commission for Educational Exchange, Herengracht 430, 1017 BZ Amsterdam. Telephone: 20-627-5421; Fax: 20-620-7269; Cable: Amembassy, The Hague; Telex: Attn: CAO 84431016 Pass Fulb-Comm. E-mail: nacee@nacee.nl/

NEW ZEALAND
Executive Director, New Zealand-United States Educational Foundation, Level 4, General Finance Building, 120 124 Featherston Street, P.O. Box 3465, Wellington, C.T. Telephone: 4-472-2065; Fax: 4-499-5364. E-mail: jennifer@fulbright.org.nz/ or educate@fulbright.org.nz/

NICARAGUA
Cultural Affairs Officer, American Embassy, Km 4½ Carretera Sur, Managua. Telephone: 2-666-036; Fax: 2-663-861.

NIGER
Public Affairs Officer, U.S. Information Service, Centre Culturel Américain, Avenue de la Liberté Niamey. Telephone: 734-107; Fax: 733-167.

NIGERIA
Public Affairs Officer, American Embassy, No. L, Kings College Road, Lagos. Telephone: 1-2635611; Fax: 1-2635379.

NORWAY
Executive Director, U.S.-Norway Fulbright Foundation for Educational Exchange, Arbinsgate 2, 0253 Oslo. Telephone: 22-83-26-00 or 03; Fax: 22-83-26-07; Cable: Fulnor; Telex: 85618470 Attn: Fulbright Foundation. E-mail: fulbright@extern.uio.no/

PAKISTAN
Executive Director, United States Educational Foundation in Pakistan, House 2, St. 84, Ataturk Avenue, G-614, P.O. Box 1128, Islamabad. Telephone: 51-21-346 or 27-1563; Fax: 51-211-563 or 825-514; Cable: USEFP Islamabad; Telex: 54143 ASIAF PK.

PALESTINE
Under a cooperative agreement with USIA, America-Mideast Educational and Training Services, Inc. (AMIDEAST) administers the Fulbright Program for students from the Middle East and North Africa. AMIDEAST has offices in Algeria, Bahrain, Egypt, Jordan, Kuwait, Lebanon, Morocco, Syria, Tunisia, the United Arab Emirates, the West Bank/Gaza Strip, and Yemen. For further information including field office addresses, please consult the AMIDEAST Web site. AMIDEAST has headquarters at 1730 M Street NW, suite 1100, Washington, D.C. 20036-4505. Telephone: 202-776-9600; Fax: 202-776-7000.

PANAMA
Cultural Affairs Officer, American Embassy, Avenida Balboa y Calle 39, Apartado 6959, Torre Miramar, Panama City. Telephone: 227-1777; Fax: 227-4515.

PAPUA NEW GUINEA AND THE PACIFIC ISLANDS
Public Affairs Officer, American Embassy, Amit Street, P.O. Box 1492, Port Moresby, Papua New Guinea. Telephone: 5-321-1759; Fax: 5-321-4593. E-mail: 103260.3203@CompuServe.com/

PARAGUAY
Cultural Affairs Officer, American Embassy, Avenida Mcal. Lopez 1776, Asuncion. Telephone: 21-213-715, ext. 247; Fax: 21-212-312.

PERU
Executive Director, Commission for Educational Exchange Between the United States of America and Peru, Coronel Inclan 806, Miraflores, Lima 18. Telephone: 511-445-4746 or 241-5320; Fax: 511-241-5319; Cable: Fulbright Lima. E-mail: commission@fulbrt.org.pe/ Office Hours: 8 a.m–5 p.m. (Monday–Friday).

PHILIPPINES
Program Officer, Philippine-American Educational Foundation, 3rd Floor, Accelerando Building, 395 Senator Gil Puyat Avenue, 1200 Makati, Metro Manila. Telephone: 63-2-895-2993 or 895-3037 (Educational Advising Center); Fax: 63-2-895-3215; Cable: Fulbright Manila. E-mail: fulbrght@mnl.sequel.net/

POLAND
Executive Director, U.S.-Polish Fulbright Commission, ul. Nowy Swiat 4, Roo 113, 00-497 Warsaw. Telephone: 22-628-79-50; Fax: 22-628-79-43. E-mail: oee@plearn.edu.pl/

Student Advising Centers: Warsaw University, 26/28 Krakowskie Przedmiescie, 00-927 Warsaw. Telephone: 22-268-148; Fax: 22-268-148.

PORTUGAL
Executive Director, Luso-American Educational Commission, Avenida Elias Garcia, 59-5, 1000 Lisbon. Telephone: 796-7976 or 8626; Fax: 1-796-8921; Cable: Fulcom, Lisbon; Telex: 83212528 Attn: Lopes da Silva. E-mail: rbacelad@fulbright.eunet.pt

ROMANIA
Executive Director, The Fulbright Commission for Romania (Biroul de Schimburi Romano-Americane), Strada Austrului nr. 15, 73112 Bucharest. Telephone: 252-6913 or 4449; Fax: 252-6915.

Student Advising Centers: International Research and Exchanges Board (IREX), Str. Dem. I. Dobrescu 11, Bucharest. Tel/ Fax: 1-312-0041.

RWANDA
Public Affairs Officer, American Embassy, Rue des Grands Lacs, Kigali. Telephone: 73-206; Fax: 72-128.

SAUDI ARABIA
Under a cooperative agreement with USIA, America-Mideast Educational and Training Services, Inc. (AMIDEAST) administers the Fulbright Program for students from the Middle East and North Africa. AMIDEAST has offices in Algeria, Bahrain, Egypt, Jordan, Kuwait, Lebanon, Morocco, Syria, Tunisia, the United Arab Emirates, the West Bank/Gaza Strip, and Yemen. For further information including field office addresses, please consult the AMIDEAST Web site. AMIDEAST has headquarters at 1730 M Street NW, suite 1100, Washington, D.C. 20036-4505. Telephone: 202-776-9600; Fax: 202-776-7000.

SENEGAL
Public Affairs Officer, U.S. Information Service, Centre Culturel Américain de Dakar, Rue Carnot (cross Avenue Roumée) (Boîte Postale 49), Dakar. Telephone: 231185; Fax: 222345.

SIERRA LEONE
Public Affairs Officer, American Embassy, Street Walpole & Siaka Stevens Street, Freetown. Telephone: 22-6481; Fax: 22-5471.

SINGAPORE
Cultural Affairs Officer, American Embassy, FPO AP 96534-001. Street address for express mail: U.S. Information Service, MPH Building, Level 4, 71-77 Stamford Road, Singapore 0617. Telephone: 65-334-0910; Fax: 65-334-2780. E-mail: apao@slip.technet.sg/ or clsing@usia.gov/

SLOVAK REPUBLIC
Executive Director, J. Fulbright Commission for Educational Exchange in the Slovak Republic, Hviezdoslavovo nam. 14, 811-02 Bratislava. Telephone: 7-542-5606; Fax: 7-526-7491; E-mail: nora@fulb.sanet.sk/

Student Advising Centers: Slovak Academic Information Agency (SAIA), Hviezdoslavovo nam. 14, PO Box 108, 810-00 Bratislava 1. Telephone: 7-333-010; Fax: 7-335-827 or 332-192.

SLOVENIA
Public Affairs Officer, American Embassy, Cankarjeva 11, 61000 Ljubljana. Telephone: 61-210-190 or 258-226; Fax: 61-264-284.

SOLOMON ISLANDS
Public Affairs Officer, American Embassy, Amit Street, P.O. Box 1492, Port Moresby, Papua New Guinea. Telephone: 5-321-1759; Fax: 5-321-4593. E-mail: 103260.3203@CompuServe.com/

SOUTH AFRICA
Senior Cultural Specialist, American Embassy, 877 Pretorius Street, Arcadia 86. Telephone: 12-342-3006; Fax: 12-342-2092.

SPAIN
Executive Director, Commission for Educational Exchange Between the United States of America and Spain (Comisión de Intercambio Cultural, Educativo y Científico entre España y los Estados Unidos de

América), Paseo General Martinez Campos, 24 bis, Primera Planta, 28010 Madrid. Telephone: 91-308-2646, 308-2436, or 308-2647; Fax: 91-308-5704; Cable: USEDUCOM (Note: Cable only for embassy); Telex: 83149429 USEDE; E-mail: postmaster@comision. fulbright.es/

SRI LANKA
Executive Director, United States Educational Foundation in Sri Lanka, 39 Sir Ernest De Silva Mawatha, Colombo 7. Telephone: 1-697-835; Fax: 1-697-834. E-mail: tissaj@sri.lanka.net/ Back-up Fax: 1-499-070.

SURINAME
Eric Dennen, CAS, American Embassy, Dr. Sophie Redmonstraat 129, Paramaribo, Suriname. Telephone: 4-75051; Fax: 4-10025.

SWAZILAND
Public Affairs Officer, American Embassy, Embassy House, Mbabane. Telephone: 42445; Fax: 45846.

SWEDEN
Executive Director, Commission for Educational Exchange Between the United States of America and Sweden, Vasagatan 15-17, 4th Floor, S-111 20, Stockholm. Telephone: 8-24-85-81; Fax: 08-14-10-64; Cable: FULBRIGHTCOM, Stockholm. E-mail: ceeus@fulbright. se.

SWITZERLAND
Program Assistant, Central Office of the Swiss Universities, Seidenweg 68, CH-3012, Bern. Telephone: 31-302-23-50; Fax: 31-302-68-11.

SYRIA
Under a cooperative agreement with USIA, America-Mideast Educational and Training Services, Inc. (AMIDEAST) administers the Fulbright Program for students from the Middle East and North Africa. AMIDEAST has offices in Algeria, Bahrain, Egypt, Jordan, Kuwait, Lebanon, Morocco, Syria, Tunisia, the United Arab Emirates, the West Bank/Gaza Strip, and Yemen. For further information including field office addresses, please consult the AMIDEAST Web site. AMIDEAST has headquarters at 1730 M Street NW, suite 1100, Washington, D.C. 20036-4505. Telephone: 202-776-9600; Fax: 202-776-7000.

TAIWAN
Executive Director, Foundation for Scholarly Exchange, 2nd Floor, 1-A Chuan Chow Street, Taipei 100, Taiwan. Telephone: 2-332-8188; Fax: 2-332-5455; Cable: Fulbright Taipei. E-mail: fse@arc.org.tw/

TANZANIA
Public Affairs Officer, American Embassy, Pergeot House, Upanga Road, Box 9170, Dar Es Salaam. Telephone: 51-37101; Fax: 51-37202.

THAILAND
Executive Director, Thailand-United States Educational Foundation, 21/5 Thai Wah Tower 1, 3rd floor, South Sathorn Road, Bangkok 10120, Thailand. Telephone: 2-285-0581; Fax: 2-286-4783; Telex: Attn: Fulbright 020567 AMACO. E-mail: oipsk@chulkn.chula.ac.th/

TOGO
Public Affairs Officer, American Embassy, Centre Culturel Américain, Rue Pelletier et Rue Vauban, Boîte Postale 852, Lomé. Telephone: 212-166; Fax: 217-794.

TRINIDAD AND TOBAGO
Cultural Affairs Officer, American Embassy, 7-9 Marli Street, P.O. Box 752, Port of Spain. Telephone: 622-6627 or 622-6371; Fax: 628-7944.

TUNISIA
Under a cooperative agreement with USIA, America-Mideast Educational and Training Services, Inc. (AMIDEAST) administers the Fulbright Program for students from the Middle East and North Africa. AMIDEAST has offices in Algeria, Bahrain, Egypt, Jordan, Kuwait, Lebanon, Morocco, Syria, Tunisia, the United Arab Emirates, the West Bank/Gaza Strip, and Yemen. For further information including field office addresses, please consult the AMIDEAST Web site. AMIDEAST has headquarters at 1730 M Street NW, suite 1100, Washington, D.C. 20036-4505. Telephone: 202-776-9600; Fax: 202-776-7000.

TURKEY
Executive Director, Commission for Educational Exchange Between the United States of America and Turkey, Sehit Ersan Caddesi, #28/4, Cankaya, 06680 Ankara. Telephone: 312-428-4824; Fax: 312-468-1560; Cable: Fulbright Ankara. E-mail: fulb-ank@tr-net.tr/

UGANDA
Public Affairs Officer, American Embassy, 21 Mackinon Road, Nakasero, Kampala. Telephone: 41-230-507; Fax: 41-250-314.

UNITED ARAB EMIRATES
Under a cooperative agreement with USIA, America-Mideast Educational and Training Services, Inc. (AMIDEAST) administers the Fulbright Program for students from the Middle East and North Africa. AMIDEAST has offices in Algeria, Bahrain, Egypt, Jordan, Kuwait, Lebanon, Morocco, Syria, Tunisia, the United Arab Emirates, the West Bank/Gaza Strip,

and Yemen. For further information including field office addresses, please consult the AMIDEAST Web site. AMIDEAST has headquarters at 1730 M Street NW, suite 1100, Washington, D.C. 20036-4505. Telephone: 202-776-9600; Fax: 202-776-7000.

UNITED KINGDOM
Executive Director, United States-United Kingdom Educational Commission, Fulbright House, 62 Doughty Street, London WC1N 2LS. Telephone: 0171-404-6994; Fax: 0171-404-6874; Cable: Attn: Fulbright AmEmbassy London (England). E-mail contacts: Program Director (scholar and fellow inquiries): education@fulbright.co.uk/

URUGUAY
Executive Director, Commission for Educational Exchange Between the United States of America and Uruguay, Paraguay 1217, Montevideo. Telephone: 2-91-4160; Fax: 2-93-2031, 92-1621 (USIS); Cable: American Embassy. E-mail: fulbrigh@chasque.apc.org/ Office Hours: 9 a.m–1 p.m. (Monday–Friday).

VENEZUELA
Cultural Affairs Officer, Embajada de los Estados Unidos de America, Colinas de Valle Arriba—Municipio Baruto, Caracas. Telephone: 2-977-1077 or 977-2011, ext. 2013; Fax: 2-977-3717.

VIETNAM
Center for Educational Exchange with Vietnam, 91 Pho Tho Nhuom, Hanoi, S.R. Vietnam. Telephone: 4-243014; Fax: 4-244614.

YEMEN
Under a cooperative agreement with USIA, America-Mideast Educational and Training Services, Inc. (AMIDEAST) administers the Fulbright Program for students from the Middle East and North Africa. AMIDEAST has offices in Algeria, Bahrain, Egypt, Jordan, Kuwait, Lebanon, Morocco, Syria, Tunisia, the United Arab Emirates, the West Bank/Gaza Strip, and Yemen. For further information including field office addresses, please consult the AMIDEAST Web site. AMIDEAST has headquarters at 1730 M Street NW, suite 1100, Washington, D.C. 20036-4505. Telephone: 202-776-9600; Fax: 202-776-7000.

ZAMBIA
Public Affairs Officer, American Embassy, Veritas House, Heroes Place, Lusaka. Telephone: 1-227-993; Fax: 1-226-523.

ZIMBABWE
Public Affairs Officer, American Embassy, Century House, E. Mez. Fl., Baker Avenue, P.O. Box 4010, Harare. Telephone: 4-758-798, 758-799 or 758-800; Fax: 4-758-802.

WHAT INTERNATIONAL STUDENTS NEED TO KNOW ABOUT LOANS IN FINANCING AN AMERICAN EDUCATION

▲

by Dwight Peterson, President, International Education Finance Corporation

Editorials in major newspapers throughout the United States have focused on students who study outside of their home country and the importance of the international student to the local and international economies. Universities and colleges throughout the world have turned to the international student to introduce their own country's students to a well-rounded cultural education and to embrace one aspect of globalization. Universities feel that students from overseas enrich student life and bring new ideas, attitudes, and experiences to the campus. International study is here to stay and will only increase as it is promoted and the barriers to study are removed.

Students react differently when asked what is the biggest obstacle to studying at a foreign institution. Barriers to study are many and range from the language issue to the cost of travel. However, as the cost of education increases all over the world, the issue of how to pay for an education will become more prominent. United States students or permanent residents may use the United States federal student financial aid programs to study outside the U.S. More than 75,000 American students *do* study for a semester or a year abroad. Further, approximately 40,000 U.S. students are enrolled at a foreign institution on a full-time basis. These students have available the standard U.S. federal programs as well as the International Student Loan Program (ISLP), combining the federal loan programs with alternative loans offered by the International Education Finance Corporation (IEFC).

In 1995, more than 450,000 students from other countries entered the U.S. to study at American academic institutions. Students are becoming increasingly mobile and willing to travel, and it can be projected that the number of international students studying in the U.S. will continue to increase. However, since these students receive little aid from their own countries, international students face more difficulty than their American counterparts in paying for their education. In the past, students have relied on their own and family resources to pay for most of their education. As the cost of education continues to escalate in the United States, however, this mode of payment becomes more difficult. Loans, which allow families to stretch out the cost of education, become an alternative to using all of their resources at once.

Loans for students entering the U.S. to study should be the last alternative investigated. The prospect of obtaining grants or scholarships is uncertain at best. Graduate students have a better opportunity of receiving help from their academic institution than undergraduate students. However, graduate students usually receive only a portion of their total cost of education in this form. In all cases, students should first approach their university and college and review their financial aid situation with the student financial aid officer at the school. Students should search out all alternatives prior to inquiring about a loan program to pay for their education.

Planning for one's education and paying for it should begin at least one year prior to entering the United States to study. As most international students realize, the time it takes to receive an application, process the application, and receive the funds is often slowed by international postal service. Furthermore, most loan programs require the college or university to certify the amount of the cost of education at their institution and that the student is enrolled. The cost of education includes the tuition, room, board, living expenses, travel, and other expenses related to a student's education. A student can obtain the estimated cost of education from the college's or university's admissions materials or by calling the institution's financial aid office. Once the student knows the cost of education, he or she will need to review his or her current financial situation to determine what may be his or her need for financing through a loan. If a student is able to pay for a portion of his or her educational costs through a personal source, the student may enhance his or her ability to find the remaining portion. In trying to obtain financial aid for an education, the international student should access all sources available. In recent years, the Internet has become a major source of information. The use of electronic mail offered in many computer network services allows students to contact many sources without incurring large charges in their search. Financial companies that offer services and loans to international students have identified the Internet as a major opportunity to connect with these students. Use the key words *international education, student loans, international student loans,* and *financial aid* in accessing these companies.

Loan programs in the United States charge interest rates that are variable and tied to the United States Prime Rate, which can be found in the *Wall Street Journal* or the 90-day Treasury Bill, also found in the *Wall Street Journal*. These rates can include an additional factor and will be shown as Prime + 1% or T-bill + 3.25%. Be sure to call or e-mail to find the correct rate for the particular loan program. Furthermore, most loans will charge a guarantee fee. The guarantee fee is paid to a corporation that will insure or guarantee the payment of the loan to the lending institution. Without the guarantor, the program would not be available at such favorable rates. Students will usually have up to twenty years to repay, depending on the amount borrowed. Amounts that can be borrowed vary by program. Students should calculate what they need to borrow but try to keep that amount to a minimum, if possible. Borrowing for education results in the student taking on a very important responsibility.

When a student has determined that a loan is necessary, a few preliminary steps must be taken to make sure that he or she is eligible to receive a loan through the companies that have been identified. These loan programs are still evolving and inevitably will become easier and friendlier for the international student. However, at the current stage, receiving a loan usually requires a coborrower who is a United States citizen or permanent resident of the United States. A holder of a "green card" is usually classified as a permanent resident.

Once you have identified a coborrower or cosigner of the loan, you should investigate to find out if the coborrower will meet the creditworthiness criteria of the lending institution. The general criteria used by the lending institutions include a review of the coborrower's debt repayment history. This can be done by obtaining a credit bureau report from a credit reporting agency. Credit reporting agencies gather information from credit providers on a continuous basis on individuals in the United States. To meet the standard of consistent payment of debts, the coborrower must usually be on time with payments and rarely more than thirty days late with a payment. The coborrower may want to review the credit bureau report before applying. Next, after a satisfactory credit bureau report, the coborrower must have at least a two-year history of employment with one company. Lenders will also require that the coborrower have an income that is sufficient to allow them to live and pay their debts. Although most will not identify a minimum income level, they will deny loans if the income is not sufficient to allow them to pay for the necessities of life and also make the loan payment. Finally, a debt-to-income ratio will be calculated to make sure that there is sufficient income left to take on additional payments. Debt is defined as monthly payments to credit card providers, consumer loans, and mortgages and/or rent. Income is calculated as the annual income divided by twelve months. Income includes salary as well as interest or dividend payments received from investments. Lenders will require that the income be verified through federal tax returns and/or pay statements from the company where the coborrower works. In general, the debt-to-income ratio should not exceed 40 percent of the monthly income. The most frequent problem incurred when applying with a coborrower is the inability of the coborrower to meet these extensive criteria. The student should investigate whether or not the coborrower can meet them before applying.

Make sure that your application is complete and that the required documents are sent to the lender. Both the student and the coborrower must sign all documents.

When a loan is approved, the student and the coborrower become equally responsible for the payment of the debt. Graduate students are usually provided the opportunity to defer the payment of both principal and interest until after graduation. Most undergraduate students are required to pay interest while they are in school. Monthly payments are calculated by taking the interest rate and multiplying by the principal or amount borrowed divided by 12. If this is a requirement of the loan, it must be taken seriously. Failure to pay the interest will result in the loan going into default; the possibility of receiving further funding will be very remote. If the student fails to make payments, the coborrower will be notified and will be required to make the payments. If the coborrower fails to make payments, the coborrower, as well as the student, will receive calls from collection agencies or may be sued to force payment of the debt. Students who return home to work should be aware that there are methods used to attempt collection all over the world. In most cases, the lender will use all available methods to collect the debt from the student and the coborrower. To summarize, students should choose their coborrowers wisely and make them aware of all the criteria of the loan and their responsibilities.

When a student returns to his or her country, the payment of the debt must be in U.S. dollars. Therefore, he or she should make arrangements with the lender to establish a mechanism to make payment. It may be easier for the coborrower to make the payments and for the student to transfer the required payments to the coborrower. However, electronic payment can be accomplished on a worldwide basis, with the local bank in most countries transferring payment to the account of the lender. To alleviate any potential problems, these details should be worked out with the bank or its servicer before leaving the country.

Lenders in the United States usually will use an outside company to service the debt. The servicer in this case is required by the lender to send out invoices for the payment, calculate the interest, and, if payment is not made, try to collect the debt. You can find out the name of the servicer of your loan by contacting the lender or by reviewing your invoice for the number and address. It is very important to make sure that the lender or its servicer has your correct current address to send you information pertaining to the loan. When you leave school, you are required to provide the lender with your new address if it is different from the permanent address on your application.

Students entering the U.S. from Canada may borrow through Canadian federal and provincial programs. The amounts that can be borrowed depend on your grade level and if the U.S. school you are attending is approved to participate in the program. Check with your local banks or federal student loan program representative to inquire about a school's eligibility.

The IEFC has developed a program for international students to help them meet a portion of their needs. Undergraduate and graduate students may borrow through the ISLP (International Student Loan Program). They must have a U.S. citizen or permanent resident act as coborrower. The students are able to borrow up to the cost of their education. IEFC also has announced a new program for Canadian citizens

to borrow without the use of a U.S. citizen acting as a coborrower. This program, called the CanHELP program, was designed after exhaustive study of Canada's laws and regulations. Undergraduate students may borrow up to the cost of education with a creditworthy Canadian citizen as a coborrower. Graduate students who are Canadian citizens have the opportunity to borrow on their own signature. This is the first program of its kind. It is the purpose of IEFC to develop programs similar to this for other students from other parts of the world.

United Kingdom students who study in the United States may be able to obtain a private loan through one of their local banks. In most cases these loans are for graduate study. It is important to talk with one of those institutions to check the requirements and loan criteria.

Students from Venezuela may borrow through a program called Fundayaucho. This program is administered through a group called LASPAU located in Cambridge, Massachusetts.

Other organizations can assist an international student in obtaining information. One is The Education Resources Institute (TERI) located in Boston, Massachusetts. TERI can provide students with the names of lending institutions that participate and an application. Finally, the Massachusetts Education Finance Authority (MEFA) provides loans for students studying in America from specific countries. If you are studying in Massachusetts, contact MEFA to find out if your home country is eligible.

Although many loan programs in the U.S. require an application to be made within six months of enrollment, the loan programs mentioned in this article do not have any deadline for applying.

The following are the addresses and phone and fax numbers for the organizations mentioned above:

International Education Finance Corporation 424 Adams Street, Milton, MA 02186; Telephone: 617-696-7840 or 888-296-IEFC; Fax: 617-698-3001; World Wide Web: http://www.iefc.com

The Education Resources Institute—TERI 330 Stuart Street, Suite 500, Boston, MA 02116-5237; Telephone: 617-426-0681 or 800-255-TERI; Fax: 617-351-6013; World Wide Web: http://www.teri.org

LASPAU 25 Mount Auburn Street, Cambridge, MA 02138-6095; Telephone: 617-495-5255; Fax: 617-495-8990; World Wide Web: http://www.lapsau.harvard.edu

Massachusetts Education Finance Authority—MEFA 125 Summer Street, Suite 1450, Boston, MA 02110; Telephone: 617-261-9760 or 800-449-MEFA; Fax: 617-261-9765; World Wide Web: http://mefa.org

Scholarship Frauds: Advice for International Students

▲

by Mark Kantrowitz, Publisher, FinAid Page, Inc.

You want to study in the United States or Canada but cannot afford to pay the expenses yourself. You are desperately seeking potential sponsors and sources of funding. You are probably not very familiar with business as usual in the United States and Canada, especially when it concerns private-ssector scholarship programs. This makes you vulnerable to fraudulent businesses or, in American slang, scams that through deception and fraud will convince you to give them what little money you *do* have. You may never discover that you have been fooled, but if you do, you will have no way to reclaim your lost money.

Opportunities for financial aid for study in the United States and Canada by international students are extremely limited. The United States government does not provide much money for students who are not U.S. citizens or permanent residents. U.S. government funding is generally limited to the Fulbright program and a handful of small special purpose programs. Funding from the preponderance of private scholarship programs is likewise restricted to U.S. citizens and permanent residents. Most colleges and universities do not provide financial aid for international students, and most of the aid they do provide is restricted to graduate students. Only about fifty schools give money to more than 50 non-U.S. undergraduate students per year, and the typical award at these schools is only about 20 percent to 30 percent of the cost of attendance.

According to the NAFSA: Association of International Educators, two thirds of international students in the U.S. finance their education using their own resources and the resources of their family.

In order to get a student visa, you will need to demonstrate that you have enough money to pay for the first year of study. If you do not have enough financial resources to cover the rest of your educational program, do not assume that you will be able to find funding after you arrive in the United States. Most off-campus jobs, for example, are restricted to U.S. citizens and permanent residents. Too many international students arrive in the U.S. only to run out of money after the first year. Desperate for any source of funding, they can become victims of the many scams that target international students.

Common Types of Scams

The most common type of scam is the guaranteed scholarship matching service. For a fee that ranges from $30 to $300 or more, a service will guarantee to find you funding for school. They may even insist that non-U.S. students are eligible. This sounds like a risk-free proposition, doesn't it? But most students who use such services do not get any money. Many of these services match the student's profile (i.e., academic record, hobbies, career interests, and ethnic background) against a database of private scholarships and provide the student with a list of addresses of the scholarship sponsors. However, consider that only 1 in 25 U.S. students wins a private scholarship, averaging only about $1600. The success rate for international students is worse, especially since the majority of the awards listed in most search services' databases are restricted to U.S. citizens. In the list of scholarships, there may be only a handful of awards for which international students are eligible. If you try to take advantage of the guarantee, you will find that you have to submit copies of the rejection letters (most scholarship sponsors do not send rejection letters), or that the refund is in the form of a U.S. savings bond with an immediate redemption value worth half its face value, or that the company just does not honor its guarantee. So you are better off saving your money and not wasting it on scholarship matching services.

You probably will hear that billions of dollars of private sector scholarships went unclaimed last year. This is a myth. The National Commission on Student Financial Assistance, a congressionally charted commission, held a hearing on November 10, 1983, in which it presented a report it had issued earlier that year. In the public testimony section of this report, the National Institute of Work and Learning summarized a 1976–77 academic year study, in which it estimated that a potential $7 billion in tuition assistance was available from employers for their employees (i.e., if every employee were to go to school or have dependents in school), but that only about $400 million was used each year. Thus, a wildly exaggerated figure is based on a 20-year-old estimate of potential employer tuition assistance, not actual private-sector scholarships, and that money goes unclaimed because it can-

not be claimed. Very little actual scholarship money, if any, ever goes unclaimed. The hard reality is that scholarship sponsors are not going to give you money simply for breathing.

Another common type of scam is the scholarship with an application fee. With these scams, you hear about a wonderful financial aid opportunity, but when you write asking for application materials, you find that there is an application fee. Or, you might get a letter that says you have been selected for an award, but the sponsors "unfortunately" have had to institute an application fee. The application fee might be a nominal amount, such as $25, $10, or even $5. This may seem insignificant to you, but the typical scam has 5,000 to 10,000 victims, and some extraordinary ones have had as many as 100,000 victims. This can yield a substantial profit, even if the scam artist gives away a few $1000 scholarships to keep the operation legal. If you send in your application fee to a fraudulent scholarship sponsor, you can expect that it will cash your check, but you will never receive any money.

You might start receiving similar offers from other organizations. After all, if you were gullible enough to become a victim of one scam, you are a likely prospect for other scams. Scam artists trade the names of their victims to try to extract as much money as possible from them. Or it may be the same scam artist, operating under many different names. You may even get a letter from another company, offering to help you recover your money for a small fee. This, too, is a scam.

There are many other types of scams, and they all involve your paying money to the scam operation. An advance-fee loan scam requires the up-front payment of application, processing, origination, and guarantee fees (most legitimate student loan programs deduct the fees from the disbursement check); a scholarship prize that requires you to first pay the taxes, a redemption fee, or a disbursement fee. An honor-and-recognition book scam congratulates you for being nominated for inclusion in their "nationally recognized" publication. If there is not a fee for inclusion, you can be sure that they will try to sell you a copy of the book. About 10 percent of the students who are included in the book will buy a copy. The common thread in all scams, whether aimed at college students or anyone else, is that the person attempting the fraud will want you to give them some money first.

Protecting Yourself from Scams

So how do you identify the difference between a scam and a legitimate offer? How do you protect yourself from scams?

The first tip is to remember the following common-sense rules:

- If it sounds too good to be true, it probably is.
- If you have to pay money to get money, it might be a scam.

If you receive an offer that seems suspicious, ask people you trust for their advice. Your family, friends, and school officials will all be able to help you. If nobody you know has ever heard of the program, let alone won the award, it probably is not legitimate. Trust your instincts. If you feel uneasy about an offer, do not pursue it.

- Call the Better Business Bureau located closest to the address of the organization. A satisfactory rating does not mean that the organization is legitimate. However, an unsatisfactory rating is a sure sign of problems.
- Call directory assistance to see if the company has a listing.
- Never give out your checking or savings account number or other personal information.
- Get an offer and guarantee in writing before sending money, and read the fine print.
- Read the information on the Internet Financial Aid Information Page: http://www.finaid.org/

If you are the victim of a scam, report it to the National Fraud Information Center at 800-876-7060 or http://www.fraud.org/. The center passes on the information it receives to the Federal Trade Commission and the State Attorney General. Also inform your school's financial aid office and student newspaper.

GLOSSARY OF SPECIAL TERMINOLOGY

▲

The terms and acronyms in this glossary are used in this book with some special meaning to scholarships or are terms that we believe may be unfamiliar or confusing to a student who does not reside in the U.S. We have not included the acronyms of professional accrediting bodies and associations in the belief that students involved in the relevant professional fields will either be familiar with the acronyms or easily be able to discover what the association may be. In looking through the program profiles, please be aware that sponsoring organizations frequently refer to their own organization as an acronym. The glossary is not an exhaustive list, so you should be sure to contact the sponsor for clarification of any words or terms whose meanings are unclear to you.

ACCREDITED PROGRAM; ACCREDITED COLLEGE
Indicates that an academic institution has been recognized as providing an adequate education. There are general regional accrediting agencies and specific academic-area accrediting agencies. Regional accreditation guarantees a minimum of adequacy in terms of academic facilities and programs. Many awards are for use only in colleges or universities that have regional accreditation. Awards for study in specific subject or career preparation fields frequently must be used in programs that have been accredited by a federally recognized professional education accrediting body or association. (Before coming to study in the United States, confirm with the appropriate government agency of your country that the accreditation of your selected American institution and program is recognized.)

ACT
A standardized test offered by American College Testing, Inc., required for admission to some American colleges. (see also *SAT*)

AFRICAN AMERICAN
A U.S. citizen who is regarded as having Negroid racial identity. U.S. citizens with Negroid racial identity who have ancestry from countries outside of Africa usually are considered by sponsors to be African American. U.S. citizens with ancestry from countries in Africa, but who have a racial identity other than Negroid, are usually not considered to be African American.

AK
Two-letter abbreviation for the state of Alaska.

AL
Two-letter abbreviation for the state of Alabama.

AMERICAN
In U.S. usage, an American is a native, inhabitant, or citizen of the United States. People from other countries of the Western Hemisphere are referred to by the name of their specific country (e.g., Canadian, Mexican, Colombian, Brazilian, Argentine, etc.). Citizens or immigrants to the U.S. who are identified by their origin or ancestry from a particular place outside of the U.S. typically are referred to by whatever may be the name for an inhabitant of that country or region attached to the word American (e.g., Mexican American, German American, Korean American, Asian American).

AR
Two-letter abbreviation for the state of Arkansas.

ASIAN AMERICAN
A U.S. citizen or resident immigrant who is identified by ancestry from East Asia or the countries of the Indian subcontinent. In typical usage, people identified with ancestry from the countries west of Pakistan or of central Asia or Siberia are not called Asian American. This term sometimes is restricted to citizens with Mongoloid racial identity. If national distinctions are important to you in relation to award eligibility, please contact the sponsor to ascertain its definition.

AWARD
A general term for gift aid that encompasses scholarships, grants, fellowships, and prizes. Awards do not have to be repaid.

AZ
Two-letter abbreviation for the state of Arizona.

BACCALAUREATE, BACHELOR'S DEGREE
The degree awarded upon successful completion of three to five years of study in the liberal arts and sciences in professional or in preprofessional areas.

CA
Two-letter abbreviation for the state of California.

CLASS RANK
Students' standing in the secondary school class relative to their peers. It is reported as a raw number (such as 3rd out of a class of 30) or in a percentile (top third, top 10 percent, etc.).

CLASSICS
A course of study specializing in the languages and literature of ancient Greece and Rome.

CO
Two-letter abbreviation for the state of Colorado.

COMMUNITY COLLEGE
A postsecondary institution governed by a local governmental agency (usually county or city) at which the associate degree is the highest credential awarded. A typical course of study is two years. Community college curricula are often are characterized by career and vocational training programs and nondegree continuing education programs. Community colleges usually lack residential facilities, and their students often commute to classes. Many students begin their higher education at community colleges with plans to eventually transfer to a four-year college or university program to obtain their bachelor's degree.

CONTEST
Awards given on the basis of a contest typically require the applicant to submit material (an essay, documentation of research, a creative work, a portfolio, autobiographical information) that is judged. The candidate whose material is deemed by the judges to be superior is awarded the gift aid. Contests in the performing arts may require actual competitive performances.

COUNTY
In the U.S., this is a governmental division smaller than and subordinate to the state level and, with only very few exceptions, larger than the municipal level. Some provinces of eastern Canada also have counties.

CREDIT, CREDIT HOURS, CREDITS
The unit of measurement of academic work successfully completed. There are several different credit systems. Under one system, a course might be worth 1 credit, while in another system the same course would be worth 3 "credit hours" or "hours," indicating the amount of time spent each week in class. Sometimes courses that are more advanced—or that meet for more hours—offer greater credit.

CT
Two-letter abbreviation for the state of Connecticut.

CURRICULUM VITAE
A summary account of one's life. Familiarly called a "c.v.". In academe, this is a relatively lengthy document. In addition to basic biographical data, it typically covers an individual's education, employment, teaching or research positions, administrative responsibilities, ongoing research, delivered and published papers, lengthier publications, awards and honors, professional memberships and posts, and other relevant accomplishments.

DC
Two-letter abbreviation for the District of Columbia.

DE
Two-letter abbreviation for the state of Delaware.

DEADLINE
The time by which something must be done or submitted. The deadlines announced by scholarship sponsors should be taken very seriously. If you anticipate a delay in your mail response reaching an American address, you may be able to use a fax as a means of communication. Check first with the sponsor to be sure that this is acceptable.

DEMONSTRATED FINANCIAL NEED
Proof that one's income and assets are insufficient to cover college expenses. This is usually a formal document on which an applicant will provide required information and backup documentation concerning income and assets. This form may supplied by the sponsor. Although you are disqualified from U.S. federal aid if you are not a U.S. citizen, an award sponsor may request a copy of the Free Application for Federal Student Aid (FAFSA) that American students submit to the U.S. Department of Education.

DEPENDENT, DEPENDENT CHILD
Usually a dependent is considered to be an immediate family member or spouse who receives over half of his or her support from another family member. The actual definitions of which family members may qualify and how old they can be may differ from sponsor to sponsor. Be sure to check with the sponsor

to find out its particular definition of dependent status if this is a factor in your eligibility.

DISABILITY, DISABILITIES, DISABLED

A disability is a limitation in one or more life functions, including seeing, hearing, thinking, walking, breathing, performing manual tasks, or speaking. Some disabilities are obvious physical impediments. In the U.S., there is also widespread recognition of disabilities, such as learning disabilities and attention deficit disorders, that can greatly affect a student's ability to perform well academically.

ENTERING STUDENTS, ENTERING FRESHMEN

Students who have been recently enrolled by a postsecondary institution but who may or may not have begun to attend classes.

FINANCIAL NEED ANALYSIS

The formula for calculating a student's financial need. This may be individual to a scholarship sponsor or be one of numerous standardized formulas. See *demonstrated financial need*, above.

FL

Two-letter abbreviation for the state of Florida.

FOREIGN

In the context of this book, this describes someone or something from a country other than the home country of the sponsor.

FOUR-YEAR INSTITUTION

A postsecondary institution or college that offers one or more four-year programs of study leading to a bachelor's degree. A four-year institution may be a unit within a university or an independent college.

FREELANCE

Describes independent workers who are hired to perform specific jobs but have no long-term employment agreement or commitments with the employer.

FRESHMAN, FRESHMEN

A student in the first year or with first-year standing at a college or secondary school. The term applies to both men and women students.

FULL-TIME, FULL-TIME COURSE LOAD, FULL-TIME STUDY

This denotes a student who meets a specific minimal criterion regarding the number of credits being taken in a particular period. Current U.S. Immigration and Naturalization Service regulations require that an international student pursue a full-time course of study. Colleges differ in the standards that they use to determine full-time status, and they apply different standards to different levels of study. A typical undergraduate program requires 12 credit hours or four courses each term to qualify as full-time. This standard is reduced, usually progressively, for each graduate level. You will have to check with the specific institution to find out how it defines a "full-time" course load.

GA

Two-letter abbreviation for the state of Georgia.

GPA

Grade point average. This is a system of scoring student achievement used by many colleges and universities. A student's GPA is computed by multiplying the numerical grade received in each course by the number of credits offered for each course, then dividing by the total number of credit hours studied. Most institutions use the following grade conversion scale: A = 4, B = 3, C = 2, D = 1, and E and F = 0.

GRADUATE STUDENT, GRADUATE STUDY

Refers to the level of higher education that will lead to a master's or doctoral degree. Graduate degrees are required to enter professional careers in medicine, business, college or university teaching, and many other fields. Among other requirements, admission to a graduate program requires a bachelor's degree or its equivalent.

GRANT

Gift aid, usually awarded to support research or specific projects. Grants provide funds directly related to carrying out proposed research but can include funds for travel and living expenses while conducting research away from a home institution. Many grant programs support doctoral dissertation research, and some can be applied to research related to a master's thesis. The term "grant" often is used imprecisely to refer to any form of gift aid, including scholarships and fellowships.

HANDICAPPED

Alternative term for "disabled." See *disability*, above.

HI

Two-letter abbreviation for the state of Hawaii.

HISPANIC

Used to refer to people, regardless of race, who identify with ancestry in Mexico, Puerto Rico, Cuba, Central or South America, and other countries with Spanish cultural roots. There is confusion as to whether Europeans of the Iberian Peninsula, Brazilians, and American Indians with a mixed heritage of Mexican or Central or South American tribes are included in this category. If these distinctions are important to you, check with the specific award sponsor to find out its definition.

HUMANITIES
Courses of study related to cultural heritage. The term "humanities" includes, but is not limited to the study of the languages; linguistics; literature; history; jurisprudence; philosophy; archaeology; comparative religion; ethics; the history, criticism, and theory of the arts; and those aspects of social sciences that have humanistic content and employ humanistic methods.

IA
Two-letter abbreviation for the state of Iowa.

ID
Two-letter abbreviation for the state of Idaho.

IL
Two-letter abbreviation for the state of Illinois.

IMPAIRED, IMPAIRMENT
Alternative terms for "disabled" or "disability." See *disability*, above.

IN
Two-letter abbreviation for the state of Indiana.

INTERNATIONAL
In this book, "international" is the adjective used generally to describe students from outside the U.S. or Canada who are planning study at U.S. or Canadian institutions.

INTERNSHIP
The opportunity for recipients to gain practical experience in their field of interest by working with and under the supervision of the professional staff of an organization. Paid internships offer a wage or fixed allowance to the student during the period of internship. Often an intern works on projects of interest to the host organization or learns specific techniques. Internships can range in length up to an entire academic year.

INTERVIEW
A conversation between the candidate for an award and the individual or group that will decide who receives the award. Usually this is an actual meeting of the parties that is conducted at the sponsor's offices. The purpose is to allow the judges the opportunity to better evaluate the suitability of the candidate in accordance with the program's goals.

JUNIOR
A student in the third year or with third-year standing at a college or secondary school.

KS
Two-letter abbreviation for the state of Kansas.

KY
Two-letter abbreviation for the state of Kentucky.

LA
Two-letter abbreviation for the state of Louisiana.

LETTER OF RECOMMENDATION
A document written and signed by an individual of professional authority or credence, typically a teacher, school administrator, or professional in a subject field that attests to the quality of an applicant's qualifications, work, character, or abilities. The letter may be specifically addressed or written to any recipient who may be interested. Sponsors may request that the signer send the letter directly.

MA
Two-letter abbreviation for the state of Massachusetts.

MAJOR
The academic area in which a student chooses to concentrate. Generally, major course requirements take up one quarter to one half of the student's undergraduate studies and are combined with other general education requirements.

MD
Two-letter abbreviation for the state of Maryland.

ME
Two-letter abbreviation for the state of Maine.

MERIT-BASED
Describes awards that are given on the basis of academic, creative, athletic, or community service–related achievement or ability.

MI
Two-letter abbreviation for the state of Michigan.

MINORITY
In the context of this book, this is a group with a coherent identity that historically has been frustrated in achieving parity with groups that comprise the U.S. "majority." The traditional and most common usage of the term is in reference to racial or ethnic populations, specifically African Americans and other people with a Negroid racial identity, Hispanics, and Native Americans. In higher education and other areas of public interaction, the "minority" label has been

attached to or claimed by other groups, such as women, homosexuals, and people with disabilities, that have experienced bias or relative lack of economic opportunity or progress.

MN
Two-letter abbreviation for the state of Minnesota.

MO
Two-letter abbreviation for the state of Missouri.

MS
Two-letter abbreviation for the state of Mississippi.

MT
Two-letter abbreviation for the state of Montana.

NATIVE AMERICAN
denotes identity with one of the aboriginal tribal populations of the Americas, excluding Inuit or Eskimo people. American Indian is a widely used alternative term. If this is used as a criterion for a scholarship award, proof of tribal membership usually will be required.

NC
Two-letter abbreviation for the state of North Carolina.

ND
Two-letter abbreviation for the state of North Dakota.

NE
Two-letter abbreviation for the state of Nebraska.

NH
Two-letter abbreviation for the state of New Hampshire.

NJ
Two-letter abbreviation for the state of New Jersey.

NM
Two-letter abbreviation for the state of New Mexico.

NOMINATED, NOMINATION
Applicants are 'nominated' when they are brought to the consideration of a sponsor by a third party or organization. Usually the nominator must be in a position of professional authority or high reputation, be unrelated to the candidate, and be familiar with the candidate's academic achievements, community service record, talents, or character.

NONRENEWABLE
Used to describe awards that will not be awarded more than once to the same recipient.

NV
Two-letter abbreviation for the state of Nevada.

NY
Two-letter abbreviation for the state of New York.

OH
Two-letter abbreviation for the state of Ohio.

OK
Two-letter abbreviation for the state of Oklahoma.

ONE-TIME AWARD
Used to describe awards that have a term limit of coverage. Check with the sponsor to find out if reapplication for a new award is allowed when the current award period ceases.

OR
Two-letter abbreviation for the state of Oregon.

PA
Two-letter abbreviation for the state of Pennsylvania.

PERFORMING ARTS
The fields of dance, music, and theater.

POSTSECONDARY
Used to describe any organized education above grade twelve of the secondary (high school or preparatory school) level in the American educational system.

PR
Two-letter abbreviation for the commonwealth of Puerto Rico.

PRIZE
Gift aid given for outstanding achievement or winning a competition.

QUARTER
A division of a college or university's academic year if the institution divides its year into four terms (quarters).

REAPPLICATION, REAPPLY
Indicates that a new application is required to secure renewal of an award. Frequently in a reapplication you have no intrinsic advantage over other applicants for the award.

RECOMMENDATION
see *letter of recommendation*, above

REGISTRATION FEE
A fee charged by certain sponsors to consider your application.

RENEWABLE
Describes awards that either may automatically be renewed for a length of study beyond a single year or can be renewed with a new application.

RESIDENT, RESIDENTS

Many awards require that recipients be residents of a specific state. Each state of the United States sets its own criteria for what conditions must be met to be considered a "legal" resident. Typically, this consists of having one's primary place of residence within the state for a specified length of time. Non-U.S. citizens who have "permanent resident" status from the U.S. Immigration and Naturalization Service can be considered legal residents of one of the United States if they can meet that specific state's criteria.

RESUME

A summary account of one's life, education, and experience. Typically this is shorter than a *curriculum vitae,* usually between one and two pages in length. In addition to basic biographical data, it typically covers an individual's education, employment, teaching or research positions, responsibilities, and other relevant information.

RI

Two-letter abbreviation for the state of Rhode Island.

SASE

A stamped self-addressed envelope to be included with inquiry or application material to ensure a response. If you are mailing internationally, you will need to acquire the proper amount of U.S. postage to secure delivery from the U.S. to your country.

SAT

A standardized test, offered by the College Board through the Educational Testing Service, required for admission to many American colleges.

SC

Two-letter abbreviation for the state of South Carolina.

SCHOLARSHIP

Precisely defined, this is gift aid used to cover tuition and fees for undergraduate study. However, "scholarship" is frequently used generically to describe all forms of gift aid, including fellowships and grants. You will need to read the full description of a scholarship award program in order to ascertain to what level of study it may apply.

SCHOOL

In the context of this publication, the word school is a general term used to refer to any institution of secondary or higher education. This includes high schools, colleges, universities, and graduate or professional institutions.

SD

Two-letter abbreviation for the state of South Dakota.

SEMESTER

A division of a college or university's academic year if the institution divides its year into two terms (semesters).

SEMINAR

An advanced or graduate-level class or course of study on a particular subject in which each student does original research under the guidance of a faculty member.

SEMINARY

A professional school or other institution of higher education for training in religion, usually as preparation for priesthood, ministry, or rabbinate.

SENIOR

A student in the fourth year or with fourth-year standing at a college or secondary school.

SOPHOMORE

A student in the second year or with second-year standing at a college or secondary school.

TN

Two-letter abbreviation for the state of Tennessee.

TRANSCRIPT

The record of your academic work. Many award programs will require the submission of an official copy, translated into English, of your secondary school transcript.

TRIMESTER

A division of a college or university's academic year if the institution divides its year into three terms (trimesters).

TUITION

The fees that cover academic expenses. Other expenses, such as those for room and board (lodging and meals), health insurance, activities, and transportation, are not included in tuition figures.

TWO-YEAR INSTITUTION

A postsecondary institution at which the associate degree is the highest credential awarded. A typical course of study is two years. Credits earned at an accredited two-year institution generally will be transferable for study at a four-year college or university.

TX

Two-letter abbreviation for the state of Texas.

UNDERGRADUATE

An associate or bachelor's degree candidate or a description of such a candidate's courses. Once students have earned a bachelor's degree, they are eligible for entry to graduate programs at the master's and doctoral levels.

UNIVERSITY

A large educational institution comprising a number of divisions, including graduate and professional schools. Academic offerings are usually more comprehensive than at colleges. A few universities have no professional schools or offer no doctoral programs.

UT

Two-letter abbreviation for the state of Utah.

VA

Two-letter abbreviation for the state of Virginia.

VETERAN

A former member of the armed forces. Awards to veterans usually require service in one of the U.S. armed service branches (Army, Air Force, Navy, Marines) and an honorable discharge.

VI

Two-letter abbreviation for the territory of the U.S. Virgin Islands.

VOCATIONAL-TECHNICAL SCHOOLS

Institutions of postsecondary education that offer certificates or diplomas requiring fewer than two years of study. Programs of study usually are directly related to preparation for specific careers.

VT

Two-letter abbreviation for the state of Vermont.

WA

Two-letter abbreviation for the state of Washington.

WI

Two-letter abbreviation for the state of Wisconsin.

WV

Two-letter abbreviation for the state of West Virginia.

WY

Two-letter abbreviation for the state of Wyoming.

UNDERGRADUATE AWARDS

ACADEMIC/CAREER AREAS–UNDERGRADUATE

▲

AGRIBUSINESS

▼ SOCIETY FOR RANGE MANAGEMENT

Masonic Range Science Scholarship • 1

Award provides a cash payment to institution of student's choice. Applicant must be nominated by a Society for Range Management member, a Soil and Water Conservation District, or a National Association of Conservation District. One-time award for the study of range science. For use in freshman year.

Academic/Career Areas: Agribusiness; Agriculture; Animal/Veterinary Sciences; Earth Science; Natural Resources; Physical Sciences and Math.

Award: Scholarship for use in freshman year; not renewable. *Number:* 1. *Amount:* $1000–$1800.

Application Requirements: Application, autobiography, references, transcript. **Deadline:** January 15.

E-mail: srmden@ix.netcom.com

Phone: 303-355-7070 **Fax:** 303-355-5059

World Wide Web: http://www.srm.org

Contact: J. C. Whittekiend, Executive Vice President
Society for Range Management
1839 York Street
Denver, CO 80206-1213

▼ UNITED AGRIBUSINESS LEAGUE

United Agribusiness League Scholarship Program • 2

One-time award of $1000-$4000 available to students enrolled or planning to enroll in a degree program in agribusiness at a two- or four-year institution. Contact for further information.

Academic/Career Areas: Agribusiness.

Award: Scholarship for use in any year; not renewable. *Amount:* $1000–$4000.

Eligibility Requirements: Applicant must be enrolled at a two-year or four-year institution.

Application Requirements: Application, essay, financial need analysis, references, test scores, transcript. **Deadline:** April 20.

Phone: 714-975-1424 **Fax:** 714-975-1671

Contact: Paula Lopez, Administrative Assistant
United Agribusiness League
54 Corporate Park
Irvine, CA 92606-5105

AGRICULTURE

▼ AMERICAN ASSOCIATION OF CEREAL CHEMISTS FOUNDATION

American Association of Cereal Chemists Undergraduate Scholarships • 3

Award for full-time undergraduates with minimum 3.0 GPA preparing for a career in cereal chemistry and technology. Must have passed at least one term and have at least one term remaining at approved institution. Submit department head endorsement, essay in form of letter of application for scholarship.

Academic/Career Areas: Agriculture; Applied Sciences; Food Science/Nutrition; Physical Sciences and Math.

Award: Scholarship for use in freshman, sophomore, junior, or senior year; not renewable. *Number:* 12–15. *Amount:* $1000–$2000.

Eligibility Requirements: Applicant must be enrolled at a four-year institution and must have an interest in leadership.

Application Requirements: Application, essay, references, test scores, transcript. **Deadline:** April 1.

Contact: Dr. Elwood F. Caldwell, Scholarship/
Fellowship Jury Chairman
American Association of Cereal Chemists
Foundation
3340 Pilot Knob Road
St. Paul, MN 55121-2097

▼ CHARLES A. AND ANNE MORROW LINDBERGH FOUNDATION

Lindbergh Grants Program • 4

Grant for research in area addressing balance between technological advance and preservation of human/natural environment. Open to all nationalities. Apply in English. Submit proposal. Institutional affiliation not required. One-time award of up to $10,580.

Academic/Career Areas: Agriculture; Animal/Veterinary Sciences; Applied Sciences; Area/Ethnic Studies; Arts; Aviation/Aerospace; Biology; Education; Health and Medical Sciences; Horticulture/Floriculture; Humanities; Nursing.

Award: Grant for use in any year; not renewable. *Number:* 10. *Amount:* up to $10,580.

Application Requirements: Application, references, self-addressed stamped envelope. **Deadline:** June 16.

E-mail: lindfdtn@mtn.org

Phone: 612-338-1703 **Fax:** 612-338-6826

World Wide Web: http://www.mtn.org/lindfdtn

Contact: Marlene White, Grants Administrator
Charles A. and Anne Morrow Lindbergh Foundation
708 South Third Street, Suite 110
Minneapolis, MN 55415-1141

▼ GARDEN CLUB OF AMERICA

Garden Club of America-"GCA Awards in Environmental Studies" • 5

One-time award available to students following their first, second, or third year of college who are majoring in environmental studies, ecology, or related field for credit in a summer course at a U.S. college or university. Submit course plan. For use in summer only. Funds two or more students annually.

Academic/Career Areas: Agriculture; Earth Science; Meteorology/Atmospheric Science; Natural Resources; Physical Sciences and Math.

Award: Scholarship for use in freshman, sophomore, or junior year; not renewable. *Number:* 2. *Amount:* $1500.

Application Requirements: Application, essay, references, self-addressed stamped envelope, transcript. **Deadline:** February 15.

World Wide Web: http://www.users.interport.net/~gca

Contact: Scholarship Committee
Garden Club of America
14 East 60th Street
New York, NY 10022

▼ KENTUCKY NATURAL RESOURCES AND ENVIRONMENTAL PROTECTION CABINET

Environmental Protection Scholarships • 6

Renewable awards for college juniors, seniors, and graduate students for tuition, fees, and room and board at a Kentucky state university. Awards of $3000 to $3500 per semester for up to four semesters. Six awards given in 1997 for a total of $23,000. Minimum 2.5 GPA required. Must agree to work full-time for the Kentucky Natural Resources and Environmental Protection Cabinet upon graduation.

Academic/Career Areas: Agriculture; Chemical Engineering; Civil Engineering; Earth Science; Health and Medical Sciences; Natural Resources.

Award: Scholarship for use in junior, senior, or graduate years; renewable. *Number:* 3–5.

Eligibility Requirements: Applicant must be enrolled at a four-year institution and studying in Kentucky.

Application Requirements: Application, essay, interview, references, transcript. **Deadline:** February 15.

E-mail: kipp@pop.uky.edu

Phone: 606-257-1299 **Fax:** 606-323-1049

Contact: Scholarship Program Coordinator
Kentucky Natural Resources and
Environmental Protection Cabinet
233 Mining/Mineral Resources Building
University of Kentucky
Lexington, KY 40506-0107

▼ MASTER BREWERS ASSOCIATION SCHOLARSHIP FOUNDATION, INC.

Master Brewers Association-America's Scholarships • 7

Students must either have a parent employed for five years in the brewing industry or have been employed for two years in the industry themselves. Must be junior/senior studying a science related to the technical areas of malting/brewing.

Academic/Career Areas: Agriculture; Biology; Chemical Engineering; Electrical/Electronic Engineering; Engineering/Technology; Food Science/Nutrition; Mechanical Engineering; Physical Sciences and Math.

Award: Scholarship for use in junior or senior year; renewable. *Number:* 2. *Amount:* $2000.

Eligibility Requirements: Applicant must be enrolled at a four-year institution and have employment experience in brewing industry.

Application Requirements: Application, references, transcript.
Deadline: February 28.
Contact: Master Brewers Association Scholarship
Foundation, Inc.
2421 North Mayfair Road, Suite 310
Wauwatosa, WI 53226

▼ SIGMA XI, THE SCIENTIFIC RESEARCH SOCIETY

Sigma Xi Grants-in-Aid of Research • 8
One-time award for scientific investigation in the sciences. Must be undergraduate or graduate student enrolled at an accredited institution. Faculty adviser must be member of Sigma Xi. Deadlines: February 1, May 1, and November 1.
Academic/Career Areas: Agriculture; Animal/Veterinary Sciences; Biology; Earth Science; Engineering/Technology; Health and Medical Sciences; Meteorology/Atmospheric Science; Physical Sciences and Math; Social Sciences.
Award: Grant for use in freshman, sophomore, junior, senior, or graduate years; not renewable. *Number:* 850–900. *Amount:* $100–$1000.
Eligibility Requirements: Applicant must be enrolled at a two-year or four-year institution.
Application Requirements: Application, references.
E-mail: giar@sigmaxi.org
Phone: 919-547-5206 **Fax:** 919-549-0090
World Wide Web: http://www.sigmaxi.org
Contact: Deborah Donati, Programs Coordinator
Sigma Xi, The Scientific Research Society
99 Alexander Drive
Box 13975
Research Triangle Park, NC 27709

▼ SOCIETY FOR RANGE MANAGEMENT

Masonic Range Science Scholarship see number 1

▼ WOMEN GROCERS OF AMERICA

Mary Macey Scholarship • 9
Award for students intending to pursue a grocery industry-related career. Includes majors in such areas as food marketing management, agricultural economics, food service technology, communications, or business management/administration. Does not include majors in such areas as public health or hotel/restaurant management. One-time award for students who have completed fresh-man year. Submit statement and recommendation from sponsor in the grocery industry.
Academic/Career Areas: Agriculture; Business/Consumer Services; Communications; Economics; Food Service/Hospitality.
Award: Scholarship for use in sophomore, junior, senior, or graduate years; not renewable. *Number:* 2. *Amount:* $1000.
Eligibility Requirements: Applicant must be enrolled at a two-year or four-year institution.
Application Requirements: Application, transcript. **Deadline:** June 1.
Phone: 703-437-5300 **Fax:** 703-437-7768
Contact: Ms. Anne Wintersteen, Director of Administration
Women Grocers of America
1825 Samuel Morse Drive
Reston, VA 20190-5317

ANIMAL/VETERINARY SCIENCES

▼ APPALOOSA HORSE CLUB-APPALOOSA YOUTH PROGRAM

Lew & JoAnn Eklund Educational Scholarship • 10
One-time award for college juniors and seniors and graduate students studying a field related to the equine industry. Must be member or dependent of member of the Appaloosa Horse Club. Submit picture and three recommendations. Award based on merit.
Academic/Career Areas: Animal/Veterinary Sciences.
Award: Scholarship for use in junior, senior, or graduate years; not renewable. *Number:* 1. *Amount:* $2000.
Eligibility Requirements: Applicant must be enrolled at a four-year institution and member of Appaloosa Horse Club/Appaloosa Youth Association.
Application Requirements: Application, photo, references, transcript. **Deadline:** June 10.
E-mail: aphc@appaloosa.com
Phone: 208-882-5578 **Fax:** 208-882-8150

ACADEMIC/CAREER AREAS–UNDERGRADUATE

Lew & JoAnn Eklund Educational Scholarship (continued)

Contact: Appaloosa Youth Foundation Scholarship
Committee
Appaloosa Horse Club-Appaloosa Youth
Program
PO Box 8403
Moscow, ID 83843

▼ CHARLES A. AND ANNE MORROW LINDBERGH FOUNDATION

Lindbergh Grants Program   *see number 4*

▼ DOG WRITERS' EDUCATIONAL TRUST

Dog Writers' Educational Trust Scholarship • 11

For students and immediate relatives of those who have participated in dog shows (including junior showmanship, obedience training, or field training), raised guide dogs, or worked with a humane group. Application fee: $25. Merit considered. Five copies of application, information about dog-related and work-related experience, 250-word essay on college and career goals, 250-word essay on "Why People Own Dogs," and official transcripts required.
Academic/Career Areas: Animal/Veterinary Sciences; Communications.
Award: Scholarship for use in any year; not renewable. *Number:* 10. *Amount:* $1000.
Eligibility Requirements: Applicant must have an interest in animal/agricultural competition.
Application Requirements: Application, essay, financial need analysis, self-addressed stamped envelope, transcript.
Fee: $25. **Deadline:** December 31.
Contact: Roger Alan Au, Executive Director
Dog Writers' Educational Trust
PO 760
North Olmsted, OH 44070

▼ MANOMET CENTER FOR CONSERVATION SCIENCES

Kathleen S. Anderson Award   • 12

One-time award for research projects in the Western Hemisphere involving the ecological and behavioral activities of birds, and especially for projects relevant to bird conservation. Must submit two copies of proposal with budget and references.
Academic/Career Areas: Animal/Veterinary Sciences; Biology.

Award: Scholarship for use in any year; not renewable.
Number: 1–2. *Amount:* $1000.
Eligibility Requirements: Applicant must be enrolled at a four-year institution.
Application Requirements: Application, essay, references.
Deadline: December 1.
Phone: 508-224-6521 **Fax:** 508-224-9220
Contact: Jennie Robbins, Administrative Assistant
Manomet Center for Conservation Sciences
PO Box 1770
Manomet, MA 02345-1770

▼ SIGMA XI, THE SCIENTIFIC RESEARCH SOCIETY

National Academy of Science Grants-in-Aid of Research   • 13

One-time award for scientific investigation in natural or physical sciences. Must be graduate or undergraduate student enrolled at an accredited institution. Deadlines are February 1, May 1, and November 1.
Academic/Career Areas: Animal/Veterinary Sciences; Biology; Earth Science; Health and Medical Sciences; Meteorology/Atmospheric Science; Natural Resources; Physical Sciences and Math.
Award: Grant for use in freshman, sophomore, junior, senior, or graduate years; not renewable. *Number:* 850–900. *Amount:* $100–$2500.
Eligibility Requirements: Applicant must be enrolled at a two-year or four-year institution.
Application Requirements: Application, references.
E-mail: giar@sigmaxi.org
Phone: 919-547-5206 **Fax:** 919-549-0090
World Wide Web: http://www.sigmaxi.org
Contact: Deborah Donati, Programs Coordinator
Sigma Xi, The Scientific Research Society
99 Alexander Drive
Box 13975
Research Triangle Park, NC 27709

Sigma Xi Grants-in-Aid of Research   *see number 8*

▼ SOCIETY FOR RANGE MANAGEMENT

Masonic Range Science Scholarship *see number 1*

⏎

▼ WILSON ORNITHOLOGICAL SOCIETY

Louis Agassiz Fuertes Award • 14

One-time award for scientific research on birds. Available to all ornithologists although graduate students and young professionals are preferred. Must submit research proposal.
Academic/Career Areas: Animal/Veterinary Sciences; Biology; Natural Resources.
Award: Grant for use in any year; not renewable. *Number:* up to 1. *Amount:* $600.
Application Requirements: Application, references. **Deadline:** January 15.
E-mail: jhinshaw@umich.edu
Phone: 313-764-0457
World Wide Web: http://www.ummz.lsa.umich.edu/birds/wos.html
Contact: Janet Hinshaw, Librarian
Wilson Ornithological Society
Museum of Zoology
University of Michigan
Ann Arbor, MI 48109-1079

Margaret Morse Nice Award • 15

One-time award for scientific research on birds. Available to independent researchers without access to funds or facilities at a college or university. Must be a nonprofessional to apply. Submit research proposal.
Academic/Career Areas: Animal/Veterinary Sciences; Biology; Natural Resources.
Award: Grant for use in any year; not renewable. *Number:* 1. *Amount:* $200.
Application Requirements: Application, references. **Deadline:** January 15.
E-mail: jhinshaw@umich.edu
Phone: 313-764-0457
World Wide Web: http://www.ummz.lsa.umich.edu/birds/wos.html
Contact: Janet Hinshaw, Librarian
Wilson Ornithological Society
Museum of Zoology
University of Michigan
Ann Arbor, MI 48109-1079

Paul A. Stewart Awards • 16

One-time award for studies of bird movements based on banding, analysis of recoveries, and returns of banded birds, or research with an emphasis on economic ornithology. Submit research proposal.
Academic/Career Areas: Animal/Veterinary Sciences; Biology; Natural Resources.
Award: Grant for use in any year; not renewable. *Number:* 4–6. *Amount:* $200.
Application Requirements: Application, references. **Deadline:** January 15.
E-mail: jhinshaw@umich.edu
Phone: 313-764-0457
World Wide Web: http://www.ummz.lsa.umich.edu/birds/wos.html
Contact: Janet Hinshaw, Librarian
Wilson Ornithological Society
Museum of Zoology
University of Michigan
Ann Arbor, MI 48109-1079

APPLIED SCIENCES

▼ AMERICAN ASSOCIATION OF CEREAL CHEMISTS FOUNDATION

American Association of Cereal Chemists Undergraduate Scholarships see number 3

▼ AMERICAN SOCIETY FOR PHOTOGRAMMETRY AND REMOTE SENSING

Earth Observation Satellite Company Award for Application of Digital Landsat TM Data • 17

Award for undergraduate or graduate students to stimulate development of applications of digital Landsat Thematic Mapper (TM) data. For applied research with digital Landset data. Contact for details and deadlines.
Academic/Career Areas: Applied Sciences; Engineering/Technology; Physical Sciences and Math.
Award: Scholarship for use in freshman, sophomore, junior, senior, or graduate years; not renewable. *Number:* 1. *Amount:* up to $4000.
Application Requirements: Application, autobiography, references.
E-mail: wendyw@asprs.org
Phone: 301-493-0290 Ext. 20 **Fax:** 301-493-0208
World Wide Web: http://www.asprs.org/asprs

Earth Observation Satellite Company Award for Application of Digital Landsat TM Data (continued)

Contact: Wendy Wattman, Awards Coordinator
American Society for Photogrammetry and
Remote Sensing
5410 Grosvenor Lane, Suite 210
Bethesda, MD 20814

▼ ASSOCIATED WESTERN UNIVERSITIES, INC.

Associated Western Universities Student Research Fellowships • 18

One-time award for college undergraduates to participate in science/technology research with experienced scientists/engineers at participating universities. Submit application, transcript, and references by February 1. Write for further information. Must have completed at least one year of study.
Academic/Career Areas: Applied Sciences; Chemical Engineering; Civil Engineering; Computer Science/Data Processing; Earth Science; Electrical/Electronic Engineering; Engineering/Technology; Mechanical Engineering; Meteorology/Atmospheric Science; Natural Resources; Nuclear Science; Physical Sciences and Math.
Eligibility Requirements: Applicant must be enrolled at a four-year institution.
Application Requirements: Application, references, transcript.
Deadline: February 1.
E-mail: info@awu.org
Phone: 801-273-8900 **Fax:** 801-277-5632
World Wide Web: http://www.awu.org
Contact: Associated Western Universities, Inc.
4190 South Highland Drive, Suite 211
Salt Lake City, UT 84124-4234

▼ CAMPUS SAFETY DIVISION

Campus Safety Scholarship • 19

Two awards for full-time undergraduate and graduate students who are majoring in academic programs leading to degrees in safety, health, or environmental affairs. One-time award of $1000. Financial Aid Administrator must attest to financial need. Must include self-addressed stamped envelope. Deadline: March 31.
Academic/Career Areas: Applied Sciences; Biology; Engineering-Related Technologies; Health Administration; Health and Medical Sciences; Nursing; Physical Sciences and Math; Science, Technology & Society.

Award: Scholarship for use in sophomore, junior, senior, or graduate years; not renewable. *Number:* 2. *Amount:* $1000.
Eligibility Requirements: Applicant must be enrolled at a two-year or four-year institution.
Application Requirements: Application, essay, self-addressed stamped envelope. **Deadline:** March 31.
E-mail: brouwere@nsc.org
Contact: Campus Safety Division
1121 Spring Lake Drive
Itasca, IL 60143

▼ CHARLES A. AND ANNE MORROW LINDBERGH FOUNDATION

Lindbergh Grants Program see number 4

▼ CHEMICAL HERITAGE FOUNDATION

Chemical Heritage Foundation Travel Grants • 20

Travel grants to interested individuals to make use of research resources of Beckman Center for History of Chemistry, Othmer Library of Chemical History, and associated facilities. Deadlines vary. Submit proposal, curriculum vitae, and resume for each visit.
Academic/Career Areas: Applied Sciences; Business/Consumer Services; Chemical Engineering; History; Physical Sciences and Math.
Award: Scholarship for use in any year; not renewable. *Amount:* up to $500.
Application Requirements: References. **Deadline:** Continuous.
Phone: 215-925-2222 Ext. 224 **Fax:** 215-925-1954
World Wide Web: http://www.chem.heritage.org
Contact: Program Manager
Chemical Heritage Foundation
315 Chestnut Street
Philadelphia, PA 19106

▼ INTERNATIONAL SOCIETY FOR OPTICAL ENGINEERING-SPIE

SPIE Educational Scholarships and Grants in Optical Engineering • 21

One-time awards for the study of optics and optical engineering. Contact International Society for Optical Engineering for applications and further information.
Academic/Career Areas: Applied Sciences; Engineering/Technology; Health and Medical Sciences; Physical Sciences and Math.

Award: Scholarship for use in any year; not renewable. *Number:* 15–20. *Amount:* $500–$7000.
Application Requirements: Application, references. **Deadline:** April 4.
E-mail: education@spie.org
Phone: 360-676-3290 **Fax:** 360-647-1445
Contact: Ali Khounsary, Chair, Scholarship
Committee
International Society for Optical
Engineering-SPIE
PO Box 10
Bellingham, WA 98227-0010

▼ INVENTURE PLACE, NATIONAL INVENTORS HALL OF FAME

BFGoodrich Collegiate Inventors Program • 22

Competition to recognize and reward full-time college and university students who have produced outstanding research, innovations, and discoveries. Must be an individual or team and have a university adviser. Adviser receives additional prize money. Write for application or visit Web site and download application.
Academic/Career Areas: Applied Sciences; Engineering/Technology; Physical Sciences and Math.
Award: Prize for use in any year; not renewable. *Number:* 1–6. *Amount:* $3000–$7500.
Application Requirements: Application, applicant must enter a contest, essay. **Deadline:** June 2.
E-mail: pkunce@invent.org
Phone: 330-849-6887 **Fax:** 330-762-6313
World Wide Web: http://www.invent.org/bfg/bfghome.html
Contact: Paul Kunce, Program Coordinator
Inventure Place, National Inventors Hall of
Fame
221 South Broadway Street
Akron, OH 44308-1505

▼ MCDERMOTT, INCORPORATED

McDermott Scholarship • 23

Applicants must be high school seniors who are children of eligible employees of McDermott International, Inc., or its subsidiaries. For undergraduate study in science, engineering, or business at four-year institution. Renewable award of $1500.
Academic/Career Areas: Applied Sciences; Business/Consumer Services; Computer Science/Data Processing; Engineering/Technology; Physical Sciences and Math.

Award: Scholarship for use in freshman, sophomore, junior, or senior year; renewable. *Number:* 20. *Amount:* $1500.
Eligibility Requirements: Applicant must be high school student and enrolled at a four-year institution.
Application Requirements: Application, essay, financial need analysis, test scores, transcript. **Deadline:** March 31.
Contact: Don Washington, Manager, Corporate
Communications
McDermott, Incorporated
PO Box 60035
New Orleans, LA 70160

ARCHITECTURE

▼ AMERICAN INSTITUTE OF ARCHITECTS

American Institute of Architects/AHA Fellowship in Health Facilities Design • 24

One-time award for scholars who have earned and received a professional degree in architecture or are in the final year of undergraduate work leading to a degree. Must be a citizen of the U.S., Canada, or Mexico. Several types of fellowships available. Write for details.
Academic/Career Areas: Architecture.
Award: Scholarship for use in senior or graduate years; not renewable.
Application Requirements: Application. **Deadline:** January 15.
Phone: 202-626-7511 **Fax:** 202-626-7420
World Wide Web: http://www.aiaonline.com
Contact: Mary Felber, Director, Scholarship Programs
American Institute of Architects
1735 New York Avenue, NW
Washington, DC 20006-5292

▼ AMERICAN INSTITUTE OF ARCHITECTS/AMERICAN ARCHITECTURAL FOUNDATION

American Institute of Architects/American Architectural Foundation Scholarship for Professional Degree Candidates • 25

Available to students in the final two years of a professional degree, NAAB-accredited program leading to a Bachelor of Arts or Master's. Applications available from head of department. One-time award.

American Institute of Architects/American Architectural Foundation Scholarship for Professional Degree Candidates (continued)

Academic/Career Areas: Architecture.
Award: Scholarship for use in junior, senior, or graduate years; not renewable. *Number:* 250. *Amount:* $500–$2500.
Eligibility Requirements: Applicant must be enrolled at a four-year institution.
Application Requirements: Application, essay, financial need analysis, references, transcript. **Deadline:** February 1.
Phone: 202-626-7511 **Fax:** 202-626-7420
Contact: Mary Felber, Director, Scholarship Programs
American Institute of Architects/American
Architectural Foundation
1735 New York Avenue, NW
Washington, DC 20006-5292

▼ JOHN F. KENNEDY LIBRARY FOUNDATION

Kennedy Research Grants • 26

One-time grants for students and scholars to help defray costs incurred while doing research in the Kennedy Library. Must include ten-page writing sample, project budget and a vita. See application for further details.
Academic/Career Areas: Architecture; Criminal Justice/Criminology; Economics; Education; History; Humanities; Library Sciences; Literature/English/Writing; Political Science; Social Sciences.
Award: Grant for use in any year; not renewable. *Number:* 15–20. *Amount:* $500–$1500.
Eligibility Requirements: Applicant must be studying in Massachusetts.
Application Requirements: Application, driver's license, essay, financial need analysis, references, transcript.
Deadline: Continuous.
E-mail: library@kennedy.nara.gov
Contact: William Johnson, Chief Archivist
John F. Kennedy Library Foundation
Columbia Point
Boston, MA 02125

▼ NATIONAL ASSOCIATION OF WOMEN IN CONSTRUCTION

National Association of Women in Construction Undergraduate Scholarships • 27

One-time award for any student having at least one year of study remaining in a construction-related program leading to an associate or higher degree. Awards range from $500-$2000. Submit academic advisor evaluation, application, and transcript of grades.
Academic/Career Areas: Architecture; Civil Engineering; Drafting; Electrical/Electronic Engineering; Engineering/Technology; Engineering-Related Technologies; Landscape Architecture; Mechanical Engineering; Trade/Technical Specialties.
Award: Scholarship for use in any year; not renewable. *Number:* 40–50. *Amount:* $500–$2000.
Eligibility Requirements: Applicant must be ages 17-70.
Application Requirements: Application, financial need analysis, interview, transcript. **Deadline:** February 1.
Phone: 800-552-3506
Contact: Joan Mehos, Administrator
National Association of Women in
Construction
327 South Adams Street
Fort Worth, TX 76104

▼ NATIONAL ASSOCIATION OF WOMEN IN CONSTRUCTION FOUNDER'S SCHOLARSHIP FOUNDATION

National Association of Women in Contruction Founder's Scholarship Award • 28

Scholarship available to those interested in pursuing a construction-related degree. Scholarship is not limited to women. One-time award available to college sophomores, juniors, and seniors. Contact office for details.
Academic/Career Areas: Architecture; Civil Engineering; Engineering/Technology; Mechanical Engineering; Trade/Technical Specialties.
Award: Scholarship for use in sophomore, junior, or senior year; not renewable. *Number:* 40–50. *Amount:* $500–$2500.
Application Requirements: Application, interview, references, self-addressed stamped envelope, transcript.
Deadline: February 1.
E-mail: nawic@onramp.net
Phone: 914-961-7879
Contact: Joan Mehos, Administrator
National Association of Women in
Construction Founder's Scholarship
Foundation
327 South Adams Street
Fort Worth, TX 76104

▼ SKIDMORE, OWINGS, AND MERRILL FOUNDATION

Interior Architecture Traveling Fellowship Program • 29

Award for graduating seniors in accredited U.S. architectural/interior design schools, to study interior design abroad. Must be nominated. Submit portfolio and itinerary. Write for deadlines and more information. One-time award of $7500.
Academic/Career Areas: Architecture.
Application Requirements: Application, portfolio.
E-mail: somfoundation@som.com
Contact: Lisa Westerfield, Administrative Director
Skidmore, Owings, and Merrill Foundation
224 South Michigan Avenue, Suite 1000
Chicago, IL 60604

AREA/ETHNIC STUDIES

▼ AMERICAN SCHOOLS OF ORIENTAL RESEARCH

Endowment for Biblical Research and American Schools of Oriental Research Summer Research Grants and Travel Scholarships • 30

EBR awards may be used for research in the Holy Land on projects involving archaeological survey or excavation, textual or linguistic study, anthropology or natural sciences, or interpretation or analysis of excavated materials or manuscripts. Research into Biblical periods is especially encouraged. Deadline: February 1.
Academic/Career Areas: Area/Ethnic Studies; History; Museum Studies; Social Sciences.
Award: Grant for use in any year; not renewable. *Number:* 1. *Amount:* $1500.
Application Requirements: Application, references, transcript.
Deadline: February 1.
E-mail: asor@bu.edu
Phone: 617-353-6570 **Fax:** 617-353-6575
World Wide Web: http://www.asor.org/
Contact: Holly Andrews, Administrative Assistant
American Schools of Oriental Research
656 Beacon Street, 5th Floor
Boston, MA 02215-2010

▼ ARMENIAN PROFESSIONAL SOCIETY OF THE BAY AREA

Armenian Professional Society of the Bay Area Scholarships • 31

One-time award for full-time college juniors or seniors, or teachers of Armenian subjects studying on a part-time basis. Must have 3.2 GPA and substantial involvement in Armenian affairs. Include resume, program of study, transcript, two letters of recommendation, and evidence of Armenian community affairs.
Academic/Career Areas: Area/Ethnic Studies; Education; Filmmaking; Journalism; Literature/English/Writing; Performing Arts; Social Sciences.
Award: Scholarship for use in junior, senior, or graduate years; not renewable.
Eligibility Requirements: Applicant must be enrolled at a four-year institution.
Application Requirements: Application, references, transcript.
Deadline: November 15.
Contact: Armenian Professional Society of the Bay Area
839 Marina Boulevard
San Francisco, CA 94123

▼ CHARLES A. AND ANNE MORROW LINDBERGH FOUNDATION

Lindbergh Grants Program see number 4

▼ SOCIETY FARSAROTUL

Society Farsarotul Financial Awards • 32

Must have at least one Arumanian parent or grandparent. Must be at least a college junior with minimum 3.0 GPA. Submit written request and three references. Undergraduate applicants must be members of Society Farsarotul. Must study an area concerned with Arumanian heritage.
Academic/Career Areas: Area/Ethnic Studies; Foreign Language; Humanities.
Award: Scholarship for use in junior, senior, or graduate years; not renewable. *Number:* 2. *Amount:* $1000.
Eligibility Requirements: Applicant must be Arumanian/Ulacedo-Romanian and enrolled at a four-year institution.
Application Requirements: Application, essay, references, transcript. **Deadline:** February 1.
Contact: Society Farsarotul
799 Silver Lane
PO Box 753
Trumbull, CT 06611

▼ ST. DAVID'S SOCIETY OF THE STATE OF NEW YORK

St. David's Society of the State of New York Scholarships • 33

Available to students of Welsh descent, or to students either studying in Wales or studying the Welsh language or literature. One-time award. Write for further information.
Academic/Career Areas: Area/Ethnic Studies.
Award: Scholarship for use in any year; not renewable. *Number:* 8–12. *Amount:* $300–$1000.
Eligibility Requirements: Applicant must be Welsh.
Application Requirements: Application, references, transcript.
Deadline: May 30.
Contact: Scholarship Administrator
St. David's Society of the State of New York
3 West 51st Street
New York, NY 10019

ART HISTORY

▼ ASSOCIATION OF UNIVERSITIES AND COLLEGES OF CANADA

Canada-Taiwan Student Exchange Program • 34

One-time award for Chinese faculty and doctoral students to spend four to twelve months in Canada to increase their knowledge in the field of Canadian studies. Includes a stipend of 1,100 Canadian dollars per month. Must be citizen of China.
Academic/Career Areas: Art History; Arts; Foreign Language; Natural Resources; Performing Arts.
Award: Scholarship for use in freshman, sophomore, junior, or senior year; not renewable. *Number:* 20.
Application Requirements: Application. **Deadline:** March 15.
World Wide Web: http://www.aucc.ca
Contact: Jeanne Gallagher
Association of Universities and Colleges of Canada
350 Albert Street, Suite 600
Ottawa, ON K1R 1B1
Canada

ARTS

▼ ALLIANCE FOR YOUNG ARTISTS AND WRITERS, INC.

Scholastic Art and Writing Awards-Art Section • 35

Award for students in grades 7-12. Winners of preliminary judging advance to national level. Contact regarding application fee and deadlines, which vary.
Academic/Career Areas: Arts; Literature/English/Writing.
Award: Scholarship for use in freshman, sophomore, junior, or senior year; not renewable. *Amount:* $100–$5000.
Eligibility Requirements: Applicant must be high school student; enrolled at a two-year or four-year institution and must have an interest in art.
Application Requirements: Application, applicant must enter a contest, essay, portfolio, references, transcript.
Contact: Alliance for Young Artists and Writers, Inc.
555 Broadway
New York, NY 10012-1396

Scholastic Art and Writing Awards-Writing Section • 36

Award for students in grades 7-12. Winners of preliminary judging advance to national level. Contact regarding application fee and deadlines, which vary.
Academic/Career Areas: Arts; Literature/English/Writing.
Award: Scholarship for use in freshman, sophomore, junior, or senior year; not renewable. *Amount:* $100–$5000.
Eligibility Requirements: Applicant must be high school student; enrolled at a two-year or four-year institution and must have an interest in writing.
Application Requirements: Application, applicant must enter a contest, essay, transcript.
Contact: Alliance for Young Artists and Writers, Inc.
555 Broadway
New York, NY 10012-1396

▼ ASSOCIATION OF UNIVERSITIES AND COLLEGES OF CANADA

Canada-Taiwan Student Exchange Program
see number 34

▼ CHARLES A. AND ANNE MORROW LINDBERGH FOUNDATION

Lindbergh Grants Program
see number 4

▼ ELIZABETH GREENSHIELDS FOUNDATION

Elizabeth Greenshields Award/Grant • 37

10,000 Canadian dollar grant available to candidates working in painting, drawing, printmaking, or sculpture. Work must be representational or figurative. Must submit at least one color slide of each of six works. Must reapply to renew.
Academic/Career Areas: Arts.
Award: Grant for use in any year; not renewable. *Number:* 40–60.
Eligibility Requirements: Applicant must have an interest in art.
Application Requirements: Application. **Deadline:** Continuous.
Phone: 514-937-9225 **Fax:** 514-937-0141
Contact: Diane Pitcher, Applications Coordinator
Elizabeth Greenshields Foundation
1814 Sherbrooke Street West, Suite 1
Montreal, PQ H3H 1E4
Canada

▼ FINE ARTS WORK CENTER IN PROVINCETOWN, INC.

Fine Arts Work Center Fellowships • 38

Seven-month residency fellowship for emerging artists and writers at the Fine Arts Work Center in Provincetown, Massachusetts. Provided with living expenses, stipend, and studio space. Have opportunity to work independently with support. Application fee: $35.
Academic/Career Areas: Arts; Literature/English/Writing.
Eligibility Requirements: Applicant must be studying in Massachusetts and must have an interest in art or writing.
Application Requirements: Application, essay, self-addressed stamped envelope. **Fee:** $35. **Deadline:** February 1.
E-mail: fawc@capecod.net
Phone: 508-487-9960 **Fax:** 508-487-8873
Contact: Writing or Visual Coordinator
Fine Arts Work Center in Provincetown, Inc.
24 Pearl Street
Provincetown, MA 02657

▼ FOUNDATION OF FLEXOGRAPHIC TECHNICAL ASSOCIATION

Flexography Scholarships • 39

Award for study of graphic arts. Institution must offer courses in flexography. Applicants must be high school seniors, college freshmen, sophomores, or juniors. Must be interested in career in flexography and have minimum 3.0 GPA. Thirty-seven renewable awards of $1000 each.
Academic/Career Areas: Arts.
Award: Scholarship for use in sophomore or junior year; renewable. *Number:* 37. *Amount:* $1000.
Application Requirements: Application, references, transcript.
Deadline: March 15.
E-mail: srubin@vax.fta.ffta.org
World Wide Web: http://www.fta.ffta.org
Contact: Shelley Rubin, Educational Coordinator
Foundation of Flexographic Technical Association
900 Marconi Avenue
Ronkonkoma, NY 11779-7212

▼ HAYSTACK MOUNTAIN SCHOOL OF CRAFTS

Technical Assistant Scholarships • 40

One-time award for artists 18 and older, to provide assistance to Haystack Mountain School of Crafts faculty for shop maintenance and organization. Submit list of technical abilities. Must submit slides. Write for more information. Application fee: $25.
Academic/Career Areas: Arts.
Award: Scholarship for use in any year; not renewable. *Number:* 30–35. *Amount:* $760–$1030.
Eligibility Requirements: Applicant must be age 18 or over and studying in Maine.
Application Requirements: Application, autobiography, photo, references, self-addressed stamped envelope.
Fee: $25. **Deadline:** March 25.
E-mail: haystack@haystack-mtn.org
Phone: 207-348-2306 **Fax:** 207-348-2307
World Wide Web: http://www.haystack-mtn.org
Contact: Mr. Stuart Kestenbaum, Director
Haystack Mountain School of Crafts
PO Box 518
Deer Isle, ME 04627-0518

▼ JAPANESE AMERICAN CITIZENS LEAGUE

Henry and Chiyo Kuwahara Creative Arts Scholarship • 41

One-time award to encourage creative arts projects that reflect the Japanese-American experience and culture. All technical work of the applicant should be college level. Community service considered. Professional artists ineligible. Submit relevant materials. Send self-addressed stamped envelope for application, specifying application category.

Henry and Chiyo Kuwahara Creative Arts Scholarship (continued)

Academic/Career Areas: Arts.
Award: Scholarship for use in freshman, sophomore, junior, senior, or graduate years; not renewable. *Number:* 1. *Amount:* $5000.
Eligibility Requirements: Applicant must be member of Japanese-American Citizens League.
Application Requirements: Application, essay, references, transcript. **Deadline:** April 1.
E-mail: jacl@jacl.org
Phone: 415-921-5225 **Fax:** 415-931-4671
Contact: Scholarship Administrator
Japanese American Citizens League
1765 Sutter Street
San Francisco, CA 94115

▼ NATIONAL SCHOLARSHIP TRUST FUND OF THE GRAPHIC ARTS

National Scholarship Trust Fund of the Graphic Arts • 42

Renewable award for high school seniors and undergraduates majoring in graphic art/communication, leading to printing/publishing career. Must have minimum 3.0 GPA. Deadline is March 1 for high school seniors, and April 1 for college students.
Academic/Career Areas: Arts; Communications; Trade/Technical Specialties.
Award: Scholarship for use in freshman, sophomore, junior, or senior year; renewable. *Number:* 250–300. *Amount:* $500–$1500.
Eligibility Requirements: Applicant must be enrolled at a two-year or four-year institution and must have an interest in art.
Application Requirements: Application, references, test scores, transcript.
Phone: 412-741-6860 **Fax:** 412-741-2311
Contact: Kristiin Winkowski, Program Coordinator
National Scholarship Trust Fund of the
Graphic Arts
200 Deer Run Road
Sewickley, PA 15143

▼ NATIONAL SCULPTURE SOCIETY

National Sculpture Competition for Young Sculptors • 43

For any sculptors age 18-35. Must submit slides of five to ten works with biography. Slides will be returned if self-addressed stamped envelope is included. There are one medal and six monetary awards.
Academic/Career Areas: Arts.
Award: Prize for use in any year; not renewable. *Number:* 6. *Amount:* $200–$1000.
Eligibility Requirements: Applicant must be ages 18-35 and must have an interest in art.
Application Requirements: Application, applicant must enter a contest, autobiography, photo, self-addressed stamped envelope. **Deadline:** Continuous.
Phone: 212-764-5645 **Fax:** 212-764-5651
Contact: Gwen Pier, Executive Director
National Sculpture Society
1177 Avenue of the Americas, 15th Floor
New York, NY 10036

National Sculpture Society Alex J. Ettl Grant • 44

Grant awarded to a figurative or realist sculptor who has demonstrated a commitment to sculpting and an outstanding ability through his or her life's work. Must submit photos of work. Not available to NSS members. One-time award.
Academic/Career Areas: Arts.
Award: Prize for use in any year; not renewable. *Number:* 1. *Amount:* $4000–$5000.
Eligibility Requirements: Applicant must have employment experience in experience in career field and must have an interest in art.
Application Requirements: Application, applicant must enter a contest, autobiography, self-addressed stamped envelope. **Deadline:** October 31.
Phone: 212-764-5645 **Fax:** 212-764-5651
Contact: Gwen Pier, Executive Director
National Sculpture Society
1177 Avenue of the Americas, 15th Floor
New York, NY 10036

▼ PRINCESS GRACE AWARDS

Dance, Theater, Film, and Playwright Grants • 45

One-time award for young aspiring artists. Scholarships for college seniors or graduate students; fellowships to artists who have been in a dance or theater company for less than five years. Invited schools may nominate one candidate. Deadlines: theater/playwright, March 31; dance, April 30; film, June 1. Submit photo, work samples/tapes, videos.
Academic/Career Areas: Arts; Filmmaking; Performing Arts.

Award: Scholarship for use in senior or graduate years; not renewable. *Number:* 15–20. *Amount:* $3000–$15,000.
Eligibility Requirements: Applicant must be enrolled at a four-year institution and must have an interest in art, photography/photogrammetry/filmmaking, or writing.
Application Requirements: Application, autobiography, essay, portfolio, references, self-addressed stamped envelope.
E-mail: pgfusa@pgfusa.com
Phone: 212-317-1470 **Fax:** 212-317-1473
World Wide Web: http://www.pgfusa.com
Contact: Toby E. Boshak, Executive Director
Princess Grace Awards
105 East 58th Street, 21st Floor
New York, NY 10155

▼ UNIVERSITY FILM AND VIDEO ASSOCIATION

University Film and Video Association Carole Fielding Student Grants • 46
One-time award for film, video, or multimedia production or research in historical, critical, theoretical, or experimental studies of film or video. Must be sponsored by a University Film and Video Association member. Must submit statement and resume.
Academic/Career Areas: Arts; Communications; Filmmaking; TV/Radio Broadcasting.
Award: Grant for use in any year; not renewable. *Amount:* $1000–$5000.
Application Requirements: Application, essay, references, self-addressed stamped envelope. **Deadline:** January 1.
World Wide Web: http://raven.ubalt.edu/simon/ufvagrants.html
Contact: Julie Simon, Chairperson
University Film and Video Association
1420 North Charles Street
Baltimore, MD 21201

AVIATION/AEROSPACE

▼ AIRCRAFT ELECTRONICS ASSOCIATION EDUCATIONAL FOUNDATION

Bud Glover Memorial Scholarship • 47
Award for anyone who plans to or is attending an accredited school in an avionics or aircraft repair program. Minimum 2.5 GPA required. One-time award of $1000.

Academic/Career Areas: Aviation/Aerospace; Trade/Technical Specialties.
Award: Scholarship for use in any year; not renewable. *Number:* 1. *Amount:* $1000.
Application Requirements: Application, essay, references, test scores, transcript. **Deadline:** February 2.
E-mail: aea@microlink.net
Phone: 816-373-6565 **Fax:** 816-478-3100
World Wide Web: http://www.aeaavnews.org
Contact: Ms. Tracy Lykins, Educational Foundation
Coordinator
Aircraft Electronics Association Educational
Foundation
4217 South Hocker
Independence, MO 64055-0963

Castleberry Instruments Scholarship • 48
Award for anyone who plans to attend or is attending an accredited school in avionics or aircraft repair program. Minimum 2.5 GPA required. One-time award of $2500.
Academic/Career Areas: Aviation/Aerospace; Trade/Technical Specialties.
Award: Scholarship for use in freshman, sophomore, junior, or senior year; not renewable. *Number:* 1. *Amount:* $2500.
Application Requirements: Application, essay, references, test scores, transcript. **Deadline:** February 2.
E-mail: aea@microlink.net
Phone: 816-373-6565 **Fax:** 816-478-3100
World Wide Web: http://www.aeaavnews.org
Contact: Ms. Tracy Lykins, Educational Foundation
Coordinator
Aircraft Electronics Association Educational
Foundation
4217 South Hocker
Independence, MO 64055-0963

College of Aeronautics Scholarship • 49
One-time award for students in the two-year avionics program at the College of Aeronautics in Flushing, New York. Minimum 2.5 GPA required.
Academic/Career Areas: Aviation/Aerospace.
Award: Scholarship for use in freshman or sophomore year; not renewable. *Number:* 1. *Amount:* $3000.
Eligibility Requirements: Applicant must be enrolled at a two-year institution and studying in New York.
Application Requirements: Application, essay, references, test scores, transcript. **Deadline:** February 2.
E-mail: aea@microlink.net
Phone: 816-373-6565 **Fax:** 816-478-3100

College of Aeronautics Scholarship (continued)

World Wide Web: http://www.aeaavnews.org
Contact: Ms. Tracy Lykins, Educational Foundation
Coordinator
Aircraft Electronics Association Educational
Foundation
4217 South Hocker
Independence, MO 64055-0963

David Arver Memorial Scholarship • 50

One-time award for any student who plans to attend an accredited vocational/technical school in Illinois, Indiana, Iowa, Kansas, Michigan, Minnesota, Missouri, Nebraska, North Dakota, South Dakota, or Wisconsin. Must plan to study aviation electronics and have a minimum 2.5 GPA.
Academic/Career Areas: Aviation/Aerospace.
Award: Scholarship for use in any year; not renewable. *Number:* 1. *Amount:* $1000.
Eligibility Requirements: Applicant must be enrolled at a technical institution and studying in Illinois, Indiana, Iowa, Kansas, Michigan, Minnesota, Missouri, Nebraska, North Dakota, South Dakota, or Wisconsin.
Application Requirements: Application, essay, references, test scores, transcript. **Deadline:** February 2.
E-mail: aea@microlink.net
Phone: 816-373-6565 **Fax:** 816-478-3100
World Wide Web: http://www.aeaavnews.org
Contact: Ms. Tracy Lykins, Educational Foundation
Coordinator
Aircraft Electronics Association Educational
Foundation
4217 South Hocker
Independence, MO 64055-0963

Dutch and Ginger Arver Scholarship • 51

Award for anyone who plans to attend or is attending an accredited school in an avionics program. Must have minimum 2.5 GPA. One-time award of $1000.
Academic/Career Areas: Aviation/Aerospace.
Award: Scholarship for use in any year; not renewable. *Number:* 1. *Amount:* $1000.
Application Requirements: Application, essay, references, test scores, transcript. **Deadline:** February 2.
E-mail: aea@microlink.net
Phone: 816-373-6565 **Fax:** 816-478-3100
World Wide Web: http://www.aeaavnews.org

Contact: Ms. Tracy Lykins, Educational Foundation
Coordinator
Aircraft Electronics Association Educational
Foundation
4217 South Hocker
Independence, MO 64055-0963

Mid-Continent Instrument Scholarship • 52

Award for anyone who plans to attend or is attending an accredited school in an avionics program. Minimum 2.5 GPA required. One-time award of $1000.
Academic/Career Areas: Aviation/Aerospace.
Award: Scholarship for use in any year; not renewable. *Number:* 1. *Amount:* $1000.
Application Requirements: Application, essay, references, test scores, transcript. **Deadline:** February 2.
E-mail: aea@microlink.net
Phone: 816-373-6565 **Fax:** 816-478-3100
World Wide Web: http://www.aeaavnews.org
Contact: Ms. Tracy Lykins, Educational Foundation
Coordinator
Aircraft Electronics Association Educational
Foundation
4217 South Hocker
Independence, MO 64055-0963

Northern Airborne Technology Scholarship • 53

Award for high school seniors and/or college students who plan to or are attending an accredited college/ university in an avionics or aircraft repair program. Institution must be in Canada. Minimum 2.5 GPA required. One-time award of $1000.
Academic/Career Areas: Aviation/Aerospace; Trade/ Technical Specialties.
Award: Scholarship for use in freshman, sophomore, junior, or senior year; not renewable. *Number:* 1. *Amount:* $1000.
Application Requirements: Application, essay, references, test scores, transcript. **Deadline:** February 2.
E-mail: aea@microlink.net
Phone: 816-373-6565 **Fax:** 816-478-3100
World Wide Web: http://www.aeaavnews.org
Contact: Ms. Tracy Lykins, Educational Foundation
Coordinator
Aircraft Electronics Association Educational
Foundation
4217 South Hocker
Independence, MO 64055-0963

Paul and Blanche Wulfsberg Scholarship • 54

Award for anyone who plans to or is attending an accredited school in an avionics or aircraft repair program. Minimum 2.5 GPA required. One-time award of $1000.
Academic/Career Areas: Aviation/Aerospace; Trade/Technical Specialties.
Award: Scholarship for use in any year; not renewable. *Number:* 1. *Amount:* $1000.
Application Requirements: Application, essay, references, test scores, transcript. **Deadline:** February 2.
E-mail: aea@microlink.net
Phone: 816-373-6565 **Fax:** 816-478-3100
World Wide Web: http://www.aeaavnews.org
Contact: Ms. Tracy Lykins, Educational Foundation Coordinator
Aircraft Electronics Association Educational Foundation
4217 South Hocker
Independence, MO 64055-0963

Plane & Pilot Magazine/GARMIN Scholarship • 55

Award for high school, college or vocational/technical school students who plan to or are attending an accredited vocational/technical school in an avionics or aircraft repair program. Minimum 2.5 GPA required. One-time award of $2000.
Academic/Career Areas: Aviation/Aerospace; Trade/Technical Specialties.
Award: Scholarship for use in any year; not renewable. *Number:* 1. *Amount:* $2000.
Eligibility Requirements: Applicant must be enrolled at a technical institution.
Application Requirements: Application, essay, references, test scores, transcript. **Deadline:** February 2.
E-mail: aea@microlink.net
Phone: 816-373-6565 **Fax:** 816-478-3100
World Wide Web: http://www.aeaavnews.org
Contact: Ms. Tracy Lykins, Educational Foundation Coordinator
Aircraft Electronics Association Educational Foundation
4217 South Hocker
Independence, MO 64055-0963

▼ CHARLES A. AND ANNE MORROW LINDBERGH FOUNDATION

Lindbergh Grants Program see number 4

▼ VERTICAL FLIGHT FOUNDATION

Vertical Flight Foundation Scholarship • 56

This award is available for undergraduate and graduate study in aerospace, electrical, or mechanical engineering. Undergraduates must be in junior or senior year. Applicants must have an interest in vertical flight technology. One-time award of $1000-$2000.
Academic/Career Areas: Aviation/Aerospace; Electrical/Electronic Engineering; Mechanical Engineering.
Award: Scholarship for use in junior, senior, or graduate years; not renewable. *Number:* 10–12. *Amount:* $1000–$2000.
Eligibility Requirements: Applicant must be enrolled at a four-year institution.
Application Requirements: Application, essay, references, transcript. **Deadline:** February 1.
E-mail: ahs703@aol.com
Phone: 703-684-6777 **Fax:** 703-739-9279
World Wide Web: http://www.vtol.org
Contact: Enid A. Nichols, Office Manager
Vertical Flight Foundation
217 North Washington Street
Alexandria, VA 22314

▼ WHIRLY-GIRLS SCHOLARSHIP FUND

International Women's Helicopter Pilots Whirly-Girls/Doris Mullen Memorial Scholarship & Memorial Flight Training Scholarship • 57

Scholarship to assist a fixed-wing, glider, or balloon pilot earn helicopter rating. To qualify, applicant must be a licensed pilot with qualifications to operate a private, or better, or a Whirly Girl aircraft. $25 application fee.
Academic/Career Areas: Aviation/Aerospace; Trade/Technical Specialties.
Award: Scholarship for use in any year; not renewable. *Number:* 5. *Amount:* $4500.
Eligibility Requirements: Applicant must be female.
Application Requirements: Application, financial need analysis, references. **Fee:** $25. **Deadline:** November 15.
Contact: Whirly-Girls Scholarship Fund
PO Box 7446
Menlo Park, CA 94026-7446

BIOLOGY

▼ AMERICAN FOUNDATION FOR AGING RESEARCH

American Foundation for Aging Research Undergraduate and Graduate Fellowships in Aging Research • 58

Available to undergraduate and graduate students who are involved in biological research on aging or age-related diseases. Applicants must submit a research proposal which may be renewed. Send $3 for application. Merit-based.

Academic/Career Areas: Biology; Health and Medical Sciences.

Award: Scholarship for use in any year; renewable. *Number:* up to 10. *Amount:* $500–$1000.

Eligibility Requirements: Applicant must be enrolled at a four-year institution.

Application Requirements: Application, references, test scores, transcript. **Fee:** $3. **Deadline:** Continuous.

Contact: Paul F. Agris, President
American Foundation for Aging Research
128 Polk Hall
North Carolina State University
Raleigh, NC 27695-7622

▼ AMERICAN SOCIETY OF CRIME LABORATORY DIRECTORS

American Society of Crime Laboratory Directors Scholarship Award • 59

For undergraduate or graduate students enrolled in a forensic science program recognized by the American Society of Crime Laboratory Directors. Must be nominated by an adviser or an American Society of Crime Laboratory Directors member. Overall B average required.

Academic/Career Areas: Biology; Health and Medical Sciences; Physical Sciences and Math.

Award: Scholarship for use in any year; not renewable. *Number:* 2. *Amount:* $1000.

Eligibility Requirements: Applicant must be enrolled at a four-year institution.

Application Requirements: Application, essay, references, transcript. **Deadline:** May 1.

Phone: 573-526-6134 **Fax:** 573-751-9382

World Wide Web: http://www.shadow.net/~datachem/ascld.html

Contact: Terry J. Luikart, Scholarship Director
American Society of Crime Laboratory Directors
Execusuites, Suite 350
15200 Shady Grove Road
Rockville, MD 20850

▼ CAMPUS SAFETY DIVISION

Campus Safety Scholarship *see number 19*

▼ CHARLES A. AND ANNE MORROW LINDBERGH FOUNDATION

Lindbergh Grants Program *see number 4*

▼ CYSTIC FIBROSIS FOUNDATION

Cystic Fibrosis Foundation Student Traineeships • 60

Traineeship for college seniors and graduate students. Number of awards varies. Must be student in or about to enter a doctoral program. Applicant must work with a faculty sponsor on a research project related to cystic fibrosis. One-time $1500 award, of which $1200 is stipend and $300 is for laboratory expenses.

Academic/Career Areas: Biology; Health and Medical Sciences.

Award: Scholarship for use in senior or graduate years; not renewable. *Amount:* $1500.

Eligibility Requirements: Applicant must be enrolled at a four-year institution.

Application Requirements: Application. **Deadline:** Continuous.

E-mail: kcurley@cff.org

Phone: 301-951-4422 **Fax:** 301-951-6378

World Wide Web: http://www.cff.org

Contact: Kathleen Curley, Office of Grants Management
Cystic Fibrosis Foundation
6931 Arlington Road
Bethesda, MD 20814

▼ EASTER SEAL RESEARCH INSTITUTE

Miriam Neveren Summer Studentship • 61

Award for full-time-students in Ontario universities to gain firsthand experience with research relating to prevention, treatment, and management of physical disabilities in children and young adults. Must submit resume and letters

from student and student's supervisor describing research to be undertaken. Deadline: March 1.
Academic/Career Areas: Biology; Health and Medical Sciences; Health Information Management/Technology; Nursing; Special Education; Therapy/Rehabilitation.
Award: Scholarship for use in freshman year; not renewable. *Number:* 5.
Application Requirements: Application, photo, references, transcript. **Deadline:** March 1.
E-mail: amichie@easterseals.org
Phone: 416-421-8377 **Fax:** 416-696-1035
Contact: Anne Michie, Executive Director
Easter Seal Research Institute
1185 Eglinton Avenue East
Suite 706
North York, ON M3C 3C6
Canada

▼ HUDSON RIVER NATIONAL ESTUARINE RESEARCH RESERVE— NEW YORK STATE DEPARTMENT OF ENVIRONMENTAL CONSERVATION AND THE HUDSON RIVER FOUNDATION

Tibor T. Polgar Fellowship • 62

Award for the support of graduate and undergraduate research projects concerning the Hudson River. Applicant may attend a two-year or four-year institution. Submit research proposal. One-time award of $3500. Contact for deadlines.
Academic/Career Areas: Biology; Earth Science; Physical Sciences and Math.
Eligibility Requirements: Applicant must be enrolled at a two-year or four-year institution.
E-mail: cnieder@ocean.nos.noaa.gov
Phone: 914-758-7010 **Fax:** 914-758-7033
Contact: Chuck Nieder, Research Coordinator
Hudson River National Estuarine Research Reserve—New York State Department of Environmental Conservation and The Hudson River Foundation
Bard College Field Station
Annandale, NY 12504

▼ MANOMET CENTER FOR CONSERVATION SCIENCES

Kathleen S. Anderson Award see number 12

▼ MASTER BREWERS ASSOCIATION SCHOLARSHIP FOUNDATION, INC.

Master Brewers Association-America's Scholarships see number 7

▼ MICROSCOPY SOCIETY OF AMERICA

Microscopy Society of America Presidential Student Awards • 63

Submit registration form, $75 application fee (refunded to successful applicants), a supporting letter from an MSA member (preferably research adviser) and a scientific paper for representation. One-time award for study of the fields of microscopy.
Academic/Career Areas: Biology; Health and Medical Sciences; Physical Sciences and Math.
Award: Prize for use in any year; not renewable.
Application Requirements: Application, applicant must enter a contest. **Fee:** $75. **Deadline:** March 15.
E-mail: businessoffice@msa.microscopy.com
Phone: 800-538-3672
Contact: Dr. Ralph Albrecht
Microscopy Society of America
1655 Linden Drive
Madison, WI 53706

▼ NORTH AMERICAN BLUEBIRD SOCIETY

Bluebird Student Research Grant • 64

One-time award for any student to study bluebirds. Must be enrolled at a four-year postsecondary institution. Submit research proposal. Write for more information.
Academic/Career Areas: Biology; Natural Resources.
Award: Grant for use in any year; not renewable. *Number:* 4–7. *Amount:* up to $1000.
Eligibility Requirements: Applicant must be enrolled at a four-year institution.
Application Requirements: Application, autobiography.
Deadline: December 1.
E-mail: bernerkl@cobleskill.edu
Phone: 518-234-5252
Contact: Kevin Berner, Research Chairman
North American Bluebird Society
SUNY
Cobleskill, NY 12043

▼ SIGMA XI, THE SCIENTIFIC RESEARCH SOCIETY

National Academy of Science Grants-in-Aid of Research   see number 13

Sigma Xi Grants-in-Aid of Research   see number 8

▼ WILSON ORNITHOLOGICAL SOCIETY

Louis Agassiz Fuertes Award   see number 14

Margaret Morse Nice Award   see number 15

Paul A. Stewart Awards   see number 16

BUSINESS/CONSUMER SERVICES

▼ APICS-EDUCATIONAL AND RESEARCH FOUNDATION

Donald W. Fogarty International Student Paper Competition   • 65

Annual competition on topics pertaining to resource management only. Must be original work of one or more authors. May submit one paper only. Must be in English. Open to full- and part-time undergraduate and graduate students. High school students ineligible.
Academic/Career Areas: Business/Consumer Services.
Award: Prize for use in any year; not renewable. *Number:* up to 164. *Amount:* $100–$1700.
Application Requirements: Applicant must enter a contest.
Deadline: May 15.
E-mail: foundation@apics-hq.org
Phone: 800-444-2742 **Fax:** 703-237-8450
World Wide Web: http://www.apics.org
Contact: Michael Lythgoe, Director
APICS-Educational and Research
Foundation
500 West Annandale Road
Falls Church, VA 22046-4274

▼ CHEMICAL HERITAGE FOUNDATION

Chemical Heritage Foundation Travel Grants   see number 20

▼ EXECUTIVE WOMEN INTERNATIONAL

Executive Women International Scholarship Program   • 66

Available to high school juniors planning careers in any business or professional field of study which requires a four-year college degree. Award is renewable based on continuing eligibility. Awards range from $50-$10,000.
Academic/Career Areas: Business/Consumer Services.
Award: Scholarship for use in any year; renewable. *Number:* 130. *Amount:* $50–$10,000.
Eligibility Requirements: Applicant must be high school student and enrolled at a four-year institution.
Application Requirements: Application, autobiography, interview, references, transcript. **Deadline:** March 1.
Phone: 801-355-2800 **Fax:** 801-362-3212
Contact: Debra G. Tucker, Scholarship Programs
Executive Women International
515 South 700 East, Suite 2E
Salt Lake City, UT 84102

▼ KARLA SCHERER FOUNDATION

Karla Scherer Foundation Scholarships   • 67

Scholarships only for women pursuing undergraduate or graduate degrees in finance or economics in preparation for careers in the private manufacturing-based sector. To request application, must provide college/university name; major; a detailed statement of career plans; and a stamped self-addressed envelope. Deadline for application request is March 1; for completed application, May 1.
Academic/Career Areas: Business/Consumer Services; Economics.
Award: Scholarship for use in any year; not renewable.
Eligibility Requirements: Applicant must be enrolled at a four-year institution and female.
Application Requirements: Application, autobiography, essay, financial need analysis, interview, photo, references, self-addressed stamped envelope, test scores, transcript.
Phone: 312-943-9191

Contact: Scholarship Administrator
Karla Scherer Foundation
737 North Michigan Avenue, Suite 2330
Chicago, IL 60611

▼ MCDERMOTT, INCORPORATED

McDermott Scholarship   see number 23

▼ SPE FOUNDATION

SPE Foundation Scholarships   • 68

For students showing a career interest in the plastics industry. Must be enrolled full-time at a two- or four-year college or university. Applicant must be in good academic standing. Must submit one to two page statement on career goals. Renewable award of $3000 to $4000.
Academic/Career Areas: Business/Consumer Services; Engineering/Technology; Engineering-Related Technologies; Physical Sciences and Math; Trade/Technical Specialties.
Award: Scholarship for use in freshman, sophomore, junior, or senior year; renewable. *Number:* 7–10. *Amount:* $3000–$4000.
Eligibility Requirements: Applicant must be enrolled at a two-year or four-year institution.
Application Requirements: Application, autobiography, financial need analysis, references, transcript. **Deadline:** December 15.
E-mail: grbristol@4spe.org
Phone: 203-740-5434 **Fax:** 203-775-8490
World Wide Web: http://4spe.org
Contact: Gail R. Bristol, Development Director
SPE Foundation
14 Fairfield Drive
Brookfield, CT 06804

▼ WOMEN GROCERS OF AMERICA

Mary Macey Scholarship   see number 9

CHEMICAL ENGINEERING

▼ AMERICAN ELECTROPLATERS AND SURFACE FINISHERS SOCIETY

American Electroplaters and Surface Finishers Society Scholarships   • 69

Award for students interested in careers in surface finishing technologies. Submit transcripts, career objectives, references, and resume with application by April 15. May reapply for up to two years. One-time award of $1000. Awards available for college juniors and seniors, as well as for graduate students.
Academic/Career Areas: Chemical Engineering; Trade/Technical Specialties.
Award: Scholarship for use in junior, senior, or graduate years; not renewable. *Amount:* $1000.
Application Requirements: Application, essay, references, transcript. **Deadline:** April 15.
Phone: 407-281-6441
Contact: American Electroplaters and Surface Finishers Society
Central Florida Research Park
12644 Research Parkway
Orlando, FL 32826-3298

▼ ASSOCIATED WESTERN UNIVERSITIES, INC.

Associated Western Universities Student Research Fellowships   see number 18

▼ CHEMICAL HERITAGE FOUNDATION

Chemical Heritage Foundation Travel Grants   see number 20

▼ CHEMICAL INSTITUTE OF CANADA

SNC LAVALIN Plant Design Competition   • 70

One prize available to a student enrolled in an undergraduate chemical engineering program at a Canadian university. Entries should include a flowsheet and summary, a final report, list of students involved, and the name of any collaborating organization. A letter authorizing the release of information in "Canadian Chemical News" is also required. Projects will be presented at the Canadian Chemical Conference. One-time prize of 1000 Canadian dollars.
Academic/Career Areas: Chemical Engineering.
Award: Prize for use in freshman, sophomore, junior, or senior year; not renewable. *Number:* 1.
Eligibility Requirements: Applicant must be enrolled at a four-year institution.
Application Requirements: Applicant must enter a contest, essay. **Deadline:** May 15.
Phone: 613-232-6252
World Wide Web: http://www.chem-inst-can.org

SNC LAVALIN Plant Design Competition (continued)

Contact: Jodie Chislett, Program Manager
Chemical Institute of Canada
130 Slater Street, Suite 550
Ottawa, ON K1P 6E2
Canada

▼ KENTUCKY NATURAL RESOURCES AND ENVIRONMENTAL PROTECTION CABINET

*Environmental Protection
Scholarships*   *see number 6*

▼ MASTER BREWERS ASSOCIATION SCHOLARSHIP FOUNDATION, INC.

*Master Brewers Association-America's
Scholarships*   *see number 7*

CIVIL ENGINEERING

▼ ASSOCIATED WESTERN UNIVERSITIES, INC.

*Associated Western Universities Student
Research Fellowships*   *see number 18*

▼ KENTUCKY NATURAL RESOURCES AND ENVIRONMENTAL PROTECTION CABINET

*Environmental Protection
Scholarships*   *see number 6*

▼ NATIONAL ASSOCIATION OF WOMEN IN CONSTRUCTION

*National Association of Women in Construction
Undergraduate Scholarships*   *see number 27*

▼ NATIONAL ASSOCIATION OF WOMEN IN CONSTRUCTION FOUNDER'S SCHOLARSHIP FOUNDATION

*National Association of Women in Contruction
Founder's Scholarship Award*   *see number 28*

COMMUNICATIONS

▼ ACADEMY OF MOTION PICTURE ARTS AND SCIENCES

*Don and Gee Nicholl Fellowships in
Screenwriting*   • 71

Fellowships open to writers in English who have not earned money writing for film or television. Must submit completed, original, noncollaborative feature film screenplay, application, and $30 fee. One-time award not for any portion of formal education program.
Academic/Career Areas: Communications; Filmmaking; Literature/English/Writing.
Eligibility Requirements: Applicant must have an interest in writing.
Application Requirements: Application, applicant must enter a contest, self-addressed stamped envelope. **Fee:** $30.
Deadline: May 1.
Phone: 310-247-3059
World Wide Web: http://www.oscars.org
Contact: Academy of Motion Picture Arts and Sciences
8949 Wilshire Boulevard
Beverly Hills, CA 90211-1972

▼ CHARLES AND LUCILLE KING FAMILY FOUNDATION, INC.

*Charles and Lucille King Family Foundation
Scholarships*   • 72

Renewable award for college undergraduates pursuing television/film/communication studies to further their education. Must attend a four-year undergraduate institution. Minimum 3.0 GPA required to renew scholarship. Must have completed at least two years of study.
Academic/Career Areas: Communications; Filmmaking; TV/Radio Broadcasting.
Award: Scholarship for use in junior or senior year; renewable. *Number:* 10–20. *Amount:* $1250–$2500.

Eligibility Requirements: Applicant must be enrolled at a four-year institution.
Application Requirements: Application, essay, financial need analysis, references, transcript. **Deadline:** March 1.
E-mail: kingedu@aol.com
Phone: 212-682-2913 **Fax:** 212-949-0728
Contact: Michael Donovan, Educational Director
Charles And Lucille King Family
Foundation, Inc.
366 Madison Avenue, 10th Floor
New York, NY 10017

▼ COUNCIL FOR ADVANCEMENT AND SUPPORT OF EDUCATION/ COMMITTEE ON OPPORTUNITY AND EQUITY

Virginia Carter Smith Scholarship • 73

Award for new advancement professionals employed at member/affiliate institutions of the Council for Advancement and Support of Education for less than three years. Must be employed full-time in alumni relations or philanthropy or be a full-time professional relocated within the past three years. One-time award of up to $500.
Academic/Career Areas: Communications.
Award: Scholarship for use in any year; not renewable. *Number:* 40. *Amount:* up to $500.
Eligibility Requirements: Applicant must be affiliated with Council for Advancement and Support of Education and have employment experience in experience in career field.
Application Requirements: Application, essay. **Deadline:** March 4.
Phone: 202-328-5915
Contact: Joanne Katlett, Director, Awards Program
Council for Advancement and Support of
Education/Committee on Opportunity
and Equity
11 Dupont Circle, Suite 400
Washington, DC 20036-1261

▼ DOG WRITERS' EDUCATIONAL TRUST

Dog Writers' Educational Trust Scholarship
see number 11

▼ INSTITUTE FOR HUMANE STUDIES

Humane Studies Fellowships • 74

One-time award for undergraduate and graduate students in selected disciplines. Applicants should have demonstrated interest in classical liberal/libertarian ideas and must intend to pursue a scholarly career. Application fee: $25.
Academic/Career Areas: Communications; Economics; History; Humanities; Legal Services; Literature/English/ Writing; Political Science; Social Sciences.
Eligibility Requirements: Applicant must be enrolled at a four-year institution.
Application Requirements: Application, autobiography, essay, references, test scores, transcript. **Fee:** $25. **Deadline:** December 31.
E-mail: ihs@gmu.edu
Phone: 703-934-6920 **Fax:** 703-352-7535
World Wide Web: http://osf1.gmu.edu/~ihs
Contact: Damon Chetson, Program Coordinator
Institute for Humane Studies
4084 University Drive, Suite 101
Fairfax, VA 22030-6812

▼ INTERNATIONAL FOODSERVICE EDITORIAL COUNCIL

International Foodservice Editorial Council Scholarship Award • 75

For undergraduate or graduate students majoring in food service or communications. Applicants should intend to focus on the development of communication skills (writing, editing, public relations) for use within the food service industry. Several one-time awards of $1000-$2500.
Academic/Career Areas: Communications; Food Science/ Nutrition; Food Service/Hospitality; Journalism; Literature/English/Writing; Photojournalism; TV/Radio Broadcasting.
Award: Scholarship for use in any year; not renewable. *Number:* 3–5. *Amount:* $1000–$2500.
Eligibility Requirements: Applicant must have employment experience in food service or journalism and must have an interest in leadership, photography/ photogrammetry/filmmaking, or writing.
Application Requirements: Application, essay, references, transcript. **Deadline:** March 15.
E-mail: ifec@aol.com
Phone: 914-452-4345 **Fax:** 914-452-0532
Contact: Carol Metz
International Foodservice Editorial Council
PO Box 491
Hyde Park, NY 12538-0491

▼ NATIONAL SCHOLARSHIP TRUST FUND OF THE GRAPHIC ARTS

National Scholarship Trust Fund of the Graphic Arts
see number 42

▼ UNIVERSITY FILM AND VIDEO ASSOCIATION

University Film and Video Association Carole Fielding Student Grants   *see number 46*

▼ WILLIAM RANDOLPH HEARST FOUNDATION

Photojournalism Competitions   • 76

Three competitions for undergraduate journalism and mass communications majors who study at member colleges/universities of the Association of Schools of Journalism and Mass Communications. Submit original photograph and three sets of slides to journalism administrator at college. Each college may submit two entries per competition, and there are three photo competitions per year.
Academic/Career Areas: Communications; Journalism; Photojournalism.
Award: Scholarship for use in freshman, sophomore, junior, or senior year; not renewable. *Number:* 30. *Amount:* $500–$5000.
Eligibility Requirements: Applicant must be enrolled at a four-year institution.
Application Requirements: Application. **Deadline:** Continuous.
Phone: 415-543-6033
Contact: Jan Watten, Program Director
William Randolph Hearst Foundation
90 New Montgomery Street, Suite 1212
San Francisco, CA 94105

▼ WOMEN GROCERS OF AMERICA

Mary Macey Scholarship   *see number 9*

COMPUTER SCIENCE/DATA PROCESSING

▼ AMERICAN SOCIETY FOR INFORMATION SCIENCE

American Society for Information Science Award of Merit   • 77

One-time award for an individual who has made significant contributions to the field of information science. Must be nominated. Submit biographical sketch and a description of the nominated work.
Academic/Career Areas: Computer Science/Data Processing; Library Sciences.
Award: Prize for use in any year; not renewable. *Number:* 1.
Application Requirements: Application, applicant must enter a contest, references. **Deadline:** July 1.
E-mail: mdevine@asis.org
Phone: 301-495-0900 **Fax:** 301-495-0810
World Wide Web: http://www.asis.org
Contact: Michele Devine, Awards Coordinator
American Society for Information Science
8720 Georgia Avenue, Suite 501
Silver Spring, MD 20910

American Society for Information Science Best Information Science Book Award   • 78

One-time award for publishers or individuals who have published the best book in the information science field the preceding year. Must be nominated. Write for more information.
Academic/Career Areas: Computer Science/Data Processing; Library Sciences.
Award: Prize for use in any year; not renewable. *Number:* 1.
Eligibility Requirements: Applicant must have an interest in writing.
Application Requirements: Application, applicant must enter a contest, references. **Deadline:** June 1.
E-mail: mdevine@asis.org
Phone: 301-495-0900 **Fax:** 301-495-0810
World Wide Web: http://www.asis.org
Contact: Michele Devine, Awards Coordinator
American Society for Information Science
8720 Georgia Avenue, Suite 501
Silver Spring, MD 20910

American Society for Information Science Research Award   • 79

One-time award for any individual in the field of information science to recognize outstanding research contributions in information science. Submit nomination statement of 200-500 words. Must be nominated. Submit publications if they contribute to an understanding of research work.
Academic/Career Areas: Computer Science/Data Processing; Library Sciences.
Award: Prize for use in any year; not renewable. *Number:* 1.
Application Requirements: Application, references. **Deadline:** June 1.

E-mail: mdevine@asis.org
Phone: 301-495-0900 **Fax:** 301-495-0810
World Wide Web: http://www.asis.org
Contact: Michele Devine, Awards Coordinator
American Society for Information Science
8720 Georgia Avenue, Suite 501
Silver Spring, MD 20910

▼ ASSOCIATED WESTERN UNIVERSITIES, INC.

Associated Western Universities Student Research Fellowships see number 18

▼ McDERMOTT, INCORPORATED

McDermott Scholarship see number 23

CRIMINAL JUSTICE/ CRIMINOLOGY

▼ JOHN F. KENNEDY LIBRARY FOUNDATION

Kennedy Research Grants see number 26

DENTAL HEALTH/SERVICES

▼ AMERICAN DENTAL HYGIENISTS' ASSOCIATION INSTITUTE FOR ORAL HEALTH

American Dental Hygienists' Association Institute-Baccalaureate Scholarship • 80

Award for full-time-students enrolled at an accredited four-year college who have completed one year of dental hygiene program or hold certificate/associate degree. Must have a 3.0 GPA and prove need of $1500. One-time award.
Academic/Career Areas: Dental Health/Services; Trade/Technical Specialties.
Award: Scholarship for use in sophomore, junior, or senior year; not renewable. *Number:* 10–25. *Amount:* up to $1500.

Eligibility Requirements: Applicant must be enrolled at a four-year institution.
Application Requirements: Application, essay, financial need analysis, references. **Deadline:** June 1.
Contact: Beatrice Pedersen, Administrator
American Dental Hygienists' Association
Institute for Oral Health
444 North Michigan Avenue, Suite 3400
Chicago, IL 60611-5063

▼ BETHESDA LUTHERAN HOMES AND SERVICES, INC.

Mental Retardation Scholastic Achievement Scholarship for Lutheran College Students • 81

One-time award for Lutheran college students who have reached sophomore year in studies related to mental retardation. Awards of up to $1000. 3.0 GPA required.
Academic/Career Areas: Dental Health/Services; Education; Food Science/Nutrition; Health Administration; Health and Medical Sciences; Health Information Management/Technology; Humanities; Legal Services; Social Services; Special Education; Sports-related; Therapy/Rehabilitation.
Award: Scholarship for use in junior or senior year; not renewable. *Number:* 1–10. *Amount:* $50–$1000.
Eligibility Requirements: Applicant must be Lutheran; enrolled at a four-year institution and have employment experience in helping handicapped.
Application Requirements: Application, autobiography, essay, references, transcript. **Deadline:** March 15.
E-mail: blhsncrc@execpc.com
Phone: 920-261-3050 Ext. 525 **Fax:** 920-261-8441
World Wide Web: http://www.bethesdainfo.org
Contact: Kevin W. Keller, Coordinator, Outreach
Programs and Services
Bethesda Lutheran Homes and Services, Inc.
National Christian Resource Center
700 Hoffmann Drive
Watertown, WI 53094-6294

▼ INTERNATIONAL ORDER OF THE KING'S DAUGHTERS AND SONS

International Order of the King's Daughters and Sons Health Careers Scholarship • 82

Award for study in the health fields. No biology, premedical, or veterinary applicants accepted. BA or BS candidates are eligible in junior year; medical/dental students must

International Order of the King's Daughters and Sons Health Careers Scholarship (continued)

have finished first year of school. Send No.10 self-addressed stamped envelope for application and information.

Academic/Career Areas: Dental Health/Services; Health and Medical Sciences; Nursing; Therapy/Rehabilitation.

Award: Scholarship for use in junior, senior, or graduate years; renewable. *Number:* 25–55. *Amount:* $500–$1000.

Eligibility Requirements: Applicant must be enrolled at a two-year or four-year institution.

Application Requirements: Application, autobiography, financial need analysis, references, self-addressed stamped envelope, transcript. **Deadline:** April 1.

Phone: 601-833-5418

Contact: Mrs. Fred Cannon
　　　　　International Order of the King's Daughters
　　　　　　and Sons
　　　　　Box 1310
　　　　　Brookhaven, MS 39601

DRAFTING

▼ NATIONAL ASSOCIATION OF WOMEN IN CONSTRUCTION

National Association of Women in Construction Undergraduate Scholarships　　　see number 27

EARTH SCIENCE

▼ ASSOCIATED WESTERN UNIVERSITIES, INC.

Associated Western Universities Student Research Fellowships　　　see number 18

▼ GARDEN CLUB OF AMERICA

Garden Club of America-"GCA Awards in Environmental Studies"　　　see number 5

▼ HUDSON RIVER NATIONAL ESTUARINE RESEARCH RESERVE— NEW YORK STATE DEPARTMENT OF ENVIRONMENTAL CONSERVATION AND THE HUDSON RIVER FOUNDATION

Tibor T. Polgar Fellowship　　　see number 62

▼ KENTUCKY NATURAL RESOURCES AND ENVIRONMENTAL PROTECTION CABINET

Environmental Protection Scholarships　　　see number 6

▼ SIGMA XI, THE SCIENTIFIC RESEARCH SOCIETY

National Academy of Science Grants-in-Aid of Research　　　see number 13

Sigma Xi Grants-in-Aid of Research　　see number 8

▼ SOCIETY FOR RANGE MANAGEMENT

Masonic Range Science Scholarship　see number 1

▼ SOCIETY OF EXPLORATION GEOPHYSICISTS FOUNDATION (SEG)

Society of Exploration Geophysicists Foundation Scholarship　　　● 83

Renewable award available to undergraduate and graduate students. Applicants must be preparing for a career in geophysics or a related earth science at a four-year college or university. High school seniors may apply. Minimum 3.0 GPA required. Average award is $1200 per year.

Academic/Career Areas: Earth Science; Physical Sciences and Math.

Award: Scholarship for use in freshman, sophomore, junior, senior, or graduate years; renewable. *Number:* 60–100. *Amount:* $500–$3000.

Eligibility Requirements: Applicant must be enrolled at a four-year institution.

Application Requirements: Application, financial need analysis, references, test scores, transcript. **Deadline:** March 1.

E-mail: mgerhart@seg.org
Phone: 918-497-5500 **Fax:** 918-497-5558
Contact: Marge Gerhart, Scholarship Coordinator
Society of Exploration Geophysicists
Foundation (SEG)
PO Box 702740
Tulsa, OK 74170-2740

▼ WOMEN'S AUXILIARY TO THE AMERICAN INSTITUTE OF MINING, METALLURGICAL AND PETROLEUM ENGINEERS

Women's Auxiliary to the American Institute of Mining, Metallurgical and Petroleum Engineers Scholarship Loan Fund • 84

One-time awards for college juniors, seniors, and graduate students pursuing earth science degrees related to the minerals industry. Dollar value of award may vary. Interview is required. Write for guidelines.
Academic/Career Areas: Earth Science; Engineering-Related Technologies; Mechanical Engineering.
Award: Scholarship, loan for use in junior, senior, or graduate years; not renewable. *Amount:* $1750–$10,000.
Eligibility Requirements: Applicant must be enrolled at a four-year institution.
Application Requirements: Application, financial need analysis, interview, references, transcript. **Deadline:** March 15.
Phone: 212-705-7692 **Fax:** 212-705-8024
Contact: Scholarship Loan Fund Committee Chair
Women's Auxiliary to the American Institute of Mining, Metallurgical and Petroleum Engineers
345 East 47th Street, 14th Floor
New York, NY 10017-2304

ECONOMICS

▼ INSTITUTE FOR HUMANE STUDIES

Humane Studies Fellowships see number 74

▼ JOHN F. KENNEDY LIBRARY FOUNDATION

Kennedy Research Grants see number 26

▼ KARLA SCHERER FOUNDATION

Karla Scherer Foundation Scholarships see number 67

▼ WOMEN GROCERS OF AMERICA

Mary Macey Scholarship see number 9

EDUCATION

▼ AMERICAN MONTESSORI SOCIETY

American Montessori Society Scholarship Fund • 85

One-time award for any aspiring Montessori teacher candidate who has been accepted into an American Montessori Society affiliated teacher education program. Submit financial aid forms, essay, references, and application.
Academic/Career Areas: Education.
Award: Scholarship for use in any year; not renewable.
Application Requirements: Application, essay, financial need analysis, references. **Deadline:** May 1.
E-mail: sweetfeld@aol.com
Phone: 212-358-1250 **Fax:** 212-358-1256
World Wide Web: http://www.seattleu.edu/~jcm/montessori/menu_link.html
Contact: Dottie Feldman, Scholarship Director
American Montessori Society
281 Park Avenue South, 6th Floor
New York, NY 10010-6102

▼ ARMENIAN PROFESSIONAL SOCIETY OF THE BAY AREA

Armenian Professional Society of the Bay Area Scholarships see number 31

▼ BETHESDA LUTHERAN HOMES AND SERVICES, INC.

Mental Retardation Scholastic Achievement Scholarship for Lutheran College Students see number 81

▼ CHARLES A. AND ANNE MORROW LINDBERGH FOUNDATION

Lindbergh Grants Program   see number 4

▼ JOHN F. KENNEDY LIBRARY FOUNDATION

Kennedy Research Grants   see number 26

▼ MEMORIAL FOUNDATION FOR JEWISH CULTURE

Memorial Foundation for Jewish Culture International Scholarship Program for Community Service   • 86

Scholarships for students preparing for careers as educators, rabbis, or religious functionaries in social services. Must be planning a career of service to small Jewish communities outside of the U.S., Israel, or Canada.
Academic/Career Areas: Education; Religion/Theology; Social Services.
Award: Scholarship for use in any year; not renewable. *Amount:* $1000–$3000.
Eligibility Requirements: Applicant must be Jewish.
Application Requirements: Application, references. **Deadline:** November 30.
Phone: 212-679-4074
Contact: Lorraine Blass, Associate Director
Memorial Foundation for Jewish Culture
15 East 26th Street, Room 1703
New York, NY 10010

▼ OKLAHOMA STATE REGENTS FOR HIGHER EDUCATION

Future Teacher Scholarship Program-Oklahoma   • 87

Open to outstanding high school graduates who agree to teach in shortage areas. Must rank in top fifteen percent of graduating class and score above 85th percentile on ACT or similar test. Students nominated by institution. Reapply to renew.
Academic/Career Areas: Education.
Award: Scholarship for use in any year; not renewable. *Amount:* up to $1500.
Eligibility Requirements: Applicant must be enrolled at a two-year or four-year institution; resident of Oklahoma and studying in Oklahoma.

Application Requirements: Application, essay, test scores, transcript. **Deadline:** May 1.
Phone: 405-524-9153 **Fax:** 405-524-9230
Contact: Dawn Scott, Research Analyst
Oklahoma State Regents for Higher Education
State Capitol Complex
500 Education Building
Oklahoma City, OK 73105

ELECTRICAL/ELECTRONIC ENGINEERING

▼ AMERICAN SOCIETY OF HEATING, REFRIGERATION, AND AIR CONDITIONING ENGINEERS, INC.

Alwin B. Newton Scholarship Fund   • 88

For full-time studies relating to heating, refrigeration, and air-conditioning. Must be for an ABET-accredited program. 3.0 GPA required. Renewable award of $2000.
Academic/Career Areas: Electrical/Electronic Engineering; Engineering/Technology; Heating, Air-Conditioning, and Refrigeration Mechanics; Trade/Technical Specialties.
Award: Scholarship for use in junior or senior year; renewable. *Number:* 1. *Amount:* $2000.
Eligibility Requirements: Applicant must have an interest in leadership.
Application Requirements: Application, financial need analysis, references, transcript. **Deadline:** December 1.
E-mail: benedict@ashrae.org
Phone: 404-636-8400 **Fax:** 404-321-5478
World Wide Web: http://www.ashrae.org
Contact: Lois Benedict
American Society of Heating, Refrigeration, and Air Conditioning Engineers, Inc.
1791 Tullie Circle, NE
Atlanta, GA 30329-1683

▼ ASSOCIATED WESTERN UNIVERSITIES, INC.

Associated Western Universities Student Research Fellowships   see number 18

▼ DEMONSTRATION OF ENERGY-EFFICIENT DEVELOPMENTS PROGRAM

Demonstration of Energy-Efficient Developments Scholarship • 89

Applicants must be in an accredited college or university studying an energy-related discipline. Must complete a research project and be sponsored by a member of the Demonstration of Energy-Efficient Developments Program. Inquire for details. Deadlines vary. Must have completed one year of study.

Academic/Career Areas: Electrical/Electronic Engineering; Engineering/Technology; Engineering-Related Technologies; Heating, Air-Conditioning, and Refrigeration Mechanics; Mechanical Engineering; Natural Resources.

Award: Scholarship for use in sophomore, junior, senior, or graduate years; not renewable. *Number:* 10. *Amount:* $3000.

Application Requirements: Application, transcript.

E-mail: hriester@appanet.org

Phone: 202-467-2960 **Fax:** 202-467-2992

World Wide Web: http://www.appanet.org

Contact: Holly Riester, Administrator
Demonstration of Energy-Efficient
Developments Program
2301 M Street, NW
Washington, DC 20037

▼ MASTER BREWERS ASSOCIATION SCHOLARSHIP FOUNDATION, INC.

Master Brewers Association-America's Scholarships *see number 7*

▼ NATIONAL ASSOCIATION OF WOMEN IN CONSTRUCTION

National Association of Women in Construction Undergraduate Scholarships *see number 27*

▼ SOCIETY OF MANUFACTURING ENGINEERS EDUCATION FOUNDATION

William E. Weisel Scholarship Fund • 90

Award for undergraduates who have completed at least thirty credit hours in manufacturing, robotics, or automated systems. Must have minimum 3.5 GPA. Submit application cover sheet, resume, transcript, essay, references, and statement of career goals. One-time award of $1000.

Academic/Career Areas: Electrical/Electronic Engineering; Engineering/Technology; Mechanical Engineering; Trade/Technical Specialties.

Award: Scholarship for use in sophomore, junior, or senior year; not renewable. *Number:* 1. *Amount:* $1000.

Application Requirements: Essay, references, transcript.

Deadline: March 1.

E-mail: murrdor@sme.org

Phone: 313-271-1500 Ext. 512 **Fax:** 313-240-6095

World Wide Web: http://www.sme.org

Contact: Dora Murray, Grants Coordinator
Society of Manufacturing Engineers
Education Foundation
One SME Drive
PO Box 930
Dearborn, MI 48121-0930

▼ VERTICAL FLIGHT FOUNDATION

Vertical Flight Foundation Scholarship *see number 56*

ENGINEERING-RELATED TECHNOLOGIES

▼ AMERICAN CONCRETE INSTITUTE INTERNATIONAL-CONCRETE RESEARCH AND EDUCATION FOUNDATION

Peter D. Courtois Concrete Construction Scholarships • 91

Two scholarships available to any undergraduate student in the U.S. or Canada. The student must have achieved senior status in a four-year or longer program in engineering, construction, or technology during the year for which the awards are presented. The student must have a course load of at least six credit hours per semester. Two one-time awards of $1000 each.

Academic/Career Areas: Engineering/Technology; Engineering-Related Technologies.

Award: Scholarship for use in senior year; not renewable. *Number:* 2. *Amount:* $1000.

Eligibility Requirements: Applicant must be enrolled at a four-year institution.

Peter D. Courtois Concrete Construction Scholarships (continued)

Application Requirements: Application, essay, references, transcript. **Deadline:** February 11.
Contact: Scholarship Council
American Concrete Institute
International-Concrete Research and
Education Foundation
38800 Country Club Drive
Farmington Hills, MI 48333

▼ CAMPUS SAFETY DIVISION

Campus Safety Scholarship   *see number 19*

▼ DEMONSTRATION OF ENERGY-EFFICIENT DEVELOPMENTS PROGRAM

Demonstration of Energy-Efficient Developments Scholarship   *see number 89*

▼ FEL-PRO, INCORPORATED

Fel-Pro Automotive Technicians Scholarship Program   • 92

Several scholarships available for qualified undergraduate students to become automotive technicians. Eligible fields of study include: auto, diesel, heavy equipment, and agricultural equipment mechanics. Renewable awards of $500 each.
Academic/Career Areas: Engineering/Technology; Engineering-Related Technologies; Trade/Technical Specialties.
Award: Scholarship for use in freshman, sophomore, junior, or senior year; renewable. *Number:* 250–340. *Amount:* $500.
Application Requirements: Application, references, transcript. **Deadline:** May 1.
E-mail: cpeurye%fel-pro@mcimail.com
Phone: 847-568-2411 **Fax:** 847-568-1997
Contact: Celene Peurye, Director, Corporate
Contributions Program
Fel-Pro, Incorporated
7450 North McCormick Boulevard
Skokie, IL 60076

▼ NATIONAL ASSOCIATION OF WOMEN IN CONSTRUCTION

National Association of Women in Construction Undergraduate Scholarships   *see number 27*

▼ SOCIETY OF BROADCAST ENGINEERS, INC.

Robert Greenberg/Harold E. Ennes Scholarship Fund and Ennes Educational Foundation Broadcast Technology Scholarship   • 93

Merit-based awards for undergraduate students to study the technical aspects of broadcast engineering. Students should apply as high school senior or college freshman and may use the award for a two- or four-year college or university program. One-time award of $1000-$2000.
Academic/Career Areas: Engineering/Technology; Engineering-Related Technologies; TV/Radio Broadcasting.
Award: Scholarship for use in freshman, sophomore, junior, or senior year; not renewable. *Number:* 2. *Amount:* $1000–$2000.
Eligibility Requirements: Applicant must be enrolled at a two-year or four-year institution.
Application Requirements: Application, essay, references, self-addressed stamped envelope, transcript. **Deadline:** July 1.
Contact: Linda Godby
Society of Broadcast Engineers, Inc.
8445 Keystone Crossing, Suite 140
Indianapolis, IN 46240

▼ SOLE—THE INTERNATIONAL LOGISTICS SOCIETY

Logistics Education Foundation Scholarship   • 94

One-time award for students pursuing a program of study in logistics. Must have minimum 3.0 GPA. Submit transcript and references with application.
Academic/Career Areas: Engineering-Related Technologies.
Award: Scholarship for use in any year; not renewable. *Number:* 5–10. *Amount:* $1000–$3000.
Eligibility Requirements: Applicant must be enrolled at a four-year institution.
Application Requirements: Application, references, transcript. **Deadline:** April 15.
World Wide Web: http://www.sole.org
Contact: Katherin O'Dea, Scholarship Coordinator
Sole—The International Logistics Society
8100 Professional Place, Suite 211
New Carrollton, MD 20785

▼ SPE FOUNDATION

SPE Foundation Scholarships   *see number 68*

▼ WOMEN'S AUXILIARY TO THE AMERICAN INSTITUTE OF MINING, METALLURGICAL AND PETROLEUM ENGINEERS

Women's Auxiliary to the American Institute of Mining, Metallurgical and Petroleum Engineers Scholarship Loan Fund   *see number 84*

ENGINEERING/TECHNOLOGY

▼ AMERICAN ASSOCIATION FOR THE ADVANCEMENT OF SCIENCE

American Association for the Advancement of Science Mass Media, Science, and Engineering Fellowship • 95

Ten-week summer program at television stations, radio stations, newspapers, or magazines. Students are given a weekly stipend and travel expenses. The main goal is for the students to help improve coverage of science-related issues. Must submit resume and have a minimum 3.0 GPA. Very competitive selection process is designed to seek out all qualified candidates, including African-American, Hispanic, and Native American students and those with disabilities.
Academic/Career Areas: Engineering/Technology; Health and Medical Sciences; Physical Sciences and Math.
Application Requirements: Application, essay, references, transcript. **Deadline:** January 15.
E-mail: aking@aaas.org
Phone: 202-326-6760 **Fax:** 202-371-9849
Contact: American Association for the Advancement of Science
1200 New York Avenue, NW
Washington, DC 20005

▼ AMERICAN CONCRETE INSTITUTE INTERNATIONAL-CONCRETE RESEARCH AND EDUCATION FOUNDATION

Peter D. Courtois Concrete Construction Scholarships   *see number 91*

▼ AMERICAN SOCIETY FOR PHOTOGRAMMETRY AND REMOTE SENSING

Earth Observation Satellite Company Award for Application of Digital Landsat TM Data   *see number 17*

▼ AMERICAN SOCIETY OF HEATING, REFRIGERATION, AND AIR CONDITIONING ENGINEERS, INC.

Alwin B. Newton Scholarship Fund see number 88

▼ ASSOCIATED WESTERN UNIVERSITIES, INC.

Associated Western Universities Student Research Fellowships   *see number 18*

▼ CATERPILLAR, INC.

Applied Power Scholarship Award Program • 96

Award for full-time undergraduate students enrolled in manufacturing engineering degree programs. Must have minimum 3.5 GPA, have completed at least 30 college credit hours, and be seeking a career in manufacturing engineering. One-time award of $1000. Must submit application cover sheet and resume.
Academic/Career Areas: Engineering/Technology.
Award: Scholarship for use in freshman, sophomore, junior, or senior year; not renewable. *Number:* 2. *Amount:* $1000.
Application Requirements: Essay, references, transcript.
Deadline: March 1.
World Wide Web: http://www.sme.org/foundation
Contact: Dora Murray or Teresa Macias, Grants Coordinator/Grants Secretary
Caterpillar, Inc.
One SME Drive
PO Box 930
Dearborn, MI 48121-0930

Caterpillar Scholars Award Program • 97

Award for full-time-students in manufacturing engineering/technical degree programs who have finished a minimum of thirty credit hours. Minimum 3.5 GPA required. Send four copies of application materials including statement

Caterpillar Scholars Award Program (continued)

outlining career goals, application cover sheet, and resume. One-time award of $2000.
Academic/Career Areas: Engineering/Technology.
Award: Scholarship for use in freshman, sophomore, junior, or senior year; not renewable. *Number:* 5. *Amount:* $2000.
Application Requirements: Essay, references, transcript.
Deadline: March 1.
World Wide Web: http://www.sme.org
Contact: Dora Murray or Teresa Macias, Grants Coordinator/Grants Secretary
Caterpillar, Inc.
One SME Drive
PO Box 930
Dearborn, MI 48121-0930

Lucile B. Kaufman Women's Scholarship • 98

Award for full-time female students enrolled in a degree program in manufacturing engineering or manufacturing engineering technology. Must have minimum 3.5 GPA and have completed at least 30 college credit hours. One-time award of $1000. Must submit application cover sheet, resume.
Academic/Career Areas: Engineering/Technology.
Award: Scholarship for use in sophomore, junior, or senior year; not renewable. *Number:* 1. *Amount:* $1000.
Eligibility Requirements: Applicant must be female.
Application Requirements: Essay, references, transcript.
Deadline: March 1.
World Wide Web: http://www.sme.org/foundation
Contact: Dora Murray or Teresa Macias, Grants Coordinator/Grants Secretary
Caterpillar, Inc.
One SME Drive
PO Box 930
Dearborn, MI 48121-0930

▼ DEMONSTRATION OF ENERGY-EFFICIENT DEVELOPMENTS PROGRAM

Demonstration of Energy-Efficient Developments Scholarship   see number 89

▼ FEL-PRO, INCORPORATED

Fel-Pro Automotive Technicians Scholarship Program   see number 92

▼ INSTITUTE OF INDUSTRIAL ENGINEERS

A.O. Putnam Memorial Scholarship • 99

One-time award for industrial engineering undergraduates at four-year accredited institutions. Applicants must be members of the Institute of Industrial Engineers, have a 3.4 GPA, and be nominated by a department head by November 15.
Academic/Career Areas: Engineering/Technology.
Award: Scholarship for use in junior or senior year; not renewable. *Number:* 1. *Amount:* $300–$750.
Eligibility Requirements: Applicant must be enrolled at a four-year institution and member of Institute of Industrial Engineers.
Application Requirements: Application, references, transcript.
Deadline: November 15.
Contact: Bisi Oyeyemi, University Operations Coordinator
Institute of Industrial Engineers
25 Technology Park/Atlanta
Norcross, GA 30092-2988

Institute of Industrial Engineers-Dwight D. Gardner Scholarship • 100

Available to industrial engineering juniors, seniors, and graduate students at four-year accredited colleges. Applicants must belong to the Institute of Industrial Engineers, have a 3.4 GPA, and be nominated by a department head by November 1. One-time award of $750-$1500.
Academic/Career Areas: Engineering/Technology.
Award: Scholarship for use in junior, senior, or graduate years; not renewable. *Number:* 5–15. *Amount:* $750–$1500.
Eligibility Requirements: Applicant must be enrolled at a four-year institution and member of Institute of Industrial Engineers.
Application Requirements: Application, references, transcript.
Deadline: November 15.
Contact: Bisi Oyeyemi, University Operations Coordinator
Institute of Industrial Engineers
25 Technology Park/Atlanta
Norcross, GA 30092-2988

UPS Scholarship for Female Students • 101

One-time award for female undergraduate students enrolled at any school in the U.S., Canada, or Mexico in an industrial engineering program. Must be a member of

Institute of Industrial Engineers, have a minimum GPA of 3.4, and be nominated by a department head.
Academic/Career Areas: Engineering/Technology.
Award: Scholarship for use in freshman, sophomore, junior, or senior year; not renewable. *Number:* 1. *Amount:* $2500.
Eligibility Requirements: Applicant must be enrolled at a four-year institution; female and member of Institute of Industrial Engineers.
Application Requirements: Application, references, transcript.
Deadline: November 15.
Contact: Bisi Oyeyemi, University Operations Coordinator
Institute of Industrial Engineers
25 Technology Park/Atlanta
Norcross, GA 30092-2988

▼ INTERNATIONAL SOCIETY FOR OPTICAL ENGINEERING-SPIE

SPIE Educational Scholarships and Grants in Optical Engineering   *see number 21*

▼ INVENTURE PLACE, NATIONAL INVENTORS HALL OF FAME

BFGoodrich Collegiate Inventors Program   *see number 22*

▼ MASTER BREWERS ASSOCIATION SCHOLARSHIP FOUNDATION, INC.

Master Brewers Association-America's Scholarships   *see number 7*

▼ MCDERMOTT, INCORPORATED

McDermott Scholarship   *see number 23*

▼ NATIONAL ASSOCIATION OF WOMEN IN CONSTRUCTION

National Association of Women in Construction Undergraduate Scholarships   *see number 27*

▼ NATIONAL ASSOCIATION OF WOMEN IN CONSTRUCTION FOUNDER'S SCHOLARSHIP FOUNDATION

National Association of Women in Contruction Founder's Scholarship Award   *see number 28*

▼ SIGMA XI, THE SCIENTIFIC RESEARCH SOCIETY

Sigma Xi Grants-in-Aid of Research *see number 8*

▼ SOCIETY OF BROADCAST ENGINEERS, INC.

Robert Greenberg/Harold E. Ennes Scholarship Fund and Ennes Educational Foundation Broadcast Technology Scholarship *see number 93*

▼ SOCIETY OF MANUFACTURING ENGINEERS EDUCATION FOUNDATION

Myrtle and Earl Walker Scholarship Fund • 102
One-time award for undergraduates seeking a career in manufacturing engineering who have completed at least thirty credit hours of college courses. Must have minimum 3.5 GPA. Submit application cover sheet, resume, transcript, essay, references, and statement of career goals.
Academic/Career Areas: Engineering/Technology; Trade/Technical Specialties.
Award: Scholarship for use in sophomore, junior, or senior year; not renewable. *Number:* 34. *Amount:* $500.
Application Requirements: Essay, references, transcript.
Deadline: March 1.
E-mail: murrdor@sme.org
Phone: 313-271-1500 Ext. 512 **Fax:** 313-240-6095
World Wide Web: http://www.sme.org
Contact: Dora Murray, Grants Coordinator
Society of Manufacturing Engineers Education Foundation
One SME Drive
PO Box 930
Dearborn, MI 48121-0930

St. Louis Chapter No. 17 Scholarship Fund • 103
Award for undergraduates pursuing studies in manufacturing engineering or industrial technology. Must attend an

St. Louis Chapter No. 17 Scholarship Fund (continued)

approved institution with a student chapter of the Society of Manufacturing Engineers, sponsored by St. Louis Chapter Number 17. One-time award of $1000. Award based on merit. Submit application cover sheet and resume.
Academic/Career Areas: Engineering/Technology.
Award: Scholarship for use in freshman, sophomore, junior, or senior year; not renewable. *Number:* 6. *Amount:* $1000.
Eligibility Requirements: Applicant must be studying in Illinois or Missouri.
Application Requirements: Essay, references, transcript.
Deadline: March 1.
E-mail: murrdor@sme.org
Phone: 313-271-1500 Ext. 512 **Fax:** 313-240-6095
World Wide Web: http://www.sme.org
Contact: Dora Murray, Grants Coordinator
Society of Manufacturing Engineers
Education Foundation
One SME Drive
PO Box 930
Dearborn, MI 48121-0930

Wayne Kay Scholarship ● 104

Award for undergraduate study in manufacturing engineering and manufacturing technology. Freshmen are not eligible. Must have minimum 3.5 GPA. Submit transcript, essay, references, application cover sheet, and statement letter with resume. One-time award of $2500.
Academic/Career Areas: Engineering/Technology; Trade/Technical Specialties.
Award: Scholarship for use in sophomore, junior, or senior year; not renewable. *Number:* 10. *Amount:* $2500.
Application Requirements: Essay, references, transcript.
Deadline: March 1.
E-mail: murrdor@sme.org
Phone: 313-271-1500 Ext. 512 **Fax:** 313-240-6095
World Wide Web: http://www.sme.org
Contact: Dora Murray, Grants Coordinator
Society of Manufacturing Engineers
Education Foundation
One SME Drive
PO Box 930
Dearborn, MI 48121-0930

William E. Weisel Scholarship
Fund see number 90

▼ SOCIETY OF PETROLEUM ENGINEERS

Gus Archie Memorial Scholarships ● 105

Renewable award for high school seniors planning to enroll in a petroleum engineering degree program at a four-year institution. Must have minimum 3.5 GPA. Write for further information.
Academic/Career Areas: Engineering/Technology.
Award: Scholarship for use in freshman, sophomore, junior, or senior year; renewable. *Amount:* $4000.
Eligibility Requirements: Applicant must be high school student and enrolled at a four-year institution.
Application Requirements: Application, autobiography, financial need analysis, photo, transcript. **Deadline:** April 30.
E-mail: twhipple@spelink.spe.org
Phone: 972-952-9393 **Fax:** 972-952-9435
Contact: Tom Whipple, Professional Development Manager
Society of Petroleum Engineers
PO Box 833836
Richardson, TX 75083

▼ SPE FOUNDATION

SPE Foundation Scholarships see number 68

▼ SPECIALTY EQUIPMENT MARKET ASSOCIATION

Specialty Equipment Market Association
Memorial Scholarship Fund ● 106

Scholarship for higher education in the automotive field for a student who has already completed one full year of study. Write for information concerning application guidelines. Several one-time awards of $2000 each.
Academic/Career Areas: Engineering/Technology; Trade/Technical Specialties.
Award: Scholarship for use in sophomore, junior, senior, or graduate years; not renewable. *Amount:* $2000.
Eligibility Requirements: Applicant must be enrolled at a four-year institution and must have an interest in automotive.
Application Requirements: Application, essay, financial need analysis, photo, references, self-addressed stamped envelope, transcript. **Deadline:** January 15.
E-mail: university@sema.org
Phone: 909-396-0289 Ext. 144 **Fax:** 909-860-0184

Contact: Dr. Harry Perden, Director of Educational
Services
Specialty Equipment Market Association
PO Box 4910
Diamond Bar, CA 91675-4910

Application Requirements: Application. **Deadline:** April 26.
Phone: 818-560-6894 **Fax:** 818-557-6702
Contact: Walt Disney Studios
500 South Buena Vista Street
Burbank, CA 91521-1735

FILMMAKING

▼ **ACADEMY OF MOTION PICTURE ARTS AND SCIENCES**
Don and Gee Nicholl Fellowships in Screenwriting see number 71

▼ **ARMENIAN PROFESSIONAL SOCIETY OF THE BAY AREA**
Armenian Professional Society of the Bay Area Scholarships see number 31

▼ **CHARLES AND LUCILLE KING FAMILY FOUNDATION, INC.**
Charles and Lucille King Family Foundation Scholarships see number 72

▼ **PRINCESS GRACE AWARDS**
Dance, Theater, Film, and Playwright Grants see number 45

▼ **UNIVERSITY FILM AND VIDEO ASSOCIATION**
University Film and Video Association Carole Fielding Student Grants see number 46

▼ **WALT DISNEY STUDIOS**
Walt Disney Studios Fellowship Program • 107
One-time award for writers in the feature film and television division. Open to all writers, but seeking culturally and ethnically diverse new writers. Submit writing samples and resume. Fellowship will take place in Los Angeles.
Academic/Career Areas: Filmmaking; Literature/English/Writing.
Eligibility Requirements: Applicant must be studying in California and must have an interest in writing.

FOOD SCIENCE/NUTRITION

▼ **AMERICAN ASSOCIATION OF CEREAL CHEMISTS FOUNDATION**
American Association of Cereal Chemists Undergraduate Scholarships see number 3

▼ **BETHESDA LUTHERAN HOMES AND SERVICES, INC.**
Mental Retardation Scholastic Achievement Scholarship for Lutheran College Students see number 81

▼ **EDUCATIONAL FOUNDATION OF THE NATIONAL RESTAURANT ASSOCIATION**
Educational Foundation of the National Restaurant Association Undergraduate Scholarship • 108
Award for students who have completed the first semester of a two- or four-year degree in a food service/hospitality program. Must have GPA of 3.0 and 1000 hours of work experience in food service/hospitality industry. Deadline: March 1.
Academic/Career Areas: Food Science/Nutrition.
Award: Scholarship for use in freshman, sophomore, or junior year; not renewable. *Number:* 75–100. *Amount:* $1000–$5000.
Eligibility Requirements: Applicant must be enrolled at a two-year or four-year institution and have employment experience in food service.
Application Requirements: Application, essay, financial need analysis, transcript. **Deadline:** March 1.
E-mail: cblasius@foodtrain.org
Phone: 312-715-6760 **Fax:** 312-715-0220
World Wide Web: http://www.restaurant.org

Educational Foundation of the National Restaurant Association
Undergraduate Scholarship (continued)

Contact: Tina Blasius
Educational Foundation of the National
Restaurant Association
250 South Wacker, #1400
Chicago, IL 60606

▼ GOLDEN GATE RESTAURANT ASSOCIATION

Golden Gate Restaurant Association Scholarship Foundation Awards • 109

One-time award for any student pursuing a food service degree at a 501(c)(3) institution. Personal interview in San Francisco is required. Write for further information.
Academic/Career Areas: Food Science/Nutrition.
Award: Scholarship for use in any year; not renewable.
Number: 1–15. *Amount:* $1000–$3000.
Application Requirements: Application, essay, financial need analysis, interview, references, self-addressed stamped envelope, transcript. **Deadline:** March 31.
E-mail: hq1@ggra.org **Fax:** 415-781-3925
Contact: Noah A. Froio, Scholarship Coordinator
Golden Gate Restaurant Association
720 Market Street, Suite 200
San Francisco, CA 94102

▼ INTERNATIONAL ASSOCIATION OF CULINARY PROFESSIONALS FOUNDATION

International Association of Culinary Professionals Foundation Scholarships • 110

One-time award for undergraduate and graduate culinary arts student pursuing professional training. Include transcript, essay, and references with application. Interview required. Application fee of $5.
Academic/Career Areas: Food Science/Nutrition.
Award: Scholarship for use in any year; not renewable.
Number: 60–65. *Amount:* $1000–$3000.
Eligibility Requirements: Applicant must be age 18 or over.
Application Requirements: Application, essay, interview, references, transcript. **Fee:** $5. **Deadline:** December 1.
Phone: 502-587-7953 **Fax:** 502-589-3602
Contact: Debbie Arnold, Director of Administration
International Association of Culinary
Professionals Foundation
304 West Liberty Street, Suite 201
Louisville, KY 40202-3068

▼ INTERNATIONAL FOODSERVICE EDITORIAL COUNCIL

International Foodservice Editorial Council Scholarship Award see number 75

▼ MASTER BREWERS ASSOCIATION SCHOLARSHIP FOUNDATION, INC.

Master Brewers Association-America's Scholarships see number 7

FOOD SERVICE/HOSPITALITY

▼ INTERNATIONAL EXECUTIVE HOUSEKEEPERS ASSOCIATION EDUCATIONAL FOUNDATION

International Executive Housekeepers Educational Foundation • 111

Award for students planning careers in the area of facilities management. Must be enrolled in IEHA-approved courses at a participating college or university. One-time award of up to $500.
Academic/Career Areas: Food Service/Hospitality; Health Administration; Home Economics; Trade/Technical Specialties.
Award: Scholarship for use in any year; not renewable.
Number: 10. *Amount:* up to $500.
Application Requirements: Application, essay, transcript.
Deadline: January 31.
E-mail: excel@ieha.org
Phone: 800-200-6342 **Fax:** 614-895-1248
World Wide Web: http://www.ieha.org
Contact: Beth Risinger, Chief Executive Officer
International Executive Housekeepers
Association Educational Foundation
1001 Eastwind Drive, Suite 301
Westerville, OH 43081-3361

▼ INTERNATIONAL FOODSERVICE EDITORIAL COUNCIL

International Foodservice Editorial Council Scholarship Award see number 75

▼ NATIONAL RESTAURANT ASSOCIATION EDUCATIONAL FOUNDATION

National Restaurant Association Educational Foundation Industry Assistance Grants • 112

One-time award for those with minimum three years food service experience who are currently employed in the industry and demonstrate commitment to industry. Contact for further information.
Academic/Career Areas: Food Service/Hospitality.
Award: Grant for use in any year; not renewable. *Number:* 18. *Amount:* up to $1000.
Eligibility Requirements: Applicant must have employment experience in food service.
Application Requirements: Application, references. **Deadline:** July 1.
E-mail: cblasius@foodtrain.org
Phone: 800-765-2122 Ext. 760 **Fax:** 312-715-0220
Contact: Tina Blasius, Scholarship Program
Coordinator
National Restaurant Association Educational
Foundation
250 South Wacker Drive, Suite 1400
Chicago, IL 60606-5834

NRAEF Undergraduate Scholarships • 113

Nonrenewable award for students pursuing an undergraduate degree in a food service/hospitality program. Must have completed first year of two- or four-year degree, 1000 hours of work experience in the industry, and have a 3.0 GPA.
Academic/Career Areas: Food Service/Hospitality.
Award: Scholarship for use in sophomore, junior, or senior year; not renewable. *Number:* 75. *Amount:* $1000–$5000.
Eligibility Requirements: Applicant must be enrolled at a two-year or four-year institution and have employment experience in food service.
Application Requirements: Application, essay, transcript.
Deadline: March 1.
E-mail: cblasius@foodtrain.org
Phone: 800-765-2122 Ext. 760 **Fax:** 312-715-0220
Contact: Tina Blasius, Scholarship Program
Coordinator
National Restaurant Association Educational
Foundation
250 South Wacker Drive, Suite 1400
Chicago, IL 60606-5834

▼ WOMEN GROCERS OF AMERICA

Mary Macey Scholarship   see number 9

FOREIGN LANGUAGE

▼ AMERICAN HISTORICAL ASSOCIATION

John E. O'Connor Film Award • 114

Award to recognize outstanding interpretations of history on film and video. Must be work done within past year. Laser disks, slides and other teaching material ineligible. Submit three copies. Write for details.
Academic/Career Areas: Foreign Language; History; Humanities.
Award: Prize for use in any year; not renewable. *Number:* 1.
Application Requirements: Applicant must enter a contest.
Deadline: June 1.
E-mail: aschulkin@theaha.org
Phone: 202-544-2422 **Fax:** 202-544-8307
World Wide Web: http://chnm.gmu.edu/aha
Contact: Andrew Schulkin, Administrative Assistant
American Historical Association
400 A Street, SE
Washington, DC 20003

▼ ASSOCIATION OF UNIVERSITIES AND COLLEGES OF CANADA

Canada-Taiwan Student Exchange Program   see number 34

▼ SOCIETY FARSAROTUL

Society Farsarotul Financial Awards   see number 32

GEMOLOGY

▼ GEMOLOGICAL INSTITUTE OF AMERICA

Cora Diamond Corporation Scholarship • 115

One-time award for anyone 17 years of age or older, with a high school diploma, currently employed in the jewelry industry or planing to enter the field. Must be used for Gemological Institute of America Distance Education gemology enrollment. Write for details.

Academic/Career Areas: Gemology.

Award: Scholarship for use in any year; not renewable. *Number:* 1. *Amount:* up to $250.

Eligibility Requirements: Applicant must be age 17 or over.

Application Requirements: Application, essay, financial need analysis, references. **Deadline:** November 1.

Phone: 760-603-4005

Contact: Office of Student Financial Assistance
Gemological Institute of America
5345 Armada Drive
Carlsbad, CA 92008-4698

Richard Kern Scholarship • 116

One-time awards for anyone over 17 years of age, with a high school diploma, currently employed in the jewelry industry or planning to enter the field. Award must be used for a Gemological Institute of America course or program enrollment. Write for details.

Academic/Career Areas: Gemology.

Award: Scholarship for use in any year; not renewable. *Number:* 2. *Amount:* up to $500.

Eligibility Requirements: Applicant must be age 17 or over.

Application Requirements: Application, references. **Deadline:** November 1.

Phone: 760-603-4005

Contact: Office of Student Financial Assistance
Gemological Institute of America
5345 Armada Drive
Carlsbad, CA 92008-4698

HEALTH ADMINISTRATION

▼ BETHESDA LUTHERAN HOMES AND SERVICES, INC.

Mental Retardation Scholastic Achievement Scholarship for Lutheran College Students see number 81

▼ CAMPUS SAFETY DIVISION

Campus Safety Scholarship see number 19

▼ INTERNATIONAL EXECUTIVE HOUSEKEEPERS ASSOCIATION EDUCATIONAL FOUNDATION

International Executive Housekeepers Educational Foundation see number 111

▼ NATIONAL ENVIRONMENTAL HEALTH ASSOCIATION

National Environmental Health Association/ AAS Scholarship • 117

One-time awards for college juniors, seniors, and graduate students pursuing studies in environmental health sciences and/or public health. Undergraduates must be enrolled in an approved program that is accredited by the Environmental Health Accreditation Council (EHAC).

Academic/Career Areas: Health Administration; Health and Medical Sciences.

Award: Scholarship for use in junior, senior, or graduate years; not renewable. *Number:* 3–4. *Amount:* $500–$2000.

Application Requirements: Application, references, transcript.

Deadline: February 1.

E-mail: neha.org@juno.com

Phone: 303-756-9090 **Fax:** 303-691-9490

World Wide Web: http://www.neha.org/~beckyr

Contact: Veronica White, NEHA Liaison
National Environmental Health Association
720 South Colorado Boulevard
Suite 970 South
Denver, CO 80246-1925

HEALTH AND MEDICAL SCIENCES

▼ AMERICAN ASSOCIATION FOR THE ADVANCEMENT OF SCIENCE

American Association for the Advancement of Science Mass Media, Science, and Engineering Fellowship see number 95

▼ AMERICAN FOUNDATION FOR AGING RESEARCH

American Foundation for Aging Research Undergraduate and Graduate Fellowships in Aging Research   see number 58

▼ AMERICAN FOUNDATION FOR UROLOGIC DISEASE, INC.

American Foundation for Urologic Disease Summer Medical Student Fellowship • 118

Introductory research fellowships to attract outstanding students to work in Urology Research Laboratories during the summer.
Academic/Career Areas: Health and Medical Sciences.
Application Requirements: Application. **Deadline:** March 15.
E-mail: lesley@afud.org
Phone: 410-468-1804 **Fax:** 410-468-1808
World Wide Web: http://www.access.digex.net/~afud
Contact: Lesley Finney, Director, Research Program
American Foundation for Urologic Disease, Inc.
1128 North Charles Street
Baltimore, MD 21201

▼ AMERICAN SOCIETY OF CRIME LABORATORY DIRECTORS

American Society of Crime Laboratory Directors Scholarship Award   see number 59

▼ BETHESDA LUTHERAN HOMES AND SERVICES, INC.

Mental Retardation Scholastic Achievement Scholarship for Lutheran College Students   see number 81

▼ CALIFORNIA COLLEGE OF PODIATRIC MEDICINE

Fund for Excellence in Podiatric Medicine • 119

Renewable scholarships for students of podiatric medicine at a four-year institution. Based on academic excellence, community service, demonstrated financial need, and a recommendation from student affairs office. Contact for more details. Minimum 3.0 GPA required. Award is renewable for an additional year.
Academic/Career Areas: Health and Medical Sciences.

Award: Scholarship for use in any year; renewable.
Number: 10–20. *Amount:* $1000–$2500.
Eligibility Requirements: Applicant must be enrolled at a four-year institution and have employment experience in community service.
Application Requirements: Application, autobiography, financial need analysis, references. **Deadline:** May 31.
Contact: John Hartnett, Director of Financial Aid
California College of Podiatric Medicine
1210 Scott Street
San Francisco, CA 94115

▼ CAMPUS SAFETY DIVISION

Campus Safety Scholarship   see number 19

▼ CHARLES A. AND ANNE MORROW LINDBERGH FOUNDATION

Lindbergh Grants Program   see number 4

▼ CROHN'S AND COLITIS FOUNDATION OF AMERICA, INC.

Crohn's and Colitis Foundation of America Student Research Fellowship Awards • 120

Awards for students at North American institutions to pursue research careers in inflammatory bowel diseases. Project must last at least ten weeks. Must have mentor. Must be working in U.S. laboratory. Submit research plan and curriculum vitae. One-time award of $2500.
Academic/Career Areas: Health and Medical Sciences.
Award: Scholarship for use in any year; not renewable.
Number: up to 16. *Amount:* $2500.
Application Requirements: Application. **Deadline:** February 1.
Phone: 800-932-2423 **Fax:** 212-779-4098
Contact: Jim Romano, Director of Research and Education
Crohn's and Colitis Foundation of America, Inc.
386 Park Avenue South, 17th Floor
New York, NY 10016

▼ CYSTIC FIBROSIS FOUNDATION

Cystic Fibrosis Foundation Student Traineeships   see number 60

▼ EASTER SEAL RESEARCH INSTITUTE

Miriam Neveren Summer
Studentship   *see number 61*

▼ EDUCATION AND RESEARCH FOUNDATION, SOCIETY OF NUCLEAR MEDICINE

Paul Cole Scholarship   • 121

One-time award for students of nuclear medicine technology at a two- or four-year institution. Academic merit considered. Application must be submitted by program director on behalf of the student. Write for more information.
Academic/Career Areas: Health and Medical Sciences; Nuclear Science.
Award: Scholarship for use in any year; not renewable. *Number:* 12. *Amount:* $1000.
Eligibility Requirements: Applicant must be enrolled at a two-year or four-year institution.
Application Requirements: Application, essay, references, transcript. **Deadline:** April 15.
E-mail: sweiss@nwu.edu
Phone: 773-880-4663 **Fax:** 773-880-4455
Contact: Ms. Susan C. Weiss, Administrative Director
Education and Research Foundation, Society
of Nuclear Medicine
2300 Children's Plaza, #42
Chicago, IL 60614

▼ INTERNATIONAL ORDER OF THE KING'S DAUGHTERS AND SONS

International Order of the King's Daughters
and Sons Health Careers
Scholarship   *see number 82*

▼ INTERNATIONAL SOCIETY FOR OPTICAL ENGINEERING-SPIE

SPIE Educational Scholarships and Grants in
Optical Engineering   *see number 21*

▼ KENTUCKY NATURAL RESOURCES AND ENVIRONMENTAL PROTECTION CABINET

Environmental Protection
Scholarships   *see number 6*

▼ MICROSCOPY SOCIETY OF AMERICA

Microscopy Society of America Presidential
Student Awards   *see number 63*

▼ NATIONAL COMMUNITY PHARMACIST ASSOCIATION (NCPA) FOUNDATION

National Community Pharmacist Association
Student Achievement Award   • 122

Award for junior or senior undergraduates pursuing their first undergraduate pharmacy degree. Must be enrolled at a four-year postsecondary institution. Minimum 2.5 GPA required. One-time award of $200.
Academic/Career Areas: Health and Medical Sciences.
Award: Prize for use in junior or senior year; not renewable. *Number:* 78–80. *Amount:* $200.
Eligibility Requirements: Applicant must be enrolled at a four-year institution.
Application Requirements: Deadline: Continuous.
Phone: 703-683-8200 **Fax:** 703-683-3619
World Wide Web: http://www.ncpanet.org
Contact: Debbie Tankersely, Foundation
Administrative Assistant
National Community Pharmacist Association
(NCPA) Foundation
205 Daingerfield Road
Alexandria, VA 22314

▼ NATIONAL ENVIRONMENTAL HEALTH ASSOCIATION

National Environmental Health Association/
AAS Scholarship   *see number 117*

▼ SIGMA XI, THE SCIENTIFIC RESEARCH SOCIETY

National Academy of Science Grants-in-Aid of
Research   *see number 13*

Sigma Xi Grants-in-Aid of Research *see number 8*

HEALTH INFORMATION MANAGEMENT/TECHNOLOGY

▼ BETHESDA LUTHERAN HOMES AND SERVICES, INC.

Mental Retardation Scholastic Achievement Scholarship for Lutheran College Students   see number 81

▼ EASTER SEAL RESEARCH INSTITUTE

Miriam Neveren Summer Studentship   see number 61

HEATING, AIR-CONDITIONING, AND REFRIGERATION MECHANICS

▼ AMERICAN SOCIETY OF HEATING, REFRIGERATION, AND AIR CONDITIONING ENGINEERS, INC.

Alwin B. Newton Scholarship Fund see number 88

▼ DEMONSTRATION OF ENERGY-EFFICIENT DEVELOPMENTS PROGRAM

Demonstration of Energy-Efficient Developments Scholarship   see number 89

HISTORY

▼ AMERICAN HISTORICAL ASSOCIATION

John E. O'Connor Film Award   see number 114

▼ AMERICAN HISTORICAL ASSOCIATION AND CANADIAN HISTORICAL ASSOCIATION

Albert Corey Prize in American-Canadian Relations   • 123

Biannual prize for the best recent book dealing with the history of Canadian-American relations or the history of both countries. Four copies of book required. Write for details.

Academic/Career Areas: History; Political Science; Social Sciences.

Award: Prize for use in any year; not renewable. *Number:* 1. *Amount:* $250–$1000.

Eligibility Requirements: Applicant must have an interest in writing.

Application Requirements: Applicant must enter a contest.

Deadline: June 1.

Contact: Administrative Assistant
American Historical Association and
     Canadian Historical Association
400 A Street, SE
Washington, DC 20003

▼ AMERICAN SCHOOLS OF ORIENTAL RESEARCH

Endowment for Biblical Research and American Schools of Oriental Research Summer Research Grants and Travel Scholarships   see number 30

▼ CHEMICAL HERITAGE FOUNDATION

Chemical Heritage Foundation Travel Grants   see number 20

▼ GENERAL COMMISSION ON ARCHIVES AND HISTORY, UNITED METHODIST CHURCH

Jesse Lee Prize   • 124

To encourage the writing of serious monographs in Methodist history, which includes studies of any antecedent bodies or offshoots of Methodism in the U.S. or its missions. Awarded every four years.

Academic/Career Areas: History; Religion/Theology.

Award: Prize for use in any year; not renewable. *Number:* 1. *Amount:* up to $2000.

Jesse Lee Prize (continued)

Eligibility Requirements: Applicant must have an interest in writing.
Application Requirements: Application, applicant must enter a contest. **Deadline:** October 1.
Phone: 732-408-3189 **Fax:** 732-408-3909
Contact: Charles Yrigoyen, Jr., General Secretary
General Commission on Archives and
History, United Methodist Church
PO Box 127
Madison, NJ 07940-0127

▼ HISTORY OF SCIENCE SOCIETY

History of Women in Science Prize • 125
One prize of $500 awarded to the author of an outstanding article on the history of women in science. Article must have appeared in the preceding three years. Contact for details.
Academic/Career Areas: History.
Award: Prize for use in any year; not renewable. *Number:* 1. *Amount:* $500.
Eligibility Requirements: Applicant must have an interest in writing.
Application Requirements: Application, applicant must enter a contest. **Deadline:** Continuous.
E-mail: hssexec@u.washington.edu
Phone: 206-543-9366 **Fax:** 206-685-9544
World Wide Web: http://weber.u.washington.edu/~hssexec
Contact: Keith Benson, Executive Secretary
History of Science Society
University of Washington
Box 351330
Seattle, WA 98195-1330

▼ INSTITUTE FOR HUMANE STUDIES

Humane Studies Fellowships *see number 74*

▼ JOHN F. KENNEDY LIBRARY FOUNDATION

Kennedy Research Grants *see number 26*

HOME ECONOMICS

▼ INTERNATIONAL EXECUTIVE HOUSEKEEPERS ASSOCIATION EDUCATIONAL FOUNDATION

International Executive Housekeepers Educational Foundation *see number 111*

HORTICULTURE/FLORICULTURE

▼ CHARLES A. AND ANNE MORROW LINDBERGH FOUNDATION

Lindbergh Grants Program *see number 4*

▼ HERB SOCIETY OF AMERICA, INC.

Herb Society Research Grants • 126
One-time award for persons conducting scientific, academic, or artistic study of herbs. Projects must be conducted in locations which may be monitored by the chairperson of the grants committee. Must include research proposal and proposed budget with application.
Academic/Career Areas: Horticulture/Floriculture.
Award: Grant for use in any year; not renewable. *Number:* 1–5. *Amount:* $5000–$10,000.
Application Requirements: Application. **Deadline:** January 31.
E-mail: herbsociet@aol.com
Phone: 440-256-0514 **Fax:** 440-256-0541
World Wide Web: http://www.herbsociety.com
Contact: Research Grants Chairperson
Herb Society of America, Inc.
9019 Kirtland Chardon Road
Kirtland, OH 44094

HUMANITIES

▼ AMERICAN HISTORICAL ASSOCIATION

John E. O'Connor Film Award *see number 114*

▼ **BETHESDA LUTHERAN HOMES AND SERVICES, INC.**

Mental Retardation Scholastic Achievement Scholarship for Lutheran College Students   *see number 81*

▼ **CHARLES A. AND ANNE MORROW LINDBERGH FOUNDATION**

Lindbergh Grants Program   *see number 4*

▼ **INSTITUTE FOR HUMANE STUDIES**

Humane Studies Fellowships   *see number 74*

▼ **JOHN F. KENNEDY LIBRARY FOUNDATION**

Kennedy Research Grants   *see number 26*

▼ **SOCIETY FARSAROTUL**

Society Farsarotul Financial Awards   *see number 32*

INTERIOR DESIGN

▼ **INTERNATIONAL FURNISHINGS AND DESIGN ASSOCIATION**

International Furnishings and Design Association Educational Foundation Scholarship   • **127**

One scholarship for student member of IFDA who has completed one-half of the requirements of an accredited program. Must be full-time-student. Submit essay and letters of recommendation with application. One-time award of $1500.
Academic/Career Areas: Interior Design.
Award: Scholarship for use in any year; not renewable. *Number:* 1. *Amount:* $1500.
Eligibility Requirements: Applicant must be member of International Furnishings and Design Association.
Application Requirements: Application, essay, references, transcript. **Deadline:** October 15.
Phone: 202-857-1897 **Fax:** 202-828-6042

Contact: International Furnishings and Design
     Association
     1200 19th Street NW, #300
     Washington, DC 20036-2422

JOURNALISM

▼ **ARMENIAN PROFESSIONAL SOCIETY OF THE BAY AREA**

Armenian Professional Society of the Bay Area Scholarships   *see number 31*

▼ **FUND FOR UFO RESEARCH, INC.**

Donald E. Keyhoe Journalism Award   • **128**

Award open to practicing journalists and freelance writers for the best print or broadcast story on UFOs. Submit published article or broadcast audio/videotape. One-time award of $500-$1000. Submissions are considered annually but award may not be given each year.
Academic/Career Areas: Journalism; Literature/English/Writing; Photojournalism; TV/Radio Broadcasting.
Award: Prize for use in any year; not renewable. *Number:* 1–2. *Amount:* $500–$1000.
Eligibility Requirements: Applicant must have employment experience in experience in career field.
Application Requirements: Application, applicant must enter a contest. **Deadline:** January 31.
Phone: 703-684-6032 **Fax:** 703-684-6032
Contact: Don Berliner, Office Manager
     Fund for UFO Research, Inc.
     PO Box 277
     Mt. Rainer, MD 20712

▼ **INTERNATIONAL FOODSERVICE EDITORIAL COUNCIL**

International Foodservice Editorial Council Scholarship Award   *see number 75*

▼ **WILLIAM RANDOLPH HEARST FOUNDATION**

Photojournalism Competitions   *see number 76*

LANDSCAPE ARCHITECTURE

▼ **NATIONAL ASSOCIATION OF WOMEN IN CONSTRUCTION**

National Association of Women in Construction Undergraduate Scholarships   see number 27

LEGAL SERVICES

▼ **BETHESDA LUTHERAN HOMES AND SERVICES, INC.**

Mental Retardation Scholastic Achievement Scholarship for Lutheran College Students   see number 81

▼ **INSTITUTE FOR HUMANE STUDIES**

Humane Studies Fellowships   see number 74

LIBRARY SCIENCES

▼ **AMERICAN SOCIETY FOR INFORMATION SCIENCE**

American Society for Information Science Award of Merit   see number 77

American Society for Information Science Best Information Science Book Award   see number 78

American Society for Information Science Research Award   see number 79

▼ **JOHN F. KENNEDY LIBRARY FOUNDATION**

Kennedy Research Grants   see number 26

▼ **SPECIAL LIBRARIES ASSOCIATION**

Special Libraries Association Scholarship • **129**

Three scholarships available to graduating college seniors and master's candidates enrolled in a program for library science. May be used for tuition, fees, research, and other related costs. Members of SLA preferred. One-time awards of $6000 each.

Academic/Career Areas: Library Sciences.
Award: Scholarship for use in senior or graduate years; not renewable. *Number:* 3. *Amount:* $6000.
Eligibility Requirements: Applicant must be enrolled at a four-year institution.
Application Requirements: Application, essay, financial need analysis, interview, references, test scores, transcript.
Deadline: October 31.
E-mail: taunya@sla.org
Phone: 202-234-4700 Ext. 641 **Fax:** 202-265-9317
World Wide Web: http://www.sla.org
Contact: Taunya Ferguson, Membership Assistant
        Special Libraries Association
        1700 18th Street, NW
        Washington, DC 20009

LITERATURE/ENGLISH/WRITING

▼ **ACADEMY OF MOTION PICTURE ARTS AND SCIENCES**

Don and Gee Nicholl Fellowships in Screenwriting   see number 71

▼ **ALLIANCE FOR YOUNG ARTISTS AND WRITERS, INC.**

Scholastic Art and Writing Awards-Art Section   see number 35

Scholastic Art and Writing Awards-Writing Section   see number 36

▼ **ARMENIAN PROFESSIONAL SOCIETY OF THE BAY AREA**

Armenian Professional Society of the Bay Area Scholarships   see number 31

▼ **CANADA COUNCIL FOR THE ARTS**

Canada Council International Translation Grants • **130**

One-time grants providing funding to foreign publishers for the translation of literary works by Canadian authors

into languages other than English or French, for publication or play production abroad.
Academic/Career Areas: Literature/English/Writing.
Award: Grant for use in any year; not renewable.
Application Requirements: Application. **Deadline:** Continuous.
Phone: 613-566-4414 Ext. 5060 **Fax:** 613-566-4390
World Wide Web: http://www.canadacouncil.ca
Contact: Canada Council for the Arts
350 Albert Street
Ottawa, ON K1P 5V8
Canada

▼ CHESTERFIELD FILM COMPANY

Chesterfield Film Company Writer's Film Project • 131

Award offering fiction, theatre, and film writers the opportunity to begin a career in screen writing. During the 12-month program, each writer creates two original, feature-length screenplays. Each writer is paired with studio executive mentors and a professional screenwriter. Up to five awards providing $20,000 stipend. Must submit samples of work. Application fee of $40.
Academic/Career Areas: Literature/English/Writing.
Application Requirements: Application. **Fee:** $40. **Deadline:** June 2.
E-mail: doug@chesterfield-co.com
Phone: 213-683-3977 **Fax:** 310-260-6116
World Wide Web: http://www.chesterfield-co.com
Contact: Doug Rosen, Director of Development
Chesterfield Film Company
1158 26th Street,
Box 544
Santa Monica, CA 90403

▼ FINE ARTS WORK CENTER IN PROVINCETOWN, INC.

Fine Arts Work Center Fellowships see number 38

▼ FUND FOR UFO RESEARCH, INC.

Donald E. Keyhoe Journalism Award see number 128

▼ GEORGE MASON UNIVERSITY

Mary Roberts Rinehart Fund • 132

One-time awards for two college students submitting the best work of poetry and fiction. Submit manuscript of work. Write for more information.

Academic/Career Areas: Literature/English/Writing.
Award: Scholarship for use in any year; not renewable.
Number: 2. *Amount:* $1000.
Eligibility Requirements: Applicant must have an interest in writing.
Application Requirements: Applicant must enter a contest.
Deadline: November 30.
Phone: 703-993-1180
Contact: Mr. William Miller, Director
George Mason University
Mail Stop 3E4, George Mason University
4400 University Drive
Fairfax, VA 22030

▼ INSTITUTE FOR HUMANE STUDIES

Humane Studies Fellowships see number 74

▼ INTERNATIONAL FOODSERVICE EDITORIAL COUNCIL

International Foodservice Editorial Council Scholarship Award see number 75

▼ JOHN F. KENNEDY LIBRARY FOUNDATION

Kennedy Research Grants see number 26

▼ POETRY SOCIETY OF AMERICA

George Bogin Memorial Award • 133

Award for a selection of four or five poems that reflect the encounter of the ordinary and extraordinary, use language in an original way, and take a stand against oppression. Write for guidelines, application, and deadlines. One-time award of $500. Application fee: $1.
Academic/Career Areas: Literature/English/Writing.
Award: Prize for use in any year; not renewable. *Number:* 1. *Amount:* $500.
Eligibility Requirements: Applicant must have an interest in writing.
Application Requirements: Applicant must enter a contest, self-addressed stamped envelope. **Fee:** $1.
E-mail: poetsocy@panix.org
Phone: 212-254-9628 **Fax:** 212-673-2352
World Wide Web: http://www.poetrysociety.org
Contact: Poetry Society of America
15 Gramercy Park South
New York, NY 10003

Norma Farber First Book Award • 134

Award for an author's first book of original poetry published during the calendar year. Send self-addressed stamped envelope for guidelines, application, and deadlines. One-time award of $500. Application fee: $1.
Academic/Career Areas: Literature/English/Writing.
Award: Prize for use in any year; not renewable. *Number:* 1. *Amount:* $500.
Eligibility Requirements: Applicant must have an interest in writing.
Application Requirements: Self-addressed stamped envelope. **Fee:** $1.
E-mail: poetsocy@panix.org
Phone: 212-254-9628 **Fax:** 212-673-2352
World Wide Web: http://www.poetrysociety.org
Contact: Poetry Society of America
15 Gramercy Park South
New York, NY 10003

Robert H. Winner Memorial Award • 135

Award for a manuscript of ten poems/twenty pages written by someone over 35 years of age. Applicant must not have published more than one book of poems. Send self-addressed stamped envelope for details, application, and deadlines. One-time award of $2500. Application fee: $1.
Academic/Career Areas: Literature/English/Writing.
Award: Prize for use in any year; not renewable. *Number:* 1. *Amount:* $2500.
Eligibility Requirements: Applicant must be age 36 or over and must have an interest in writing.
Application Requirements: Applicant must enter a contest, self-addressed stamped envelope. **Fee:** $1.
E-mail: poetsocy@panix.org
Phone: 212-254-9628 **Fax:** 212-673-2352
World Wide Web: http://www.poetrysociety.org
Contact: Poetry Society of America
15 Gramercy Park South
New York, NY 10003

William Carlos Williams Award • 136

One-time award for an author of a book of poetry published by a small, nonprofit, or university press. Value of award is between $500 and $1000. Send #10 self-addressed stamped envelope for guidelines and application. Deadline is in late December.
Academic/Career Areas: Literature/English/Writing.
Award: Prize for use in any year; not renewable. *Number:* 1. *Amount:* $500–$1000.

Eligibility Requirements: Applicant must have an interest in writing.
Application Requirements: Applicant must enter a contest, self-addressed stamped envelope.
E-mail: poetsocy@panix.org
Phone: 212-254-9628 **Fax:** 212-673-2352
World Wide Web: http://www.poetrysociety.org
Contact: Poetry Society of America
15 Gramercy Park South
New York, NY 10003

▼ WALT DISNEY STUDIOS

Walt Disney Studios Fellowship Program   *see number 107*

MECHANICAL ENGINEERING

▼ ASSOCIATED WESTERN UNIVERSITIES, INC.

Associated Western Universities Student Research Fellowships   *see number 18*

▼ DEMONSTRATION OF ENERGY-EFFICIENT DEVELOPMENTS PROGRAM

Demonstration of Energy-Efficient Developments Scholarship   *see number 89*

▼ MASTER BREWERS ASSOCIATION SCHOLARSHIP FOUNDATION, INC.

Master Brewers Association-America's Scholarships   *see number 7*

▼ NATIONAL ASSOCIATION OF WOMEN IN CONSTRUCTION

National Association of Women in Construction Undergraduate Scholarships   *see number 27*

▼ NATIONAL ASSOCIATION OF WOMEN IN CONSTRUCTION FOUNDER'S SCHOLARSHIP FOUNDATION

National Association of Women in Contruction Founder's Scholarship Award   see number 28

▼ SOCIETY OF MANUFACTURING ENGINEERS EDUCATION FOUNDATION

William E. Weisel Scholarship Fund   see number 90

▼ VERTICAL FLIGHT FOUNDATION

Vertical Flight Foundation Scholarship   see number 56

▼ WOMEN'S AUXILIARY TO THE AMERICAN INSTITUTE OF MINING, METALLURGICAL AND PETROLEUM ENGINEERS

Women's Auxiliary to the American Institute of Mining, Metallurgical and Petroleum Engineers Scholarship Loan Fund   see number 84

METEOROLOGY/ATMOSPHERIC SCIENCE

▼ ASSOCIATED WESTERN UNIVERSITIES, INC.

Associated Western Universities Student Research Fellowships   see number 18

▼ GARDEN CLUB OF AMERICA

Garden Club of America-"GCA Awards in Environmental Studies"   see number 5

▼ SIGMA XI, THE SCIENTIFIC RESEARCH SOCIETY

National Academy of Science Grants-in-Aid of Research   see number 13

Sigma Xi Grants-in-Aid of Research   see number 8

MUSEUM STUDIES

▼ AMERICAN SCHOOLS OF ORIENTAL RESEARCH

Endowment for Biblical Research and American Schools of Oriental Research Summer Research Grants and Travel Scholarships   see number 30

NATURAL RESOURCES

▼ ASSOCIATED WESTERN UNIVERSITIES, INC.

Associated Western Universities Student Research Fellowships   see number 18

▼ ASSOCIATION OF UNIVERSITIES AND COLLEGES OF CANADA

Canada-Taiwan Student Exchange Program   see number 34

▼ DEMONSTRATION OF ENERGY-EFFICIENT DEVELOPMENTS PROGRAM

Demonstration of Energy-Efficient Developments Scholarship   see number 89

▼ GARDEN CLUB OF AMERICA

Garden Club of America-"GCA Awards in Environmental Studies"   see number 5

▼ GRANDMOTHERS FOR PEACE INTERNATIONAL

Dorothy Vandercook Peace Scholarship • 137

Award for entering college freshmen or sophomores who are planning a career in which they will lobby for peace, social justice, and a healthy environment. School and community activities are considered. Send self-addressed stamped envelope for application. One-time award of $250.

Academic/Career Areas: Natural Resources; Peace and Conflict Studies; Political Science; Social Sciences.

Award: Scholarship for use in freshman or sophomore year; not renewable. *Number:* 4. *Amount:* $250.

Application Requirements: Application, autobiography, essay, references, self-addressed stamped envelope. **Deadline:** March 1.

E-mail: wiednerb@aol.com

Phone: 916-684-8744 **Fax:** 916-684-0394

World Wide Web: http://www.netcom.com/~lorjacy/gfp

Contact: Grandmothers for Peace International
9444 Medstead Way
Elk Grove, CA 95758

▼ KENTUCKY NATURAL RESOURCES AND ENVIRONMENTAL PROTECTION CABINET

Environmental Protection Scholarships see number 6

▼ NORTH AMERICAN BLUEBIRD SOCIETY

Bluebird Student Research Grant see number 64

▼ SIGMA XI, THE SCIENTIFIC RESEARCH SOCIETY

National Academy of Science Grants-in-Aid of Research see number 13

▼ SOCIETY FOR RANGE MANAGEMENT

Masonic Range Science Scholarship see number 1

▼ WILSON ORNITHOLOGICAL SOCIETY

Louis Agassiz Fuertes Award see number 14

Margaret Morse Nice Award see number 15

Paul A. Stewart Awards see number 16

NUCLEAR SCIENCE

▼ ASSOCIATED WESTERN UNIVERSITIES, INC.

Associated Western Universities Student Research Fellowships see number 18

▼ EDUCATION AND RESEARCH FOUNDATION, SOCIETY OF NUCLEAR MEDICINE

Paul Cole Scholarship see number 121

NURSING

▼ ANTHONY J. JANNETTI

Oncology Nursing Foundation/Pearl Moore Career Development Awards • 138

Several awards to reward a professional staff nurse for meritous practice by providing financial assistance to continue education. Must possess or be pursuing a BSN and be employed as a staff nurse with two years' oncology practice. Three awards of $2500 each.

Academic/Career Areas: Nursing.

Award: Scholarship for use in any year; not renewable. *Number:* 3. *Amount:* $2500.

Eligibility Requirements: Applicant must be enrolled at a four-year institution and have employment experience in experience in career field.

Application Requirements: Application, autobiography, references. **Deadline:** December 1.

Contact: Anthony J. Jannetti
501 Holiday Drive
Pittsburgh, PA 15220

▼ BETHESDA LUTHERAN HOMES AND SERVICES, INC.

Nursing Scholastic Achievement Scholarship for Lutheran College Students • 139

One-time award for college nursing students with minimum 3.0 GPA who are Lutheran and have completed the sophomore year of a four-year nursing program or one year of a two-year nursing program. Must be interested in working with people with mental retardation. Awards of up to $1000.
Academic/Career Areas: Nursing.
Award: Scholarship for use in junior, senior, or graduate years; not renewable. *Number:* 1–10. *Amount:* $50–$1000.
Eligibility Requirements: Applicant must be Lutheran; enrolled at a two-year or four-year institution and have employment experience in helping handicapped.
Application Requirements: Application, autobiography, essay, references, transcript. **Deadline:** March 15.
E-mail: blhsncrc@execpc.com
Phone: 920-261-3050 Ext. 525 **Fax:** 920-261-8441
World Wide Web: http://www.bethesdainfo.org
Contact: Kevin W. Keller, Coordinator, Outreach
Programs and Services
Bethesda Lutheran Homes and Services, Inc.
National Christian Resource Center
700 Hoffmann Drive
Watertown, WI 53094-6294

▼ CAMPUS SAFETY DIVISION

Campus Safety Scholarship see number 19

▼ CHARLES A. AND ANNE MORROW LINDBERGH FOUNDATION

Lindbergh Grants Program see number 4

▼ EASTER SEAL RESEARCH INSTITUTE

Miriam Neveren Summer Studentship see number 61

▼ INTERNATIONAL ORDER OF THE KING'S DAUGHTERS AND SONS

International Order of the King's Daughters and Sons Health Careers Scholarship see number 82

▼ ONCOLOGY NURSING FOUNDATION/ONCOLOGY NURSING SOCIETY

Oncology Nursing Foundation Roberta Pierce Scofield Bachelor's Scholarships • 140

Three awards to improve oncology nursing by assisting registered nurses in furthering their education. Must be currently enrolled in an undergraduate nursing degree program at an NLN-accredited school of nursing and must hold a current license to practice as a registered nurse. Application fee: $5. One-time award of $2000.
Academic/Career Areas: Nursing.
Award: Scholarship for use in any year; not renewable. *Number:* 3. *Amount:* $2000.
Eligibility Requirements: Applicant must be enrolled at a four-year institution and have employment experience in experience in career field.
Application Requirements: Application, transcript. **Fee:** $5.
Deadline: February 1.
Phone: 412-921-8597 **Fax:** 412-921-6565
World Wide Web: http://www.ons.org
Contact: Oncology Nursing Foundation/Oncology
Nursing Society
501 Holiday Drive
Pittsburgh, PA 15220

Oncology Nursing Foundation/Josh Gottheil Memorial Bone Marrow Transplant Career Development Awards • 141

Several awards available to any professional registered nurse for practice of bone marrow transplant nursing by providing financial assistance to continue education that will further professional goals or to supplement tuition in a bachelor's or master's program. Submit examples of contributions to BMT nursing. Four awards of $2000 each.
Academic/Career Areas: Nursing.
Award: Scholarship for use in any year; not renewable. *Number:* 4. *Amount:* $2000.
Eligibility Requirements: Applicant must be enrolled at a four-year institution and have employment experience in experience in career field.
Application Requirements: Application, autobiography, essay, references. **Deadline:** December 1.
Phone: 412-921-8597 **Fax:** 412-921-6565
World Wide Web: http://www.ons.org
Contact: Oncology Nursing Foundation/Oncology
Nursing Society
501 Holiday Drive
Pittsburgh, PA 15220

Oncology Nursing Foundation/Oncology Nursing Certification Corporation Bachelor's Scholarships • 142

Ten awards to improve oncology nursing by assisting registered nurses in furthering their education. Must be currently enrolled in an undergraduate nursing degree program at an NLN-accredited school of nursing and must have a current license to practice as a registered nurse. Application fee: $5. One-time award of $2000.
Academic/Career Areas: Nursing.
Award: Scholarship for use in freshman, sophomore, junior, or senior year; not renewable. *Number:* 10. *Amount:* $2000.
Eligibility Requirements: Applicant must be enrolled at a four-year institution and have employment experience in experience in career field.
Application Requirements: Application, transcript. **Fee:** $5.
Deadline: February 1.
Phone: 412-921-8597 **Fax:** 412-921-6565
World Wide Web: http://www.ons.org
Contact: Oncology Nursing Foundation/Oncology
        Nursing Society
        501 Holiday Drive
        Pittsburgh, PA 15220

Oncology Nursing Foundation/Oncology Nursing Society/Cancer Public Education Projects • 143

One-time award to assist nurses in public education projects that provide information to enhance the knowledge and awareness of cancer prevention, detection, and treatment to the public. Based on projected aims, background literature review, proposal, plan, time frame, need, and budget. Two awards of $2500 each. Contact for application fee.
Academic/Career Areas: Nursing.
Award: Grant for use in any year; not renewable. *Number:* 2. *Amount:* $2500.
Eligibility Requirements: Applicant must be enrolled at a four-year institution.
Application Requirements: Application. **Deadline:** December 1.
Phone: 412-921-8597 **Fax:** 412-921-6565
World Wide Web: http://www.ons.org
Contact: Oncology Nursing Foundation/Oncology
        Nursing Society
        501 Holiday Drive
        Pittsburgh, PA 15220

PEACE AND CONFLICT STUDIES

▼ GRANDMOTHERS FOR PEACE INTERNATIONAL

Dorothy Vandercook Peace Scholarship   see number 137

PERFORMING ARTS

▼ ARMENIAN PROFESSIONAL SOCIETY OF THE BAY AREA

Armenian Professional Society of the Bay Area Scholarships   see number 31

▼ ASSOCIATION OF UNIVERSITIES AND COLLEGES OF CANADA

Canada-Taiwan Student Exchange Program   see number 34

▼ CANADA COUNCIL FOR THE ARTS

Canada Council Music Touring Grants • 144

One-time grants for Canadian and foreign professional artists, performing a wide variety of music, who perform as individuals, ensembles, bands, collectives, groups, or companies and wish to tour in Canada. Application deadlines are June 15 and December 15.
Academic/Career Areas: Performing Arts.
Award: Grant for use in any year; not renewable.
Application Requirements: Application.
Phone: 613-566-4414 **Fax:** 613-566-4390
World Wide Web: http://www.canadacouncil.ca
Contact: Canada Council for the Arts
        350 Albert Street
        Ottawa, ON K1P 5V8
        Canada

▼ CONTEMPORARY RECORD SOCIETY

Contemporary Record Society National Competition for Performing Arts • 145

Applicant may submit one performance tape of varied length with each application. May use any number of

instrumentalists and voices. First prize is commercially distributed CD. Application fee is $50.
Academic/Career Areas: Performing Arts.
Award: Prize for use in any year; not renewable. *Number:* 1. *Amount:* $1500–$5000.
Eligibility Requirements: Applicant must have an interest in music/singing.
Application Requirements: Application, applicant must enter a contest, autobiography, references, self-addressed stamped envelope. **Fee:** $50. **Deadline:** September 19.
E-mail: crsnews@erols.com
World Wide Web: http://www.erols.com/crsnews
Contact: Ms. C. Hunt, Administrative Assistant
    Contemporary Record Society
    724 Winchester Road
    Broomall, PA 19008

▼ CURTIS INSTITUTE OF MUSIC

Curtis Institute of Music Scholarships   • 146
Renewable tuition scholarships offered to outstanding students of music. Audition required. Contact Curtis Institute for eligibility guidelines and application fee amount.
Academic/Career Areas: Performing Arts.
Award: Scholarship for use in any year; renewable.
Eligibility Requirements: Applicant must have an interest in music/singing.
Application Requirements: Application, references, test scores, transcript. **Deadline:** January 15.
Contact: Rebecca Good, Director of Student
    Financial Assistance
    Curtis Institute of Music
    1726 Locust Street
    Philadelphia, PA 19103

▼ GINA BACHAUER INTERNATIONAL PIANO FOUNDATION

Gina Bachauer International Piano Competition Award   • 147
Piano competition sponsored every four years (next in 1998). Includes solo, chamber music, and orchestral performances. Prizes of over $100,000 include cash awards, concerts, a New York recital, and grand piano. $75 fee. Contact for more information.
Academic/Career Areas: Performing Arts.
Award: Prize for use in any year; not renewable. *Number:* 11. *Amount:* $100,000.
Eligibility Requirements: Applicant must have an interest in music/singing.

Application Requirements: Application, applicant must enter a contest. **Fee:** $75. **Deadline:** Continuous.
E-mail: liano@earthlink.net
Phone: 801-323-6976 **Fax:** 801-521-9202
World Wide Web: http://www.bachauer.com
Contact: Massimiliano Frani, Associate Artistic
    Director
    Gina Bachauer International Piano
    Foundation
    PO Box 11664
    Salt Lake City, UT 84147-1664

▼ GLENN MILLER BIRTHPLACE SOCIETY

Glenn Miller Instrumental Scholarship   • 148
One-time awards for high school seniors and college freshmen, awarded as competition prizes, to be used for any education-related expense. Must submit ten minute, high-quality audiotape of pieces selected for competition or those of similar style. Applicant is responsible for travel to and lodging at competition. Submit $25 fee with completed application.
Academic/Career Areas: Performing Arts.
Award: Scholarship for use in freshman or sophomore year; not renewable. *Number:* 2. *Amount:* $750–$1500.
Eligibility Requirements: Applicant must be enrolled at a four-year institution and must have an interest in music/singing.
Application Requirements: Application, applicant must enter a contest, essay, self-addressed stamped envelope. **Fee:** $25. **Deadline:** March 15.
Phone: 712-542-4439
Contact: Dr. Gene Garrett
    Glenn Miller Birthplace Society
    711 North 14th Street
    Clarinda, IA 51632-1118

Jack Pullan Memorial Scholarship   • 149
One scholarship of $500 for male or female vocalist, awarded as competition prize, to be used for any education-related expense. Must submit ten minute, high-quality audiotape of pieces selected for competition or those of similar style. Applicant is responsible for travel to and lodging at competition. One-time award for high school seniors and college freshmen. Application fee: $25.
Academic/Career Areas: Performing Arts.
Award: Scholarship for use in freshman or sophomore year; not renewable. *Number:* 1. *Amount:* $500.

Jack Pullan Memorial Scholarship (continued)

Eligibility Requirements: Applicant must be enrolled at a four-year institution and must have an interest in music/singing.
Application Requirements: Application, applicant must enter a contest, self-addressed stamped envelope. **Fee:** $25.
Deadline: March 15.
Phone: 712-542-4439
Contact: Dr. Gene Garrett
Glenn Miller Birthplace Society
711 North 14th Street
Clarinda, IA 51632-1118

Ralph Brewster Vocal Scholarship • 150

One scholarship of $1000 for male or female vocalist, awarded as competition prize, to be used for any education-related expense. Must submit ten minute, high-quality audiotape of pieces selected for competition or those of similar style. Applicant is responsible for travel to and lodging at competition. One-time award for high school seniors and college freshmen. Application fee: $25.
Academic/Career Areas: Performing Arts.
Award: Scholarship for use in freshman or sophomore year; not renewable. *Number:* 1. *Amount:* $1000.
Eligibility Requirements: Applicant must be enrolled at a four-year institution and must have an interest in music/singing.
Application Requirements: Application, applicant must enter a contest, self-addressed stamped envelope. **Fee:** $25.
Deadline: March 15.
Phone: 712-542-4439
Contact: Dr. Gene Garrett
Glenn Miller Birthplace Society
711 North 14th Street
Clarinda, IA 51632-1118

▼ KOSCIUSZKO FOUNDATION

Kosciuszko Foundation Chopin Piano Competition • 151

Three awards for students majoring/planning to major in piano studies who are between the ages of 16 and 25. Must submit recital program of 65-70 minutes. Live audition and $35 fee required. Send curriculum vitae, references, proof of age, and photo.
Academic/Career Areas: Performing Arts.
Award: Prize for use in any year; not renewable. *Number:* 3. *Amount:* $1000–$2500.

Eligibility Requirements: Applicant must be ages 16-25; enrolled at a four-year institution and must have an interest in music/singing.
Application Requirements: Application, applicant must enter a contest, photo, references. **Fee:** $35. **Deadline:** March 8.
Phone: 212-734-2130 **Fax:** 212-628-4552
Contact: Thomas J. Pniewski, Director of Cultural Affairs
Kosciuszko Foundation
15 East 65th Street
New York, NY 10021-6595

▼ MARYLAND SUMMER INSTITUTE FOR THE CREATIVE AND PERFORMING ARTS, UNIVERSITY OF MARYLAND, COLLEGE PARK

University of Maryland International Leonard Rose Cello Competition and Festival • 152

One-time prize earned through a competitive international music competition. Cello competition takes place every four years. Award for those ages 18 to 30. Next competition is in 2001. Application fee: $80. Submit audition tape.
Academic/Career Areas: Performing Arts.
Award: Prize for use in any year; not renewable. *Number:* up to 12. *Amount:* $1000–$20,000.
Eligibility Requirements: Applicant must be ages 18-30 and must have an interest in music/singing.
Application Requirements: Application, applicant must enter a contest, autobiography, photo, portfolio, references.
Fee: $80. **Deadline:** March 15.
E-mail: intlcomp@umdacc.umd.edu
Phone: 301-403-8370 **Fax:** 301-403-8375
World Wide Web: http://www.inform.umd.edu/conted/
Contact: Don Reinhold
Maryland Summer Institute for the Creative and Performing Arts, University of Maryland, College Park
4321 Hartwick Road, Suite 220
College Park, MD 20740

University of Maryland International Marian Anderson Vocal Arts Competition and Festival • 153

One-time prize earned through a competitive international music competition. Voice competition takes place every four years. Next competition is in 1999. Submit audiocassette audition tape. Award for those 21 through 39 years of age. $80 application fee.

Academic/Career Areas: Performing Arts.
Award: Prize for use in any year; not renewable. *Number:* up to 12. *Amount:* $1000–$20,000.
Eligibility Requirements: Applicant must be ages 21-39 and must have an interest in music/singing.
Application Requirements: Application, applicant must enter a contest, autobiography, photo, portfolio, references.
Fee: $80. **Deadline:** March 15.
E-mail: intlcomp@umdacc.umd.edu
Phone: 301-403-8370 **Fax:** 301-403-8375
World Wide Web: http://www.inform.umd.edu/conted/
Contact: Don Reinhold
　　　　Maryland Summer Institute for the Creative
　　　　and Performing Arts, University of
　　　　Maryland, College Park
　　　　4321 Hartwick Road, Suite 220
　　　　College Park, MD 20740

University of Maryland International William Kapell Piano Competition and Festival • 154

One-time prize earned through a competitive international music competition. Piano competition takes place in July of even-numbered years. Submit audiocassette audition. For those ages 18-33. $80 application fee.
Academic/Career Areas: Performing Arts.
Award: Prize for use in any year; not renewable. *Number:* up to 12. *Amount:* $1000–$20,000.
Eligibility Requirements: Applicant must be ages 18-33 and must have an interest in music/singing.
Application Requirements: Application, applicant must enter a contest, autobiography, photo, portfolio, references.
Fee: $80. **Deadline:** March 15.
E-mail: intlcomp@umdacc.umd.edu
Phone: 301-403-8370 **Fax:** 301-403-8375
World Wide Web: http://www.inform.umd.edu/conted/
Contact: Don Reinhold
　　　　Maryland Summer Institute for the Creative
　　　　and Performing Arts, University of
　　　　Maryland, College Park
　　　　4321 Hartwick Road, Suite 220
　　　　College Park, MD 20740

▼ NEW JERSEY STATE OPERA

New Jersey State Opera Vocal Competition • 155

Vocal competition sponsored by the New Jersey State Opera is open to those between the ages of 22 to 34. Awards range from $1000 to $5000. Write for further information. One-time award. Application fee: $20.

Academic/Career Areas: Performing Arts.
Award: Prize for use in any year; not renewable. *Number:* 4–6. *Amount:* $1000–$5000.
Eligibility Requirements: Applicant must be ages 22-34 and must have an interest in music/singing.
Application Requirements: Application, applicant must enter a contest, autobiography, photo, references, self-addressed stamped envelope. **Fee:** $20. **Deadline:** February 28.
Phone: 973-623-5757 **Fax:** 973-623-5761
World Wide Web: http://pobox.com/~njsopera
Contact: Wanda Anderton, Director, Vocal
　　　　Competition
　　　　New Jersey State Opera
　　　　Robert Treat Center
　　　　50 Park Place, 10th Floor
　　　　Newark, NJ 07102

▼ PREMIO MUSICALE CITTA DI TRIESTE

International Competition for Symphonic Composition • 156

Musical competition for composers of any age. Must submit original composition for chamber orchestra. Award is 10,000,000 lire. Previous winners not eligible. Contact address in Italy for more information.
Academic/Career Areas: Performing Arts.
Award: Prize for use in any year; not renewable. *Number:* 1.
Eligibility Requirements: Applicant must have an interest in music/singing.
Application Requirements: Applicant must enter a contest.
Deadline: April 30.
Phone: Ext. 040366030 **Fax:** Ext. 040636969
Contact: Dr. Adriano Dugulin, General Secretary
　　　　Premio Musicale Citta Di Trieste
　　　　Palazzo Municipale
　　　　Piazza Dell'Unita D'Italia 4-1-34121
　　　　Trieste
　　　　Italy

▼ PRINCESS GRACE AWARDS

Dance, Theater, Film, and Playwright Grants
see number 45

▼ THELONIUS MONK INSTITUTE OF JAZZ

Thelonious Monk International Jazz Competition • 157

Competitions are open to all jazz musicians who plan to pursue jazz performance as a career. Musicians who have recorded as leaders on or have a contract with a major label are not eligible. Application fee is $25. Submit audiotape.

Academic/Career Areas: Performing Arts.
Award: Prize for use in any year; not renewable. *Number:* 3. *Amount:* $5000–$20,000.
Eligibility Requirements: Applicant must have an interest in music/singing.
Application Requirements: Application, applicant must enter a contest. **Fee:** $25. **Deadline:** August 1.
E-mail: sfischer@tmonkinst.org
Phone: 202-364-7272 **Fax:** 202-364-0176
Contact: Ms. Shelby Fischer, Executive Producer
Thelonius Monk Institute of Jazz
5225 Wisconsin Avenue, NW, Suite 605
Washington, DC 20015

PHOTOJOURNALISM

▼ FUND FOR UFO RESEARCH, INC.

Donald E. Keyhoe Journalism Award *see number 128*

▼ INTERNATIONAL FOODSERVICE EDITORIAL COUNCIL

International Foodservice Editorial Council Scholarship Award *see number 75*

▼ WILLIAM RANDOLPH HEARST FOUNDATION

Photojournalism Competitions *see number 76*

PHYSICAL SCIENCES AND MATH

▼ AMERICAN ASSOCIATION FOR THE ADVANCEMENT OF SCIENCE

American Association for the Advancement of Science Mass Media, Science, and Engineering Fellowship *see number 95*

▼ AMERICAN ASSOCIATION OF CEREAL CHEMISTS FOUNDATION

American Association of Cereal Chemists Undergraduate Scholarships *see number 3*

▼ AMERICAN SOCIETY FOR PHOTOGRAMMETRY AND REMOTE SENSING

Earth Observation Satellite Company Award for Application of Digital Landsat TM Data *see number 17*

▼ AMERICAN SOCIETY OF CRIME LABORATORY DIRECTORS

American Society of Crime Laboratory Directors Scholarship Award *see number 59*

▼ ASSOCIATED WESTERN UNIVERSITIES, INC.

Associated Western Universities Student Research Fellowships *see number 18*

▼ CAMPUS SAFETY DIVISION

Campus Safety Scholarship *see number 19*

▼ CHEMICAL HERITAGE FOUNDATION

Chemical Heritage Foundation Travel Grants *see number 20*

▼ GARDEN CLUB OF AMERICA

Garden Club of America-"GCA Awards in Environmental Studies" *see number 5*

▼ **HUDSON RIVER NATIONAL ESTUARINE RESEARCH RESERVE— NEW YORK STATE DEPARTMENT OF ENVIRONMENTAL CONSERVATION AND THE HUDSON RIVER FOUNDATION**

Tibor T. Polgar Fellowship   see number 62

▼ **INTERNATIONAL SOCIETY FOR OPTICAL ENGINEERING-SPIE**

SPIE Educational Scholarships and Grants in Optical Engineering   see number 21

▼ **INVENTURE PLACE, NATIONAL INVENTORS HALL OF FAME**

BFGoodrich Collegiate Inventors Program   see number 22

▼ **MASTER BREWERS ASSOCIATION SCHOLARSHIP FOUNDATION, INC.**

Master Brewers Association-America's Scholarships   see number 7

▼ **MCDERMOTT, INCORPORATED**

McDermott Scholarship   see number 23

▼ **MICROSCOPY SOCIETY OF AMERICA**

Microscopy Society of America Presidential Student Awards   see number 63

▼ **SIGMA XI, THE SCIENTIFIC RESEARCH SOCIETY**

National Academy of Science Grants-in-Aid of Research   see number 13

Sigma Xi Grants-in-Aid of Research   see number 8

▼ **SOCIETY FOR RANGE MANAGEMENT**

Masonic Range Science Scholarship see number 1

▼ **SOCIETY OF EXPLORATION GEOPHYSICISTS FOUNDATION (SEG)**

Society of Exploration Geophysicists Foundation Scholarship   see number 83

▼ **SPE FOUNDATION**

SPE Foundation Scholarships   see number 68

POLITICAL SCIENCE

▼ **AMERICAN HISTORICAL ASSOCIATION AND CANADIAN HISTORICAL ASSOCIATION**

Albert Corey Prize in American-Canadian Relations   see number 123

▼ **GRANDMOTHERS FOR PEACE INTERNATIONAL**

Dorothy Vandercook Peace Scholarship   see number 137

▼ **INSTITUTE FOR HUMANE STUDIES**

Humane Studies Fellowships   see number 74

▼ **JOHN F. KENNEDY LIBRARY FOUNDATION**

Kennedy Research Grants   see number 26

REAL ESTATE

▼ **REAL ESTATE EDUCATORS ASSOCIATION**

Harwood Memorial Real Estate Scholarship   • 158

Cash scholarship given to students pursuing a career in any facet of real estate. One-time merit-based award of

Harwood Memorial Real Estate Scholarship (continued)

$250-$500 for students who have completed at least one year of study. Must have Real Estate Educators Association member on campus.
Academic/Career Areas: Real Estate.
Award: Scholarship for use in sophomore, junior, senior, or graduate years; not renewable. *Number:* 3. *Amount:* $250–$500.
Eligibility Requirements: Applicant must be enrolled at a two-year or four-year institution.
Application Requirements: Application, references, self-addressed stamped envelope, transcript. **Deadline:** December 31.
E-mail: reea@washingtongroupinc.com
Phone: 703-352-6688 **Fax:** 703-352-6767
World Wide Web: http://www.reea.org
Contact: Real Estate Educators Association
10565 Lee Highway #104
Fairfax, VA 22030

RELIGION/THEOLOGY

▼ **GENERAL COMMISSION ON ARCHIVES AND HISTORY, UNITED METHODIST CHURCH**

Jesse Lee Prize   *see number 124*

▼ **MEMORIAL FOUNDATION FOR JEWISH CULTURE**

Memorial Foundation for Jewish Culture International Scholarship Program for Community Service   *see number 86*

▼ **OPAL DANCEY MEMORIAL FOUNDATION**

Opal Dancey Memorial Foundation   • 159
Grants for students seeking a master of divinity degree from an accredited theological school or seminary. Preference for Midwestern states and for several specified schools. Grant is primarily for students who will be serving in a local church ministry and is renewable up to four years. Ph.D. students ineligible. Submit recommendation from your pastor and others with whom you have worked. Applications available January through May 31. Write for application and further information.

Academic/Career Areas: Religion/Theology.
Award: Grant for use in any year; renewable. *Number:* 5–25. *Amount:* $3000.
Eligibility Requirements: Applicant must be Christian and ages 25-55.
Application Requirements: Application, essay, photo, references, transcript. **Deadline:** June 15.
Phone: 810-679-4729 **Fax:** 810-679-4729
Contact: Opal Dancey Memorial Foundation
45 South Street
Croswell, MI 48422

SCIENCE, TECHNOLOGY & SOCIETY

▼ **CAMPUS SAFETY DIVISION**

Campus Safety Scholarship   *see number 19*

SOCIAL SCIENCES

▼ **AMERICAN HISTORICAL ASSOCIATION AND CANADIAN HISTORICAL ASSOCIATION**

Albert Corey Prize in American-Canadian Relations   *see number 123*

▼ **AMERICAN SCHOOLS OF ORIENTAL RESEARCH**

Endowment for Biblical Research and American Schools of Oriental Research Summer Research Grants and Travel Scholarships   *see number 30*

▼ **ARMENIAN PROFESSIONAL SOCIETY OF THE BAY AREA**

Armenian Professional Society of the Bay Area Scholarships   *see number 31*

▼ GRANDMOTHERS FOR PEACE INTERNATIONAL

Dorothy Vandercook Peace Scholarship　　　　see number 137

▼ INSTITUTE FOR HUMANE STUDIES

Humane Studies Fellowships　　see number 74

▼ JOHN F. KENNEDY LIBRARY FOUNDATION

Kennedy Research Grants　　see number 26

▼ LAMBDA ALPHA NATIONAL COLLEGIATE HONORS SOCIETY FOR ANTHROPOLOGY

Lambda Alpha National Collegiate Honor Society of Anthropology National Dean's List Award　　● 160

Award for juniors majoring in anthropology to encourage them to continue their studies in the field. One award of $1000. Deadline: March 1.
Academic/Career Areas: Social Sciences.
Award: Scholarship for use in junior year; not renewable. *Number:* 1. *Amount:* $1000.
Eligibility Requirements: Applicant must be enrolled at a four-year institution.
Application Requirements: Application, references, transcript.
Deadline: March 1.
E-mail: 01bkswartz@bsuuc.bsu.edu
Phone: 765-285-1575 **Fax:** 765-285-2163
World Wide Web: http://www.geocities.com/collegepark/3022
Contact: B.K. Swartz, Jr., National Executive Secretary
Lambda Alpha National Collegiate Honors
Society for Anthropology
Dept. of Anthropology, Ball State University
Muncie, IN 47306-1099

▼ MEMORIAL FOUNDATION FOR JEWISH CULTURE

Soviet Jewry Community Service Scholarship Program　　● 161

One-time award for Jewish scholars from the former Soviet Union who are training for careers to serve the Jewish community in the former Soviet Union. Write for more information and deadline.

Academic/Career Areas: Social Sciences; Social Services.
Award: Scholarship for use in any year; not renewable.
Eligibility Requirements: Applicant must be Jewish.
Application Requirements: Application, references.
Phone: 212-679-4074
Contact: Lorraine Blass, Associate Director
Memorial Foundation for Jewish Culture
15 East 26th Street, Room 1703
New York, NY 10010

▼ PARAPSYCHOLOGY FOUNDATION

Eileen J. Garrett Scholarship for Parapsychological Research　　● 162

Applicants must show an academic interest in the science of parapsychology through research, term papers, and courses for which credit was received. Those with only a general interest will not be considered.
Academic/Career Areas: Social Sciences.
Award: Scholarship for use in any year; not renewable. *Number:* 1. *Amount:* $3000.
Application Requirements: Application, references, transcript.
Deadline: July 15.
Phone: 212-628-1550 **Fax:** 212-628-1559
World Wide Web: http://www.parapsychology.org
Contact: Lisette Coly, Vice President
Parapsychology Foundation
228 East 71st Street
New York, NY 10021

▼ SIGMA XI, THE SCIENTIFIC RESEARCH SOCIETY

Sigma Xi Grants-in-Aid of Research　　see number 8

SOCIAL SERVICES

▼ BETHESDA LUTHERAN HOMES AND SERVICES, INC.

Mental Retardation Scholastic Achievement Scholarship for Lutheran College Students　　see number 81

▼ MEMORIAL FOUNDATION FOR JEWISH CULTURE

Memorial Foundation for Jewish Culture International Scholarship Program for Community Service   *see number 86*

Soviet Jewry Community Service Scholarship Program   *see number 161*

SPECIAL EDUCATION

▼ BETHESDA LUTHERAN HOMES AND SERVICES, INC.

Mental Retardation Scholastic Achievement Scholarship for Lutheran College Students   *see number 81*

▼ EASTER SEAL RESEARCH INSTITUTE

Miriam Neveren Summer Studentship   *see number 61*

SPORTS-RELATED

▼ BETHESDA LUTHERAN HOMES AND SERVICES, INC.

Mental Retardation Scholastic Achievement Scholarship for Lutheran College Students   *see number 81*

THERAPY/REHABILITATION

▼ AMERICAN ASSOCIATION FOR RESPIRATORY THERAPY

William W. Burgin Educational Recognition Awards   • 163

Award for second-year students enrolled in accredited respiratory therapy program leading to associate degree. Must submit original referenced paper on some aspect of respiratory care and original essay of at least 1200 words describing how award will assist applicant in attaining career objective.

Academic/Career Areas: Therapy/Rehabilitation.
Award: Prize for use in sophomore year; not renewable. *Number:* 1. *Amount:* $2500.
Application Requirements: Application, applicant must enter a contest, essay, references, transcript. **Deadline:** June 30.
E-mail: demayo@aarc.org
Phone: 972-243-2272 **Fax:** 972-484-2720
World Wide Web: http://www.aarc.org
Contact: Brenda DeMayo, Administrative Assistant
American Association for Respiratory Therapy
11030 Ables Lane
Dallas, TX 75229-4593

▼ BETHESDA LUTHERAN HOMES AND SERVICES, INC.

Mental Retardation Scholastic Achievement Scholarship for Lutheran College Students   *see number 81*

▼ EASTER SEAL RESEARCH INSTITUTE

Miriam Neveren Summer Studentship   *see number 61*

▼ INTERNATIONAL ORDER OF THE KING'S DAUGHTERS AND SONS

International Order of the King's Daughters and Sons Health Careers Scholarship   *see number 82*

TRADE/TECHNICAL SPECIALTIES

▼ AIRCRAFT ELECTRONICS ASSOCIATION EDUCATIONAL FOUNDATION

Bud Glover Memorial Scholarship see number 47

Castleberry Instruments Scholarship see number 48

Northern Airborne Technology Scholarship see number 53

Paul and Blanche Wulfsberg Scholarship see number 54

Plane & Pilot Magazine/GARMIN Scholarship see number 55

▼ AMERICAN DENTAL HYGIENISTS' ASSOCIATION INSTITUTE FOR ORAL HEALTH

American Dental Hygienists' Association Institute-Baccalaureate Scholarship see number 80

▼ AMERICAN ELECTROPLATERS AND SURFACE FINISHERS SOCIETY

American Electroplaters and Surface Finishers Society Scholarships see number 69

▼ AMERICAN SOCIETY OF HEATING, REFRIGERATION, AND AIR CONDITIONING ENGINEERS, INC.

Alwin B. Newton Scholarship Fund see number 88

▼ FEL-PRO, INCORPORATED

Fel-Pro Automotive Technicians Scholarship Program see number 92

▼ GEMOLOGICAL INSTITUTE OF AMERICA

Eunice Miles Scholarship • 164

Award for a jewelry industry professional or those planning to enter the gemology field. Must be at least seventeen years of age and have a high school diploma or equivalent. To be used for enrollment in a Gemological Institute of America program of study. One-time award of $500.
Academic/Career Areas: Trade/Technical Specialties.
Award: Scholarship for use in any year; not renewable. *Number:* 1. *Amount:* $500.
Eligibility Requirements: Applicant must be age 17 or over and enrolled at a technical institution.
Application Requirements: Application. **Deadline:** November 1.
Phone: 760-603-4005
Contact: Office of Student Financial Assistance
Gemological Institute of America
5345 Armada Drive
Carlsbad, CA 92008-4698

Morris Hanauer and Irene Mack Scholarships • 165

One-time award for jewelry industry professionals or those planning to enter the gemology field. Must be at least seventeen years of age and have a high school diploma or equivalent. To be used for enrollment in a Gemological Institute of America program of study.
Academic/Career Areas: Trade/Technical Specialties.
Award: Scholarship for use in any year; not renewable. *Number:* 1–2. *Amount:* $500–$600.
Eligibility Requirements: Applicant must be age 17 or over.
Application Requirements: Application, references. **Deadline:** November 1.
Phone: 760-603-4005
Contact: Office of Student Financial Assistance
Gemological Institute of America
5345 Armada Drive
Carlsbad, CA 92008-4698

▼ INTERNATIONAL EXECUTIVE HOUSEKEEPERS ASSOCIATION EDUCATIONAL FOUNDATION

International Executive Housekeepers Educational Foundation see number 111

▼ NATIONAL ASSOCIATION OF WOMEN IN CONSTRUCTION

National Association of Women in Construction Undergraduate Scholarships see number 27

▼ NATIONAL ASSOCIATION OF WOMEN IN CONSTRUCTION FOUNDER'S SCHOLARSHIP FOUNDATION

National Association of Women in Contruction Founder's Scholarship Award   *see number 28*

▼ NATIONAL SCHOLARSHIP TRUST FUND OF THE GRAPHIC ARTS

National Scholarship Trust Fund of the Graphic Arts   *see number 42*

▼ PROFESSIONAL AVIATION MAINTENANCE ASSOCIATION

Professional Aviation Maintenance Association Student Scholarship Program   • 166

For students enrolled in an airframe and powerplant licensing program. Must have a B average and have completed 25 percent of the program. Must reapply each year. Apply after July 1 and up until October 31.
Academic/Career Areas: Trade/Technical Specialties.
Award: Scholarship for use in sophomore, junior, or senior year; not renewable. *Amount:* $1000.
Application Requirements: Application, financial need analysis, references, self-addressed stamped envelope, transcript. **Deadline:** October 31.
Phone: 202-216-9220 **Fax:** 202-216-9224
Contact: Scholarship Program Director
Professional Aviation Maintenance
Association
636 I Street, NW
Suite 300
Washington, DC 20001-3736

▼ SOCIETY OF MANUFACTURING ENGINEERS EDUCATION FOUNDATION

Myrtle and Earl Walker Scholarship Fund   *see number 102*

Wayne Kay Scholarship   *see number 104*

William E. Weisel Scholarship Fund   *see number 90*

▼ SPE FOUNDATION

SPE Foundation Scholarships   *see number 68*

▼ SPECIALTY EQUIPMENT MARKET ASSOCIATION

Specialty Equipment Market Association Memorial Scholarship Fund   *see number 106*

▼ WHIRLY-GIRLS SCHOLARSHIP FUND

International Women's Helicopter Pilots Whirly-Girls/Doris Mullen Memorial Scholarship & Memorial Flight Training Scholarship   *see number 57*

TRAVEL/TOURISM

▼ AMERICAN SOCIETY OF TRAVEL AGENTS SCHOLARSHIP FOUNDATION

A.J. (Andy) Spielman Scholarships   • 167

Must be re-entering work force in travel field and be enrolled in recognized travel school. Applicant must write a 500-word essay explaining why they chose the travel profession for re-entry to work force. Write for application by sending self-addressed stamped business-size envelope.
Academic/Career Areas: Travel/Tourism.
Award: Scholarship for use in any year; not renewable. *Number:* 1. *Amount:* $3000.
Eligibility Requirements: Applicant must be enrolled at a technical institution.
Application Requirements: Application, essay, references, self-addressed stamped envelope, transcript. **Deadline:** July 28.
World Wide Web: http://www.astanet.com
Contact: Scholarship Manager
American Society of Travel Agents
Scholarship Foundation
1101 King Street
Suite 200
Alexandria, VA 22314-2187

Air Travel Card Grant • 168

Must write a 500-word essay defining the importance and challenges of managing business travel and be enrolled in a travel curriculum at an accredited two- or four-year college or university. Canadian students eligible. Write for application by sending a self-addressed stamped business-size envelope.
Academic/Career Areas: Travel/Tourism.
Award: Grant for use in any year; not renewable. *Number:* 1. *Amount:* $3000.
Eligibility Requirements: Applicant must be enrolled at a two-year or four-year institution.
Application Requirements: Application, essay, references, self-addressed stamped envelope, transcript. **Deadline:** July 28.
World Wide Web: http://www.astanet.com
Contact: Scholarship Manager
American Society of Travel Agents
Scholarship Foundation
1101 King Street
Suite 200
Alexandria, VA 22314-2187

Alaska Airlines Scholarships • 169

One-time award for college students who are travel/tourism majors. Must write a 500-word essay and have minimum 2.5 GPA. Write for application by sending self-addressed stamped business-size envelope.
Academic/Career Areas: Travel/Tourism.
Award: Scholarship for use in freshman, sophomore, junior, or senior year; not renewable. *Number:* 1. *Amount:* $2000.
Eligibility Requirements: Applicant must be enrolled at a four-year institution.
Application Requirements: Application, essay, references, self-addressed stamped envelope, transcript. **Deadline:** July 28.
World Wide Web: http://www.astanet.com
Contact: Scholarship Manager
American Society of Travel Agents
Scholarship Foundation
1101 King Street
Suite 200
Alexandria, VA 22314-2187

American Express Travel Scholarship • 170

Candidate must be enrolled in a travel/tourism program in either a two- or four-year college or university or proprietary travel school. Must do 500-word essay on student's view of travel industry's future. Merit-based. Write for application by sending self-addressed stamped business-size envelope.
Academic/Career Areas: Travel/Tourism.
Award: Scholarship for use in freshman, sophomore, junior, or senior year; not renewable. *Number:* 1. *Amount:* $2500.
Eligibility Requirements: Applicant must be enrolled at a two-year or four-year or technical institution.
Application Requirements: Application, essay, references, self-addressed stamped envelope, transcript. **Deadline:** July 28.
World Wide Web: http://www.astanet.com
Contact: Scholarship Manager
American Society of Travel Agents
Scholarship Foundation
1101 King Street
Suite 200
Alexandria, VA 22314-2187

George Reinke Scholarships • 171

For a student enrolled in proprietary travel school or junior college. Applicant must write a 500-word essay on career goals in the travel/tourism industry. Write for application by sending a self-addressed stamped business-size envelope. Deadlines are July 28 and December 22.
Academic/Career Areas: Travel/Tourism.
Award: Scholarship for use in freshman or sophomore year; not renewable. *Number:* 5. *Amount:* $2000.
Eligibility Requirements: Applicant must be enrolled at a two-year or technical institution.
Application Requirements: Application, essay, financial need analysis, references, transcript.
World Wide Web: http://www.astanet.com
Contact: Scholarship Manager
American Society of Travel Agents
Scholarship Foundation
1101 King Street
Suite 200
Alexandria, VA 22314-2187

Healy Scholarship • 172

One-time award for a college undergraduate pursuing a travel/tourism degree. Must submit essay suggesting improvements for the travel industry. Write for application by sending a self-addressed stamped business-size envelope.
Academic/Career Areas: Travel/Tourism.
Award: Scholarship for use in freshman, sophomore, junior, or senior year; not renewable. *Number:* 1. *Amount:* $2000.

Healy Scholarship (continued)

Eligibility Requirements: Applicant must be enrolled at a four-year institution.
Application Requirements: Application, essay, references, self-addressed stamped envelope, transcript. **Deadline:** July 28.
World Wide Web: http://www.astanet.com
Contact: Scholarship Manager
American Society of Travel Agents
Scholarship Foundation
1101 King Street
Suite 200
Alexandria, VA 22314-2187

Holland-American Line Westours Scholarships • 173

Students must write 500-word essay on the future of the cruise industry and must be enrolled in travel/tourism program at a two- or four-year college or proprietary travel school. Write for application by sending a self-addressed stamped business-size envelope.
Academic/Career Areas: Travel/Tourism.
Award: Scholarship for use in any year; not renewable. *Number:* 2. *Amount:* $3000.
Eligibility Requirements: Applicant must be enrolled at a two-year or four-year or technical institution.
Application Requirements: Application, essay, references, self-addressed stamped envelope, transcript. **Deadline:** July 28.
World Wide Web: http://www.astanet.com
Contact: Scholarship Manager
American Society of Travel Agents
Scholarship Foundation
1101 King Street
Suite 200
Alexandria, VA 22314-2187

Joseph R. Stone Scholarships • 174

One-time award for high school senior or college undergraduate pursuing a travel/tourism degree. Must have a parent in the industry and proof of employment. Must submit 500-word essay explaining career goals. Write for application by sending a self-addressed business-size envelope.
Academic/Career Areas: Travel/Tourism.
Award: Scholarship for use in freshman, sophomore, junior, or senior year; not renewable. *Number:* 3. *Amount:* $2400.

Eligibility Requirements: Applicant must be enrolled at a four-year institution and have employment experience in experience in career field.
Application Requirements: Application, essay, references, self-addressed stamped envelope, transcript. **Deadline:** July 28.
World Wide Web: http://www.astanet.com
Contact: Scholarship Manager
American Society of Travel Agents
Scholarship Foundation
1101 King Street
Suite 200
Alexandria, VA 22314-2187

Pollard Scholarships • 175

Available to a person re-entering the job market. Must be enrolled in a travel/tourism curriculum at a proprietary travel school or junior college. Write for application and send self-addressed stamped business-size envelope. Deadlines are July 28 and December 22.
Academic/Career Areas: Travel/Tourism.
Award: Scholarship for use in any year; not renewable. *Number:* 2. *Amount:* $2000.
Eligibility Requirements: Applicant must be enrolled at a two-year or technical institution.
Application Requirements: Application, essay, references, self-addressed stamped envelope, transcript.
World Wide Web: http://www.astanet.com
Contact: Scholarship Manager
American Society of Travel Agents
Scholarship Foundation
1101 King Street
Suite 200
Alexandria, VA 22314-2187

Princess Cruises and Princess Tours Scholarship • 176

Merit-based award for student accepted or enrolled as an undergraduate in a travel/tourism program. Submit 300-word essay on two features cruise ships will need to offer passengers in the next ten years. Write for application by sending a self-addressed stamped business-size envelope.
Academic/Career Areas: Travel/Tourism.
Award: Scholarship for use in freshman, sophomore, junior, or senior year; not renewable. *Number:* 2. *Amount:* $2000.
Eligibility Requirements: Applicant must be enrolled at a two-year or four-year or technical institution.

Application Requirements: Application, essay, references, self-addressed stamped envelope, transcript. **Deadline:** July 28.
World Wide Web: http://www.astanet.com
Contact: Scholarship Manager
American Society of Travel Agents
Scholarship Foundation
1101 King Street
Suite 200
Alexandria, VA 22314-2187

Southern California Chapter/Pleasant Hawaiian Holidays Scholarship • 177

Two awards for students enrolled in a four-year college or university pursuing travel/tourism degrees. One award given to a student attending a college or university in southern California. Send a self-addressed stamped business-size envelope for application.
Academic/Career Areas: Travel/Tourism.
Award: Scholarship for use in freshman, sophomore, junior, or senior year; not renewable. *Number:* 2. *Amount:* $1500.
Eligibility Requirements: Applicant must be enrolled at a four-year institution.
Application Requirements: Application, essay, references, self-addressed stamped envelope, transcript. **Deadline:** July 28.
World Wide Web: http://www.astanet.com
Contact: Scholarship Manager
American Society of Travel Agents
Scholarship Foundation
1101 King Street
Suite 200
Alexandria, VA 22314-2187

▼ TRAVEL AND TOURISM RESEARCH ASSOCIATION

J. Desmond Slattery Undergraduate Student Award • 178

Award for the best original research study directly related to the travel and tourism field. Student's institution will designate recipient. Award of $700 cash; $300 travel allowance to conference; plaque; and one-year Travel and Tourism Research Association student membership.
Academic/Career Areas: Travel/Tourism.
Award: Prize for use in any year; not renewable. *Number:* 1. *Amount:* $1000.
Application Requirements: Application. **Deadline:** March 1.
E-mail: dornuf@mgtserv.com

Phone: 606-226-4344 **Fax:** 606-226-4355
Contact: Cynde Dornuf, Awards Committee
Travel and Tourism Research Association
546 East Main Street
Lexington, KY 40508

Travel and Tourism Research Association Student Research Award • 179

One-time prizes for master's and undergraduate students who submit recently written research papers on travel and tourism completed between March 1, 1997, and March 1, 1998. Submit the abstract and paper of a completed, original research survey. Five awards given; first prize is $1000; registration and travel allowance for conference; and plaque.
Academic/Career Areas: Travel/Tourism.
Award: Prize for use in freshman, sophomore, junior, senior, or graduate years; not renewable. *Number:* 5.
Application Requirements: Deadline: March 1.
E-mail: dornuf@mgtserv.com
Phone: 606-226-4344 **Fax:** 606-226-4355
Contact: Cynde Dornuf, Awards Committee
Travel and Tourism Research Association
546 East Main Street
Lexington, KY 40508

TV/RADIO BROADCASTING

▼ CHARLES AND LUCILLE KING FAMILY FOUNDATION, INC.

Charles and Lucille King Family Foundation Scholarships   *see number 72*

▼ FUND FOR UFO RESEARCH, INC.

Donald E. Keyhoe Journalism Award   *see number 128*

▼ INTERNATIONAL FOODSERVICE EDITORIAL COUNCIL

International Foodservice Editorial Council Scholarship Award   *see number 75*

▼ SOCIETY OF BROADCAST
   ENGINEERS, INC.

Robert Greenberg/Harold E. Ennes Scholarship
Fund and Ennes Educational Foundation
Broadcast Technology Scholarship see number 93

▼ UNIVERSITY FILM AND VIDEO
   ASSOCIATION

University Film and Video Association Carole
Fielding Student Grants see number 46

NONACADEMIC/NONCAREER CRITERIA—UNDERGRADUATE

▲

ASSOCIATION AFFILIATION

▼ **AIRCRAFT ELECTRONICS ASSOCIATION EDUCATIONAL FOUNDATION**

Terra-By-Trimble Avionics Collegiate Scholarship • 180

Award for high school seniors and college students who are children or grandchildren of employees of Aircraft Electronics Association regular members who are planning to attend or are attending an accredited college. Award is based on essay competition. One-time award of $2500.

Award: Scholarship for use in freshman, sophomore, junior, or senior year; not renewable. *Number:* 1. *Amount:* $2500.

Eligibility Requirements: Applicant must be member of Aircraft Electronics Association.

Application Requirements: Application, essay, references, test scores, transcript. **Deadline:** February 2.

E-mail: aea@microlink.net

Phone: 816-373-6565 **Fax:** 816-478-3100

World Wide Web: http://www.aeaavnews.org

Contact: Ms. Tracy Lykins, Educational Foundation
Coordinator
Aircraft Electronics Association Educational
Foundation
4217 South Hocker
Independence, MO 64055-0963

▼ **AMERICAN LEGION AUXILIARY NATIONAL HEADQUARTERS**

American Legion Auxiliary Girl Scout Achievement Award • 181

One scholarship available to recipients of Girl Scout Gold Award. Must be active in religious institution and have received appropriate religious emblem, Cadet or Senior Scout level. Must show practical citizenship in religious institution, community, and school. One-time award of $1000.

Award: Scholarship for use in freshman year; not renewable. *Number:* 1. *Amount:* $1000.

Eligibility Requirements: Applicant must be high school student; female; member of Girl Scouts and have employment experience in community service.

Application Requirements: Application, applicant must enter a contest, references, self-addressed stamped envelope.

Deadline: February 14.

Phone: 317-635-6291 **Fax:** 317-636-5590

World Wide Web: http://www.legion-aux.org

Contact: Peggy Sappenfield, National Secretary
American Legion Auxiliary National
Headquarters
777 North Meridian Street
Indianapolis, IN 46204

▼ **DAUGHTERS OF PENELOPE**

Alexandra Apostolides Sonenfeld Award • 182

Award for female high school seniors or recent graduates applying to postsecondary institution or college undergraduates. Award made upon receipt of proof of registration. Applicant must have immediate family member who has been member of Daughters of Penelope or Order of Ahepa for two years, or herself have been member of Daughters of Penelope or Maids of Athena for two years. Must verify membership. One-time award of $1500, based on financial need and academic merit. Must submit student's or parents' IRS forms. Deadline: June 20.

Award: Scholarship for use in freshman, sophomore, junior, or senior year; not renewable. *Number:* 1. *Amount:* $1500.

Eligibility Requirements: Applicant must be female and member of Daughters of Penelope/Maids of Athena/Order of Ahepa.

Alexandra Apostolides Sonenfeld Award (continued)

Application Requirements: Application, essay, financial need analysis, photo, references, test scores, transcript. **Deadline:** June 20.
Contact: Daughters of Penelope
1909 Q Street, NW, Suite 500
Washington, DC 20009

Daughters of Penelope Past Grand Presidents' Award • 183

Award for female high school seniors or recent graduates applying to postsecondary institution, or college undergraduates. Award made upon receipt of proof of registration. Applicant must have immediate family member who has been member of Daughters of Penelope or Order of Ahepa for two years, or herself have been member of Daughters of Penelope or Maids of Athena for two years. Must verify membership. One-time award of $1500, based on financial need and academic merit. Must submit student's or parents' IRS forms. Deadline: June 20.
Award: Scholarship for use in freshman, sophomore, junior, or senior year; not renewable. *Number:* 1. *Amount:* $1500.
Eligibility Requirements: Applicant must be female and member of Daughters of Penelope/Maids of Athena/Order of Ahepa.
Application Requirements: Application, essay, financial need analysis, photo, references, test scores, transcript. **Deadline:** June 20.
Contact: Daughters of Penelope
1909 Q Street, NW, Suite 500
Washington, DC 20009

Joanne V. Hologgitas Scholarship • 184

Award for female high school senior or recent graduate applying to postsecondary institution, or college undergraduate. Award made upon receipt of proof of registration. Applicant must have immediate family member who has been member of Daughters of Penelope or Order of Ahepa for two years, or herself have been member of Daughters of Penelope or Maids of Athena for two years. Must verify membership. One-time award of $1000, based on academic merit. Deadline: June 20.
Award: Scholarship for use in freshman, sophomore, junior, or senior year; not renewable. *Number:* 1. *Amount:* $1000.
Eligibility Requirements: Applicant must be female and member of Daughters of Penelope/Maids of Athena/Order of Ahepa.

Application Requirements: Application, essay, references, transcript. **Deadline:** June 20.
Contact: Daughters of Penelope
1909 Q Street, NW, Suite 500
Washington, DC 20009

Kottis Family Award • 185

Award for female high school seniors or recent graduates applying to postsecondary institution, or college undergraduates. Award made upon receipt of proof of registration. Applicant must have immediate family member who has been member of Daughters of Penelope or Order of Ahepa for two years, or herself have been member of Daughters of Penelope or Maids of Athena for two years. Must verify membership. One-time award of $1000, based on academic merit. Deadline: June 20.
Award: Scholarship for use in freshman, sophomore, junior, or senior year; not renewable. *Number:* 1. *Amount:* $1000.
Eligibility Requirements: Applicant must be female and member of Daughters of Penelope/Maids of Athena/Order of Ahepa.
Application Requirements: Application, essay, photo, references, test scores, transcript. **Deadline:** June 20.
Contact: Daughters of Penelope
1909 Q Street, NW, Suite 500
Washington, DC 20009

Mary M. Verges Award • 186

Award for female high school seniors or recent graduates applying to postsecondary institution, or college undergraduates. Award made upon receipt of proof of registration. Applicant must have immediate family member who has been member of Daughters of Penelope or Order of Ahepa for two years, or herself have been member of Daughters of Penelope or Maids of Athena for two years. Must verify membership. Award of $1000, based on academic merit. Deadline: June 20.
Award: Scholarship for use in freshman, sophomore, junior, or senior year; renewable. *Number:* 1. *Amount:* $1000.
Eligibility Requirements: Applicant must be female and member of Daughters of Penelope/Maids of Athena/Order of Ahepa.
Application Requirements: Application, essay, photo, references, test scores, transcript. **Deadline:** June 20.
Contact: Daughters of Penelope
1909 Q Street, NW, Suite 500
Washington, DC 20009

Past Grand Presidents' Memorial Scholarship Award • 187

Award for female high school seniors or recent graduates applying to postsecondary institution, or college undergraduates. Award made upon receipt of proof of registration. Applicant must have immediate family member who has been member of Daughters of Penelope or Order of Ahepa for two years, or herself have been member of Daughters of Penelope or Maids of Athena for two years. Must verify membership. One-time award of $1000, based on academic merit. Deadline: June 20.

Award: Scholarship for use in freshman, sophomore, junior, or senior year; not renewable. *Number:* 1. *Amount:* $1000.

Eligibility Requirements: Applicant must be female and member of Daughters of Penelope/Maids of Athena/ Order of Ahepa.

Application Requirements: Application, essay, references, test scores, transcript. **Deadline:** June 20.

Contact: Daughters of Penelope
1909 Q Street, NW, Suite 500
Washington, DC 20009

▼ DELTA PHI EPSILON EDUCATIONAL FOUNDATION

Delta Phi Epsilon Educational Foundation Scholarships • 188

One-time award for members of Delta Phi Epsilon or their children to further their educational pursuits. Based on financial need, scholarship, service to community, and service to sorority. Application deadline: March 15.

Award: Scholarship for use in any year; not renewable. *Number:* 4–6. *Amount:* $500.

Eligibility Requirements: Applicant must have employment experience in community service.

Application Requirements: Application, autobiography, financial need analysis, photo, references, transcript. **Deadline:** March 15.

E-mail: ealper@dephie.org

World Wide Web: http://www.dphie.org

Contact: Ms. Ellen Alper, Treasurer
Delta Phi Epsilon Educational Foundation
734 West Port Plaza, Suite 271
St. Louis, MO 63146

▼ GIRLS INCORPORATED

Girls Incorporated Donna Brace Ogilvie-Zelda Gitlin Poetry Program Awards • 189

For young women ages 14-18 who are members of Girls Incorporated. Submit poems for local judging. Two one-time awards of $500 each.

Award: Prize for use in any year; not renewable. *Number:* 2. *Amount:* $500.

Eligibility Requirements: Applicant must be high school student; ages 14-18; female; member of Girls Incorporated and must have an interest in writing.

Application Requirements: Application, applicant must enter a contest. **Deadline:** December 15.

Contact: Girls Incorporated
120 Wall Street
New York, NY 10005

Girls Incorporated/Scholars Program • 190

For young women in 10th, 11th, or 12th grades who are members of Girls Incorporated affiliates and under the age of 19. Must complete an application form. Judging is done first locally and then nationally. Up to twenty-three one-time awards of $1000-$10,000. Must plan to enroll at a two- or four-year postsecondary institution.

Award: Scholarship for use in any year; not renewable. *Number:* up to 23. *Amount:* $1000–$10,000.

Eligibility Requirements: Applicant must be high school student; age 19 or under; female and member of Girls Incorporated.

Application Requirements: Application, essay, references, transcript. **Deadline:** December 15.

Contact: Girls Incorporated
120 Wall Street
New York, NY 10005

▼ HEBREW IMMIGRANT AID SOCIETY

Hebrew Immigrant Aid Society Scholarship Awards • 191

Must be Hebrew Immigrant Aid Society-sponsored refugee or child thereof who migrated to the U.S. after 1985. Must have completed two semesters at a U.S. high school, college, or graduate school. Send self-addressed stamped envelope for application in February.

Award: Scholarship for use in any year; not renewable. *Number:* 50–75. *Amount:* $1000.

Eligibility Requirements: Applicant must be member of Hebrew Immigrant Aid Society.

Hebrew Immigrant Aid Society Scholarship Awards (continued)

Application Requirements: Application, essay, financial need analysis, self-addressed stamped envelope, transcript.
Deadline: April 15.
Contact: Sally Hespe, Associate Director, Member and
      Board Services
      Hebrew Immigrant Aid Society
      333 Seventh Avenue
      New York, NY 10001-5004

▼ INTERNATIONAL BROTHERHOOD OF BOILERMAKERS, IRON SHIP BUILDERS, BLACKSMITHS, FORGERS AND HELPERS, AFL-CIO

International Brotherhood of Boilermakers Scholarship Program • 192

Several scholarships for high school seniors who are the children of members of the International Brotherhood of Boilermakers. Based on academic merit, career goals, extracurricular activities, and essay. Submit birth certificate, ACT/SAT scores, transcript, essay, and application. One-time award.
Award: Scholarship for use in freshman year; not renewable. *Number:* 14. *Amount:* $2500–$5000.
Eligibility Requirements: Applicant must be high school student; enrolled at a two-year or four-year institution and member of International Brotherhood of Boilermakers.
Application Requirements: Application, essay, test scores, transcript. **Deadline:** March 31.
E-mail: tracy@boilermakers.org
Phone: 913-371-2640 **Fax:** 913-281-8104
World Wide Web: http://www.boilermakers.org
Contact: Tracy France, Administrative Secretary
      International Brotherhood of Boilermakers,
      Iron Ship Builders, Blacksmiths, Forgers
      and Helpers, AFL-CIO
      753 State Avenue, Suite 570
      Kansas City, KS 66101

▼ INTERNATIONAL SOCIETY FOR CLINICAL LABORATORY TECHNOLOGY

David Birenbaum Scholarship Fund • 193

One-time award based on merit for members or dependents of members of the International Society for Clinical Laboratory Technology for study in any discipline for any academic year. Submit two character references.

Award: Scholarship for use in any year; not renewable.
Number: 1–5.
Eligibility Requirements: Applicant must be member of Transportation Club International.
Application Requirements: Application, essay, financial need analysis, references, transcript. **Deadline:** April 1.
E-mail: isclt@aol.com
Phone: 314-241-1445 **Fax:** 314-241-1449
Contact: Scholarship Coordinator
      International Society for Clinical Laboratory
      Technology
      917 Locust Street, Suite 1100
      St. Louis, MO 63101-1413

▼ JAPANESE AMERICAN CITIZENS LEAGUE

Abe and Ester Hagiwara Student Aid Award • 194

One-time award for students with strong financial need. Applicants will be evaluated as to whether they show need as well as whether they meet the requirements. Send self-addressed stamped envelope for application, specifying application category.
Award: Scholarship for use in any year; not renewable.
Number: 1. *Amount:* $2500.
Eligibility Requirements: Applicant must be member of Japanese-American Citizens League.
Application Requirements: Application, essay, financial need analysis, references, transcript. **Deadline:** April 1.
E-mail: jacl@jacl.org
Phone: 415-921-5225 **Fax:** 415-931-4671
Contact: Scholarship Administrator
      Japanese American Citizens League
      1765 Sutter Street
      San Francisco, CA 94115

▼ NORTHEASTERN LOGGERS' ASSOCIATION, INC.

Northeastern Loggers' Association Scholarships • 195

Scholarships available to those whose family belongs to the Northeastern Loggers' Association or whose family member is an employee of the Industrial and Associate Members of the Northeastern Loggers' Association. Must submit paper on topic of "What it means to grow up in the forest industry."
Award: Scholarship for use in freshman, sophomore, junior, or senior year; not renewable. *Number:* 3.
Amount: $500.

Eligibility Requirements: Applicant must be member of Northeastern Loggers Association.
Application Requirements: Application, autobiography, essay, transcript. **Deadline:** March 31.
E-mail: mlincoln_nela@mailcity.com
Phone: 315-369-3078 **Fax:** 315-369-3736
Contact: Norene Lincoln, Training and Safety
　　　Coordinator
　　　Northeastern Loggers' Association, Inc.
　　　PO Box 69
　　　Old Forge, NY 13420

▼ **UNITED PAPERWORKERS INTERNATIONAL UNION**

United Paperworkers International Union Scholarship Awards Program • 196

For high school seniors who are dependents of an active United Paperworkers International Union member in good standing. Must take a course in labor studies. Must submit two letters of reference from two teachers. For use at four-year colleges or universities.
Award: Scholarship for use in freshman year; not renewable. *Number:* 22. *Amount:* $1000.
Eligibility Requirements: Applicant must be high school student; enrolled at a four-year institution and member of United Paperworkers International Union.
Application Requirements: Application, autobiography, financial need analysis, references, test scores, transcript. **Deadline:** March 15.
Phone: 615-834-8590 **Fax:** 615-781-0428
Contact: Debi Taylor, Executive Secretary
　　　United Paperworkers International Union
　　　PO Box 1475
　　　Nashville, TN 37202-1475

CORPORATE AFFILIATION

▼ **CLARA ABBOTT FOUNDATION**

Educational Grant Program • 197

One-time award for employees of Abbott Laboratories and their children. Must be under age 30. Submit copy of Forms 1040 and W-2. Deadline: March 16.
Award: Grant for use in freshman, sophomore, junior, or senior year; not renewable. *Amount:* $500–$13,000.
Eligibility Requirements: Applicant must be age 29 or under and affiliated with Abbott Laboratories.

Application Requirements: Application, financial need analysis, transcript. **Deadline:** March 16.
Phone: 847-937-3294 **Fax:** 847-938-6511
Contact: Jeriann Dosemagen, Educational Grant
　　　Analyst
　　　Clara Abbott Foundation
　　　200 Abbott Park Road, D579, J37
　　　Abbott Park, IL 60064

EMPLOYMENT EXPERIENCE

▼ **AMERICAN LEGION AUXILIARY NATIONAL HEADQUARTERS**

American Legion Auxiliary Girl Scout Achievement Award see number 181

▼ **DELTA PHI EPSILON EDUCATIONAL FOUNDATION**

Delta Phi Epsilon Educational Foundation Scholarships see number 188

▼ **HARNESS TRACKS OF AMERICA**

Harness Tracks of America Scholarship • 198

One-time, merit-based award for students actively involved in harness racing or the children of licensed drivers, trainers, breeders, or caretakers, living or deceased. Applicant must be actively involved in harness racing.
Award: Scholarship for use in any year; not renewable. *Number:* 5. *Amount:* $4000.
Eligibility Requirements: Applicant must have employment experience in harness racing.
Application Requirements: Application, essay, financial need analysis, transcript. **Deadline:** June 15.
Phone: 520-529-2525 **Fax:** 520-529-3235
Contact: Mary Griffin, Director of Administrative
　　　Affairs
　　　Harness Tracks of America
　　　4640 East Sunrise Avenue, Suite 200
　　　Tucson, AZ 85718

▼ INTERNATIONAL ASSOCIATION OF BRIDGE, STRUCTURAL, ORNAMENTAL, AND REINFORCING IRON WORKERS

John H. Lyons Sr. Scholarship Program • 199

For sons and daughters of current or deceased members of International Association of Ironworkers. Award based on extracurricular activities, community involvement, academic achievement, and essay. One award given to a man and one to a woman. Must be high school senior to apply.

Award: Scholarship for use in freshman, sophomore, junior, or senior year; renewable. *Number:* 2. *Amount:* $2500.

Eligibility Requirements: Applicant must be high school student; enrolled at a four-year institution and have employment experience in community service.

Application Requirements: Application, essay, references, test scores, transcript. **Deadline:** March 31.

Phone: 800-368-0105 **Fax:** 202-638-4856

Contact: LeRoy E. Worley, Trustee
International Association of Bridge,
Structural, Ornamental, and Reinforcing
Iron Workers
1750 New York Avenue, NW, Suite 400
Washington, DC 20006

IMPAIRMENT

▼ ALEXANDER GRAHAM BELL ASSOCIATION FOR THE DEAF

Alexander Graham Bell Scholarship Award • 200

Several scholarships for applicants who were born with profound or severe hearing loss (of at least 60dB) or have experienced such a loss before acquiring language. Must use speech or speechreading to communicate. Must be attending or have been admitted to a college or university that primarily enrolls students with normal hearing. Application requests must be made between May 1 and December 1. May renew once.

Award: Scholarship for use in any year; not renewable. *Amount:* $250–$1000.

Eligibility Requirements: Applicant must have an interest in leadership. Applicant must be hearing impaired.

Application Requirements: Application, essay, financial need analysis, references, transcript. **Deadline:** March 15.

World Wide Web: http://www.agbell.org

Contact: Dr. Veronica Boutte, Financial Aid
Coordinator
Alexander Graham Bell Association for the
Deaf
3417 Volta Place, NW
Washington, DC 20007-2778

▼ NATIONAL AMPUTATION FOUNDATION, INC.

National Amputation Foundation Scholarships • 201

Renewable award for students who have a major limb amputation. Must attend a U.S. college. Submit letter from doctor confirming amputation. Send self-addressed stamped envelope for application.

Award: Scholarship for use in freshman, sophomore, junior, or senior year; renewable. *Number:* 20. *Amount:* up to $125.

Eligibility Requirements: Applicant must be physically disabled.

Application Requirements: Application, self-addressed stamped envelope. **Deadline:** Continuous.

Phone: 516-887-3600 **Fax:** 516-887-3667

Contact: Sol Kaminsky, Scholarship Director
National Amputation Foundation, Inc.
38-40 Church Street
Malverne, NY 11565

▼ OPTIMIST INTERNATIONAL FOUNDATION

Optimist International Communication Contest for the Deaf and Hard of Hearing • 202

Winners at club level compete in oratorical contest at district level for 53 to 106 scholarships of $1500 each. Must be deaf or hard of hearing and compete by signing, orally, or a combination of both. Must be 19 or younger as of December 31 of senior year of high school. Open to residents of the U.S., Canada, and Jamaica. Contact for application deadline.

Award: Scholarship for use in any year; not renewable. *Number:* 53–106. *Amount:* $1500.

Eligibility Requirements: Applicant must be age 19 or under. Applicant must be hearing impaired.

Application Requirements: Application, applicant must enter a contest.

Contact: Optimist Club in your town
Optimist International Foundation
4494 Lindell Boulevard
St. Louis, MO 63108

▼ SISTER KENNY INSTITUTE

International Art Show for Disabled Artists   • 203

One-time award for artwork submitted by artists with visual, hearing, physical, or learning impairment. Contact Sister Kenny Institute for show information.
Award: Prize for use in any year; not renewable. *Number:* 40–60. *Amount:* $25–$500.
Eligibility Requirements: Applicant must have an interest in art. Applicant must be hearing impaired, learning disabled, physically disabled, or visually impaired.
Application Requirements: Application. **Deadline:** March 15.
Phone: 612-863-4446 **Fax:** 612-863-3299
Contact: Kathy Schultz, Art Show Coordinator
Sister Kenny Institute
800 East 28th Street
Minneapolis, MN 55407-3799

MILITARY SERVICE: GENERAL

▼ DEPARTMENT OF VETERANS AFFAIRS (VA)

Survivors and Dependents Educational Assistance (Chapter 35)-VA   • 204

Monthly $404 benefits for up to 45 months. Must be spouses or children under 26 of current veterans missing in action or of deceased or totally and permanently disabled (service-related) service persons. Contact regional Veterans Affairs office for more information.
Award: Scholarship for use in any year; renewable.
Eligibility Requirements: Applicant must be age 26 or under.
Military Service: General.
Application Requirements: Application. **Deadline:** Continuous.
E-mail: co22@vba.va.gov
World Wide Web: http://www.va.gov/education
Contact: Celia P. Dollarhide, Director, Education
Service
Department of Veterans Affairs (VA)
810 Vermont Avenue, NW
Washington, DC 20420

Veterans Educational Assistance Program (VEAP)   • 205

Benefits for 36 months to students not covered by GI Bill who initially served on active duty between January 1977 and July 1985. Must have contributed to program fund. Entitlement varies, average $225/month. For use within ten years of discharge. Restricted to those already enrolled in program.
Award: Scholarship for use in any year; renewable.
Eligibility Requirements: Military Service: General.
Application Requirements: Application. **Deadline:** Continuous.
E-mail: co22@vba.va.gov
World Wide Web: http://www.va.gov/education
Contact: Celia P. Dollarhide, Director, Education
Service
Department of Veterans Affairs (VA)
810 Vermont Avenue, NW
Washington, DC 20420

▼ VETERANS BENEFIT ADMINISTRATION

Veterans Benefits Grants-General   • 206

Many renewable awards are available to veterans and their dependents for education, vocational rehabilitation, and work training. Contact your local Veteran's Affairs office for details or call 800-827-1000.
Award: Scholarship for use in any year; renewable.
Eligibility Requirements: Military Service: General.
Application Requirements: Application. **Deadline:** Continuous.
E-mail: vaedusve@patriot.net
Phone: 800-827-1000
World Wide Web: http://www.va.gov/education
Contact: Celia P. Dollarhide, Director, Education
Service
Veterans Benefit Administration
810 Vermont Avenue, NW
Washington, DC 20420

NATIONAL OR ETHNIC BACKGROUND

▼ AMERICAN HELLENIC EDUCATIONAL PROGRESSIVE ASSOCIATION

American Hellenic Educational Progressive Association Educational Scholarships • 207

One-time award for any student who is of Hellenic descent or a member of the American Hellenic Educational Progressive association. Submit transcript, autobiography, test scores, references, and photo with application. Must be at least a high school senior to apply.

Award: Scholarship for use in freshman year; not renewable. *Number:* 30–50. *Amount:* $500–$1000.

Eligibility Requirements: Applicant must be Greek and high school student.

Application Requirements: Application, autobiography, essay, photo, references, test scores, transcript. **Deadline:** June 1.

Phone: 202-232-6300 **Fax:** 202-232-2140

World Wide Web: http://www.ahepa.org

Contact: American Hellenic Educational Progressive Association
1909 Q Street, NW, Suite 500
Washington, DC 20009

▼ ASSOCIATION OF UNIVERSITIES AND COLLEGES OF CANADA

Russian Federation Presidential Scholarships • 208

One-time award to allow Russian graduate and undergraduate university students to study in Canada for one year. Must be a citizen of Russia. Submit application to Ministry of General and Professional Education in Moscow.

Award: Scholarship for use in any year; not renewable. *Number:* up to 10.

Eligibility Requirements: Applicant must be Russian.

Application Requirements: Application, autobiography, references, test scores, transcript. **Deadline:** Continuous.

World Wide Web: http://www.aucc.ca

Contact: Alison Craig, Program Officer
Association of Universities and Colleges of Canada
350 Albert Street, Suite 600
Ottawa, ON K1R 1B1
Canada

▼ CYPRUS CHILDREN'S FUND SCHOLARSHIP ENDOWMENT

Cyprus Children's Fund Scholarship Endowment • 209

Award for students of Greek origin. Minimum 3.0 GPA required. One to two awards of $1000 for one college semester. Deadline: May 5.

Award: Scholarship for use in any year; not renewable. *Number:* 1–2. *Amount:* $1000.

Eligibility Requirements: Applicant must be Greek.

Application Requirements: Application, autobiography, financial need analysis, photo, portfolio, references, transcript. **Deadline:** May 5.

Phone: 212-696-4590 **Fax:** 212-532-9640

Contact: Kyriaki Christodoulou, Executive Director
Cyprus Children's Fund Scholarship Endowment
13 East 40th Street
New York, NY 10016

▼ FLORIDA DEPARTMENT OF EDUCATION

Nicaraguan and Haitian Scholarship Program • 210

One-time award for one Nicaraguan and one Haitian student to attend a Florida state university system school. Must live in Florida and be a U.S. citizen or permanent resident. Permanent residents qualify provided they are either citizens of Nicaragua or Haiti. Minimum 3.0 GPA. Must demonstrate service to the community. May reapply. Deadline: July 1.

Award: Scholarship for use in any year; not renewable. *Number:* 2. *Amount:* $4000–$5000.

Eligibility Requirements: Applicant must be Haitian or Nicaraguan; enrolled at a four-year institution; resident of Florida and studying in Florida.

Application Requirements: Application, financial need analysis. **Deadline:** July 1.

Contact: Joseph Simma
Florida Department of Education
1344 Florida Education Center
Tallahassee, FL 32399

▼ MAKARIOS SCHOLARSHIP FUND INC.

Cyprus Children's Fund Scholarship Endowment • 211

Ten one-time awards of $1000 for college undergraduate or graduate students aged 18 to 30 pursuing any field of study. Must be of Greek origin. Must submit application and other materials by May 5.
Award: Scholarship for use in freshman, sophomore, junior, senior, or graduate years; not renewable. *Number:* 10. *Amount:* $1000.
Eligibility Requirements: Applicant must be Greek and ages 18-30.
Application Requirements: Application, autobiography, photo, references, test scores, transcript. **Deadline:** May 5.
Phone: 212-696-4590 **Fax:** 212-447-1988
Contact: Kyriaki Christodoulou, Executive Director
Makarios Scholarship Fund Inc.
13 East 40th Street
New York, NY 10016

Makarios Scholarship Fund Inc. Scholarships • 212

Ten one-time awards of $1000 for college undergraduate or graduate student aged 18 to 30 pursuing any field of study. Must be of Cypriot heritage and maintain residence on the island of Cyprus. Must submit application and other materials by May 5.
Award: Scholarship for use in freshman, sophomore, junior, senior, or graduate years; not renewable. *Number:* 10. *Amount:* $1000.
Eligibility Requirements: Applicant must be Cypriot and ages 18-30.
Application Requirements: Application, autobiography, financial need analysis, photo, references, test scores, transcript. **Deadline:** May 5.
Phone: 212-696-4590 **Fax:** 212-447-1988
Contact: Kyriaki Christodoulou, Executive Director
Makarios Scholarship Fund Inc.
13 East 40th Street
New York, NY 10016

▼ SIKH EDUCATION AID FUND

Sikh Education Aid Fund • 213

Interest-free loan/scholarship to enable deserving Sikh students to complete postsecondary education. Must have Sikh religious affiliation and heritage. Submit application, test scores, financial need analysis, and photo.
Award: Scholarship, loan for use in any year; renewable. *Number:* 18–25. *Amount:* $400–$2500.
Eligibility Requirements: Applicant must be Other Specific Denomination; Asian and enrolled at a four-year institution.
Application Requirements: Application, financial need analysis, photo, test scores. **Deadline:** June 20.
Phone: 804-541-9279 **Fax:** 804-452-1270
Contact: Dr. Garpal S. Bhuller, Director
Sikh Education Aid Fund
PO Box 140
Hopewell, VA 23860

▼ ST. ANDREW'S SOCIETY OF WASHINGTON, DC

Donald Malcolm MacArthur Scholarship • 214

One-time award for college juniors, seniors, or graduate students of Scottish descent to pursue studies in the U.S. or Scotland. Available to residents of specified states in the U.S. and the U.K. Send self-addressed stamped envelope for application.
Award: Scholarship for use in junior, senior, or graduate years; not renewable. *Number:* 1. *Amount:* $2500.
Eligibility Requirements: Applicant must be Scottish; enrolled at a four-year institution and resident of Delaware, District of Columbia, Maryland, New Jersey, North Carolina, Pennsylvania, Virginia, or West Virginia.
Application Requirements: Application, essay, financial need analysis, references, self-addressed stamped envelope.
Deadline: March 15.
E-mail: mcleodjim@aol.com
Phone: 301-229-6140 **Fax:** 301-656-5130
Contact: James S. McLeod, Chairman
St. Andrew's Society of Washington, DC
7012 Arandale Road
Bethesda, MD 20817-4702

James and Mary Dawson Scholarship • 215

One-time award for college juniors, seniors, and graduate students who are Scottish natives and citizens of the U.K. to study in the U.S. Submit essay, references, and financial aid form with application. Send self-addressed, stamped envelope for application.
Award: Scholarship for use in junior, senior, or graduate years; not renewable. *Number:* 1–3. *Amount:* $1000–$5000.
Eligibility Requirements: Applicant must be Scottish and enrolled at a four-year institution.

James and Mary Dawson Scholarship (continued)

Application Requirements: Application, essay, financial need analysis, references, self-addressed stamped envelope. **Deadline:** March 15.
E-mail: mcleodjim@aol.com
Phone: 301-229-6140 **Fax:** 301-656-5130
Contact: James S. McLeod, Chairman
St. Andrew's Society of Washington, DC
7012 Arandale Road
Bethesda, MD 20817-4702

▼ STUDENTENWERK HAMBURG AMT FUR AUSBILDUNGSFOERDERUNG

Bafoeg for Study Abroad • 216

One-time award for students at German institution who have permanent residency in Germany to travel to the U.S. to conduct research at U.S. institution. Courses must be eligible for credit at German institution.
Award: Scholarship for use in junior, senior, or graduate years; not renewable.
Eligibility Requirements: Applicant must be German.
Application Requirements: Application, test scores, transcript.
Deadline: Continuous.
Contact: Studentenwerk Hamburg Amt fur
Ausbildungsfoerderung
Von-Melle-Park 2
20146 Hamburg
Germany

▼ SWISS BENEVOLENT SOCIETY OF NEW YORK

Medicus Student Exchange • 217

One-time award to students of Swiss nationality or parentage. U.S. residents study in Switzerland and Swiss residents study in the U.S. Awards to undergraduates are based on merit and need; those to graduates based only on merit. Open to U.S. residents of New York, New Jersey, Connecticut, Pennsylvania, and Delaware. Must be proficient in a foreign language.
Award: Scholarship for use in junior, senior, or graduate years; not renewable. *Number:* 1–5. *Amount:* $2000–$10,000.
Eligibility Requirements: Applicant must be Swiss; enrolled at a four-year institution; resident of Connecticut, Delaware, New Jersey, New York, or Pennsylvania and must have an interest in foreign language.

Application Requirements: Application, financial need analysis, references, test scores, transcript. **Deadline:** January 31.
Contact: Ann Marie Gilman, Scholarship Director
Swiss Benevolent Society of New York
608 Fifth Avenue, #309
New York, NY 10020

▼ TEXAS HIGHER EDUCATION COORDINATING BOARD

Students from Other Nations of the American Hemisphere-Texas • 218

Renewable aid for students residing in Texas who are citizens of another country of the Americas. Must attend public college in Texas. Student will be exempt from tuition.
Award: Scholarship for use in any year; not renewable.
Eligibility Requirements: Applicant must be Canadian or Latin American/Caribbean; enrolled at a two-year or four-year institution and studying in Texas.
Application Requirements: Application, test scores, transcript.
Deadline: Continuous.
Phone: 512-427-6331 **Fax:** 512-427-6420
Contact: Gustavo DeLeon, Asst. Director of Grants
Texas Higher Education Coordinating
Board
PO Box 12788
Austin, TX 78711-2788

▼ WELSH SOCIETY OF PHILADELPHIA

Cymdeithas Gymreig/Philadelphia Scholarship • 219

Awards for undergraduate students of Welsh descent. Must live or attend college within 150 miles of Philadelphia. Proof of Welsh heritage required. Merit and participation in Welsh organizations or events are required.
Award: Scholarship for use in freshman, sophomore, junior, or senior year; not renewable. *Number:* 4. *Amount:* $1000.
Eligibility Requirements: Applicant must be Welsh; enrolled at a two-year or four-year institution; resident of Delaware, Maryland, New Jersey, or Pennsylvania and studying in Delaware, Maryland, New Jersey, Pennsylvania, or Virginia.
Application Requirements: Application, autobiography, essay, references, self-addressed stamped envelope, test scores, transcript. **Deadline:** March 1.
Phone: 717-822-4871

Contact: Daniel E. Williams, Ysgrifennydd
Welsh Society of Philadelphia
Hen Dy Haplis, 367 South River Street
Wilkes-Barre, PA 18702

RELIGIOUS AFFILIATION

▼ SIKH EDUCATION AID FUND

Sikh Education Aid Fund   *see number 213*

STATE OF RESIDENCE

▼ ALABAMA COMMISSION ON HIGHER EDUCATION

Alabama Prepaid Tuition Program • 220

Renewable award to guarantee four years of fully paid undergraduate tuition at an Alabama institution.
Award: Scholarship for use in freshman, sophomore, junior, or senior year; renewable.
Eligibility Requirements: Applicant must be studying in Alabama.
Application Requirements: Application. **Deadline:** Continuous.
Phone: 334-242-7515
Contact: Ms. Brenda Emfinger, Director of ALAPACT
Alabama Commission on Higher Education
PO Box 302000
Montgomery, AL 36130

▼ CENTER FOR THE EDUCATION OF WOMEN

Center for the Education of Women Scholarship for Returning Women • 221

One-time award for women who have interrupted their education for at least four consecutive years. Must enroll in a program at any campus at the University of Michigan. Applications available at CEW every first working day of October. Up to thirty-five scholarships of $1000-$10,000.
Award: Scholarship for use in any year; not renewable.
Number: up to 35. *Amount:* $1000-$10,000.
Eligibility Requirements: Applicant must be female and studying in Michigan.
Application Requirements: Application, essay, financial need analysis, references, transcript. **Deadline:** January 15.

Phone: 734-998-7210 **Fax:** 734-998-6203
World Wide Web: http://www.umich.edu/~cew
Contact: Lisa Tulin-Silver and Doreen Murasky,
Senior Counselor/Program Specialist
Center for the Education of Women
330 East Liberty Street
Ann Arbor, MI 48104-2289

▼ DEVRY INC.

DeVry President's Scholarships • 222

Full-tuition award based on SAT/ACT scores, scholastic achievement, extracurricular activities, essay. Renewable if GPA is maintained. Application fee: $25.
Award: Scholarship for use in any year; renewable.
Number: 26. *Amount:* $18,300-$32,860.
Eligibility Requirements: Applicant must be high school student and studying in Arizona, California, Georgia, Illinois, Missouri, New Jersey, New York, Ohio, or Texas.
Application Requirements: Application, essay, interview, references, test scores, transcript. **Fee:** $25. **Deadline:** March 1.
Phone: 630-571-7700 **Fax:** 630-571-0317
Contact: Scholarship Coordinator
DeVry Inc.
One Tower Lane
Oak Brook Terrace, IL 60181

▼ ENDOWMENT FUND OF THE ALLIED JEWISH FEDERATION OF COLORADO

Charles and Louise Rosenbaum Scholarship Loan Fund • 223

One-time, interest-free loan for Colorado high school seniors planning to enter their freshmen year of college. Submit application and financial aid form. Write for more information. Deadline is March 31.
Award: Scholarship, loan for use in freshman year; not renewable. *Amount:* $500-$2000.
Eligibility Requirements: Applicant must be high school student and resident of Colorado.
Application Requirements: Application, financial need analysis. **Deadline:** March 31.
Phone: 303-321-3399 **Fax:** 303-321-8328
Contact: Evelyn Binsky, Endowment Associate
Endowment Fund of the Allied Jewish
Federation of Colorado
300 South Dahlia Street
Denver, CO 80246

▼ FLORIDA DEPARTMENT OF EDUCATION

Nicaraguan and Haitian Scholarship Program   *see number 210*

▼ ILLINOIS STUDENT ASSISTANCE COMMISSION (ISAC)

Higher Education License Plate Program— HELP • 224

Need-based grants for students at institutions participating in program, whose funds are raised by sale of special license plates commemorating the institutions. Deadline: June 30.
Award: Grant for use in freshman, sophomore, junior, or senior year; not renewable. *Amount:* up to $2000.
Eligibility Requirements: Applicant must be resident of Illinois and studying in Illinois.
Application Requirements: Financial need analysis. **Deadline:** June 30.
Phone: 847-948-8500 Ext. 2305
Contact: Barb Levin, Client Information
Illinois Student Assistance Commission (ISAC)
1755 Lake Cook Road
Deerfield, IL 60015-5209

Illinois Incentive for Access Program • 225

Award for eligible first-time freshmen enrolling in approved Illinois institution. One-time grant of up to $500 may be used for any educational expense. Deadline: October 1.
Award: Grant for use in freshman year; not renewable. *Number:* 18,000–20,000. *Amount:* up to $500.
Eligibility Requirements: Applicant must be resident of Illinois and studying in Illinois.
Application Requirements: Financial need analysis. **Deadline:** October 1.
Phone: 847-948-8500 Ext. 2305
Contact: Barb Levin, Client Information
Illinois Student Assistance Commission (ISAC)
1755 Lake Cook Road
Deerfield, IL 60015-5209

▼ MONTANA GUARANTEED STUDENT LOAN PROGRAM

Montana Guaranteed Student Loan Program Montana High School Honor Scholarship • 226

Award for graduating high school seniors desiring to attend unit of Montana unversity system. Must rank within top one-fourth of graduating class. Non-renewable waiver of cost of registration and incidental (tuition) fees for two semesters. Contact for deadline and further information.
Award: Scholarship for use in freshman year; not renewable.
Eligibility Requirements: Applicant must be high school student and studying in Montana.
Application Requirements: Application, transcript.
Phone: 406-444-0078 **Fax:** 406-444-1469
World Wide Web: http://www.mgslp.state.mt.us
Contact: Mary Taylor
Montana Guaranteed Student Loan Program
2500 Broadway, PO Box 203101
Helena, MT 59620-3101

▼ ST. ANDREW'S SOCIETY OF WASHINGTON, DC

Donald Malcolm MacArthur Scholarship   *see number 214*

▼ STATE COLLEGE AND UNIVERSITY SYSTEMS OF WEST VIRGINIA, CENTRAL OFFICE

Tuition and Fee Waiver Program-West Virginia • 227

Award for students attending West Virginia public colleges or universities. Based on financial need and academic merit. Deadlines vary. Must contact specific institution for information and application. Renewable.
Award: Scholarship for use in any year; renewable.
Eligibility Requirements: Applicant must be enrolled at a two-year or four-year institution and studying in West Virginia.
Application Requirements: Application, financial need analysis, test scores, transcript.
E-mail: jenkins@scusco.wvnet.edu
Phone: 304-558-4618 **Fax:** 304-558-4622
World Wide Web: http://www.scusco.wvnet.edu

Contact: Tammy Jenkins, Scholarship Coordinator
State College and University Systems of West
Virginia, Central Office
1018 Kanawha Boulevard East, Suite 700
Charleston, WV 25301

▼ SWISS BENEVOLENT SOCIETY OF NEW YORK

Medicus Student Exchange   see number 217

▼ TEXAS HIGHER EDUCATION COORDINATING BOARD

Students from Other Nations of the American Hemisphere-Texas   see number 218

Texas Public Educational Grant   • 228

Renewable aid for students currently enrolled in a public college or university in Texas. Based on need. Amount of award is determined by the financial aid office of each school. Texas residence not necessary. Deadlines vary.
Award: Scholarship for use in any year; not renewable.
Eligibility Requirements: Applicant must be studying in Texas.
Application Requirements: Application, financial need analysis.
Contact: Texas Higher Education Coordinating Board
PO Box 12788
Austin, TX 78711-2788

▼ UTAH STATE BOARD OF REGENTS

Utah Tuition Waiver   • 229

Renewable awards ranging from partial to full tuition waivers at eligible Utah institutions. A limited number of waivers are available for nonresidents. Deadlines vary by institution.
Award: Scholarship for use in any year; renewable.
Eligibility Requirements: Applicant must be enrolled at a two-year or four-year institution and studying in Utah.
Application Requirements: Application, financial need analysis, interview.
Contact: FA office of participating Utah school or
Associate Commissioner for SFA
Utah State Board of Regents
3 Triad, Suite 550
355 West North Temple
Salt Lake City, UT 84180-1205

▼ VERMONT STUDENT ASSISTANCE CORPORATION

Vermont Incentive Grants   • 230

Renewable grants for Vermont residents based on financial need. Must meet needs test. Must be college undergraduate or graduate student enrolled full-time at an approved postsecondary institution. Only available to U.S. citizens or permanent residents.
Award: Grant for use in freshman, sophomore, junior, senior, or graduate years; renewable. *Amount:* $500–$5200.
Eligibility Requirements: Applicant must be resident of Vermont.
Application Requirements: Application, financial need analysis. **Deadline:** March 1.
Phone: 802-655-9602 **Fax:** 802-654-3765
World Wide Web: http://www.vsac.org
Contact: Grant Program
Vermont Student Assistance Corporation
PO Box 2000
Winooski, VT 05404-2000

▼ WELSH SOCIETY OF PHILADELPHIA

Cymdeithas Gymreig/Philadelphia Scholarship   see number 219

TALENT

▼ ALEXANDER GRAHAM BELL ASSOCIATION FOR THE DEAF

Alexander Graham Bell Scholarship Award   see number 200

▼ AMERICAN BOWLING CONGRESS

Chuck Hall Star of Tomorrow Scholarship • 231

Award available to male, amateur bowlers 21 and under. Must be high school senior or undergraduate student. Merit taken into account as well. Application deadline is January 15.
Award: Scholarship for use in any year; not renewable. *Number:* 1. *Amount:* $4000.
Eligibility Requirements: Applicant must be age 21 or under; male and must have an interest in bowling.

Chuck Hall Star of Tomorrow Scholarship (continued)

Application Requirements: Application, essay, references, self-addressed stamped envelope, transcript. **Deadline:** January 15.
E-mail: yabascholarships@juno.com
Contact: Ed Gocha, Scholarship Administrator
American Bowling Congress
5301 South 76th Street
Greendale, WI 53129-1192

▼ AMERICAN GUILD OF ORGANISTS

American Guild of Organists Regional Competitions for Young Organists • 232

Organ performance competition open to organists under the age of 23. Must submit proof of age, $25 registration fee, biography, and photo. Several one-time awards for different levels of competition. Deadlines: October 15 for Chapter competition; January 31 for Regional competition.
Award: Prize for use in any year; not renewable.
Eligibility Requirements: Applicant must be age 22 or under and must have an interest in music/singing.
Application Requirements: Application, applicant must enter a contest, autobiography, photo. **Fee:** $25. **Deadline:** January 31.
E-mail: info@agogq.org
Phone: 212-870-2310 **Fax:** 212-870-2163
World Wide Web: http://www.agohq.org
Contact: James E. Thomashower, Executive Director
American Guild of Organists
475 Riverside Drive, Suite 1260
New York, NY 10115

▼ AMERICAN INSTITUTE FOR FOREIGN STUDY

American Institute for Foreign Study International Scholarships • 233

One-time award for college undergraduates to participate in study abroad programs. Must demonstrate leadership potential and have minimum 3.0 cumulative GPA. Fifty $1000 scholarships for a semester, ten $500 scholarships for summer studies. Must meet AIFS program requirements. Submit essay and application by March 15 for summer semester, April 15 for fall semester, and October 15 for spring semester. Application fee: $50.
Award: Scholarship for use in freshman, sophomore, junior, or senior year; not renewable. *Amount:* $500–$1000.

Eligibility Requirements: Applicant must have an interest in leadership.
Application Requirements: Application, essay, photo, references, transcript. **Fee:** $50.
E-mail: ygarcia@aifs.com
Phone: 800-727-2437 Ext. 6084
World Wide Web: http://www.aifs.org
Contact: Yesenia Garcia, Admissions Consultant
American Institute for Foreign Study
102 Greenwich Avenue
Greenwich, CT 06830

▼ AMERICAN-SCANDINAVIAN FOUNDATION

American-Scandinavian Foundation Translation Prize • 234

Two prizes available to bring into English translation a work of Scandinavian literature written in the last 200 years. One-time awards of $2000 and $500.
Award: Prize for use in any year; not renewable. *Number:* 2. *Amount:* $500–$2000.
Eligibility Requirements: Applicant must have an interest in Scandinavian language.
Application Requirements: Application, applicant must enter a contest. **Deadline:** Continuous.
E-mail: emckey@amscan.org
Phone: 212-879-9779 **Fax:** 212-249-3444
World Wide Web: http://www.amscan.org
Contact: Ellen McKey, Director of Fellowships and Grants
American-Scandinavian Foundation
725 Park Avenue
New York, NY 10021

▼ ASSOCIATION OF FORMER INTELLIGENCE OFFICERS (AFIO) SAN DIEGO CHAPTER

Lieutenant General Eugene F. Tighe, Jr., United States Air Force Memorial Scholarship • 235

One-time award based on judged quality of a 1000-1500-word essay written on a stipulated topic within the general area of intelligence and national security. Up to three scholarships of $1000. Must send No. 10 self-addressed, stamped envelope by December 1 to receive entry package.
Award: Scholarship for use in any year; not renewable. *Number:* 1–3. *Amount:* $1000.

Eligibility Requirements: Applicant must be enrolled at a two-year or four-year institution and must have an interest in writing.

Application Requirements: Application, applicant must enter a contest, self-addressed stamped envelope. **Deadline:** January 10.

Phone: 760-432-8844

Contact: J. T. Strong, Scholarship Administrator
Association of Former Intelligence Officers
(AFIO) San Diego Chapter
1142 Miramonte Glen
Escondido, CA 92026

▼ ASSOCIATION OF UNIVERSITIES AND COLLEGES OF CANADA

Programme Canadian de Bourses de la Francophone • 236

Renewable award for non-Canadian students from developing countries in the Francophonie. Open to students of all disciplines likely to contribute to the students' country. Must be fluent in French.

Award: Scholarship for use in freshman, sophomore, junior, senior, or graduate years; renewable.

Eligibility Requirements: Applicant must be enrolled at a four-year institution and must have an interest in French language.

Application Requirements: Application, essay, references, transcript. **Deadline:** December 15.

World Wide Web: http://www.aucc.ca

Contact: Jeanne Gallagher
Association of Universities and Colleges of Canada
350 Albert Street, Suite 600
Ottawa, ON K1R 1B1
Canada

▼ BMI FOUNDATION, INCORPORATED

BMI Student Composer Awards • 237

One-time award for composition contest for young student composers who are under age 26 and citizens of the western hemisphere. Must submit original musical score by February 7. Write for further information.

Award: Prize for use in any year; not renewable. *Number:* 5–10. *Amount:* $500–$3000.

Eligibility Requirements: Applicant must be age 26 or under and must have an interest in music/singing.

Application Requirements: Application, applicant must enter a contest. **Deadline:** February 7.

E-mail: tzavin@bmi.com

Phone: 212-830-2537 **Fax:** 212-246-2163

Contact: Ralph Jackson
BMI Foundation, Incorporated
320 West 57th Street
New York, NY 10019

▼ CONTEMPORARY RECORD SOCIETY

Contemporary Record Society National Festival for the Performing Arts • 238

Renewable award for composers/performing artists who demonstrate a high level of artistic skill. Must submit copy of work that has not been previously recorded in the U.S. $50 application fee required. Submit self-addressed stamped envelope if outside the U.S.

Award: Scholarship for use in any year; renewable. *Number:* 1. *Amount:* $1900–$5500.

Eligibility Requirements: Applicant must have an interest in music/singing.

Application Requirements: Applicant must enter a contest, references, self-addressed stamped envelope. **Fee:** $50.

Deadline: Continuous.

E-mail: crsnews@erols.com

World Wide Web: http://www.erols.com/crsnews

Contact: Ms. C. Hunt, Administrative Assistant
Contemporary Record Society
724 Winchester Road
Broomall, PA 19008

National Competition for Composers Recording • 239

Work must be nonpublished and not commercially recorded. First prize is CD recording grant. Limit of nine performers and twenty-five minutes. One work may be submitted. Send self-addressed stamped envelope with $3.00 postage if applicant wants work returned. Application fee is $50.

Award: Prize for use in any year; not renewable. *Number:* 1. *Amount:* $1500–$5000.

Eligibility Requirements: Applicant must have an interest in music/singing.

Application Requirements: Application, applicant must enter a contest, autobiography, references, self-addressed stamped envelope. **Fee:** $50. **Deadline:** July 19.

E-mail: crsnews@erols.com

World Wide Web: http://www.erols.com/crsnews

National Competition for Composers Recording (continued)

Contact: Ms. C. Hunt, Administrative Assistant
Contemporary Record Society
724 Winchester Road
Broomall, PA 19008

▼ DELIUS ASSOCIATION OF FLORIDA, INC.

Delius Composition Contest • 240

One-time prize for the new composition of vocal, keyboard, and chamber music. Categories for high school and open division. Write for brochure explaining entry guidelines. Deadline of October 1. Entry fee of $20 for open division and $5 for high school.

Award: Prize for use in any year; not renewable. *Number:* 5–7. *Amount:* $100–$500.

Eligibility Requirements: Applicant must have an interest in music/singing.

Application Requirements: Application, applicant must enter a contest. **Deadline:** October 1.

Phone: 904-745-7370

Contact: Prof. William McNeiland
Delius Association of Florida, Inc.
College of Fine Arts
2800 University Boulevard North
Jacksonville, FL 32211

▼ FOREST ROBERTS THEATRE

Mildred and Albert Panowski Playwriting Award • 241

Prize designed to encourage and stimulate artistic growth among playwrights. Winner receives a cash prize and a world premiere of their play. Write for further information. One-time award.

Award: Prize for use in any year; not renewable.

Eligibility Requirements: Applicant must have an interest in writing.

Application Requirements: Application, applicant must enter a contest, self-addressed stamped envelope. **Deadline:** November 20.

Phone: 906-227-2559 **Fax:** 906-227-2567

Contact: Erica Milkovich, Playwriting Award
Coordinator
Forest Roberts Theatre
Northern Michigan University
1401 Presque Isle Avenue
Marquette, MI 49855-5364

▼ FORT COLLINS SYMPHONY ASSOCIATION

Adeline Rosenberg Memorial Prize • 242

Senior Division (25 years or under): Instrumental competitions held in 1999, 2001, etc.; piano competitions held in 1998, 2000, etc. Auditions required. Must submit proof of age. Application fee: $35.

Award: Prize for use in any year; not renewable. *Number:* 3. *Amount:* $1000–$3000.

Eligibility Requirements: Applicant must be age 25 or under and must have an interest in music/singing.

Application Requirements: Application, applicant must enter a contest, autobiography. **Fee:** $35. **Deadline:** January 20.

E-mail: leehill@fcsymphony.org

Phone: 970-482-4823 **Fax:** 970-482-4858

World Wide Web: http://www.fcsymphony.org

Contact: Lee Hill, Executive Director
Fort Collins Symphony Association
PO Box 1963
Fort Collins, CO 80522

▼ GAY, LESBIAN, AND BISEXUAL TASK FORCE OF THE AMERICAN LIBRARY ASSOCIATION

American Library Association Gay, Lesbian and Bisexual Book Award • 243

Nonrenewable award available to authors whose books were published December 1, 1997-November 30, 1998. Book must promote gay/lesbian/bisexual awareness. Books selected by nomination; write for details.

Award: Prize for use in any year; not renewable. *Number:* 2. *Amount:* $200.

Eligibility Requirements: Applicant must have an interest in writing.

Application Requirements: Applicant must enter a contest. **Deadline:** November 30.

Contact: Faye Chadwell, Chair
Gay, Lesbian, and Bisexual Task Force of the
American Library Association
50 East Huron Street
Chicago, IL 60611

▼ GIRLS INCORPORATED

Girls Incorporated Donna Brace Ogilvie-Zelda Gitlin Poetry Program Awards see number 189

▼ GLAMOUR MAGAZINE

Glamour's Top Ten College Competition • 244

Award for female college juniors who have mastered leadership skills, participated in and initiated volunteer and campus activities, excelled in academics, and extended themselves beyond typical college experience. Honors women with unique goals and the steps used in achieving those goals. Deadline: January 31.
Award: Prize for use in junior year; not renewable. *Number:* 10. *Amount:* $1000.
Eligibility Requirements: Applicant must be enrolled at a four-year institution; female and must have an interest in leadership.
Application Requirements: Application, applicant must enter a contest, essay, photo, references, transcript. **Deadline:** January 31.
E-mail: ttcw@glamour.com
Phone: 800-244-4526 **Fax:** 212-880-6922
Contact: Glamour Magazine
350 Madison Avenue
New York, NY 10017

▼ GUIDEPOSTS MAGAZINE

GUIDEPOSTS Young Writer's Contest • 245

Award for high school juniors and seniors. Must submit an original manuscript in first person on a true, moving, or memorable experience in which the narrator's faith in God played a part. Top eight win cash; top twenty-five win typewriters. Send self-addressed stamped envelope.
Award: Prize for use in freshman year; not renewable. *Number:* 8. *Amount:* $1000–$8000.
Eligibility Requirements: Applicant must be high school student and must have an interest in writing.
Application Requirements: Applicant must enter a contest, essay, self-addressed stamped envelope. **Deadline:** November 27.
Phone: 212-251-8100
Contact: James McDermott
GUIDEPOSTS Magazine
16 East 34th Street
New York, NY 10016

▼ LIGHT WORK

Light Work Artist-in-Residence Program • 246

The Light Work Artist-in-Residence Program was established to promote new work by emerging artists. Artists are invited to live and work in Syracuse at Light Work for one month. They receive a $1200 stipend. Students are ineligible to apply. Applications taken on rolling basis.
Award: Grant for use in any year; not renewable.
Number: 12–15. *Amount:* $1200.
Eligibility Requirements: Applicant must have an interest in art.
Application Requirements: Application, portfolio, self-addressed stamped envelope. **Deadline:** Continuous.
Phone: 315-443-1300 **Fax:** 315-443-9516
World Wide Web: http://sumweb.syr.edu/com_dark/lw.html
Contact: Jeffrey Hoone, Director
Light Work
316 Waverly Avenue
Syracuse, NY 13244

▼ MILKWEED EDITIONS

Milkweed National Fiction Prize • 247

One award to a writer of previously unpublished fiction. Content must follow guidelines set by Milkweed Editions; see guidelines for details. Applicant must submit manuscript. One-time award of $2000 against royalties. Send legal-sized self-addressed stamped envelope for guidelines.
Award: Prize for use in any year; not renewable. *Number:* 1. *Amount:* $2000.
Eligibility Requirements: Applicant must have an interest in writing.
Application Requirements: Self-addressed stamped envelope. **Deadline:** Continuous.
Phone: 612-332-3192 **Fax:** 612-332-6248
World Wide Web: http://www.milkweed.org
Contact: Milkweed Editions
430 First Avenue North, Suite 400
Minneapolis, MN 55401-1743

▼ NATIONAL ASSOCIATION FOR CAMPUS ACTIVITIES EDUCATIONAL FOUNDATION

National Association for Campus Activities Educational Foundation Scholarships for Student Leaders • 248

Award for full-time college undergraduate students holding significant leadership positions on their campus. Must have made contributions to their campus communities and have demonstrated leadership skills. Renewable award of $300.
Award: Scholarship for use in freshman, sophomore, junior, or senior year; renewable. *Number:* 16. *Amount:* $300.

National Association for Campus Activities Educational Foundation
Scholarships for Student Leaders (continued)

Eligibility Requirements: Applicant must have an interest in leadership.
Application Requirements: Application, essay, references, transcript. **Deadline:** November 1.
E-mail: dionneb@naca.org
Phone: 803-732-6222 **Fax:** 803-749-1047
Contact: Dionne Blakeney, Development Staff
　　Assistant
　　National Association for Campus Activities
　　Educational Foundation
　　13 Harbison Way
　　Columbia, SC 29212-3401

▼ NATIONAL LIBRARY OF POETRY

North American Open Poetry Contest • 249
Open to any poet submitting one original poem of no more than twenty lines. Poems may be of any style and on any subject. The poet's name and address should appear at the top of the page. 500 one-time awards of $50-$1000.
Award: Prize for use in any year; not renewable. *Number:* 500. *Amount:* $50–$1000.
Eligibility Requirements: Applicant must have an interest in writing.
Application Requirements: Applicant must enter a contest.
Deadline: Continuous.
Contact: Darlene Mullen
　　National Library of Poetry
　　One Poetry Plaza
　　PO Box 704-1941
　　Owings Mills, MD 21117

▼ NATIONAL SCULPTURE SOCIETY

National Sculpture Society Scholarship • 250
Scholarships available for students of figurative or representational sculpture. Scholarships are paid directly to the academic institution through which the student applies. Applicant must submit 8-10 photographs of at least three different works.
Award: Scholarship for use in any year; not renewable. *Number:* 1–6. *Amount:* $1000.
Eligibility Requirements: Applicant must have an interest in art.
Application Requirements: Application, financial need analysis, references, self-addressed stamped envelope, transcript. **Deadline:** May 31.
Phone: 212-764-5645 **Fax:** 212-764-5651

Contact: Gwen Pier, Executive Director
　　National Sculpture Society
　　1177 Avenue of the Americas, 15th Floor
　　New York, NY 10036

▼ OMAHA SYMPHONY GUILD

Omaha Symphony Guild New Music Competition • 251
One-time award for those 25 and over for the best composition of symphony music. Prize also includes possible performance of winning composition by the Omaha Symphony Chamber Orchestra. Submit two copies of score with application. Application fee $25.
Award: Prize for use in any year; not renewable. *Number:* 1. *Amount:* up to $2500.
Eligibility Requirements: Applicant must be age 25 or over and must have an interest in music/singing.
Application Requirements: Application, applicant must enter a contest. **Fee:** $25. **Deadline:** May 15.
Phone: 402-342-3836 **Fax:** 402-342-3819
Contact: Omaha Symphony Guild
　　1605 Howard Street
　　Omaha, NE 68102

▼ OPTIMIST INTERNATIONAL FOUNDATION

Optimist International Oratorical Contest • 252
Winners at club level compete in oratorical contest at district level for 106 scholarships of $1500 each. Must be 16 or younger. Open to residents of the U.S., Canada, and Jamaica. Must present speech.
Award: Scholarship, prize for use in any year; not renewable. *Number:* 106. *Amount:* $1500.
Eligibility Requirements: Applicant must be age 16 or under; enrolled at a four-year or technical institution and must have an interest in public speaking.
Application Requirements: Application, applicant must enter a contest. **Deadline:** Continuous.
Contact: Optimist Club in your town
　　Optimist International Foundation
　　4494 Lindell Boulevard
　　St. Louis, MO 63108

▼ PACIFIC TELECOMMUNICATIONS COUNCIL

Pacific Telecommunications Council Essay Prize Competition • 253
One-time award of $2000 for original, unpublished essay on the communications need and concerns of the Pacific

region: Asia, Oceania, and the Americas. Winning entrants will be invited to present their papers at the Pacific Telecommunications Conference in Honolulu, Hawaii. **Award:** Prize for use in any year; not renewable. *Number:* 1–3. *Amount:* $2000.
Eligibility Requirements: Applicant must be enrolled at a four-year or technical institution and must have an interest in writing.
Application Requirements: Application, essay. **Deadline:** July 1.
E-mail: puja@ptc.org
Phone: 808-941-3789 **Fax:** 808-944-4874
World Wide Web: http://www.ptc.org
Contact: Puja Borries, Publications and Publicity
Coordinator
Pacific Telecommunications Council
2454 South Beretania Street, Suite 302
Honolulu, HI 96826-1596

▼ QUILL AND SCROLL FOUNDATION

Quill and Scroll National Writing/Photo Contest • 254
One-time contest for best essay and photographs in several categories. Only high school students may enter. Prize for sweepstakes winner in each category is an electric typewriter. Other winners receive gold key in addition to being eligible to apply for journalism scholarships. Contact Quill and Scroll for more details and application. Application fee: $2 per entry.
Award: Prize for use in any year; not renewable.
Eligibility Requirements: Applicant must be high school student and must have an interest in photography/photogrammetry/filmmaking or writing.
Application Requirements: Application, applicant must enter a contest, essay, photo. **Fee:** $2. **Deadline:** February 5.
E-mail: quill-scroll@uiowa.edu
Phone: 319-335-3321 **Fax:** 319-335-5210
World Wide Web: http://www.uiowa.edu/~quill-sc
Contact: Richard Johns, Executive Director
Quill and Scroll Foundation
University of Iowa
Iowa City, IA 52242

▼ SIGMA ALPHA IOTA PHILANTHROPIES, INC.

Inter-American Music Award Competition • 255
Prize for best composition for solo piano. Open to any composer over 18 (male or female, member or nonmember).

Winning composition is premiered at triennial national convention and published. Send manuscript. One-time award of $1000. Application fee: $25.
Award: Prize for use in any year; not renewable. *Number:* 1. *Amount:* $1000.
Eligibility Requirements: Applicant must be age 19 or over and must have an interest in music/singing.
Application Requirements: Application, applicant must enter a contest. **Fee:** $25. **Deadline:** April 30.
Phone: 704-251-0606 **Fax:** 704-251-0644
World Wide Web: http://sai-national.org
Contact: Ms. Ruth Sieber, Secretary
Sigma Alpha Iota Philanthropies, Inc.
7 Hickey Drive
Framingham, MA 01701-8812

▼ SISTER KENNY INSTITUTE

International Art Show for Disabled Artists see number 203

▼ SONS OF THE REPUBLIC OF TEXAS

Texas History Essay Contest • 256
Awarded to encourage the study of early Texans and the pioneer spirit. Must submit a 1500-2000-word essay on specified topic. Contest open only to high school seniors. One-time awards of $1000-$3000.
Award: Prize for use in freshman year; not renewable. *Number:* 3. *Amount:* $1000–$3000.
Eligibility Requirements: Applicant must be high school student and must have an interest in writing.
Application Requirements: Applicant must enter a contest, essay. **Deadline:** February 3.
E-mail: srttexas@tgn.net
Phone: 409-245-6644 **Fax:** 409-245-6644
Contact: Ms. Melinda Williams, Executive Secretary
Sons of the Republic of Texas
1717 8th Street
Bay City, TX 77414

▼ STANLEY DRAMA AWARD

Stanley Drama Award • 257
Award for an original, full-length play/musical or series of one-act plays that has not been professionally produced. Write for more information and specific application requirements. One-time award of $2000. Application fee: $20.
Award: Prize for use in any year; not renewable. *Number:* 1. *Amount:* $2000.

Stanley Drama Award (continued)

Eligibility Requirements: Applicant must have an interest in writing.
Application Requirements: Application, applicant must enter a contest. **Fee:** $20. **Deadline:** September 1.
Phone: 718-390-3325 **Fax:** 718-390-3323
Contact: Liz Terry, Director
Stanley Drama Award
Howard Avenue and Campus Road
Staten Island, NY 10301

▼ SWISS BENEVOLENT SOCIETY OF NEW YORK

Medicus Student Exchange   see number 217

▼ UNITED STATES NAVAL INSTITUTE

International Navies Essay Contest   • 258

Nonrenewable prize for the best 3000-word essay discussing strategic, geographic, and cultural influences on individual or regional navies, their commitments and capabilities, and relationships with other navies. Authors of all nationalities invited to enter.
Award: Prize for use in any year; not renewable. *Number:* 3. *Amount:* $500–$1000.
Eligibility Requirements: Applicant must have an interest in writing.
Application Requirements: Applicant must enter a contest.
Deadline: August 1.
E-mail: kclarke@usni.org
Phone: 410-295-1058
World Wide Web: http://www.usni.org
Contact: Kevin Clarke, Public Relations Manager
United States Naval Institute
118 Maryland Avenue
Annapolis, MD 21402-5035

▼ WOMEN'S INTERNATIONAL BOWLING CONGRESS

Alberta E. Crow Star of Tomorrow Scholarship   • 259

Award available to female, amateur bowler 21 and under. Must be high school senior or undergraduate student. Must have a minimum 2.5 GPA.

Award: Scholarship for use in freshman, sophomore, junior, or senior year; not renewable. *Number:* 1. *Amount:* $4000.
Eligibility Requirements: Applicant must be age 21 or under; female and must have an interest in bowling.
Application Requirements: Application, essay, references, self-addressed stamped envelope, transcript. **Deadline:** January 15.
E-mail: yabascholarships@juno.com
Contact: Ed Gocha, Scholarship Administrator
Women's International Bowling Congress
5301 South 76th Street
Greendale, WI 53129-1192

▼ WRITER'S DIGEST

Writer's Digest Writing Competition   • 260

Writing contest in various categories: articles, short stories, poetry, and scripts. Must be original, unpublished, unproduced, and not previously submitted to Writer's Digest. Submit entry form plus $10 manuscript fee per entry.
Award: Prize for use in any year; not renewable. *Number:* 100. *Amount:* $25–$1000.
Eligibility Requirements: Applicant must have an interest in writing.
Application Requirements: Application, applicant must enter a contest, self-addressed stamped envelope. **Fee:** $10.
Deadline: May 31.
Contact: Dan Boer, Competition Assistant
Writer's Digest
1507 Dana Avenue
Cincinnati, OH 45207

MISCELLANEOUS CRITERIA–UNDERGRADUATE

▲

▼ CONCERT ARTISTS GUILD

Concert Artists Guild Competition • 261

Award for professional-level classical musicians age 35 and under. Concert Artists Guild presents and manages prize-winning artists. Submit two tapes. Application fee is $50; late fee is $60. Deadline: October 1.

Award: Prize for use in any year; not renewable.
Eligibility Requirements: Applicant must be age 35 or under.
Application Requirements: Application, applicant must enter a contest. **Fee:** $50. **Deadline:** October 1.
E-mail: caguild@aol.com
Phone: 212-333-5200 **Fax:** 212-977-7149
World Wide Web: http://www.concertartists.org
Contact: Mary G. Madigan, Competition Manager
Concert Artists Guild
850 7th Avenue, Suite 1205
New York, NY 10019-5230

▼ DATATEL SCHOLARS FOUNDATION

Datatel Scholars Foundation • 262

One-time award for students attending institutions which use Datatel administrative software. Must apply through college/university. Available for part-time and full-time-students.

Award: Scholarship for use in any year; not renewable. *Amount:* $700–$2000.
Application Requirements: Application, essay, references, transcript. **Deadline:** February 15.
E-mail: scholars@datatel.com
Phone: 703-968-9000 **Fax:** 703-968-4573
Contact: Director
Datatel Scholars Foundation
4375 Fair Lakes Court
Fairfax, VA 22033

▼ HUDSON RIVER FOUNDATION

Tibor T. Polgar Fellowships • 263

Several fellowships available to graduate or undergraduate students to conduct research on the Hudson River. Applicants must submit five copies of the application includ-

ing a letter of interest and a letter of support from an adviser. Eight one-time awards of $3500 each.

Application Requirements: Application, essay, references.
Deadline: March 4.
E-mail: dennis@hudsonriver.org
Phone: 212-924-8290
World Wide Web: http://www.hudsonriver.org
Contact: Science Director
Hudson River Foundation
40 West 20th Street, 9th Floor
New York, NY 10011

▼ OPTIMIST INTERNATIONAL FOUNDATION

Optimist International Essay Contest • 264

Fifty-three winners at club and district level awarded all-expense paid trip to Freedom Foundation Leadership Conference, Valley Forge, Pennsylvania. Top three essays at international level win College scholarships of $5000, $3000, and $2000. Must be 19 or younger as of December 31 of senior year of high school. Open to residents of the U.S., Canada, and Jamaica. Deadline: January 31. Must submit driver's license or photo ID.

Award: Scholarship for use in any year; not renewable. *Number:* 3. *Amount:* $2000–$5000.
Eligibility Requirements: Applicant must be high school student and age 19 or under.
Application Requirements: Application, applicant must enter a contest, driver's license, essay, photo. **Deadline:** January 31.
Contact: Optimist Club in your town
Optimist International Foundation
4494 Lindell Boulevard
St. Louis, MO 63108

▼ PILOT INTERNATIONAL FOUNDATION

Ruby Newhall Memorial Scholarship Program • 265

One-time award for foreign students studying in the U.S. or Canada who plan to return to their home country. Must

Ruby Newhall Memorial Scholarship Program (continued)

have completed at least one semester of undergraduate work. Must be sponsored by a local Pilot Club.

Award: Scholarship for use in sophomore, junior, senior, or graduate years; not renewable. *Number:* 5–20. *Amount:* $500–$1500.

Eligibility Requirements: Applicant must be enrolled at a two-year or four-year institution.

Application Requirements: Application, financial need analysis, references, self-addressed stamped envelope, transcript. **Deadline:** March 1.

Contact: Awards Director
Pilot International Foundation
244 College Street, Box 5600
Macon, GA 31208-5600

▼ SHASTRI INDO-CANADIAN INSTITUTE

Shastri Distinguished Speakers Programme ● 266

Two awards available to distinguished non-academic speakers (one from Canada and one from India) to do a two- to three-week speaking tour in the other country. Two one-time awards of varying amounts. Must be a citizen of India or Canada.

Award: Scholarship for use in any year; not renewable. *Number:* 2.

Application Requirements: Application. **Deadline:** October 15.

E-mail: sici@acs.ucalgary.ca

Phone: 403-220-7467

Contact: Shastri Indo-Canadian Institute
2500 University Drive, NW
1402 Education Tower
Calgary, AB T2N 1N4
Canada

GRADUATE AWARDS

ACADEMIC/CAREER AREAS–GRADUATE

▲

AGRIBUSINESS

▼ **AMERICAN AGRICULTURAL ECONOMICS ASSOCIATION**

Outstanding Doctoral and Master's Thesis Awards • 267

One-time $250 award for graduate students of agriculture, natural resources, or rural economics who have written outstanding master's/doctoral theses. Must be nominated by department of participating institution. Write for further details.

Academic/Career Areas: Agribusiness; Agriculture.
Award: Prize for use in graduate years; not renewable. *Number:* 3–6. *Amount:* $250.
Application Requirements: Deadline: February 1.
E-mail: lchristo@iastate.edu
Phone: 515-233-3306 **Fax:** 515-233-3101
World Wide Web: http://www.aaea.org
Contact: Lona Christoffers
    American Agricultural Economics
      Association
    1110 Buckeye Avenue
    Ames, IA 50010-8063

AGRICULTURE

▼ **AMERICAN AGRICULTURAL ECONOMICS ASSOCIATION**

Outstanding Doctoral and Master's Thesis Awards see number 267

▼ **AMERICAN ASSOCIATION OF CEREAL CHEMISTS FOUNDATION**

American Association of Cereal Chemists Graduate Fellowships • 268

Fellowships for graduate students with minimum 3.0 GPA involved in research on cereal and oilseed related areas.

Students must be enrolled at an institution that is conducting fundamental investigation in this field. Submit department head endorsement and essay in form of letter of application.

Academic/Career Areas: Agriculture; Food Science/Nutrition.
Eligibility Requirements: Applicant must have an interest in leadership.
Application Requirements: Application, essay, references, transcript. **Deadline:** April 1.
Contact: Dr. Elwood F. Caldwell, Scholarship/
      Fellowship Jury Chairman
    American Association of Cereal Chemists
      Foundation
    3340 Pilot Knob Road
    St. Paul, MN 55121-2097

▼ **KENTUCKY NATURAL RESOURCES AND ENVIRONMENTAL PROTECTION CABINET**

Environmental Protection Scholarships • 269

Renewable awards for college juniors, seniors, and graduate students for tuition, fees, and room and board at a Kentucky state university. Awards of $3000 to $3500 per semester for up to four semesters. Six awards given in 1997 for a total of $23,000. Minimum 2.5 GPA required. Must agree to work full-time for the Kentucky Natural Resources and Environmental Protection Cabinet upon graduation.

Academic/Career Areas: Agriculture; Chemical Engineering; Civil Engineering; Earth Science; Health and Medical Sciences; Natural Resources.
Award: Scholarship for use in junior, senior, or graduate years; renewable. *Number:* 3–5.
Eligibility Requirements: Applicant must be enrolled at a four-year institution and studying in Kentucky.
Application Requirements: Application, essay, interview, references, transcript. **Deadline:** February 15.
E-mail: kipp@pop.uky.edu
Phone: 606-257-1299 **Fax:** 606-323-1049

Environmental Protection Scholarships (continued)

Contact: Scholarship Program Coordinator
Kentucky Natural Resources and
    Environmental Protection Cabinet
233 Mining/Mineral Resources Building
University of Kentucky
Lexington, KY 40506-0107

▼ NATIONAL DAIRY SHRINE-DAIRY MANAGEMENT INCORPORATED

H.H. Kildee Scholarship   • 270

Top twenty-five contestants in the National Intercollegiate Dairy Cattle Judging Contest are eligible to apply for a $3000 one-time scholarship for graduate study in field related to dairy cattle production at school of choice.
Academic/Career Areas: Agriculture.
Award: Scholarship for use in graduate years; not renewable. *Number:* 1. *Amount:* $3000.
Application Requirements: Application. **Deadline:** March 15.
Phone: 614-878-5333 **Fax:** 614-870-2622
Contact: Mr. Maurice E. Core, Executive Director
National Dairy Shrine-Dairy Management
    Incorporated
1224 Alton Darby Creek Road
Columbus, OH 43228-9792

▼ SIGMA XI, THE SCIENTIFIC RESEARCH SOCIETY

Sigma Xi Grants-in-Aid of Research   • 271

One-time award for scientific investigation in the sciences. Must be undergraduate or graduate student enrolled at an accredited institution. Faculty adviser must be member of Sigma Xi. Deadlines: February 1, May 1, and November 1.
Academic/Career Areas: Agriculture; Animal/Veterinary Sciences; Biology; Earth Science; Engineering/Technology; Health and Medical Sciences; Meteorology/Atmospheric Science; Physical Sciences and Math; Social Sciences.
Award: Grant for use in freshman, sophomore, junior, senior, or graduate years; not renewable. *Number:* 850–900. *Amount:* $100–$1000.
Eligibility Requirements: Applicant must be enrolled at a two-year or four-year institution.
Application Requirements: Application, references.
E-mail: giar@sigmaxi.org
Phone: 919-547-5206 **Fax:** 919-549-0090
World Wide Web: http://www.sigmaxi.org

Contact: Deborah Donati, Programs Coordinator
Sigma Xi, The Scientific Research Society
99 Alexander Drive
Box 13975
Research Triangle Park, NC 27709

▼ WOMAN'S NATIONAL FARM AND GARDEN ASSOCIATION

Sarah Bradley Tyson Memorial Fellowships   • 272

Renewable award for graduate students for advanced study in agriculture, horticulture, and allied subjects. Must submit autobiography, photo, and self-addressed stamped envelope with application. Write for details and deadline. $500 award.
Academic/Career Areas: Agriculture; Biology; Horticulture/Floriculture; Landscape Architecture; Natural Resources.
Application Requirements: Application, autobiography, photo, references, self-addressed stamped envelope.
Deadline: April 15.
Contact: Mrs. Elmer Braun, Awards Chairman
Woman's National Farm and Garden
    Association
13 Davis Drive
Saginaw, MI 48602

▼ WOMEN GROCERS OF AMERICA

Mary Macey Scholarship   • 273

Award for students intending to pursue a grocery industry-related career. Includes majors in such areas as food marketing management, agricultural economics, food service technology, communications, or business management/administration. Does not include majors in such areas as public health or hotel/restaurant management. One-time award for students who have completed freshman year. Submit statement and recommendation from sponsor in the grocery industry.
Academic/Career Areas: Agriculture; Business/Consumer Services; Communications; Economics; Food Service/Hospitality.
Award: Scholarship for use in sophomore, junior, senior, or graduate years; not renewable. *Number:* 2. *Amount:* $1000.
Eligibility Requirements: Applicant must be enrolled at a two-year or four-year institution.
Application Requirements: Application, transcript. **Deadline:** June 1.
Phone: 703-437-5300 **Fax:** 703-437-7768

Contact: Ms. Anne Wintersteen, Director of
Administration
Women Grocers of America
1825 Samuel Morse Drive
Reston, VA 20190-5317

ANIMAL/VETERINARY SCIENCES

▼ APPALOOSA HORSE CLUB-APPALOOSA YOUTH PROGRAM

Lew & JoAnn Eklund Educational Scholarship • 274

One-time award for college juniors and seniors and graduate students studying a field related to the equine industry. Must be member or dependent of member of the Appaloosa Horse Club. Submit picture and three recommendations. Award based on merit.

Academic/Career Areas: Animal/Veterinary Sciences.
Award: Scholarship for use in junior, senior, or graduate years; not renewable. *Number:* 1. *Amount:* $2000.
Eligibility Requirements: Applicant must be enrolled at a four-year institution and member of Appaloosa Horse Club/Appaloosa Youth Association.
Application Requirements: Application, photo, references, transcript. **Deadline:** June 10.
E-mail: aphc@appaloosa.com
Phone: 208-882-5578 **Fax:** 208-882-8150
Contact: Appaloosa Youth Foundation Scholarship
Committee
Appaloosa Horse Club-Appaloosa Youth
Program
PO Box 8403
Moscow, ID 83843

▼ CANADIAN FOUNDATION FOR THE STUDY OF INFANT DEATHS

Dr. Sydney Segal Research Grants • 275

Awards for graduate and postgraduate students studying the effects, causes and/or prevention of Sudden Infant Death Syndrome (SIDS). Award may only be given to students attending Canadian postsecondary institutions. Write for more information. One-time award of up to 35,000 Canadian dollars.

Academic/Career Areas: Animal/Veterinary Sciences; Area/Ethnic Studies; Health Administration; Health and Medical Sciences; Health Information Management/Technology; Nursing.
Award: Grant for use in graduate years; not renewable. *Number:* 1–10.
Application Requirements: Application, financial need analysis, references, transcript. **Deadline:** June 1.
E-mail: sidscanada@inforamp.net
Phone: 416-488-3260 **Fax:** 416-488-3864
World Wide Web: http://www.sidscanada.org/sids.html
Contact: Beverly DeBruyn, Executive Director
Canadian Foundation for the Study of
Infant Deaths
586 Eglinton Avenue East, Suite 308
Toronto, ON M4P 1P2
Canada

▼ INTERNATIONAL WOMEN'S FISHING ASSOCIATION SCHOLARSHIP TRUST

International Women's Fishing Association Graduate Scholarships in the Marine Sciences • 276

Renewable award for matriculated graduate students pursuing master's or Ph.D. in a marine science. Must be studying at a U.S. institution. Award based upon ability and financial need. Write for more information.

Academic/Career Areas: Animal/Veterinary Sciences; Biology; Natural Resources.
Award: Scholarship for use in graduate years; renewable. *Number:* 1–20. *Amount:* $500–$2000.
Application Requirements: Application, autobiography, essay, financial need analysis, photo, references, transcript.
Deadline: March 1.
Contact: Chairman, Scholarship Trust
International Women's Fishing Association
Scholarship Trust
PO Drawer 3125
Palm Beach, FL 33480

▼ L.S.B. LEAKEY FOUNDATION

L.S.B. Leakey Foundation General Research Grants • 277

One-time award for postdoctoral and senior scientists for study of paleoanthropology and primatology and for research into hunting and gathering. All funding is for

L.S.B. Leakey Foundation General Research Grants (continued)

research relating to human origins. Submit curriculum vitae, budget, and full research proposal. Deadlines: August 15 and January 5.
Academic/Career Areas: Animal/Veterinary Sciences; Biology; Social Sciences.
Award: Grant for use in postdoctoral years; not renewable. *Amount:* $3000–$12,000.
Application Requirements: Application, financial need analysis, references.
World Wide Web: http://www.leakeyfoundation.org
Contact: Dr. Karla Savage, Program and Grants
Officer
L.S.B. Leakey Foundation
PO Box 29346
Presidio Building #1002A, O'Reilly Avenue
San Francisco, CA 94129

Leakey Foundation Fellowship for Great Ape Research and Conservation ● 278

Award for pre-doctoral students and senior scientists for research in behavior and ecology of wild populations of great apes that contributes to development or testing of models of human evolution. Must submit full research proposal. Pre-application due October 15 and full application on January 5.
Academic/Career Areas: Animal/Veterinary Sciences; Biology; Social Sciences.
Award: Grant for use in graduate years; not renewable. *Number:* 1. *Amount:* $20,000.
Application Requirements: Application, financial need analysis, references. **Deadline:** October 15.
World Wide Web: http://www.leakeyfoundation.org
Contact: Dr. Karla Savage, Program and Grants
Officer
L.S.B. Leakey Foundation
PO Box 29346
Presidio Building #1002A, O'Reilly Avenue
San Francisco, CA 94129

Leakey Foundation Study of Foraging Peoples Fellowship ● 279

Award for postdoctoral or senior scientists to study foraging peoples in order to understand human origins. Include letter of intent, full research proposal, budget, and schedule with application. Write for more information. One-time award of $20,000.
Academic/Career Areas: Animal/Veterinary Sciences; Biology; Social Sciences.

Award: Grant for use in postdoctoral years; not renewable. *Number:* 1. *Amount:* $20,000.
Application Requirements: Application, financial need analysis, references. **Deadline:** October 15.
World Wide Web: http://www.leakeyfoundation.org
Contact: Dr. Karla Savage, Program and Grants
Officer
L.S.B. Leakey Foundation
PO Box 29346
Presidio Building #1002A, O'Reilly Avenue
San Francisco, CA 94129

▼ PARALYZED VETERANS OF AMERICA—SPINAL CORD RESEARCH FOUNDATION

Fellowships in Spinal Cord Injury Research ● 280

Award for research done in U.S. or Canadian laboratory and dedicated to improving quality of life for individuals with spinal cord injury and spinal cord dysfunction and to finding an eventual cure for paralysis. Must submit curriculum vitae, ten copies of grant application. Deadlines: June 1, December 1.
Academic/Career Areas: Animal/Veterinary Sciences; Biology; Health and Medical Sciences; Therapy/ Rehabilitation.
Application Requirements: Application, references.
Contact: Paralyzed Veterans of America—Spinal Cord
Research Foundation
801 18th Street, NW
Washington, DC 20006

▼ SIGMA XI, THE SCIENTIFIC RESEARCH SOCIETY

National Academy of Science Grants-in-Aid of Research ● 281

One-time award for scientific investigation in natural or physical sciences. Must be graduate or undergraduate student enrolled at an accredited institution. Deadlines are February 1, May 1, and November 1.
Academic/Career Areas: Animal/Veterinary Sciences; Biology; Earth Science; Health and Medical Sciences; Meteorology/Atmospheric Science; Natural Resources; Physical Sciences and Math.
Award: Grant for use in freshman, sophomore, junior, senior, or graduate years; not renewable. *Number:* 850–900. *Amount:* $100–$2500.

Eligibility Requirements: Applicant must be enrolled at a two-year or four-year institution.
Application Requirements: Application, references.
E-mail: giar@sigmaxi.org
Phone: 919-547-5206 **Fax:** 919-549-0090
World Wide Web: http://www.sigmaxi.org
Contact: Deborah Donati, Programs Coordinator
Sigma Xi, The Scientific Research Society
99 Alexander Drive
Box 13975
Research Triangle Park, NC 27709

Sigma Xi Grants-in-Aid of Research **see number 271**

▼ WHITEHALL FOUNDATION, INC.

Whitehall Foundation, Inc. Grants-in-Aid • 282
Designed for researchers at the assistant professor level. Current preference for research in neurobiology. Write for further information. Submit preliminary proposal by deadlines of January 15, April 15, October 1. Judged on scientific merit of proposal, past performance, and continued productivity. Application deadlines are June 1, September 1, February 15. One-time award of up to $30,000.
Academic/Career Areas: Animal/Veterinary Sciences; Biology; Health and Medical Sciences.
Award: Grant for use in postdoctoral years; not renewable. *Number:* up to 9. *Amount:* up to $30,000.
Application Requirements: Application, references.
E-mail: whitehallf@aol.com
Phone: 561-655-4474 **Fax:** 561-659-4978
World Wide Web: http://www.whitehall.org
Contact: Laurel Baker, Corporate Secretary
Whitehall Foundation, Inc.
251 Royal Palm Way, Suite 211
Palm Beach, FL 33480

Whitehall Foundation, Inc. Research Grants • 283
Renewable grants for established scientists working at accredited institutions. Principal investigator must hold no less than position of assistant professor or equivalent. Current preference for research in neurobiology. Submit preliminary proposal by deadlines of January 15, April 15, October 1. Judged on scientific merit of proposal, past performance, and continued productivity. Application deadlines are June 1, September 1, February 15.

Academic/Career Areas: Animal/Veterinary Sciences; Biology; Health and Medical Sciences.
Award: Grant for use in postdoctoral years; renewable. *Number:* 28–32. *Amount:* $30,000–$75,000.
Application Requirements: Application, references.
E-mail: whitehallf@aol.com
Phone: 561-655-4474 **Fax:** 561-659-4978
World Wide Web: http://www.whitehall.com
Contact: Laurel Baker, Corporate Secretary
Whitehall Foundation, Inc.
251 Royal Palm Way, Suite 211
Palm Beach, FL 33480

APPLIED SCIENCES

▼ AMERICAN GEOPHYSICAL UNION

American Geophysical Union Horton Research Grant • 284
Grant for research in hydrology and/or water resources by Ph.D. candidate. Proposals may be in hydrology (physics, chemistry, or biology aspects) or water resource policy sciences (economics, systems analysis, sociology, or law). Must submit executive summary. Two one-time awards of $1000 each.
Academic/Career Areas: Applied Sciences; Biology; Civil Engineering; Earth Science; Economics; Engineering/Technology; Legal Services; Natural Resources; Social Sciences.
Award: Grant for use in postdoctoral years; not renewable. *Number:* 2. *Amount:* $1000.
Eligibility Requirements: Applicant must be enrolled at a four-year institution.
Application Requirements: Application. **Deadline:** March 1.
E-mail: wsinghateh@kosmos.agu.org
Phone: 202-939-3223 **Fax:** 202-328-0566
Contact: Wynetta Singhateh, Education and Research Department
American Geophysical Union
2000 Florida Avenue, NW
Washington, DC 20009-9202

▼ AMERICAN SOCIETY FOR PHOTOGRAMMETRY AND REMOTE SENSING

Earth Observation Satellite Company Award for Application of Digital Landsat TM Data • 285

Award for undergraduate or graduate students to stimulate development of applications of digital Landsat Thematic Mapper (TM) data. For applied research with digital Landset data. Contact for details and deadlines.
Academic/Career Areas: Applied Sciences; Engineering/Technology; Physical Sciences and Math.
Award: Scholarship for use in freshman, sophomore, junior, senior, or graduate years; not renewable. *Number:* 1. *Amount:* up to $4000.
Application Requirements: Application, autobiography, references.
E-mail: wendyw@asprs.org
Phone: 301-493-0290 Ext. 20 **Fax:** 301-493-0208
World Wide Web: http://www.asprs.org/asprs
Contact: Wendy Wattman, Awards Coordinator
American Society for Photogrammetry and Remote Sensing
5410 Grosvenor Lane, Suite 210
Bethesda, MD 20814

▼ AMERICAN WATER WORKS ASSOCIATION

American Water Works Association/Abel Wolman Fellowship • 286

One fellowship for graduate students pursuing advanced training and research in field related to water supply and treatment. Application must include curriculum and research plans. One $15,000 fellowship renewable for second year.
Academic/Career Areas: Applied Sciences; Biology; Engineering/Technology; Natural Resources.
Application Requirements: Application, references, test scores, transcript. **Deadline:** January 15.
E-mail: vbaca@awwa.org
Phone: 303-347-6202 **Fax:** 303-794-8915
World Wide Web: http://www.awwa.org
Contact: Veronica Baca, Scholarship Coordinator
American Water Works Association
6666 Quincy Avenue
Denver, CO 80235

American Water Works Association/Holly A. Cornell Scholarship • 287

One scholarship for female and/or minority students researching water supply and treatment. Applicant must submit GRE scores, proposed curriculum of studies, and career objectives. One-time award of $5000 for master's degree study.
Academic/Career Areas: Applied Sciences; Biology; Engineering/Technology; Natural Resources.
Award: Scholarship for use in graduate years; not renewable. *Number:* 1. *Amount:* $5000.
Application Requirements: Application, references, test scores, transcript. **Deadline:** December 15.
E-mail: vbaca@awwa.org
Phone: 303-347-6202 **Fax:** 303-794-8915
World Wide Web: http://www.awwa.org
Contact: Veronica Baca, Scholarship Coordinator
American Water Works Association
6666 Quincy Avenue
Denver, CO 80235

American Water Works Association/Larson Aquatic Research Support Scholarship • 288

Two scholarships for applicants pursuing an advanced degree relating to public drinking water. For study at institution in Canada, Guam, Mexico, Puerto Rico, or U.S. Must include educational plans. Must submit resume, GRE scores, and plan of study. Deadlines November 15 for M.S., January 15 for Ph.D. One-time awards of $3000 and $5000.
Academic/Career Areas: Applied Sciences; Biology; Health and Medical Sciences; Natural Resources.
Award: Scholarship for use in graduate years; not renewable. *Number:* 2. *Amount:* $3000–$5000.
Application Requirements: Application, references, test scores, transcript.
E-mail: vbaca@awwa.org
Phone: 303-347-6202 **Fax:** 303-794-8915
World Wide Web: http://www.awwa.org
Contact: Veronica Baca, Scholarship Coordinator
American Water Works Association
6666 Quincy Avenue
Denver, CO 80235

American Water Works Association/Thomas R. Camp Memorial Scholarship • 289

One scholarship for graduate research related to drinking water. Applicant must include a one-page statement of

educational plans, career objectives, a two-page research proposal, GRE scores, and resume. One-time award of $5000.
Academic/Career Areas: Applied Sciences; Biology; Health and Medical Sciences; Natural Resources.
Award: Scholarship for use in graduate years; not renewable. *Number:* 1. *Amount:* $5000.
Application Requirements: Application, references, test scores, transcript. **Deadline:** January 15.
E-mail: vbaca@awwa.org
Phone: 303-347-6202 **Fax:** 303-794-8915
World Wide Web: http://www.awwa.org
Contact: Veronica Baca, Scholarship Coordinator
American Water Works Association
6666 Quincy Avenue
Denver, CO 80235

▼ ASSOCIATED WESTERN UNIVERSITIES, INC.

Associated Western Universities-DOE Post-Graduate Fellowship • 290
One-time award for postgraduates to participate in and contribute to research and technology at cooperating facilities. Designed to encourage the selection of a professional career in science or engineering. Submit transcript and references with application.
Academic/Career Areas: Applied Sciences; Chemical Engineering; Civil Engineering; Computer Science/Data Processing; Earth Science; Electrical/Electronic Engineering; Engineering/Technology; Mechanical Engineering; Meteorology/Atmospheric Science; Nuclear Science; Physical Sciences and Math.
Application Requirements: Application, references, transcript.
Deadline: Continuous.
E-mail: info@awu.org
Phone: 801-273-8900 **Fax:** 801-277-5632
World Wide Web: http://www.awu.org
Contact: Associated Western Universities, Inc.
4190 South Highland Drive, Suite 211
Salt Lake City, UT 84124-4234

Associated Western Universities/DOE Faculty Fellowships • 291
One-time award for faculty members of universities to contribute to research and development at a participating university. Submit application, and references by February 1. Write for further information. Amount of award depends on recipient's salary.

Academic/Career Areas: Applied Sciences; Chemical Engineering; Civil Engineering; Computer Science/Data Processing; Earth Science; Engineering/Technology; Mechanical Engineering; Meteorology/Atmospheric Science; Nuclear Science; Physical Sciences and Math.
Eligibility Requirements: Applicant must have employment experience in teaching.
Application Requirements: Application, references. **Deadline:** February 1.
E-mail: info@awu.org
Phone: 801-273-8900 **Fax:** 801-277-5632
World Wide Web: http://www.awu.org
Contact: Associated Western Universities, Inc.
4190 South Highland Drive, Suite 211
Salt Lake City, UT 84124-4234

Associated Western Universities/DOE Laboratory Graduate Research Fellowships • 292
One-time award for graduate students to conduct thesis/dissertation research at a participating university. Submit application, transcript, and references by February 1. Write for further information.
Academic/Career Areas: Applied Sciences; Chemical Engineering; Civil Engineering; Computer Science/Data Processing; Earth Science; Engineering/Technology; Mechanical Engineering; Meteorology/Atmospheric Science; Nuclear Science; Physical Sciences and Math.
Application Requirements: Application, references, transcript.
Deadline: February 1.
E-mail: info@awu.org
Phone: 801-273-8900 **Fax:** 801-277-5632
World Wide Web: http://www.awu.org
Contact: Associated Western Universities, Inc.
4190 South Highland Drive, Suite 211
Salt Lake City, UT 84124-4234

▼ CAMPUS SAFETY DIVISION

Campus Safety Scholarship • 293
Two awards for full-time undergraduate and graduate students who are majoring in academic programs leading to degrees in safety, health, or environmental affairs. One-time award of $1000. Financial Aid Administrator must attest to financial need. Must include self-addressed stamped envelope. Deadline: March 31.
Academic/Career Areas: Applied Sciences; Biology; Engineering-Related Technologies; Health Administra-

Campus Safety Scholarship (continued)

tion; Health and Medical Sciences; Nursing; Physical Sciences and Math; Science, Technology & Society.
Award: Scholarship for use in sophomore, junior, senior, or graduate years; not renewable. *Number:* 2. *Amount:* $1000.
Eligibility Requirements: Applicant must be enrolled at a two-year or four-year institution.
Application Requirements: Application, essay, self-addressed stamped envelope. **Deadline:** March 31.
E-mail: brouwere@nsc.org
Contact: Campus Safety Division
1121 Spring Lake Drive
Itasca, IL 60143

▼ CENTER FOR FIELD RESEARCH

Center for Field Research Grants for Field Research • 294

Private grants for field research anywhere in the world. Research projects must be labor intensive and suitable for the involvement of non-specialist, volunteer field workers provided by affiliate, Earthwatch. Each volunteer pays a share of the expedition's costs in return for the opportunity to assist and learn in the field. Renewable grants for varying amounts. Must submit a preliminary proposal form.
Academic/Career Areas: Applied Sciences; Architecture; Area/Ethnic Studies; Art History; Biology; Earth Science; Historic Preservation and Conservation; Humanities; Meteorology/Atmospheric Science; Natural Resources; Physical Sciences and Math; Social Sciences.
Award: Grant for use in graduate years; renewable. *Number:* 50–150. *Amount:* $7000–$50,000.
Application Requirements: Financial need analysis. **Deadline:** Continuous.
E-mail: chanley@earthwatch.org
Phone: 617-926-8200 **Fax:** 617-926-8532
World Wide Web: http://www.earthwatch.org
Contact: Charlotte Hanley, Program Assistant
Center for Field Research
Box 9104
680 Mount Auburn Street
Watertown, MA 02272

▼ FIGHT FOR SIGHT, INC.

Fight for Sight- Grants-in-Aid • 295

One-time awards for researchers to fund pilot projects and studies of priority interest to Fight for Sight, Inc.

Applications generally not considered from residents, fellows, and researchers who already have significant research support.
Academic/Career Areas: Applied Sciences; Health and Medical Sciences.
Award: Grant for use in graduate years; not renewable. *Number:* 15–20. *Amount:* $1000–$12,000.
Application Requirements: Application. **Deadline:** March 1.
E-mail: preventblindness@compuserve.com
Phone: 847-843-2020
Contact: Program Coordinator
Fight for Sight, Inc.
500 East Remington Road
Schaumburg, IL 60173

Fight for Sight-NSPB Postdoctoral Research Fellowships • 296

One-time award for individuals with doctorate who are interested in careers involving clinical or basic research in ophthalmology, vision, or related sciences. Residents or persons receiving fellowships from other sources are ineligible, as are individuals having two or more years doctoral training.
Academic/Career Areas: Applied Sciences; Health and Medical Sciences.
Application Requirements: Application. **Deadline:** March 1.
E-mail: preventblindness@compuserve.com
Phone: 847-843-2020
Contact: Program Coordinator
Fight for Sight, Inc.
500 East Remington Road
Schaumburg, IL 60173

▼ FOUNDATION FOR SCIENCE AND DISABILITY

Foundation for Science and Disability-Student Grant • 297

Available to graduate students who have some physical disability. Awards are given for an assistive device or as financial support for scientific research. Seniors may apply. One-time award. Electronic application is available.
Academic/Career Areas: Applied Sciences; Biology; Chemical Engineering; Civil Engineering; Computer Science/Data Processing; Electrical/Electronic Engineering; Engineering/Technology; Health and Medical Sciences; Mechanical Engineering; Physical Sciences and Math.
Award: Grant for use in graduate years; not renewable. *Number:* 1–3. *Amount:* $1000.

ACADEMIC/CAREER AREAS–GRADUATE

Eligibility Requirements: Applicant must be hearing impaired, physically disabled, or visually impaired.
Application Requirements: Application, essay, references, transcript. **Deadline:** December 1.
E-mail: rmankin@gainesville.usda.ufl.edu
Phone: 352-374-5774 **Fax:** 352-374-5781
Contact: Richard Mankin, Grants Committee Chair
Foundation for Science and Disability
503 NW 89th Street
Gainesville, FL 32607

▼ INTERNATIONAL DESALINATION ASSOCIATION

International Desalination Association Scholarship • 298

Award to assist young engineers and scientists to further their education in subjects related to desalination. Provides assistance for graduate students. One to three renewable awards of $3000 to $6000.
Academic/Career Areas: Applied Sciences; Biology; Chemical Engineering; Civil Engineering; Electrical/ Electronic Engineering; Engineering/Technology; Engineering-Related Technologies; Mechanical Engineering; Natural Sciences.
Award: Scholarship for use in graduate years; renewable. *Number:* 1–3. *Amount:* $3000–$6000.
Application Requirements: Application, photo, references, transcript. **Deadline:** Continuous.
Phone: Ext. 441546605500 **Fax:** Ext. 441546605501
World Wide Web: http://www.ida.bm
Contact: Prof. William Hanbury, Scholarship
Chairman
International Desalination Association
PO Box 387
Topsfield, MA 01983

▼ INTERNATIONAL UNION FOR VACUUM SCIENCE, TECHNIQUE AND APPLICATIONS

Welch Foundation Scholarship • 299

One scholarship available to a promising scholar who wishes to contribute to the study of vacuum science techniques or their application in any field. Candidates should hold at least a bachelor's degree and plan to spend a year in a research lab in another country. Must submit curriculum vitae, two recommendations, and a research proposal. One-time award of $12,500.

Academic/Career Areas: Applied Sciences; Chemical Engineering; Electrical/Electronic Engineering; Engineering/Technology.
Award: Scholarship for use in graduate years; not renewable. *Number:* 1. *Amount:* $12,500.
Application Requirements: Application, autobiography, references, transcript. **Deadline:** April 15.
World Wide Web: http://www.vacuum.org/iuvsta/ welchann.html
Contact: International Union for Vacuum Science,
Technique and Applications
Advanced Technology Laboratory, BNR
7 Mohawk Crescent
Nepean, ON K2H 7G7
Canada

▼ SMITHSONIAN INSTITUTION NATIONAL AIR AND SPACE MUSEUM

Guggenheim Fellowship • 300

One-time award for graduate students and postdoctoral candidates studying the history of aviation and space flight. Stipend of $16,000 for predoctoral candidates; $28,000 for postdoctoral candidates. Fellows also receive $1000 research fund and return airfare to Washington. Fellowship will be at the National Air and Space Museum, lasting six to twelve months.
Academic/Career Areas: Applied Sciences; Aviation/ Aerospace; History.
Eligibility Requirements: Applicant must be studying in District of Columbia.
Application Requirements: Application, references, transcript. **Deadline:** January 15.
Phone: 202-357-2515 **Fax:** 202-786-2447
Contact: Ms. Anita Mason, Fellowship Coordinator
Smithsonian Institution National Air and
Space Museum
Aeronautics Department
MRC 312
Washington, DC 20560

Peterson's Scholarships for Study in the USA & Canada 1999 **133**

ARCHITECTURE

▼ **AMERICAN CONCRETE INSTITUTE INTERNATIONAL-CONCRETE RESEARCH AND EDUCATION FOUNDATION**

American Concrete Institute Fellowship Awards • 301

Two fellowships available to students who, at the time of acceptance of the awards, have been accepted for graduate study. Applicant must be studying in an engineering, architectural, or materials science program at an accredited institution in the U.S. or Canada. One-time awards of $3000 each.
Academic/Career Areas: Architecture; Engineering/Technology; Engineering-Related Technologies.
Application Requirements: Application. **Deadline:** February 11.
Contact: Scholarship Council
American Concrete Institute
International-Concrete Research and
Education Foundation
38800 Country Club Drive
Farmington Hills, MI 48333

Katharine and Bryant Mather Fellowship • 302

One fellowship available to a student who, at the time of acceptance of the fellowship, has been accepted for graduate study. Applicant must be studying in an engineering, architectural, or materials science program at an accredited institution in the U.S. or Canada. One-time award of $3000.
Academic/Career Areas: Architecture; Engineering/Technology; Engineering-Related Technologies.
Application Requirements: Application. **Deadline:** February 11.
Contact: Scholarship Council
American Concrete Institute
International-Concrete Research and
Education Foundation
38800 Country Club Drive
Farmington Hills, MI 48333

W. R. Grace Fellowship • 303

One fellowship available to students who, at the time of acceptance of the fellowship, have been accepted for graduate study. Applicant must be studying in an engineer-ing, architectural, or materials science program at an accredited college or university in the U.S. or Canada. One-time award of $3000.
Academic/Career Areas: Architecture; Engineering/Technology; Engineering-Related Technologies.
Application Requirements: Application. **Deadline:** February 11.
Contact: Scholarship Council
American Concrete Institute
International-Concrete Research and
Education Foundation
38800 Country Club Drive
Farmington Hills, MI 48333

▼ **AMERICAN INSTITUTE OF ARCHITECTS**

American Institute of Architects/AHA Fellowship in Health Facilities Design • 304

One-time award for scholars who have earned and received a professional degree in architecture or are in the final year of undergraduate work leading to a degree. Must be a citizen of the U.S., Canada, or Mexico. Several types of fellowships available. Write for details.
Academic/Career Areas: Architecture.
Award: Scholarship for use in senior or graduate years; not renewable.
Application Requirements: Application. **Deadline:** January 15.
Phone: 202-626-7511 **Fax:** 202-626-7420
World Wide Web: http://www.aiaonline.com
Contact: Mary Felber, Director, Scholarship Programs
American Institute of Architects
1735 New York Avenue, NW
Washington, DC 20006-5292

American Institute of Architects/American Hospital Association Fellowship in Health Facilities Design • 305

Award for graduate study or independent graduate-level study or research in health facilities design. Must be citizen of the U.S., Canada, or Mexico. Write for further requirements. Deadline: January 15.
Academic/Career Areas: Architecture.
Application Requirements: Application, essay, references, transcript. **Deadline:** January 15.
Phone: 202-626-7511 **Fax:** 202-626-7420
World Wide Web: http://www.aiaonline.com

Contact: Mary Felber, Director, Scholarship Programs
American Institute of Architects
1735 New York Avenue, NW
Washington, DC 20006-5292

▼ AMERICAN INSTITUTE OF ARCHITECTS/AMERICAN ARCHITECTURAL FOUNDATION

American Institute of Architects/American Architectural Foundation Scholarship for Advanced Study and Research • 306

Award for postprofessional degree in architecture. Submit project proposal to be conducted under the direction of a U.S. university. Applicant must have either a bachelor's or master's degree in architecture.
Academic/Career Areas: Architecture.
Award: Scholarship for use in graduate years; not renewable. *Number:* 6–12. *Amount:* $1000–$2500.
Application Requirements: Application, essay, references, transcript. **Deadline:** February 15.
Phone: 202-626-7511 **Fax:** 202-626-7420
Contact: Mary Felber, Director, Scholarship Programs
American Institute of Architects/American
Architectural Foundation
1735 New York Avenue, NW
Washington, DC 20006-5292

American Institute of Architects/American Architectural Foundation Scholarship for Professional Degree Candidates • 307

Available to students in the final two years of a professional degree, NAAB-accredited program leading to a Bachelor of Arts or Master's. Applications available from head of department. One-time award.
Academic/Career Areas: Architecture.
Award: Scholarship for use in junior, senior, or graduate years; not renewable. *Number:* 250. *Amount:* $500–$2500.
Eligibility Requirements: Applicant must be enrolled at a four-year institution.
Application Requirements: Application, essay, financial need analysis, references, transcript. **Deadline:** February 1.
Phone: 202-626-7511 **Fax:** 202-626-7420
Contact: Mary Felber, Director, Scholarship Programs
American Institute of Architects/American
Architectural Foundation
1735 New York Avenue, NW
Washington, DC 20006-5292

▼ CENTER FOR FIELD RESEARCH

Center for Field Research Grants for Field Research   **see number 294**

▼ HAGLEY MUSEUM AND LIBRARY

Hagley Museum and Library Grants-in-Aid • 308

Award for graduate research using the Hagley Library and Museum. Research must be relevant to the Library's collections. Submit curriculum vitae and five-page proposal of research project. Maximum amount of award $2400, minimum $300 per week.
Academic/Career Areas: Architecture; Art History; Arts; Humanities; Landscape Architecture; Museum Studies.
Application Requirements: Application. **Deadline:** Continuous.
Contact: Hagley Museum and Library
PO Box 3630
Wilmington, DE 19807-0630

Henry Belin du Pont Dissertation Fellowship • 309

One-time award for graduate students to conduct research at the Hagley Museum and Library. Research must be relevant to the Library's collections. Submit curriculum vitae and five-page project description. Deadlines are March 31, June 30, and October 31.
Academic/Career Areas: Architecture; Art History; Arts; Humanities; Landscape Architecture; Museum Studies.
Application Requirements: Application.
Contact: Hagley Museum and Library
PO Box 3630
Wilmington, DE 19807-0630

▼ JAPAN FOUNDATION

Japan Foundation Cultural Properties Specialist Fellowship • 310

Award provides specialists in the conservation and restoration of cultural properties (e.g., artistic objects, handicrafts, old documents, films, and records) the chance to conduct joint research with Japanese specialists or to develop their professional skills. One-time award.
Academic/Career Areas: Architecture; Area/Ethnic Studies; Historic Preservation and Conservation; Landscape Architecture.
Eligibility Requirements: Applicant must have employment experience in experience in career field.

Japan Foundation Cultural Properties Specialist Fellowship (continued)

Application Requirements: Application, essay, references. **Deadline:** December 1.
E-mail: chris_watanabe@jfny.org
Phone: 212-489-0299 **Fax:** 212-489-0409
World Wide Web: http://www.jfny.org
Contact: Christopher Watanabe, Program Assistant
Japan Foundation
152 West 57th Street, 39th Floor
New York, NY 10019

▼ NATIONAL GALLERY OF ART

Center for Advanced Study in the Visual Arts Senior Fellowship Program • 311

Award for those who have held the Ph.D. for five years or more or who possess equivalent record of professional accomplishment, for study in the visual arts. Fellows are expected to reside in Washington. Contact for deadlines.
Academic/Career Areas: Architecture; Art History; Landscape Architecture.
Application Requirements: Application, autobiography, essay, references.
E-mail: k-rodeffer@nga.gov
Phone: 202-842-6482 **Fax:** 202-842-6733
World Wide Web: http://www.nga.gov/resources/casva. htm
Contact: Kim Rodeffer, Assistant to Fellowship
Program
National Gallery of Art
Center for Advanced Study In the Visual
Arts
Washington, DC 20565

▼ NATIONAL GALLERY OF ART, CENTER FOR ADVANCED STUDY IN THE VISUAL ARTS

Robert H. and Clarice Smith Fellowship • 312

Award for twelve months of research in Dutch or Flemish art, intended for advancement or completion of doctoral dissertation or of resulting publication. May be used either in U.S. or abroad. Must obtain departmental sponsorship. Must be competent in two foreign languages. Open to U.S. citizens or those enrolled in U.S. university. Deadline: November 15.
Academic/Career Areas: Architecture; Art History; Landscape Architecture.

Application Requirements: Application, autobiography, essay, interview, references, transcript. **Deadline:** November 15.
E-mail: k-rodeffer@nga.gov
Phone: 202-842-6482 **Fax:** 202-842-6733
World Wide Web: http://www.nga.gov/resources/casva. htm
Contact: Kim Rodeffer, Fellowship Program Assistant
National Gallery of Art, Center for
Advanced Study in the Visual Arts
Center for Advanced Study in the Visual
Arts
Washington, DC 20565

▼ SKIDMORE, OWINGS, AND MERRILL FOUNDATION

Chicago Institute of Architecture & Urbanism Award • 313

Award for the best unpublished essay/research paper addressing the sustainability of the physical development of American cities. Papers are nominated by accredited U.S. graduate programs in architecture, urban design, or physical planning. Faculty and students in these fields may apply. One-time award of $5000. Submit curriculum vitae. Contact for deadlines.
Academic/Career Areas: Architecture.
Award: Prize for use in graduate years; not renewable. *Number:* 1. *Amount:* $5000.
Application Requirements: Applicant must enter a contest, essay.
E-mail: somfoundation@som.com
Contact: Lisa Westerfield, Administrative Director
Skidmore, Owings, and Merrill Foundation
224 South Michigan Avenue, Suite 1000
Chicago, IL 60604

Mechanical/Electrical Traveling Fellowship Program • 314

Award to a recent bachelor's or master's recipient in architectural, mechanical, or electrical engineering to allow recipient to travel to observe to any innovative building systems and technologies in the world. Candidate must be attending a U.S. school. Must be nominated by faculty of degree-granting institution and must intend to enter professional building engineer practice. Submit curriculum vitae, brief paper with abstract, proposed travel itinerary, and signed copyright release. Contact for further information and application deadline.

Academic/Career Areas: Architecture; Electrical/Electronic Engineering; Engineering/Technology; Mechanical Engineering.
Application Requirements: Essay, references, transcript.
E-mail: somfoundation@som.com
Contact: Lisa Westerfield, Administrative Director
Skidmore, Owings, and Merrill Foundation
224 South Michigan Avenue, Suite 1000
Chicago, IL 60604

Structural Engineering Traveling Fellow.
Program • 315
Award for a recent graduate with a master's or Ph.D. in civil or architectural engineering and a specialization in structural engineering to allow recipient to experience buildings, bridges, and other structures firsthand. Must have attended a U.S. school and must be nominated by faculty of degree-granting institution. Submit curriculum vitae, proposed travel itinerary, and signed copyright release. Contact for further information and application deadline.
Academic/Career Areas: Architecture; Civil Engineering; Engineering/Technology.
Application Requirements: Essay, references, transcript.
E-mail: somfoundation@som.com
Contact: Lisa Westerfield, Administrative Director
Skidmore, Owings, and Merrill Foundation
224 South Michigan Avenue, Suite 1000
Chicago, IL 60604

Urban Design Traveling Fellowship
Program • 316
Award for architect with a bachelor's in architecture, landscape architecture, or urban design, and a master's concentrating in urban design to be used to broaden recipient's knowledge of the design of modern, high-density cities. Must be a student or recent graduate and must be nominated by faculty of degree-granting institution. Submit curriculum vitae, proposed travel itinerary, and signed copyright release. Contact for further information and application deadline.
Academic/Career Areas: Architecture; Landscape Architecture.
Application Requirements: Portfolio, references, transcript.
E-mail: somfoundation@som.com
Contact: Lisa Westerfield, Administrative Director
Skidmore, Owings, and Merrill Foundation
224 South Michigan Avenue, Suite 1000
Chicago, IL 60604

▼ **SOCIETY OF ARCHITECTURAL HISTORIANS**

Architectural Study Tour Scholarship • 317
One-time award for one graduate student of art history, architecture, or historic preservation to participate in the Society of Architectural Historians annual domestic tour. Submit essay, references, and resume with application.
Academic/Career Areas: Architecture; Art History; Historic Preservation and Conservation.
Application Requirements: Application, essay, references.
Deadline: Continuous.
E-mail: info@sah.org
Phone: 312-573-1365 **Fax:** 312-573-1141
World Wide Web: http://www.sah.org
Contact: Lisa Torrance, Assistant Director
Society of Architectural Historians
1365 North Astor Street
Chicago, IL 60610-2144

Edilia and Francois-Auguste de Montequin Fellowship in Iberian and Latin American Architecture • 318
Award to be used for research at the graduate level. Research must focus on Spanish, Portuguese, or Ibero-American architecture. Submit curriculum vitae with application. One-time award of $1000.
Academic/Career Areas: Architecture; Art History.
Application Requirements: Application, essay, references.
Deadline: December 15.
E-mail: info@sah.org
Phone: 312-573-1365 **Fax:** 312-573-1141
World Wide Web: http://www.sah.org
Contact: Lisa Torrance, Assistant Director
Society of Architectural Historians
1365 North Astor Street
Chicago, IL 60610-2144

Keepers Preservation Education Fund Fellowship • 319
Award for one graduate student of art history, architecture, or historic preservation to attend the annual meeting of the Society of Architectural Historians. Submit essay, references, and resume with application. One-time award of $500.
Academic/Career Areas: Architecture; Art History; Historic Preservation and Conservation.
Application Requirements: Application, essay, references.
Deadline: December 15.
E-mail: info@sah.org

Keepers Preservation Education Fund Fellowship (continued)

Phone: 312-573-1365 **Fax:** 312-573-1141
World Wide Web: http://www.sah.org
Contact: Lisa Torrance, Assistant Director
Society of Architectural Historians
1365 North Astor Street
Chicago, IL 60610-2144

Rosann S. Berry Annual Meeting Fellowship • 320

Award for an advanced graduate student of architecture or art history to attend the annual meeting of the Society of Architectural Historians. Submit essay, references, and resume with application. One-time award of $500.
Academic/Career Areas: Architecture; Art History.
Application Requirements: Application, essay, references.
Deadline: December 15.
E-mail: info@sah.org
Phone: 312-573-1365 **Fax:** 312-573-1141
World Wide Web: http://www.sah.org
Contact: Lisa Torrance, Assistant Director
Society of Architectural Historians
1365 North Astor Street
Chicago, IL 60610-2144

▼ WINTERTHUR MUSEUM, GARDEN, AND LIBRARY

NEH Fellowships • 321

One-time fellowships for postgraduate students to conduct advanced research at Winterthur Library. Research must coincide with the Library's resources. Must be a U.S. resident or a non-resident living in the U.S. for at least three years prior to application. Write for details.
Academic/Career Areas: Architecture; Art History; Arts; Historic Preservation and Conservation; History; Home Economics; Interior Design; Landscape Architecture; Literature/English/Writing; Museum Studies; Travel/Tourism.
Eligibility Requirements: Applicant must be studying in Delaware.
Application Requirements: Application, essay, references.
Deadline: January 15.
E-mail: gtbug@udel.edu
Phone: 302-888-4640 **Fax:** 302-888-4870
Contact: Gretchen Buggeln
Winterthur Museum, Garden, and Library
Advanced Studies Office
Winterthur, DE 19735

Winterthur Research Fellowships • 322

One-time fellowships for academic, museum, and independent scholars to use library archival materials for dissertation research and other study. Research must coincide with Winterthur's available resources. Submit application, essay, and references. Write for more details. Research must take place at the Winterthur Library.
Academic/Career Areas: Architecture; Art History; Arts; Historic Preservation and Conservation; History; Home Economics; Interior Design; Landscape Architecture; Literature/English/Writing; Museum Studies; Travel/Tourism.
Eligibility Requirements: Applicant must be studying in Delaware.
Application Requirements: Application, essay, references.
Deadline: January 15.
E-mail: gtbug@udel.edu
Phone: 302-888-4640 **Fax:** 302-888-4870
Contact: Gretchen Buggeln
Winterthur Museum, Garden, and Library
Advanced Studies Office
Winterthur, DE 19735

AREA/ETHNIC STUDIES

▼ ARCHAEOLOGICAL INSTITUTE OF AMERICA AND THE AMERICAN FRIENDS OF APHRODISIAS

Archaeological Institute of America/Kenan T. Erim Award • 323

One award for Ph.D. candidates or holders of the Ph.D. to assist with research relating to the site of ancient Aphrodisias. One-time a cash award of $4000.
Academic/Career Areas: Area/Ethnic Studies; Arts; Humanities; Social Sciences.
Award: Grant for use in graduate years; not renewable. *Number:* 1. *Amount:* $4000.
Application Requirements: Application, references, transcript.
Deadline: November 1.
E-mail: aia@bu.edu
Phone: 617-353-9361 **Fax:** 617-353-6550
Contact: Mark Meister, Executive Director
Archaeological Institute of America and the American Friends of Aphrodisias
656 Beacon Street, 4th Floor
Boston, MA 02215-2010

▼ ARMENIAN PROFESSIONAL SOCIETY OF THE BAY AREA

Armenian Professional Society of the Bay Area Scholarships • 324

One-time award for full-time college juniors or seniors, or teachers of Armenian subjects studying on a part-time basis. Must have 3.2 GPA and substantial involvement in Armenian affairs. Include resume, program of study, transcript, two letters of recommendation, and evidence of Armenian community affairs.

Academic/Career Areas: Area/Ethnic Studies; Education; Filmmaking; Journalism; Literature/English/Writing; Performing Arts; Social Sciences.

Award: Scholarship for use in junior, senior, or graduate years; not renewable.

Eligibility Requirements: Applicant must be enrolled at a four-year institution.

Application Requirements: Application, references, transcript.

Deadline: November 15.

Contact: Armenian Professional Society of the Bay
Area
839 Marina Boulevard
San Francisco, CA 94123

▼ ASSOCIATION TO UNITE THE DEMOCRACIES

Mayme and Herbert Frank Educational Fund • 325

Renewable award of $500-$2000 for graduate scholars interested in federalism to pursue the study of federalism and international integration. Must provide thesis, evidence of relevant course work, and/or independent project research. Deadlines are April 1 for fall term and October 1 for spring term.

Academic/Career Areas: Area/Ethnic Studies; Political Science.

Award: Grant for use in graduate years; renewable. *Number:* 1–8. *Amount:* $500–$2000.

Application Requirements: Application, essay, transcript.

E-mail: atunite@aol.com

Phone: 202-544-5150 **Fax:** 202-544-3742

World Wide Web: http://msx4.pha.jhu.edu/aud.html

Contact: Virginie Klon, Office Manager
Association to Unite the Democracies
1506 Pennsylvania Avenue, SE
Washington, DC 20003-3116

▼ CANADIAN FOUNDATION FOR THE STUDY OF INFANT DEATHS

Dr. Sydney Segal Research Grants *see number 275*

▼ CANADIAN INSTITUTE OF UKRANIAN STUDIES—PETER JACYK CENTRE FOR UKRANIAN HISTORICAL RESEARCH

Neporany Research Teaching Fellowship • 326

One-time award for Ph.D. holders, or those with equivalent professional achievement, in Ukrainian Studies to conduct research which will enable candidate to teach a course related to the specialty. Include research proposal, recommendation letters, letter of support from host institution, and information on course to be taught.

Academic/Career Areas: Area/Ethnic Studies; Social Sciences.

Application Requirements: Application, references. **Deadline:** March 1.

Phone: 403-492-2972 **Fax:** 403-492-4967

Contact: Olia Britts
Canadian Institute of Ukranian Studies—
Peter Jacyk Centre for Ukranian
Historical Research
352 Athabasca Hall
Edmonton, AB T6G 2E8
Canada

▼ CENTER FOR FIELD RESEARCH

Center for Field Research Grants for Field Research *see number 294*

▼ CENTER FOR HELLENIC STUDIES

Center for Hellenic Studies Fellowships • 327

One-time fellowships for postdoctoral scholars of ancient Greek studies. Contact the Center for Hellenic Studies for more information and deadline. Ten awards of $18,000.

Academic/Career Areas: Area/Ethnic Studies; Humanities; Social Sciences.

Application Requirements: Application.

Contact: Fellowship Director
Center for Hellenic Studies
3100 Whitehaven Street, NW
Washington, DC 20008

▼ DUMBARTON OAKS

Bliss Prize Fellowship in Byzantine Studies • 328

Renewable award for college graduate or graduating senior from a U.S. or Canadian college or university to pursue graduate studies in Byzantine civilization and culture. Must be graduate school applicant. Must have completed one year of ancient or medieval Greek and be nominated by scholastic adviser by October 15. Fellowship covers graduate school tuition and living expenses for two years. Additional $5000 available for summer travel. Submit writing sample, application letter, and personal and scholarly data. Contact for further details.

Academic/Career Areas: Area/Ethnic Studies; Art History; Arts; History; Humanities.
Application Requirements: Application, references, transcript.
Deadline: November 1.
Contact: Office of the Director
Dumbarton Oaks
1703 32nd Street, NW
Washington, DC 20007

▼ HARRY FRANK GUGGENHEIM FOUNDATION

H. F. Guggenheim Foundation Research Grants • 329

One-time postdoctoral grants for research related to dominance, aggression, and violence. Graduate students are not eligible. Grants are not awarded in the spring. Contact for further information.

Academic/Career Areas: Area/Ethnic Studies; Biology; Criminal Justice/Criminology; Health and Medical Sciences; History; Humanities; Peace and Conflict Studies; Physical Sciences and Math; Political Science; Social Sciences.
Award: Grant for use in postdoctoral years; not renewable. *Number:* 15–30. *Amount:* $15,000–$30,000.
Application Requirements: Application, references. **Deadline:** August 1.
Phone: 212-644-4907 **Fax:** 212-644-5110
World Wide Web: http://www.hfg.org
Contact: Harry Frank Guggenheim Foundation
527 Madison Avenue, 15th Floor
New York, NY 10222-4304

▼ IRISH-AMERICAN CULTURAL INSTITUTE

Irish Research Funds • 330

One-time award for research which has an Irish-American theme in any discipline of humanities and social science. Primary research preferred but will fund such projects as museum exhibits, curriculum development, and the compilation of bibliographies. Submit proposal.

Academic/Career Areas: Area/Ethnic Studies; Humanities; Social Sciences.
Award: Grant for use in graduate years; not renewable. *Number:* 1–10. *Amount:* $1000–$5000.
Application Requirements: Application. **Deadline:** October 1.
E-mail: irishwaynj@aol.com
Phone: 973-605-1991 **Fax:** 973-605-8875
Contact: Katie Finn, Irish Research Funds Coordinator
Irish-American Cultural Institute
1 Lackawanna Place
Morristown, NJ 07960

▼ JACOB RADER MARCUS CENTER OF THE AMERICAN JEWISH ARCHIVES

American Jewish Archives Fellowships • 331

One-time award for doctoral and postdoctoral scholars interested in pursuing American Jewish studies at the American Jewish Archives in Cincinnati, Ohio. Application deadline of April 1; write for details.

Academic/Career Areas: Area/Ethnic Studies.
Eligibility Requirements: Applicant must be studying in Ohio.
Application Requirements: Application. **Deadline:** April 1.
Phone: 513-221-1875 **Fax:** 513-221-7812
Contact: Director
Jacob Rader Marcus Center of the American Jewish Archives
3101 Clifton Avenue
Cincinnati, OH 45220-2488

▼ JAPAN FOUNDATION

Japan Foundation Cultural Properties Specialist Fellowship see number 310

▼ PHI BETA KAPPA SOCIETY

Mary Isabel Sibley Fellowship for Greek and French Studies • 332

Awarded alternately in the fields of Greek and French. Must be used for the study of Greek language, literature,

history, or archaeology; or of French language and literature. Must be single female age 25-35 in post-doctoral study program. Submit project description.
Academic/Career Areas: Area/Ethnic Studies; Art History; Arts; Foreign Language; History; Humanities; Literature/English/Writing; Religion/Theology; Social Sciences.
Eligibility Requirements: Applicant must be ages 25-35; single female and must have an interest in French language or Greek language.
Application Requirements: Application, references, transcript. **Deadline:** January 15.
E-mail: lsurles@pbk.org
Phone: 202-265-3808 **Fax:** 202-986-1601
World Wide Web: http://www.pbk.org
Contact: Linda Surles, Program Officer
Phi Beta Kappa Society
1811 Q Street, NW
Washington, DC 20009-1696

▼ SOCIETY FARSAROTUL

Society Farsarotul Financial Awards • 333

Must have at least one Arumanian parent or grandparent. Must be at least a college junior with minimum 3.0 GPA. Submit written request and three references. Undergraduate applicants must be members of Society Farsarotul. Must study an area concerned with Arumanian heritage.
Academic/Career Areas: Area/Ethnic Studies; Foreign Language; Humanities.
Award: Scholarship for use in junior, senior, or graduate years; not renewable. *Number:* 2. *Amount:* $1000.
Eligibility Requirements: Applicant must be Arumanian/Ulacedo-Romanian and enrolled at a four-year institution.
Application Requirements: Application, essay, references, transcript. **Deadline:** February 1.
Contact: Society Farsarotul
799 Silver Lane
PO Box 753
Trumbull, CT 06611

▼ UNITED STATES DEPARTMENT OF HOUSING AND URBAN DEVELOPMENT, OFFICE OF POLICY DEVELOPMENT AND RESEARCH

Doctoral Dissertation Research Grant (HUD) • 334

Grant is limited to Ph.D. candidates whose dissertation topic is on a HUD-related subject. Applicants must have completed all degree requirements except the dissertation. One-time award. Must submit letters from school and adviser and a statement of qualifications and experience.
Academic/Career Areas: Area/Ethnic Studies; Economics; Legal Services; Political Science; Social Sciences; Social Services.
Award: Grant for use in graduate years; not renewable. *Number:* 15. *Amount:* $15,000.
Application Requirements: Application, essay. **Deadline:** January 15.
World Wide Web: http://oup.aspensys.com
Contact: Ms. Virginia Der
United States Department of Housing and Urban Development, Office of Policy Development and Research
451 7th Street SW, Room 8230
Washington, DC 20410

ART HISTORY

▼ ASIAN CULTURAL COUNCIL

Ford Foundation Fellowships • 335

One-time award for graduate support to Asian individuals for training, travel, and research in the U.S. Individuals must be engaged in the documentation and preservation of Asian traditional arts. Write for more information.
Academic/Career Areas: Art History; Arts; Filmmaking; Historic Preservation and Conservation; Museum Studies; Performing Arts.
Eligibility Requirements: Applicant must be Asian.
Application Requirements: Application. **Deadline:** Continuous.
E-mail: acc@accny.org **Fax:** 212-315-0996
Contact: Ralph Samuelson, Director
Asian Cultural Council
1290 Avenue of the Americas, Room 3450
New York, NY 10104

▼ CENTER FOR FIELD RESEARCH

Center for Field Research Grants for Field Research — see number 294

▼ DUMBARTON OAKS

Bliss Prize Fellowship in Byzantine Studies — see number 328

▼ GETTY GRANT PROGRAM

J. Paul Getty Postdoctoral Fellowships in the
History of Art and the Humanities • 336

One-time award for outstanding scholars who have earned a doctoral degree (or the equivalent in countries outside the U.S.) within the past six years and who are undertaking interpretive research projects that promise to make a substantial contribution to the understanding of art and its history. Fellowships are awarded once a year and generally support a research period of twelve months. Award may be used wherever necessary to complete project.
Academic/Career Areas: Art History.
Eligibility Requirements: Applicant must be enrolled at a four-year institution.
Application Requirements: Application, references. **Deadline:** November 1.
Phone: 310-440-7320 **Fax:** 310-440-7703
World Wide Web: http://www.getty.edu/grant
Contact: Joan Weinstein, Program Officer
Getty Grant Program
1200 Getty Center Drive, Suite 800
Los Angeles, CA 90049-1685

▼ HAGLEY MUSEUM AND LIBRARY

Hagley Museum and Library
Grants-in-Aid see number 308

Henry Belin du Pont Dissertation
Fellowship see number 309

▼ NATIONAL GALLERY OF ART

Center for Advanced Study in the Visual Arts
Senior Fellowship Program see number 311

▼ NATIONAL GALLERY OF ART, CENTER FOR ADVANCED STUDY IN THE VISUAL ARTS

Robert H. and Clarice Smith
Fellowship see number 312

▼ PHI BETA KAPPA SOCIETY

Mary Isabel Sibley Fellowship for Greek and
French Studies see number 332

▼ SAMUEL H. KRESS FOUNDATION

Kress Travel Fellowships • 337

One-time award for predoctoral candidates to travel to view materials essential for the completion of dissertation research. Must be nominated by art history department. Several fellowships of up to $10,000.
Academic/Career Areas: Art History.
Application Requirements: Application, references, transcript.
Deadline: November 30.
Contact: Samuel H. Kress Foundation
174 East 80th Street
New York, NY 10021

▼ SOCIETY OF ARCHITECTURAL HISTORIANS

Architectural Study Tour
Scholarship see number 317

Edilia and Francois-Auguste de Montequin
Fellowship in Iberian and Latin American
Architecture see number 318

Keepers Preservation Education Fund
Fellowship see number 319

Rosann S. Berry Annual Meeting
Fellowship see number 320

▼ WINTERTHUR MUSEUM, GARDEN, AND LIBRARY

NEH Fellowships see number 321

Winterthur Research Fellowships see number 322

ARTS

▼ ARCHAEOLOGICAL INSTITUTE OF AMERICA AND THE AMERICAN FRIENDS OF APHRODISIAS

Archaeological Institute of America/Kenan T.
Erim Award see number 323

▼ ASIAN CULTURAL COUNCIL

Ford Foundation Fellowships   *see number 335*

▼ DUMBARTON OAKS

Bliss Prize Fellowship in Byzantine Studies   *see number 328*

▼ HAGLEY MUSEUM AND LIBRARY

Hagley Museum and Library Grants-in-Aid   *see number 308*

Henry Belin du Pont Dissertation Fellowship   *see number 309*

▼ JAPANESE AMERICAN CITIZENS LEAGUE

Henry and Chiyo Kuwahara Creative Arts Scholarship   • 338

One-time award to encourage creative arts projects that reflect the Japanese-American experience and culture. All technical work of the applicant should be college level. Community service considered. Professional artists ineligible. Submit relevant materials. Send self-addressed stamped envelope for application, specifying application category.
Academic/Career Areas: Arts.
Award: Scholarship for use in freshman, sophomore, junior, senior, or graduate years; not renewable. *Number:* 1. *Amount:* $5000.
Eligibility Requirements: Applicant must be member of Japanese-American Citizens League.
Application Requirements: Application, essay, references, transcript. **Deadline:** April 1.
E-mail: jacl@jacl.org
Phone: 415-921-5225 **Fax:** 415-931-4671
Contact: Scholarship Administrator
Japanese American Citizens League
1765 Sutter Street
San Francisco, CA 94115

▼ LESLIE T. AND FRANCIS U. POSEY FOUNDATION

Posey Foundation Graduate Art Scholarship   • 339

Must have bachelor's degree and be full-time graduate student majoring in painting or sculpture of "traditional kind" at school known for teaching this method. Submit ten to fifteen slides of work done in last two years, photo of best work, three essays, and personal photo (optional).
Academic/Career Areas: Arts.
Award: Scholarship for use in graduate years; not renewable. *Amount:* $1000–$4000.
Application Requirements: Application, essay, photo, references, transcript. **Deadline:** March 1.
Phone: 941-957-0442 **Fax:** 941-957-3135
Contact: Cathy Earl
Leslie T. and Francis U. Posey Foundation
1800 Second Street, Suite 905
Sarasota, FL 34236

▼ MEMORIAL FOUNDATION FOR JEWISH CULTURE

International Fellowships in Jewish Culture Program   • 340

Fellowship awarded to individuals for pursuing independent work in Jewish literature, Jewish scholarship, or Jewish art. Number of fellowships awarded varies by year. Request application in writing with a short description of the proposed project. Application deadline is January 31.
Academic/Career Areas: Arts; Literature/English/Writing; Religion/Theology.
Application Requirements: Application, photo, references.
Deadline: January 31.
Phone: 212-679-4074
Contact: Lorraine Blass, Associate Director
Memorial Foundation for Jewish Culture
15 East 26th Street, Room 1703
New York, NY 10010

▼ PHI BETA KAPPA SOCIETY

Mary Isabel Sibley Fellowship for Greek and French Studies   *see number 332*

▼ POLLOCK-KRASNER FOUNDATION, INC.

Pollock-Krasner Grants   • 341

One-time award for professional artists for personal and art-related expenses. Specifically available to visual artists. Selection is based upon artistic merit, professional record, and financial need. Submit resume and slides with application.
Academic/Career Areas: Arts.

Pollock-Krasner Grants (continued)

Award: Grant for use in graduate years; not renewable. *Amount:* $5000–$30,000.
Eligibility Requirements: Applicant must have employment experience in experience in career field.
Application Requirements: Application, financial need analysis. **Deadline:** Continuous.
E-mail: grants@pkf.org
Phone: 212-517-5400 **Fax:** 212-288-2836
World Wide Web: http://www.pkf.org
Contact: Caroline Black, Program Officer
Pollock-Krasner Foundation, Inc.
863 Park Avenue
New York, NY 10021

▼ PRINCESS GRACE AWARDS

Dance, Theater, Film, and Playwright Grants • 342

One-time award for young aspiring artists. Scholarships for college seniors or graduate students; fellowships to artists who have been in a dance or theater company for less than five years. Invited schools may nominate one candidate. Deadlines: theater/playwright, March 31; dance, April 30; film, June 1. Submit photo, work samples/tapes, videos.
Academic/Career Areas: Arts; Filmmaking; Performing Arts.
Award: Scholarship for use in senior or graduate years; not renewable. *Number:* 15–20. *Amount:* $3000–$15,000.
Eligibility Requirements: Applicant must be enrolled at a four-year institution and must have an interest in art, photography/photogrammetry/filmmaking, or writing.
Application Requirements: Application, autobiography, essay, portfolio, references, self-addressed stamped envelope.
E-mail: pgfusa@pgfusa.com
Phone: 212-317-1470 **Fax:** 212-317-1473
World Wide Web: http://www.pgfusa.com
Contact: Toby E. Boshak, Executive Director
Princess Grace Awards
105 East 58th Street, 21st Floor
New York, NY 10155

▼ SAMUEL H. KRESS FOUNDATION

Fellowships for Advanced Training in Fine Arts Conservation • 343

Ten one-time fellowships of $25,000 each for those with a master's degree in art conservation. To be used for advanced hands-on training rather than for completion of a degree. Applications must be submitted by museum or conservation research institution.
Academic/Career Areas: Arts.
Application Requirements: Application, essay, references, transcript. **Deadline:** February 28.
Contact: Samuel H. Kress Foundation
174 East 80th Street
New York, NY 10021

▼ WINTERTHUR MUSEUM, GARDEN, AND LIBRARY

NEH Fellowships   *see number 321*

Winterthur Research Fellowships   *see number 322*

AVIATION/AEROSPACE

▼ RTCA, INC.

William E. Jackson Award • 344

Award available for graduate study. Applicant must submit a thesis, project report, or technical journal on aviation, aviation electronics, or telecommunications (as related to aviation). One-time award.
Academic/Career Areas: Aviation/Aerospace; Communications; Engineering/Technology.
Award: Prize for use in graduate years; not renewable. *Number:* 1. *Amount:* $2000.
Eligibility Requirements: Applicant must be enrolled at a four-year institution.
Application Requirements: Applicant must enter a contest, autobiography, essay, references. **Deadline:** June 30.
E-mail: hmoses@rtca.org
Phone: 202-833-9339 **Fax:** 202-833-9434
World Wide Web: http://www.rtca.org
Contact: Harold E. Moses, Program Director
RTCA, Inc.
1140 Connecticut Avenue, NW, Suite 1020
Washington, DC 20036

▼ SMITHSONIAN INSTITUTION NATIONAL AIR AND SPACE MUSEUM

Guggenheim Fellowship   *see number 300*

▼ VERTICAL FLIGHT FOUNDATION

Vertical Flight Foundation Scholarship • **345**

This award is available for undergraduate and graduate study in aerospace, electrical, or mechanical engineering. Undergraduates must be in junior or senior year. Applicants must have an interest in vertical flight technology. One-time award of $1000-$2000.

Academic/Career Areas: Aviation/Aerospace; Electrical/Electronic Engineering; Mechanical Engineering.

Award: Scholarship for use in junior, senior, or graduate years; not renewable. *Number:* 10–12. *Amount:* $1000–$2000.

Eligibility Requirements: Applicant must be enrolled at a four-year institution.

Application Requirements: Application, essay, references, transcript. **Deadline:** February 1.

E-mail: ahs703@aol.com

Phone: 703-684-6777 **Fax:** 703-739-9279

World Wide Web: http://www.vtol.org

Contact: Enid A. Nichols, Office Manager
Vertical Flight Foundation
217 North Washington Street
Alexandria, VA 22314

BIOLOGY

▼ AMERICAN GEOPHYSICAL UNION

American Geophysical Union Horton Research Grant   **see number 284**

▼ AMERICAN ORCHID SOCIETY

American Orchid Society/Orchid Research Grant • **346**

Grant for graduate study in orchid research. Must submit research proposal with application. Deadlines are January 1 and August 1. Must be qualified research personnel at accredited institution or graduate student.

Academic/Career Areas: Biology; Horticulture/Floriculture.

Award: Grant for use in graduate years; renewable. *Amount:* $500–$12,000.

Application Requirements: Application, financial need analysis, references.

Phone: 561-585-8666 **Fax:** 561-585-0654

Contact: Ned Nash, Director of Education and Conservation
American Orchid Society
6000 South Olive Avenue
West Palm Beach, FL 33405

▼ AMERICAN PHYSIOLOGICAL SOCIETY

American Physiological Society Conference Student Awards • **347**

Award for outstanding abstract presentation given to graduate students who are first author of paper presented at any American Physiological Society conference. Check box on abstract paper to be considered for award. Application fee: $30.

Academic/Career Areas: Biology; Health and Medical Sciences.

Award: Prize for use in graduate years; not renewable. *Number:* 4–8. *Amount:* $500.

Eligibility Requirements: Applicant must be enrolled at a four-year institution.

Application Requirements: Application, applicant must enter a contest. **Fee:** $30. **Deadline:** Continuous.

E-mail: mmatyas@aps.faseb.org

Phone: 301-530-7132 **Fax:** 301-571-8305

World Wide Web: http://www.faseb.org/aps

Contact: Dr. Marsha Matyas, Education Officer
American Physiological Society
9650 Rockville Pike
Bethesda, MD 20814-3991

▼ AMERICAN SOCIETY OF MICROBIOLOGY & NATIONAL CENTER FOR INFECTIOUS DISEASES

American Society of Microbiology & National Center for Infectious Diseases Post Doctoral Research Associates Program • **348**

Award for persons who earned doctorate degree or completed a primary residency after May, 1995. For full-time research on infectious diseases which cause public health problems. Preference given to U.S. citizen or permanent residents. One-time award of $30,800-$32,300.

Academic/Career Areas: Biology; Health and Medical Sciences.

Application Requirements: Application, essay, references, transcript. **Deadline:** December 1.

American Society of Microbiology & National Center for Infectious Diseases Post Doctoral Research Associates Program (continued)

E-mail: ihulede@asmusa.org
Phone: 202-942-9295 **Fax:** 202-942-9329
World Wide Web: http://www.asmusa.org/edusic/edu23e. htm
Contact: Irene Hulede
American Society of Microbiology &
National Center for Infectious Diseases
1325 Massachusetts Avenue, NW
Washington, DC 20005

▼ AMERICAN WATER WORKS ASSOCIATION

American Water Works Association/Abel Wolman Fellowship see number 286

American Water Works Association/Holly A. Cornell Scholarship see number 287

American Water Works Association/Larson Aquatic Research Support Scholarship see number 288

American Water Works Association/Thomas R. Camp Memorial Scholarship see number 289

▼ ARCTIC INSTITUTE OF NORTH AMERICA

Jennifer Robinson Scholarship • 349

One award for graduate student majoring in biology with concentration on North American issues. Must submit statement of research objectives, curriculum vitae, references, and current funding information. One-time award of $5000.
Academic/Career Areas: Biology.
Award: Scholarship for use in graduate years; not renewable. *Number:* 1. *Amount:* $5000.
Eligibility Requirements: Applicant must have employment experience in experience in career field.
Application Requirements: Application, references, transcript.
Deadline: May 1.
Phone: 403-220-7515 **Fax:** 403-282-4609

Contact: Mr. Michael Robinson, Executive Director
Arctic Institute of North America
University of Calgary
2500 University Drive, NW
Calgary, AB T2N 1N4
Canada

▼ ASSOCIATION FOR WOMEN IN SCIENCE EDUCATIONAL FOUNDATION

Ruth Satter Memorial Award • 350

Award for women pursuing a Ph.D. in math or science, including social science, biology, chemical engineering, and earth science, at an accredited college or university. Deadlines vary. Write for application. One-time award of $500-$1000.
Academic/Career Areas: Biology; Chemical Engineering; Earth Science; Physical Sciences and Math; Social Sciences.
Award: Scholarship for use in graduate years; not renewable. *Amount:* $500–$1000.
Eligibility Requirements: Applicant must be female.
Application Requirements: Application.
E-mail: awis@awis.org
Phone: 800-886-AWIS **Fax:** 202-326-8960
World Wide Web: http://www.awis.org
Contact: Association for Women in Science
Educational Foundation
1200 New York Avenue NW, 6th Floor
Washington, DC 20005

▼ BURROUGHS WELLCOME FUND

Wellcome Research Travel Grants for United Kingdom Citizens • 351

One-time travel grants for established researchers from the U.K. and Ireland to visit the U.S. and Canada for periods of two weeks to six months. Must be full-time researcher, with doctoral degree, in the biomedical sciences or history of medicine or science. Provides travel and subsistence for researchers to engage in collaborative projects or learn new research techniques. Deadlines: March 1, July 1, November 1.
Academic/Career Areas: Biology; Health and Medical Sciences.
Award: Grant for use in postdoctoral years; not renewable. *Number:* up to 45. *Amount:* $1000–$15,000.
Eligibility Requirements: Applicant must be English or Irish and have employment experience in experience in career field.

Application Requirements: Application.
World Wide Web: http://www.bwfund.org/bwfund/
Contact: Burroughs Wellcome Fund
183 Euston Road
London NW 2BE
England

▼ CAMPUS SAFETY DIVISION
Campus Safety Scholarship   see number 293

▼ CENTER FOR FIELD RESEARCH
Center for Field Research Grants for Field Research   see number 294

▼ COOLEY'S ANEMIA FOUNDATION, INC.
Cooley's Anemia Foundation Research Fellowship   • 352
One-time award for fellows and junior faculty members to provide research support to those studying Cooley's anemia. Must submit letters from sponsors, detailed research proposal, research support, and hypothesis to be tested. See application for details.
Academic/Career Areas: Biology; Health and Medical Sciences.
Eligibility Requirements: Applicant must be age 20.
Application Requirements: Application, autobiography, references. **Deadline:** March 9.
E-mail: ncaf@aol.com
Phone: 718-321-2873 **Fax:** 718-321-3340
World Wide Web: http://www.thalassemia.org
Contact: Pia LeVasseur, Special Projects
Cooley's Anemia Foundation, Inc.
129-09 26th Avenue, Suite 203
Flushing, NY 11354

▼ CYSTIC FIBROSIS FOUNDATION
Cystic Fibrosis Foundation Student Traineeships   • 353
Traineeship for college seniors and graduate students. Number of awards varies. Must be student in or about to enter a doctoral program. Applicant must work with a faculty sponsor on a research project related to cystic fibrosis. One-time $1500 award, of which $1200 is stipend and $300 is for laboratory expenses.
Academic/Career Areas: Biology; Health and Medical Sciences.

Award: Scholarship for use in senior or graduate years; not renewable. *Amount:* $1500.
Eligibility Requirements: Applicant must be enrolled at a four-year institution.
Application Requirements: Application. **Deadline:** Continuous.
E-mail: kcurley@cff.org
Phone: 301-951-4422 **Fax:** 301-951-6378
World Wide Web: http://www.cff.org
Contact: Kathleen Curley, Office of Grants Management
Cystic Fibrosis Foundation
6931 Arlington Road
Bethesda, MD 20814

▼ EASTER SEAL RESEARCH INSTITUTE
Elizabeth St. Louis Award   • 354
Award for best eligible graduate student research proposal in area of development and/or testing of assistive or prosthetic devices for physically disabled children. Must submit resume and letters from student and student's supervisor describing research to be undertaken. Deadline: April 15.
Academic/Career Areas: Biology; Health and Medical Sciences; Health Information Management/Technology; Nursing; Special Education; Therapy/Rehabilitation.
Award: Prize for use in graduate years; not renewable. *Number:* 1.
Application Requirements: Application, applicant must enter a contest, photo, references, transcript. **Deadline:** April 15.
E-mail: amichie@easterseals.org
Phone: 416-421-8377 **Fax:** 416-696-1035
Contact: Anne Michie, Executive Director
Easter Seal Research Institute
1185 Eglinton Avenue East
Suite 706
North York, ON M3C 3C6
Canada

▼ EDMUND NILES HUYCK PRESERVE AND BIOLOGICAL RESEARCH STATION
Huyck Station Research Grants   • 355
Renewable grant for graduate students to pursue research on the ecology, evolution, natural history, and conservation biology of the flora and fauna at the Huyck Preserve and its vicinity. Write for more information.
Academic/Career Areas: Biology.

Huyck Station Research Grants (continued)

Award: Grant for use in graduate years; renewable. *Number:* 8–12. *Amount:* up to $2500.
Eligibility Requirements: Applicant must be studying in New York.
Application Requirements: Application, references. **Deadline:** February 1.
E-mail: rlwyman@capital.net
Phone: 518-797-3440 **Fax:** 518-797-3440
Contact: Richard L. Wyman, Executive Director
Edmund Niles Huyck Preserve and
Biological Research Station
PO Box 189
Rennselaerville, NY 12147

▼ ENTOMOLOGICAL SOCIETY OF AMERICA

John Henry Comstock Graduate Student Award • 356

Must be pursuing graduate degree with a concentration in entomology or have acquired a degree within twelve months of application. Must have applied for society membership prior to January 1. Submit photo and documentation.
Academic/Career Areas: Biology.
Award: Prize for use in graduate years; not renewable. *Number:* 5. *Amount:* $100.
Eligibility Requirements: Applicant must be member of Entomological Society of America.
Application Requirements: Application, photo. **Deadline:** September 1.
E-mail: esa@entsoc.org
Phone: 301-731-4535 **Fax:** 301-731-4538
World Wide Web: http://www.entsoc.org
Contact: Entomological Society of America
9301 Annapolis Road
Lanham, MD 20706-3115

▼ FOUNDATION FOR SCIENCE AND DISABILITY

Foundation for Science and Disability-Student Grant see number 297

▼ HARRY FRANK GUGGENHEIM FOUNDATION

H. F. Guggenheim Foundation Research Grants see number 329

▼ HOWARD HUGHES MEDICAL INSTITUTE

Howard Hughes Medical Institute Postdoctoral Research Fellowships for Physicians • 357

Three-year fellowship for physicians doing postdoctoral training research on basic biological processes and disease mechanisms. By the beginning of fellowship, must have at least two years of postgraduate clinical training, no more than two years of postdoctoral research, and may not have faculty appointment. Provides stipend and research allowance. Submit research plan and mentor's endorsement.
Academic/Career Areas: Biology; Health and Medical Sciences.
Eligibility Requirements: Applicant must have employment experience in experience in career field.
Application Requirements: Application, references, transcript.
Deadline: December 4.
E-mail: fellows@hhmi.org
Phone: 301-215-8889 **Fax:** 301-215-8888
World Wide Web: http://www.hhmi.org
Contact: Office of Grants/Special Programs
Howard Hughes Medical Institute
Office of Grants and Special Programs
4000 Jones Bridge Road
Chevy Chase, MD 20815-6789

Howard Hughes Medical Institute Predoctoral Fellowships in Biological Sciences • 358

Five-year fellowship for full-time study towards a Ph.D. in cell biology, genetics, immunology, neuroscience, structural biology, and other eligible biology fields. College seniors and first-year graduate students may apply. Award provides annual stipend and cost-of-education allowance. Submit plan of study and notification of prior research experience.
Academic/Career Areas: Biology; Health and Medical Sciences.
Application Requirements: Application, essay, references, test scores, transcript. **Deadline:** November 15.
E-mail: fellows@hhmi.org
Phone: 202-334-2872 **Fax:** 202-334-3419
World Wide Web: http://www.hhmi.org
Contact: Office of Grants/Special Programs
Howard Hughes Medical Institute
Office of Grants and Special Programs
4000 Jones Bridge Road
Chevy Chase, MD 20815-6789

Howard Hughes Medical Institute Research Training Fellowships for Medical Students • 359

One-year fellowship for medical students in the U.S. to conduct full-time fundamental research on basic biological processes or disease mechanisms. Applicants may not be in a Ph.D. program. Provides stipend and research allowance. Continued fellowships awarded for second year of research or completion of medical studies. Submit research plan and mentor's endorsement.

Academic/Career Areas: Biology; Health and Medical Sciences.
Application Requirements: Application, references, test scores, transcript. **Deadline:** December 2.
E-mail: fellows@hhmi.org
Phone: 301-215-8889 **Fax:** 301-215-8888
World Wide Web: http://www.hhmi.org
Contact: Office of Grants/Special Programs
Howard Hughes Medical Institute
Office of Grants and Special Programs
4000 Jones Bridge Road
Chevy Chase, MD 20815-6789

▼ HUDSON RIVER NATIONAL ESTUARINE RESEARCH RESERVE— NEW YORK STATE DEPARTMENT OF ENVIRONMENTAL CONSERVATION AND THE HUDSON RIVER FOUNDATION

Tibor T. Polgar Fellowship • 360

Award for the support of graduate and undergraduate research projects concerning the Hudson River. Applicant may attend a two-year or four-year institution. Submit research proposal. One-time award of $3500. Contact for deadlines.

Academic/Career Areas: Biology; Earth Science; Physical Sciences and Math.
Eligibility Requirements: Applicant must be enrolled at a two-year or four-year institution.
E-mail: cnieder@ocean.nos.noaa.gov
Phone: 914-758-7010 **Fax:** 914-758-7033
Contact: Chuck Nieder, Research Coordinator
Hudson River National Estuarine Research Reserve—New York State Department of Environmental Conservation and The Hudson River Foundation
Bard College Field Station
Annandale, NY 12504

▼ HUMAN GROWTH FOUNDATION

Human Growth Foundation Small Grants • 361

One-time postdoctoral award for young investigators to conduct research in human growth and growth disorders, particularly chondrodystrophies, metabolic disorders, and psycho-social issues. Submit letter of intent. Write for more details.

Academic/Career Areas: Biology; Health and Medical Sciences.
Award: Grant for use in postdoctoral years; not renewable. *Number:* 1–4. *Amount:* $7500–$10,000.
Application Requirements: Application. **Deadline:** July 1.
E-mail: hgfound@erols.com
Phone: 703-883-1773 **Fax:** 703-883-1776
World Wide Web: http://www.medhelp.org/web/hgf.htm
Contact: Kimberly Frye, Executive Director
Human Growth Foundation
7777 Leesburg Pike, Suite 202S
Falls Church, VA 22043

▼ INTERNATIONAL DESALINATION ASSOCIATION

International Desalination Association Scholarship see number 298

▼ INTERNATIONAL WOMEN'S FISHING ASSOCIATION SCHOLARSHIP TRUST

International Women's Fishing Association Graduate Scholarships in the Marine Sciences see number 276

▼ L.S.B. LEAKEY FOUNDATION

L.S.B. Leakey Foundation General Research Grants see number 277

Leakey Foundation Fellowship for Great Ape Research and Conservation see number 278

Leakey Foundation Study of Foraging Peoples Fellowship see number 279

▼ LALOR FOUNDATION

Lalor Foundation Post-Doctoral Grants • 362

One-time grants for institutions to conduct basic post-doctoral research in mammalian reproductive biology, as related to the regulation of fertility. Applicant institution may name an individual grant recipient to conduct research; this person must have Ph.D. or M.D.-related training and experience. See application for details.
Academic/Career Areas: Biology; Health and Medical Sciences.
Award: Grant for use in postdoctoral years; not renewable. *Number:* 15–20. *Amount:* $10,000–$25,000.
Application Requirements: Application, references. **Deadline:** January 15.
Phone: 401-272-1973
Contact: Cynthia Patterson, Director
Lalor Foundation
PO Box 2493
Providence, RI 02906

▼ MYASTHENIA GRAVIS FOUNDATION OF AMERICA, INC.

Kermit Osserman Fellowship • 363

One-time postdoctoral award for investigators to pursue the treatment, etiology, and/or cure of myasthenia gravis. Submit autobiography and references. Write for further details.
Academic/Career Areas: Biology; Health and Medical Sciences; Physical Sciences and Math.
Application Requirements: Autobiography, references.
Deadline: November 1.
E-mail: mgfa@aol.com
Phone: 312-258-0522 **Fax:** 312-258-0461
World Wide Web: http://www.med.unc.edu/wrkunits/2depts/neurolog/mgfa/mgf-home.htm
Contact: Edward S. Trainer, Executive Director
Myasthenia Gravis Foundation of America, Inc.
222 South Riverside Plaza, Suite 1540
Chicago, IL 60606

▼ NATIONAL INSTITUTES OF HEALTH

Fogarty International Center International Research Fellowship • 364

Award for applicants who have earned a doctoral degree or the equivalent in a health science field within 10 years of application date. Provides opportunity for postdoctoral biomedical or behavioral scientists to extend research experience in laboratory in U.S. Must not be a U.S. citizen or permanent resident. Must have U.S. sponsor. Write for further details. Deadlines: July 1 and October 15.
Academic/Career Areas: Biology; Health and Medical Sciences; Social Sciences.
Application Requirements: Application.
World Wide Web: http://www.nih.gov
Contact: Levon Parker, Director
National Institutes of Health
9000 Rockwell Pike
Building 31, Room 8A19
Bethesda, MD 20892-7762

Fogarty International Center International Training and Research Program • 365

Award for pre- and postdoctoral and advanced research training in research related to population. Program enables NIH grant recipients to extend geographic base of research and training efforts to developing nations. Write for further information and deadlines.
Academic/Career Areas: Biology; Health and Medical Sciences; Social Sciences.
Award: Grant for use in graduate years; not renewable.
Application Requirements: Application.
World Wide Web: http://www.nih.gov
Contact: Levon Parker, Director
National Institutes of Health
9000 Rockwell Pike
Building 31, Room 8A19
Bethesda, MD 20892-7762

▼ NATIONAL RESEARCH COUNCIL

Howard Hughes Medical Institute Predoctoral Fellowship in Biological Sciences • 366

For students at or near the beginning of full-time graduate study toward a Ph.D. or Sc.D. degree in selected biological sciences. Fellowship based on academic records, plan of study, and GRE scores. Renewable for up to five years.
Academic/Career Areas: Biology.
Application Requirements: Application, essay, references, test scores, transcript. **Deadline:** November 12.
Contact: Fellowship Office
National Research Council
2101 Constitution Avenue
Washington, DC 20418

▼ NORTH AMERICAN BLUEBIRD SOCIETY

North American Bluebird Society Research Grant • 367

Research grants for graduate students or professional biologists studying bluebirds or other North American cavity-nesting birds. Must submit research proposal.
Academic/Career Areas: Biology; Natural Resources.
Award: Grant for use in graduate years; not renewable. *Number:* 4–7. *Amount:* $100–$1000.
Application Requirements: Application, autobiography.
Deadline: December 1.
E-mail: bernerkl@cobleskill.edu
Phone: 518-234-5252
Contact: Kevin Berner, Research Chairman
North American Bluebird Society
SUNY
Cobleskill, NY 12043

▼ OLFACTORY RESEARCH FUND, LTD.

Olfactory Research Fund Research Grants • 368

Research award for the advanced study of olfaction. Applicants must hold a doctorate degree and submit a research proposal including abstract, budget, and curriculum vitae of applicant and collaborators. Several awards of up to $45,000. Priority given to specific topics that change each year. Applicants should call organization or check Web site for current topic.
Academic/Career Areas: Biology; Health and Medical Sciences; Science, Technology & Society; Therapy/Rehabilitation.
Award: Grant for use in postdoctoral years; not renewable. *Number:* 1–6. *Amount:* up to $45,000.
Application Requirements: Deadline: January 15.
E-mail: olfactory@fragrance.org
Phone: 212-725-2755 **Fax:** 212-779-9058
World Wide Web: http://www.olfactory.org
Contact: Grants Director
Olfactory Research Fund, Ltd.
145 East 32nd Street, 14th Floor
New York, NY 10016-6002

▼ PARALYZED VETERANS OF AMERICA—SPINAL CORD RESEARCH FOUNDATION

Fellowships in Spinal Cord Injury Research see number 280

▼ SIGMA XI, THE SCIENTIFIC RESEARCH SOCIETY

National Academy of Science Grants-in-Aid of Research see number 281

Sigma Xi Grants-in-Aid of Research see number 271

▼ SOCIAL SCIENCE RESEARCH COUNCIL-MACARTHUR FOUNDATION

Postdoctoral Fellowships on Peace and Security in a Changing World • 369

Fellowship for those who hold a Ph.D. or equivalent. Position of Ph.D. is not required for lawyers, public servants, journalists, or others who can demonstrate competent research experience. Award supports innovative and interdisciplinary research on the implications for peace and security issues. One-time award of up to $37,500.
Academic/Career Areas: Biology; Humanities; Journalism; Legal Services; Physical Sciences and Math; Social Sciences.
Application Requirements: Application. **Deadline:** December 1.
Phone: 212-661-0280
Contact: Social Science Research Council-MacArthur Foundation
605 Third Avenue
New York, NY 10158

▼ SOCIETY FOR THE SCIENTIFIC STUDY OF SEXUALITY

Society for the Scientific Study of Sexuality Student Research Grant • 370

Award to support students doing scientific research related to sexuality. Purpose of research can be master's thesis or doctoral dissertation, but this is not a requirement. Must be enrolled in degree-granting program. Deadlines: February 1 and September 1. One-time award of $750.
Academic/Career Areas: Biology; Health and Medical Sciences; Social Sciences.
Award: Grant for use in graduate years; not renewable. *Number:* 3. *Amount:* $750.
Eligibility Requirements: Applicant must be enrolled at a four-year institution.
Application Requirements: Application, essay, references.
E-mail: thesociety@worldnet.att.net
Phone: 319-895-8407 **Fax:** 319-895-6203

Society for the Scientific Study of Sexuality Student Research Grant (continued)

Contact: Howard J. Ruppel, Executive Director
Society for the Scientific Study of Sexuality
PO Box 208
Mount Vernon, IA 52314-0208

▼ WHITAKER FOUNDATION

Doctoral Fellowship Program in Biomedical Engineering • 371

One-time award for graduate scholars pursuing careers in biomedical engineering. Must enroll in full-time programs leading to Ph.D. or Sc.D. degrees in biomedical engineering. Include transcript, test scores, and references with application. Recipients receive $32,000 per year for three years.
Academic/Career Areas: Biology; Health and Medical Sciences.
Application Requirements: Application, references, test scores, transcript. **Deadline:** December 10.
E-mail: info@whitaker.org
Phone: 703-528-2430 **Fax:** 703-528-2431
Contact: Carina S. Hreib, Grants Administrator
Whitaker Foundation
1700 North Moore Street, Suite 2200
Rosslyn, VA 22209

▼ WHITEHALL FOUNDATION, INC.

Whitehall Foundation, Inc. Grants-in-Aid see number 282

Whitehall Foundation, Inc. Research Grants see number 283

▼ WOMAN'S NATIONAL FARM AND GARDEN ASSOCIATION

Sarah Bradley Tyson Memorial Fellowships see number 272

▼ WOODS HOLE OCEANOGRAPHIC INSTITUTION

Woods Hole Oceanographic Institution Postdoctoral Fellowships • 372

One-time award for new or recent recipients of a doctoral degree in biology, molecular biology, microbiology, chemistry, engineering, geology, geophysics, mathematics, meteorology, physics, or oceanography. Scientists with more than three or four years postdoctoral experience not eligible. Award must be used at Woods Hole Oceanographic Institution.
Academic/Career Areas: Biology; Earth Science; Engineering/Technology; Meteorology/Atmospheric Science; Physical Sciences and Math.
Application Requirements: Application, essay, references, transcript. **Deadline:** January 15.
Phone: 508-289-2950 **Fax:** 508-457-2188
World Wide Web: http://www.whoi.edu
Contact: Lee Ann Campbell, Staff Assistant
Woods Hole Oceanographic Institution
Clark 223, Education Office
MS 31
Woods Hole, MA 02543

BUSINESS/CONSUMER SERVICES

▼ ACADEMY OF MARKETING SCIENCE FOUNDATION

Mary Kay Doctoral Dissertation Award • 373

One-time award for the best dissertation abstract in marketing science submitted. Must be no more than 30 double-spaced pages, including tables and figures.
Academic/Career Areas: Business/Consumer Services.
Award: Prize for use in graduate years; not renewable.
Application Requirements: Applicant must enter a contest.
Deadline: December 11.
Contact: Sharon Beatty
Academy of Marketing Science Foundation
University of Miami
PO Box 248012
Coral Gables, FL 33134-6536

▼ AMERICAN JEWISH COMMITTEE

Harold W. Rosenthal Fellowship in International Relations • 374

One-time award for college seniors or graduate students continuing education post-internship. Must intend to pursue career in international relations. Professional internship with Congress member or in State Department.
Academic/Career Areas: Business/Consumer Services; Communications; Foreign Language; History; Humanities; Political Science; Social Sciences; Trade/Technical Specialties.

Eligibility Requirements: Applicant must be studying in District of Columbia.
Application Requirements: Application, essay, interview, references, transcript. **Deadline:** February 1.
Phone: 202-785-4200 **Fax:** 202-785-4115
World Wide Web: http://www.ajc.org
Contact: Vera Lemons, Fellowship Coordinator
American Jewish Committee
1156 15th Street, NW, Suite 1201
Washington, DC 20005

▼ EDUCATIONAL TESTING SERVICE

Educational Testing Service Postdoctoral Fellowship Program • 375

One-time award of $35,000 for individual with doctorate in relevant discipline. Must submit current curriculum vitae and detailed proposal of research project. Candidate must provide evidence of prior research. Affirmative action goals considered.
Academic/Career Areas: Business/Consumer Services; Computer Science/Data Processing; Education; Social Sciences.
Eligibility Requirements: Applicant must be studying in New Jersey.
Application Requirements: References, transcript. **Deadline:** February 1.
E-mail: ldelauro@ets.org
Phone: 609-734-1806 **Fax:** 609-497-6032
World Wide Web: http://www.ets.org
Contact: Linda J. DeLauro, ETS Fellowship Program Administrator
Educational Testing Service
Rosedale Road
Mail Stop 16T
Princeton, NJ 08541-0001

▼ NATIONAL ASSOCIATION OF PURCHASING MANAGEMENT, INC.

National Association of Purchasing Management Doctoral Grants • 376

One-time award for Ph.D. candidates enrolled at an accredited college or university for study in business/economics. Deadline is January 31. Up to four grants of up to $10,000 each.
Academic/Career Areas: Business/Consumer Services; Economics.
Award: Grant for use in graduate years; not renewable. *Number:* up to 4. *Amount:* up to $10,000.

Eligibility Requirements: Applicant must be enrolled at a four-year institution.
Application Requirements: Application, references, transcript.
Deadline: January 31.
E-mail: rboyle@napm.org
Phone: 602-752-2277 **Fax:** 602-491-7885
World Wide Web: http://www.napm.org
Contact: Rick Boyle, Assistant Director
National Association of Purchasing Management, Inc.
PO Box 22160
Tempe, AZ 85285-2160

▼ WOMEN GROCERS OF AMERICA
Mary Macey Scholarship see number 273

CAMPUS ACTIVITIES

▼ NATIONAL ASSOCIATION FOR CAMPUS ACTIVITIES EDUCATIONAL FOUNDATION

Donald L. McCullough Memorial Scholarships • 377

One-time award of $300 for graduate students who have demonstrated experience and involvement in campus activities and are pursuing careers as campus activities professionals. Must have minimum 2.5 GPA. Application deadline is May 30.
Academic/Career Areas: Campus Activities.
Award: Scholarship for use in graduate years; not renewable. *Number:* 9. *Amount:* $300.
Application Requirements: Application, essay, references, transcript. **Deadline:** May 30.
E-mail: dionneb@naca.org
Phone: 803-732-6222 **Fax:** 803-749-1047
Contact: Dionne Blakeney, Development Staff Assistant
National Association for Campus Activities Educational Foundation
13 Harbison Way
Columbia, SC 29212-3401

CHEMICAL ENGINEERING

▼ AMERICAN ELECTROPLATERS AND SURFACE FINISHERS SOCIETY

American Electroplaters and Surface Finishers Society Scholarships • 378

Award for students interested in careers in surface finishing technologies. Submit transcripts, career objectives, references, and resume with application by April 15. May reapply for up to two years. One-time award of $1000. Awards available for college juniors and seniors, as well as for graduate students.

Academic/Career Areas: Chemical Engineering; Trade/Technical Specialties.

Award: Scholarship for use in junior, senior, or graduate years; not renewable. *Amount:* $1000.

Application Requirements: Application, essay, references, transcript. **Deadline:** April 15.

Phone: 407-281-6441

Contact: American Electroplaters and Surface
Finishers Society
Central Florida Research Park
12644 Research Parkway
Orlando, FL 32826-3298

▼ AMERICAN OIL CHEMISTS' SOCIETY

American Oil Chemists' Society Honored Student Awards • 379

One-time award for graduate students studying any area of science dealing with fats and oils, proteins, lipids, surfactants, detergents, or related materials to attend annual meeting of the American Oil Chemists' Society. Must submit abstract with application. Write for complete details.

Academic/Career Areas: Chemical Engineering; Natural Sciences.

Award: Scholarship for use in graduate years; not renewable. *Number:* 1–20. *Amount:* $400–$750.

Application Requirements: Application, references. **Deadline:** October 15.

E-mail: membership@aocs.org

Phone: 217-359-2344 **Fax:** 217-351-8091

World Wide Web: http://www.aocs.org

Contact: Karen Larson, Asst. to Area Manager of
Membership Services
American Oil Chemists' Society
PO Box 3489
Champaign, IL 61826

▼ ASSOCIATED WESTERN UNIVERSITIES, INC.

Associated Western Universities-DOE Post-Graduate Fellowship see number 290

Associated Western Universities/DOE Faculty Fellowships see number 291

Associated Western Universities/DOE Laboratory Graduate Research Fellowships see number 292

▼ ASSOCIATION FOR WOMEN IN SCIENCE EDUCATIONAL FOUNDATION

Ruth Satter Memorial Award see number 350

▼ FOUNDATION FOR SCIENCE AND DISABILITY

Foundation for Science and Disability-Student Grant see number 297

▼ INTERNATIONAL DESALINATION ASSOCIATION

International Desalination Association Scholarship see number 298

▼ INTERNATIONAL UNION FOR VACUUM SCIENCE, TECHNIQUE AND APPLICATIONS

Welch Foundation Scholarship see number 299

▼ KENTUCKY NATURAL RESOURCES AND ENVIRONMENTAL PROTECTION CABINET

Environmental Protection Scholarships see number 269

CIVIL ENGINEERING

▼ AMERICAN GEOPHYSICAL UNION

American Geophysical Union Horton Research Grant see number 284

▼ AMERICAN WATER WORKS ASSOCIATION

American Water Works Association/Academic Achievement Awards • 380

Award to encourage academic excellence by recognizing contributions to field of public water supply. Submit completed doctoral dissertation or master's thesis. One-time award.

Academic/Career Areas: Civil Engineering.
Award: Prize for use in graduate years; not renewable. *Number:* 4. *Amount:* $500–$1000.
Application Requirements: Application, applicant must enter a contest. **Deadline:** October 1.
E-mail: vbaca@awwa.org
Phone: 303-347-6202 **Fax:** 303-794-8915
World Wide Web: http://www.awwa.org
Contact: Veronica Baca, Scholarship Coordinator
American Water Works Association
6666 Quincy Avenue
Denver, CO 80235

▼ ASSOCIATED WESTERN UNIVERSITIES, INC.

Associated Western Universities-DOE Post-Graduate Fellowship see number 290

Associated Western Universities/DOE Faculty Fellowships see number 291

Associated Western Universities/DOE Laboratory Graduate Research Fellowships see number 292

▼ FOUNDATION FOR SCIENCE AND DISABILITY

Foundation for Science and Disability-Student Grant see number 297

▼ INSTITUTE OF TRANSPORTATION ENGINEERS

Burton W. Marsh Fellowship • 381

One fellowship available to graduates planning to study transportation engineering. One-time award of $4000. Minimum 3.0 GPA required.

Academic/Career Areas: Civil Engineering; Engineering-Related Technologies.
Eligibility Requirements: Applicant must be enrolled at a two-year or four-year or technical institution.
Application Requirements: Application, autobiography, essay, references, transcript. **Deadline:** March 15.
Phone: 202-554-8050 **Fax:** 202-863-5486
Contact: Institute of Transportation Engineers
525 School Street, SW, Suite 410
Washington, DC 20024

Harold F. Hammond Scholarship • 382

One fellowship available to graduates planning to study transportation engineering. One-time award of $3000. Minimum 3.0 GPA required.

Academic/Career Areas: Civil Engineering; Engineering-Related Technologies.
Award: Scholarship for use in graduate years; not renewable. *Number:* 1. *Amount:* $3000.
Eligibility Requirements: Applicant must be enrolled at a technical institution.
Application Requirements: Application, autobiography, essay, references, transcript. **Deadline:** March 15.
Phone: 202-554-8050 **Fax:** 202-863-5486
Contact: Institute of Transportation Engineers
525 School Street, SW, Suite 410
Washington, DC 20024

▼ INTERNATIONAL DESALINATION ASSOCIATION

International Desalination Association Scholarship see number 298

▼ KENTUCKY NATURAL RESOURCES AND ENVIRONMENTAL PROTECTION CABINET

Environmental Protection Scholarships see number 269

▼ SKIDMORE, OWINGS, AND MERRILL FOUNDATION

Structural Engineering Traveling Fellow.
Program   *see number 315*

COMMUNICATIONS

▼ AMERICAN JEWISH COMMITTEE

Harold W. Rosenthal Fellowship in
International Relations   *see number 374*

▼ CONSORTIUM OF COLLEGE AND UNIVERSITY MEDIA CENTERS

Consortium of College and University Media
Centers Research Awards   ● 383

One-time research award for faculty, staff, and students at constituent member institutions of the Consortium of College and University Media Centers. Submit a one- to two-page description of proposed study, budget, and resume. Research must be in progress.
Academic/Career Areas: Communications; Education; Filmmaking; Library Sciences; Photojournalism; TV/Radio Broadcasting.
Award: Grant for use in graduate years; not renewable. *Number:* 1–5. *Amount:* up to $2000.
Application Requirements: Application. **Deadline:** May 1.
E-mail: ccumc@ccumc.org
Phone: 605-697-3676 **Fax:** 605-692-3816
Contact: Gary Sheeley, Chair, Res. Awards Committee
Consortium of College and University Media Centers
121 Pearson Hall
Iowa State University
Ames, IA 50011-2203

▼ INSTITUTE FOR HUMANE STUDIES

Humane Studies Fellowships   ● 384

One-time award for undergraduate and graduate students in selected disciplines. Applicants should have demonstrated interest in classical liberal/libertarian ideas and must intend to pursue a scholarly career. Application fee: $25.
Academic/Career Areas: Communications; Economics; History; Humanities; Legal Services; Literature/English/Writing; Political Science; Social Sciences.

Eligibility Requirements: Applicant must be enrolled at a four-year institution.
Application Requirements: Application, autobiography, essay, references, test scores, transcript. **Fee:** $25. **Deadline:** December 31.
E-mail: ihs@gmu.edu
Phone: 703-934-6920 **Fax:** 703-352-7535
World Wide Web: http://osf1.gmu.edu/~ihs
Contact: Damon Chetson, Program Coordinator
Institute for Humane Studies
4084 University Drive, Suite 101
Fairfax, VA 22030-6812

▼ NATIONAL ASSOCIATION OF BROADCASTERS

National Association of Broadcasters Grants
for Research in Broadcasting   ● 385

Grants awarded to graduate students and academic personnel for pursuit of research on important issues in the U.S. commercial broadcast industry. Must submit a proposal. One-time awards average $5000.
Academic/Career Areas: Communications; Journalism; TV/Radio Broadcasting.
Award: Grant for use in graduate years; not renewable. *Number:* 4–6. *Amount:* $5000–$25,000.
Application Requirements: Application. **Deadline:** January 26.
World Wide Web: http://www.nab.org/research/grants.htm
Contact: Dr. Mark Fratrik, Vice President/Economist
National Association of Broadcasters
1771 N Street, NW
Washington, DC 20036-2891

▼ RTCA, INC.
William E. Jackson Award   *see number 344*

▼ WOMEN GROCERS OF AMERICA
Mary Macey Scholarship   *see number 273*

COMPUTER SCIENCE/DATA PROCESSING

▼ AMERICAN SOCIETY FOR INFORMATION SCIENCE

Institute for Scientific Information Doctoral Dissertation Scholarship • 386

Nonrenewable scholarship for active doctoral student in information science who has completed all course work and has dissertation approval. Purpose of scholarship is to foster research in information science by encouraging and assisting doctoral students with dissertation research. Must submit curriculum vitae, detailed research proposal, budget, and other supporting data.
Academic/Career Areas: Computer Science/Data Processing; Library Sciences.
Award: Scholarship for use in graduate years; not renewable. *Number:* 1. *Amount:* $1500.
Application Requirements: Application, references. **Deadline:** July 1.
E-mail: mdevine@asis.org
Phone: 301-495-0900 **Fax:** 301-495-0810
World Wide Web: http://www.asis.org
Contact: Michele Devine, Awards Coordinator
American Society for Information Science
8720 Georgia Avenue, Suite 501
Silver Spring, MD 20910

Pratt-Severn Student Research Award • 387

One-time award, for students at a master's degree-granting institution, to recognize substantive work in the information science field. Submit paper that falls within the scope of the "Journal of the American Society for American Science." Doctoral theses are not eligible.
Academic/Career Areas: Computer Science/Data Processing; Library Sciences.
Award: Prize for use in graduate years; not renewable.
Eligibility Requirements: Applicant must have an interest in writing.
Application Requirements: Application, references. **Deadline:** June 15.
E-mail: mdevine@asis.org
Phone: 301-495-0900 **Fax:** 301-495-0810
World Wide Web: http://www.asis.org
Contact: Michele Devine, Awards Coordinator
American Society for Information Science
8720 Georgia Avenue, Suite 501
Silver Spring, MD 20910

Special Interest Group/STI BIOSIS Student Award • 388

One-time award for an outstanding student in a program of library and/or information science with interest in the area of biological information. Must be a full-time-student. Contact for application form.
Academic/Career Areas: Computer Science/Data Processing; Library Sciences.
Award: Prize for use in graduate years; not renewable.
Application Requirements: Application. **Deadline:** February 15.
E-mail: mdevine@asis.org
Phone: 301-495-0900 **Fax:** 301-495-0810
World Wide Web: http://www.asis.org
Contact: Michele Devine, Awards Coordinator
American Society for Information Science
8720 Georgia Avenue, Suite 501
Silver Spring, MD 20910

Special Interest Group/STI Chemical Abstracts Service Student Award • 389

One-time award for an outstanding student in a program of library and/or information science with interest in the area of chemical information. Must be enrolled full-time. Contact for application form.
Academic/Career Areas: Computer Science/Data Processing; Library Sciences.
Award: Prize for use in graduate years; not renewable.
Application Requirements: Application, references. **Deadline:** February 15.
E-mail: mdevine@asis.org
Phone: 301-495-0900 **Fax:** 301-495-0810
World Wide Web: http://www.asis.org
Contact: Michele Devine, Awards Coordinator
American Society for Information Science
8720 Georgia Avenue, Suite 501
Silver Spring, MD 20910

UMI Doctoral Dissertation Award • 390

One-time award for information scientists honoring outstanding achievements in the completion of dissertation projects. Must have completed dissertation within the past year. Recognizes outstanding recent doctoral candidates whose research contributes significantly to an understanding of some aspect of information science. Submit letter of endorsement and manuscript or full dissertation.
Academic/Career Areas: Computer Science/Data Processing; Library Sciences.

UMI Doctoral Dissertation Award (continued)

Award: Prize for use in graduate years; not renewable. *Number:* 1. *Amount:* $1000.
Application Requirements: Application, references. **Deadline:** June 1.
E-mail: mdevine@asis.org
Phone: 301-495-0900 **Fax:** 301-495-0810
World Wide Web: http://www.asis.org
Contact: Michele Devine, Awards Coordinator
American Society for Information Science
8720 Georgia Avenue, Suite 501
Silver Spring, MD 20910

▼ ASSOCIATED WESTERN UNIVERSITIES, INC.

Associated Western Universities-DOE Post-Graduate Fellowship　　　*see number 290*

Associated Western Universities/DOE Faculty Fellowships　　　*see number 291*

Associated Western Universities/DOE Laboratory Graduate Research Fellowships　　　*see number 292*

▼ CHARLES BABBAGE INSTITUTE

Adelle and Erwin Tomash Fellowship in the History of Information Processing　　　• 391

One-time award for graduate students addressing a topic in the history of computer and information processing. Submit research proposal and biographical information. Priority given to students who have completed all requirements for doctoral degree except the research and writing of the dissertation.
Academic/Career Areas: Computer Science/Data Processing; Electrical/Electronic Engineering; Engineering/Technology; History; Humanities; Science, Technology & Society.
Application Requirements: Essay, references, transcript.
Deadline: January 15.
E-mail: cbi@vx.cis.umn.edu
Phone: 612-624-5050 **Fax:** 612-625-8054
Contact: Dr. Robert Seidel, Director
Charles Babbage Institute
University of Minnesota, 103 Walter Library
117 Pleasant Street, SE
Minneapolis, MN 55455

▼ EDUCATIONAL TESTING SERVICE

Educational Testing Service Postdoctoral Fellowship Program　　　*see number 375*

▼ FOUNDATION FOR SCIENCE AND DISABILITY

Foundation for Science and Disability-Student Grant　　　*see number 297*

CRIMINAL JUSTICE/ CRIMINOLOGY

▼ HARRY FRANK GUGGENHEIM FOUNDATION

H. F. Guggenheim Foundation Research Grants　　　*see number 329*

▼ PI GAMMA MU INTERNATIONAL HONOR SOCIETY IN SOCIETY SCIENCE

Pi Gamma Mu Scholarship　　　• 392

Ten scholarships available to graduate students in social services, social sciences, criminal justice, economics, history, and political science. Must have a minimum 3.0 GPA. One-time award of $1000-$2000.
Academic/Career Areas: Criminal Justice/Criminology; Economics; History; Political Science; Social Sciences; Social Services.
Award: Scholarship for use in graduate years; not renewable. *Number:* 10. *Amount:* $1000–$2000.
Application Requirements: Application, essay, references, transcript. **Deadline:** January 30.
E-mail: pgm@jinx.sckans.edu
Phone: 316-221-3128 **Fax:** 316-221-7124
World Wide Web: http://www.sckans.edu/~pgm
Contact: Sue Watters, Executive Director
Pi Gamma Mu International Honor Society
in Society Science
1001 Millington, Suite B
Winfield, KS 67156

DENTAL HEALTH/SERVICES

▼ INTERNATIONAL ORDER OF THE KING'S DAUGHTERS AND SONS

International Order of the King's Daughters and Sons Health Careers Scholarship • 393

Award for study in the health fields. No biology, premedical, or veterinary applicants accepted. BA or BS candidates are eligible in junior year; medical/dental students must have finished first year of school. Send No.10 self-addressed stamped envelope for application and information.

Academic/Career Areas: Dental Health/Services; Health and Medical Sciences; Nursing; Therapy/Rehabilitation.
Award: Scholarship for use in junior, senior, or graduate years; renewable. *Number:* 25–55. *Amount:* $500–$1000.
Eligibility Requirements: Applicant must be enrolled at a two-year or four-year institution.
Application Requirements: Application, autobiography, financial need analysis, references, self-addressed stamped envelope, transcript. **Deadline:** April 1.
Phone: 601-833-5418
Contact: Mrs. Fred Cannon
International Order of the King's Daughters and Sons
Box 1310
Brookhaven, MS 39601

EARTH SCIENCE

▼ AMERICAN GEOPHYSICAL UNION

American Geophysical Union Horton Research Grant see number 284

▼ ASSOCIATED WESTERN UNIVERSITIES, INC.

Associated Western Universities-DOE Post-Graduate Fellowship see number 290

Associated Western Universities/DOE Faculty Fellowships see number 291

Associated Western Universities/DOE Laboratory Graduate Research Fellowships see number 292

▼ ASSOCIATION FOR WOMEN GEOSCIENTISTS

Chrysalis Scholarship • 394

Award for a woman who needs to complete her master's or Ph.D., whose education has been interrupted for at least one year, and whose degree is in the geosciences. Include statement of goals, reasons for educational interruption, and plans for award use. One-time award of $250-$750.

Academic/Career Areas: Earth Science; Physical Sciences and Math.
Award: Scholarship for use in graduate years; not renewable. *Number:* 2–5. *Amount:* $250-$750.
Eligibility Requirements: Applicant must be enrolled at a four-year institution and female.
Application Requirements: Application, references. **Deadline:** March 1.
Phone: 303-534-0708 **Fax:** 303-436-0609
Contact: Ms. Jeanne Harris
Association for Women Geoscientists
518 17th Street
Denver, CO 80202

▼ ASSOCIATION FOR WOMEN IN SCIENCE EDUCATIONAL FOUNDATION

Ruth Satter Memorial Award see number 350

▼ CENTER FOR FIELD RESEARCH

Center for Field Research Grants for Field Research see number 294

▼ GEOLOGICAL SOCIETY OF AMERICA

Geological Society of America Student Research Grants • 395

Research grants in geology provide support for master's and doctoral research at universities in the U.S., Canada, Mexico, and Central America. Applications available through GSA campus representatives and geology department chairpersons. Several one-time awards of $1500 each.

Geological Society of America Student Research Grants (continued)

Academic/Career Areas: Earth Science.
Award: Grant for use in graduate years; not renewable. *Number:* 240. *Amount:* $1500.
Application Requirements: Application, references. **Deadline:** February 1.
Contact: Ms. June R. Forstrom, Research Grants Administrator
Geological Society of America
3300 Penrose Place
PO Box 9140
Boulder, CO 80301-9140

▼ HUDSON RIVER NATIONAL ESTUARINE RESEARCH RESERVE—NEW YORK STATE DEPARTMENT OF ENVIRONMENTAL CONSERVATION AND THE HUDSON RIVER FOUNDATION

Tibor T. Polgar Fellowship   *see number 360*

▼ KENTUCKY NATURAL RESOURCES AND ENVIRONMENTAL PROTECTION CABINET

Environmental Protection Scholarships   *see number 269*

▼ NATIONAL ACADEMIC ADVISING ASSOCIATION

National Academic Advising Association Research Grants   • 396

Practicing professionals (administrators and faculty), as well as graduate students seeking support for dissertation research, are eligible. Award does not support indirect or overhead costs. Submit research proposal. Renewable $5000 award.
Academic/Career Areas: Engineering/Technology; Engineering-Related Technologies; Trade/Technical Specialties.
Award: Grant for use in graduate years; renewable. *Number:* 1–5. *Amount:* up to $5000.
Application Requirements: Application. **Deadline:** March 6.
E-mail: nacada@ksu.edu
Phone: 508-235-8215 **Fax:** 508-235-8276
World Wide Web: http://www.ksu.edu/nacada

Contact: Victoria McGillin, Chair
National Academic Advising Association
2323 Anderson Avenue, Suite 225
Manhattan, KS 66502

▼ SIGMA XI, THE SCIENTIFIC RESEARCH SOCIETY

National Academy of Science Grants-in-Aid of Research   *see number 281*

Sigma Xi Grants-in-Aid of Research   *see number 271*

▼ SOCIETY OF EXPLORATION GEOPHYSICISTS FOUNDATION (SEG)

Society of Exploration Geophysicists Foundation Scholarship   • 397

Renewable award available to undergraduate and graduate students. Applicants must be preparing for a career in geophysics or a related earth science at a four-year college or university. High school seniors may apply. Minimum 3.0 GPA required. Average award is $1200 per year.
Academic/Career Areas: Earth Science; Physical Sciences and Math.
Award: Scholarship for use in freshman, sophomore, junior, senior, or graduate years; renewable. *Number:* 60–100. *Amount:* $500–$3000.
Eligibility Requirements: Applicant must be enrolled at a four-year institution.
Application Requirements: Application, financial need analysis, references, test scores, transcript. **Deadline:** March 1.
E-mail: mgerhart@seg.org
Phone: 918-497-5500 **Fax:** 918-497-5558
Contact: Marge Gerhart, Scholarship Coordinator
Society of Exploration Geophysicists Foundation (SEG)
PO Box 702740
Tulsa, OK 74170-2740

▼ WOMEN'S AUXILIARY TO THE AMERICAN INSTITUTE OF MINING, METALLURGICAL AND PETROLEUM ENGINEERS

Women's Auxiliary to the American Institute of Mining, Metallurgical and Petroleum Engineers Scholarship Loan Fund • 398

One-time awards for college juniors, seniors, and graduate students pursuing earth science degrees related to the minerals industry. Dollar value of award may vary. Interview is required. Write for guidelines.
Academic/Career Areas: Earth Science; Engineering-Related Technologies; Mechanical Engineering.
Award: Scholarship, loan for use in junior, senior, or graduate years; not renewable. *Amount:* $1750–$10,000.
Eligibility Requirements: Applicant must be enrolled at a four-year institution.
Application Requirements: Application, financial need analysis, interview, references, transcript. **Deadline:** March 15.
Phone: 212-705-7692 **Fax:** 212-705-8024
Contact: Scholarship Loan Fund Committee Chair
Women's Auxiliary to the American Institute of Mining, Metallurgical and Petroleum Engineers
345 East 47th Street, 14th Floor
New York, NY 10017-2304

▼ WOODS HOLE OCEANOGRAPHIC INSTITUTION

Woods Hole Oceanographic Institution Postdoctoral Fellowships see number 372

ECONOMICS

▼ ALEXANDER VON HUMBOLDT-STIFTUNG

Transatlantic Research Cooperation between German and American Scholars in the Human and Social Sciences, Economics, and Law • 399

One-time award for Ph.D. scholars for joint research projects involving American and German scholars in humanities, economics, law, and social sciences. At least one German and one American must participate.
Academic/Career Areas: Economics; Humanities; Legal Services; Social Sciences.
Award: Scholarship for use in graduate years; not renewable. *Number:* up to 20. *Amount:* up to $60,000.
Application Requirements: Application. **Deadline:** Continuous.
E-mail: daak@alex.avh.uni-bonn.de
Phone: 022-883-3109 **Fax:** 022-883-3216
World Wide Web: http://www.access.digex.net/ngaac/gaachome.htm
Contact: Heide Radlanski, Director
Alexander von Humboldt-Stiftung
Jean-Paul-Strasse 12
53173 Bonn
Germany

▼ AMERICAN GEOPHYSICAL UNION

American Geophysical Union Horton Research Grant see number 284

▼ INSTITUTE FOR HUMANE STUDIES

Humane Studies Fellowships see number 384

▼ NATIONAL ASSOCIATION OF PURCHASING MANAGEMENT, INC.

National Association of Purchasing Management Doctoral Grants see number 376

▼ PI GAMMA MU INTERNATIONAL HONOR SOCIETY IN SOCIETY SCIENCE

Pi Gamma Mu Scholarship see number 392

▼ POPULATION COUNCIL

Population Council Fellowships in Population Study • 400

One-time nonrenewable award for advanced training in population studies. Must have completed all course work for Ph.D. in area of social sciences. Dissertation fieldwork or writing possible. Must deal with developing world. Submit formal application form found on Internet, including three-page proposal.
Academic/Career Areas: Economics; Social Sciences.
Application Requirements: Application, references, transcript.
Deadline: January 2.
E-mail: jlam@popcouncil.org
Phone: 212-339-0671 **Fax:** 212-755-6052

Population Council Fellowships in Population Study (continued)

World Wide Web: http://www.popcouncil.org/council/fellowsh/socsci/socsci.htm
Contact: Jude H. Lam
Population Council
One Dag Hammarskjold Plaza, 9th Floor
New York, NY 10017

Population Council Postdoctoral Fellowships in the Social Sciences • 401

One-time award for persons with Ph.D. or equivalent who wish to continue postdoctoral training or research at an institution other than where Ph.D. was received. Include a letter from adviser at proposed institution. Must submit research proposal.
Academic/Career Areas: Economics; Social Sciences.
Award: Scholarship for use in postdoctoral years; not renewable. *Number:* 1–3. *Amount:* $30,000–$35,000.
Application Requirements: Application, references, transcript.
Deadline: January 2.
E-mail: jlam@popcouncil.org
Phone: 212-339-0671 **Fax:** 212-755-6052
World Wide Web: http://www.popcouncil.org
Contact: Jude H. Lam
Population Council
One Dag Hammarskjold Plaza, 9th Floor
New York, NY 10017

▼ RESOURCES FOR THE FUTURE

Gilbert F. White Postdoctoral Fellowships • 402

Two postdoctoral fellowship for social/natural scientists with Ph.D. who wish to devote a year to scholarly work in areas related to natural resources, energy, or the environment. Teaching and/or research experience at postdoctoral level preferred though not essential. May hold position in government as well as at academic institution. Must submit resume and proposal. Deadline February 27.
Academic/Career Areas: Economics; Engineering-Related Technologies; Natural Resources; Political Science; Social Sciences.
Application Requirements: Application, references. **Deadline:** February 27.
E-mail: moran@rff.org
Phone: 202-328-5067 **Fax:** 202-939-3460
World Wide Web: http://www.rff.org

Contact: Mary Moran, Coordinator for Academic Programs
Resources for the Future
1616 P Street, NW
Washington, DC 20036

Joseph L. Fisher Dissertation Awards • 403

Award intended for doctoral candidates in final year of dissertation research on issues related to the environment, natural resources, or energy. Students whose research emphasizes policy aspects of environmental issues are encouraged to apply. Proof of Ph.D. status, curriculum vita, proposal, and technical summary are required.
Academic/Career Areas: Economics; Engineering-Related Technologies; Natural Resources; Political Science; Social Sciences.
Application Requirements: Application, autobiography, essay, references, transcript. **Deadline:** February 27.
E-mail: moran@rff.org
Phone: 202-328-5067 **Fax:** 202-939-3460
World Wide Web: http://www.rff.org
Contact: Mary Moran, Coordinator for Academic Programs
Resources for the Future
1616 P Street, NW
Washington, DC 20036

▼ SOCIAL SCIENCE RESEARCH COUNCIL

Abe Fellowship Program • 404

Applicants must hold Ph.D. or the terminal degree in their field. Supports postdoctoral research on contemporary policy-relevant issues. Should spend at least one-third of fellow tenure in residence abroad in Japan or the U.S. Fellows eligible for up to twelve months of full-time support, which need not be continuous, but must be concluded within 24 months. Funds may be spent on additional residence and fieldwork in third countries as appropriate.
Academic/Career Areas: Economics; Humanities; Political Science; Social Sciences.
Application Requirements: Application. **Deadline:** September 1.
World Wide Web: http://www.ssrc.org
Contact: Social Science Research Council
810 Seventh Avenue
New York, NY 10019

▼ STATE HISTORICAL SOCIETY OF WISCONSIN

J.C. Geilfuss Fellowship • 405

Fellowship for research at graduate level and beyond in Wisconsin and U.S. business and economic history. Prefer topics on Wisconsin and American Midwest and/or research using State Historical Society of Wisconsin collection. Submit resume and proposal.
Academic/Career Areas: Economics; History.
Application Requirements: Essay. **Deadline:** February 1.
Phone: 608-264-6464
Contact: Dr. Michael Stevens, State Historian
State Historical Society of Wisconsin
816 State Street
Madison, WI 53706-1488

▼ UNITED STATES DEPARTMENT OF HOUSING AND URBAN DEVELOPMENT, OFFICE OF POLICY DEVELOPMENT AND RESEARCH

Doctoral Dissertation Research Grant (HUD) see number 334

▼ WOMEN GROCERS OF AMERICA

Mary Macey Scholarship see number 273

EDUCATION

▼ ARMENIAN PROFESSIONAL SOCIETY OF THE BAY AREA

Armenian Professional Society of the Bay Area Scholarships see number 324

▼ ASSOCIATION FOR THE STUDY OF HIGHER EDUCATION

Association for the Study of Higher Education Dissertation of the Year Award • 406

One-time award for a graduate student of education who has written an outstanding dissertation. Must be nominated. Write for further information.
Academic/Career Areas: Education; Special Education.
Award: Prize for use in graduate years; not renewable.
Number: 1–2. *Amount:* $200–$500.

Application Requirements: Applicant must enter a contest.
Deadline: Continuous.
E-mail: elpajc@showme.missouri.edu
Phone: 573-882-9645 **Fax:** 573-884-5714
World Wide Web: http://www.coe.missouri.edu/~ashe
Contact: Dr. Julie Caplow, Executive Director
Association for the Study of Higher Education
University of Missouri-Columbia, ELPA
Columbia, MO 65211

▼ CANADIAN INSTITUTE OF UKRAINIAN STUDIES—PETER JACYK CENTRE FOR UKRAINIAN HISTORICAL RESEARCH

Doctoral Thesis Fellowship in Ukrainian History • 407

One-time award for scholars to complete a thesis on Ukrainian-Canadian topics in education, history, law, humanities, social sciences, women's studies, and library sciences. Canadian citizen or permanent resident may hold fellowship at any institution. For non-Canadian applicants, preference will be given to students enrolled at the University of Alberta.
Academic/Career Areas: Education; History; Humanities; Legal Services; Library Sciences; Social Sciences.
Application Requirements: Application, references. **Deadline:** May 1.
Contact: Canadian Institute of Ukrainian Studies—
Peter Jacyk Centre for Ukrainian Historical Research
352 Athabasca Hall
Edmonton, AB T6G 2E8
Canada

Michael Dorosh Fund Master's Fellowship • 408

One-time award for scholars to complete thesis on Ukrainian or Ukrainian-Canadian topics in education, history, law, humanities, social sciences, women's studies, and library sciences. Canadian citizen or permanent resident may hold fellowship at any institution. For non-Canadian applicants, preference will be given to students enrolled at the University of Alberta.
Academic/Career Areas: Education; History; Humanities; Legal Services; Library Sciences; Social Sciences.
Application Requirements: Application, references. **Deadline:** May 1.

Michael Dorosh Fund Master's Fellowship (continued)

Contact: Canadian Institute of Ukrainian Studies—
Peter Jacyk Centre for Ukrainian
Historical Research
352 Athabasca Hall
Edmonton, AB T6G 2E8
Canada

▼ CANADIAN INSTITUTE OF UKRANIAN STUDIES—PETER JACYK CENTRE FOR UKRANIAN HISTORICAL RESEARCH

Helen Darcovich Memorial Endowment Fund Doctoral Fellowship • 409

Renewable award for doctoral students to complete a thesis on a Ukrainian or Ukrainian-Canadian topic in education, history, law, humanities, social sciences, women's studies, or library science. All other degree requirements must be completed by the time award is taken up. Canadian citizens/permanent residents may hold fellowship at any institution. For non-Canadian applicants, preference will be given to students enrolled at the University of Alberta. Must submit proposal and budget. Dissertation proposal, references, writing sample, academic grades, and publishing record are evaluated.
Academic/Career Areas: Education; History; Humanities; Legal Services; Library Sciences; Social Sciences.
Application Requirements: Application, references. **Deadline:** May 1.
Phone: 403-492-2972 **Fax:** 403-492-4967
Contact: Olia Britts
Canadian Institute of Ukrainian Studies—
Peter Jacyk Centre for Ukrainian
Historical Research
352 Athabasca Hall
Edmonton, AB T6G 2E8
Canada

▼ CONSORTIUM OF COLLEGE AND UNIVERSITY MEDIA CENTERS

Consortium of College and University Media Centers Research Awards see number 383

▼ COUNCIL OF JEWISH FEDERATIONS

Federation Executive Recruitment and Education Program • 410

Tuition awards for two years of graduate study plus a stipend. Must have minimum 3.0 GPA and pursue an MS in social work, Jewish communal service, or public administration. Must make commitment to work in the Jewish Federations System upon graduation.
Academic/Career Areas: Education; Social Services.
Award: Scholarship for use in graduate years; renewable.
Number: 7–10. *Amount:* $7500–$20,000.
Eligibility Requirements: Applicant must be Jewish; have employment experience in community service and must have an interest in leadership.
Application Requirements: Application, essay, interview, references, transcript. **Deadline:** February 1.
E-mail: susan_sherr@cjfny.org
Phone: 212-598-3583 **Fax:** 212-475-6571
Contact: Susan Sherr, Consultant
Council of Jewish Federations
730 Broadway
New York, NY 10003

▼ EDUCATIONAL TESTING SERVICE

Educational Testing Service Postdoctoral Fellowship Program see number 375

▼ NATIONAL ACADEMY OF EDUCATION

Spencer Postdoctoral Fellowship Program • 411

One-time research award for Ph.D. holders who had Ph.D. conferred between January 1, 1993 and December 31, 1998 in education, social or behavioral science, or the humanities. Must submit three recommendations. Must describe research relevant to education. Write for details.
Academic/Career Areas: Education; Humanities; Social Sciences.
Application Requirements: Application, references. **Deadline:** December 10.
Contact: Marie Rosen
National Academy of Education
Stanford University, School of Education
520 Galvez Mall
Stanford, CA 94305-3084

▼ NATIONAL ASSOCIATION FOR GIFTED CHILDREN

Hollingworth Award Competition • 412

Award for individual investigators and organizations presenting proposals for publishable research projects

concerning gifted and/or talented children. Write for guidelines and application deadline. One-time award of $2000.
Academic/Career Areas: Education.
Award: Grant for use in graduate years; not renewable. *Number:* 1–2. *Amount:* $2000.
Application Requirements: Application.
Phone: 202-785-4268
World Wide Web: http://www.nagc.org
Contact: Sally Reis, President
National Association for Gifted Children
1707 L Street NW, Suite 550
Washington, DC 20036

▼ NATIONAL ASSOCIATION FOR WOMEN IN EDUCATION

Women's Research Award • 413

Award for a woman at a graduate or post-graduate career or professional level. Submit proposal on any topic relating to educational, personal, and professional development of women and girls. Must follow APA guidelines and be less than fifty pages. Submit five copies. One-time award of $750.
Academic/Career Areas: Education; Health Information Management/Technology; Humanities; Social Sciences; Social Services.
Award: Prize for use in graduate years; not renewable. *Amount:* $750.
Eligibility Requirements: Applicant must be enrolled at a four-year institution and female.
Application Requirements: Applicant must enter a contest, essay. **Deadline:** October 1.
E-mail: nawe@clark.net
Phone: 202-659-9330 **Fax:** 202-457-0946
World Wide Web: http://www.nawe.org
Contact: Committee Chair
National Association for Women in Education
1325 18th Street, NW
Suite 210
Washington, DC 20036

▼ PHI DELTA KAPPA

Phi Delta Kappa International Graduate Fellowships in Educational Leadership • 414

One-time graduate fellowship for members of Phi Delta Kappa pursuing a degree in educational leadership. Must

have minimum 3.0 GPA. Submit all graduate transcripts, synopsis of PDK activities, position paper describing role as educational leader.
Academic/Career Areas: Education.
Application Requirements: Application, essay, portfolio, transcript. **Deadline:** May 1.
E-mail: headquarters@pdkintl.org
Phone: 812-339-1156 **Fax:** 812-339-0018
World Wide Web: http://www.pdkintl.org
Contact: George Kersey, Associate Executive Director
Phi Delta Kappa
Box 789
Bloomington, IN 47402

▼ WILLIAM T. GRANT FOUNDATION

Grant Foundation Faculty Scholars Program • 415

Renewable award for young investigators to research the causes and consequences of factors that promote or compromise healthy child development. Must be a faculty member of a university or nonprofit institution. Submit curriculum vitae, abstract, research plan, budget, and two published journal articles.
Academic/Career Areas: Education; Health and Medical Sciences.
Award: Scholarship for use in graduate years; renewable.
Eligibility Requirements: Applicant must have employment experience in teaching.
Application Requirements: Application. **Deadline:** July 1.
Phone: 212-752-0071 **Fax:** 212-752-1398
Contact: Cindy Sigal, Information Coordinator
William T. Grant Foundation
570 Lexington Avenue, 18th Floor
New York, NY 10022-5403

ELECTRICAL/ELECTRONIC ENGINEERING

▼ ASSOCIATED WESTERN UNIVERSITIES, INC.

Associated Western Universities-DOE Post-Graduate Fellowship see number 290

▼ BLUE CROSS BLUE SHIELD OF MICHIGAN FOUNDATION

Blue Cross Blue Shield of Michigan Foundation Student Award Program • 416

Awards available to students pursuing a Ph.D. or M.D. at a Michigan university. Projects can address a major public health or medical issue, quality of care, cost containment, or access to care. Projects can include research, pilot projects, intervention, feasibility studies, demonstration and evaluation projects, and must relate to improving health care in Michigan. One-time award of $3000. Submit letter from faculty adviser.

Academic/Career Areas: Electrical/Electronic Engineering; Food Science/Nutrition; Health Administration; Health and Medical Sciences; Health Information Management/Technology; Mechanical Engineering; Nuclear Science; Nursing; Social Sciences; Therapy/Rehabilitation.

Award: Scholarship for use in graduate years; not renewable. *Number:* 25–35. *Amount:* $3000.

Eligibility Requirements: Applicant must be studying in Michigan.

Application Requirements: Application, autobiography, references, transcript. **Deadline:** April 15.

E-mail: mnagel@bcbsm.com

Phone: 313-225-9099 **Fax:** 313-225-7730

World Wide Web: http://www.bcbsm.com/foundation.html

Contact: Margie Nagel, Program Officer
Blue Cross Blue Shield of Michigan Foundation
600 Lafayette East, B243
Detroit, MI 48226-2927

▼ CHARLES BABBAGE INSTITUTE

Adelle and Erwin Tomash Fellowship in the History of Information Processing see number 391

▼ DEMONSTRATION OF ENERGY-EFFICIENT DEVELOPMENTS PROGRAM

Demonstration of Energy-Efficient Developments Scholarship • 417

Applicants must be in an accredited college or university studying an energy-related discipline. Must complete a research project and be sponsored by a member of the Demonstration of Energy-Efficient Developments Program. Inquire for details. Deadlines vary. Must have completed one year of study.

Academic/Career Areas: Electrical/Electronic Engineering; Engineering/Technology; Engineering-Related Technologies; Heating, Air-Conditioning, and Refrigeration Mechanics; Mechanical Engineering; Natural Resources.

Award: Scholarship for use in sophomore, junior, senior, or graduate years; not renewable. *Number:* 10. *Amount:* $3000.

Application Requirements: Application, transcript.

E-mail: hriester@appanet.org

Phone: 202-467-2960 **Fax:** 202-467-2992

World Wide Web: http://www.appanet.org

Contact: Holly Riester, Administrator
Demonstration of Energy-Efficient Developments Program
2301 M Street, NW
Washington, DC 20037

▼ FOUNDATION FOR SCIENCE AND DISABILITY

Foundation for Science and Disability-Student Grant see number 297

▼ INTERNATIONAL DESALINATION ASSOCIATION

International Desalination Association Scholarship see number 298

▼ INTERNATIONAL UNION FOR VACUUM SCIENCE, TECHNIQUE AND APPLICATIONS

Welch Foundation Scholarship see number 299

▼ SKIDMORE, OWINGS, AND MERRILL FOUNDATION

Mechanical/Electrical Traveling Fellowship Program see number 314

▼ VERTICAL FLIGHT FOUNDATION

Vertical Flight Foundation Scholarship see number 345

ENGINEERING-RELATED TECHNOLOGIES

▼ AMERICAN CONCRETE INSTITUTE INTERNATIONAL-CONCRETE RESEARCH AND EDUCATION FOUNDATION

American Concrete Institute Fellowship Awards   see number 301

Katharine and Bryant Mather Fellowship   see number 302

Stewart C. Watson Fellowship   • 418
One fellowship available to a student who, at the time of acceptance of the fellowship, has been accepted for graduate study. Available to an applicant with a special interest in joints and bearings for concrete structures. Study must be at an accredited college or university in the U.S. or Canada. One award of $3000.
Academic/Career Areas: Engineering-Related Technologies.
Application Requirements: Application. **Deadline:** February 11.
Contact: Scholarship Council
    American Concrete Institute
      International-Concrete Research and
      Education Foundation
    38800 Country Club Drive
    Farmington Hills, MI 48333

V. Mohan Malhotra Fellowship   • 419
One fellowship available to a student who, at the time of acceptance of the fellowship, has been accepted for graduate study. Applicant must be majoring in concrete materials science research at an accredited college or university in the U.S. or Canada. One-time award of $3000.
Academic/Career Areas: Engineering-Related Technologies.
Application Requirements: Application. **Deadline:** February 11.
Contact: Scholarship Council
    American Concrete Institute
      International-Concrete Research and
      Education Foundation
    38800 Country Club Drive
    Farmington Hills, MI 48333

W. R. Grace Fellowship   see number 303

▼ AMERICAN SOCIETY FOR ENGINEERING EDUCATION

Army Research Laboratory Postdoctoral Fellowship Program   • 420
Renewable postdoctoral award for highly trained scientists and engineers to pursue scientific research and technological development at the Army Research Laboratory in Maryland (or annex in New Jersey). Must submit research proposal and have received Ph.D. or other earned research doctoral degree. Continuous deadline.
Academic/Career Areas: Engineering/Technology; Engineering-Related Technologies; Physical Sciences and Math.
Eligibility Requirements: Applicant must be studying in Maryland.
Application Requirements: Application, references, transcript.
Deadline: Continuous.
E-mail: projects@asee.org
Phone: 202-331-3525
Contact: Program Manager
    American Society for Engineering Education
    1818 N Street NW, Suite 600
    Washington, DC 20036-2479

▼ CAMPUS SAFETY DIVISION
Campus Safety Scholarship   see number 293

▼ DEMONSTRATION OF ENERGY-EFFICIENT DEVELOPMENTS PROGRAM
Demonstration of Energy-Efficient Developments Scholarship   see number 417

▼ INSTITUTE OF TRANSPORTATION ENGINEERS
Burton W. Marsh Fellowship   see number 381

Harold F. Hammond Scholarship   see number 382

▼ INTERNATIONAL DESALINATION ASSOCIATION
International Desalination Association Scholarship   see number 298

▼ NATIONAL ACADEMIC ADVISING ASSOCIATION

National Academic Advising Association Research Grants   see number 396

▼ RESOURCES FOR THE FUTURE

Gilbert F. White Postdoctoral Fellowships   see number 402

Joseph L. Fisher Dissertation Awards   see number 403

▼ WOMEN'S AUXILIARY TO THE AMERICAN INSTITUTE OF MINING, METALLURGICAL AND PETROLEUM ENGINEERS

Women's Auxiliary to the American Institute of Mining, Metallurgical and Petroleum Engineers Scholarship Loan Fund   see number 398

ENGINEERING/TECHNOLOGY

▼ AMERICAN ASSOCIATION FOR THE ADVANCEMENT OF SCIENCE

American Association for the Advancement of Science Mass Media, Science, and Engineering Fellowship   • 421

Ten-week summer program at television stations, radio stations, newspapers, or magazines. Students are given a weekly stipend and travel expenses. The main goal is for the students to help improve coverage of science-related issues. Must submit resume and have a minimum 3.0 GPA. Very competitive selection process is designed to seek out all qualified candidates, including African-American, Hispanic, and Native American students and those with disabilities.

Academic/Career Areas: Engineering/Technology; Health and Medical Sciences; Physical Sciences and Math.
Application Requirements: Application, essay, references, transcript. **Deadline:** January 15.
E-mail: aking@aaas.org
Phone: 202-326-6760 **Fax:** 202-371-9849

Contact: American Association for the Advancement of Science
1200 New York Avenue, NW
Washington, DC 20005

▼ AMERICAN CONCRETE INSTITUTE INTERNATIONAL-CONCRETE RESEARCH AND EDUCATION FOUNDATION

American Concrete Institute Fellowship Awards   see number 301

Katharine and Bryant Mather Fellowship   see number 302

W. R. Grace Fellowship   see number 303

▼ AMERICAN GEOPHYSICAL UNION

American Geophysical Union Horton Research Grant   see number 284

▼ AMERICAN SOCIETY FOR ENGINEERING EDUCATION

Army Research Laboratory Postdoctoral Fellowship Program   see number 420

▼ AMERICAN SOCIETY FOR PHOTOGRAMMETRY AND REMOTE SENSING

Earth Observation Satellite Company Award for Application of Digital Landsat TM Data   see number 285

▼ AMERICAN WATER WORKS ASSOCIATION

American Water Works Association/Abel Wolman Fellowship   see number 286

American Water Works Association/Holly A. Cornell Scholarship   see number 287

▼ ASSOCIATED WESTERN UNIVERSITIES, INC.

Associated Western Universities-DOE Post-Graduate Fellowship   see number 290

Associated Western Universities/DOE Faculty Fellowships   see number 291

Associated Western Universities/DOE Laboratory Graduate Research Fellowships   see number 292

▼ CHARLES BABBAGE INSTITUTE

Adelle and Erwin Tomash Fellowship in the History of Information Processing   see number 391

▼ DEMONSTRATION OF ENERGY-EFFICIENT DEVELOPMENTS PROGRAM

Demonstration of Energy-Efficient Developments Scholarship   see number 417

▼ FOUNDATION FOR SCIENCE AND DISABILITY

Foundation for Science and Disability-Student Grant   see number 297

▼ INSTITUTE OF ELECTRICAL AND ELECTRONICS ENGINEERS CENTER FOR THE HISTORY OF ELECTRICAL ENGINEERING

Institute of Electrical and Electronics Engineers Fellowship in Electrical History   • 422

Award for graduate or postgraduate historical study of electrical technology. Submit transcript, essay, and references with application. Write, phone, or e-mail for additional information. One-time award of $15,000.
Academic/Career Areas: Engineering/Technology; History.
Application Requirements: Application, essay, references, transcript. **Deadline:** February 1.
E-mail: history@ieee.org
Phone: 908-932-1068 **Fax:** 908-932-1193
World Wide Web: http://www.ieee.org/history_center

Contact: Sheila Plotnick, Research Coordinator
Institute of Electrical and Electronics Engineers Center for the History of Electrical Engineering
39 Union Street
New Brunswick, NJ 08903-5062

▼ INSTITUTE OF INDUSTRIAL ENGINEERS

E.J. Sierleja Memorial Fellowship   • 423

One-time award for graduate students pursuing an advanced degree in the area of transportation with priority given to the study of rail transportation. Must be member of Institute of Industrial Engineers, have a minimum GPA of 3.4, and be nominated by a department head.
Academic/Career Areas: Engineering/Technology.
Eligibility Requirements: Applicant must be member of Institute of Industrial Engineers.
Application Requirements: Application, references, transcript.
Deadline: November 15.
Contact: Bisi Oyeyemi, University Operations Coordinator
Institute of Industrial Engineers
25 Technology Park/Atlanta
Norcross, GA 30092-2988

Institute of Industrial Engineers-Dwight D. Gardner Scholarship   • 424

Available to industrial engineering juniors, seniors, and graduate students at four-year accredited colleges. Applicants must belong to the Institute of Industrial Engineers, have a 3.4 GPA, and be nominated by a department head by November 1. One-time award of $750-$1500.
Academic/Career Areas: Engineering/Technology.
Award: Scholarship for use in junior, senior, or graduate years; not renewable. *Number:* 5–15. *Amount:* $750–$1500.
Eligibility Requirements: Applicant must be enrolled at a four-year institution and member of Institute of Industrial Engineers.
Application Requirements: Application, references, transcript.
Deadline: November 15.
Contact: Bisi Oyeyemi, University Operations Coordinator
Institute of Industrial Engineers
25 Technology Park/Atlanta
Norcross, GA 30092-2988

▼ INTERNATIONAL DESALINATION ASSOCIATION

International Desalination Association Scholarship see number 298

▼ INTERNATIONAL UNION FOR VACUUM SCIENCE, TECHNIQUE AND APPLICATIONS

Welch Foundation Scholarship see number 299

▼ NATIONAL ACADEMIC ADVISING ASSOCIATION

National Academic Advising Association Research Grants see number 396

▼ RTCA, INC.

William E. Jackson Award see number 344

▼ SIGMA XI, THE SCIENTIFIC RESEARCH SOCIETY

Sigma Xi Grants-in-Aid of Research see number 271

▼ SKIDMORE, OWINGS, AND MERRILL FOUNDATION

Mechanical/Electrical Traveling Fellowship Program see number 314

Structural Engineering Traveling Fellow. Program see number 315

▼ SOCIETY OF MANUFACTURING ENGINEERS EDUCATION FOUNDATION

Wayne Kay Graduate Fellowship • 425

Award for full-time graduate students pursuing manufacturing or industrial engineering degrees. Must have 3.5 minimum GPA. Submit application cover sheet, resume, transcript, essay, references, and statement of career goals. One-time award of $5000.
Academic/Career Areas: Engineering/Technology.
Application Requirements: Essay, references, transcript.
Deadline: March 1.
E-mail: murrdor@sme.org

Phone: 313-271-1500 Ext. 512 **Fax:** 313-240-6095
World Wide Web: http://www.sme.org
Contact: Dora Murray, Grants Coordinator
Society of Manufacturing Engineers
Education Foundation
One SME Drive
PO Box 930
Dearborn, MI 48121-0930

▼ SPECIALTY EQUIPMENT MARKET ASSOCIATION

Specialty Equipment Market Association Memorial Scholarship Fund • 426

Scholarship for higher education in the automotive field for a student who has already completed one full year of study. Write for information concerning application guidelines. Several one-time awards of $2000 each.
Academic/Career Areas: Engineering/Technology; Trade/Technical Specialties.
Award: Scholarship for use in sophomore, junior, senior, or graduate years; not renewable. *Amount:* $2000.
Eligibility Requirements: Applicant must be enrolled at a four-year institution and must have an interest in automotive.
Application Requirements: Application, essay, financial need analysis, photo, references, self-addressed stamped envelope, transcript. **Deadline:** January 15.
E-mail: university@sema.org
Phone: 909-396-0289 Ext. 144 **Fax:** 909-860-0184
Contact: Dr. Harry Perden, Director of Educational Services
Specialty Equipment Market Association
PO Box 4910
Diamond Bar, CA 91675-4910

▼ TAU BETA PI ASSOCIATION

Tau Beta Pi Fellowships for Graduate Study in Engineering • 427

Award for graduate scholars pursuing engineering studies. Must be member of Tau Beta Pi or be initiated by March 1. Preference given to first-time graduate students. Must submit typewritten application and two letters of reference by January 15. One-time award of $10,000.
Academic/Career Areas: Engineering/Technology.
Award: Scholarship for use in graduate years; not renewable. *Number:* 17–22. *Amount:* $10,000.
Application Requirements: Application, essay, references.
Deadline: January 15.
E-mail: donald.s.pierre@apc.com **Fax:** 334-694-2310

World Wide Web: http://www.tbp.org
Contact: D. Stephen Pierre, Jr., Director of
Fellowships
Tau Beta Pi Association
PO Box 2687
Knoxville, TN 37901-2697

▼ WOODS HOLE OCEANOGRAPHIC INSTITUTION

*Woods Hole Oceanographic Institution
Postdoctoral Fellowships*   *see number 372*

FILMMAKING

▼ ARMENIAN PROFESSIONAL SOCIETY OF THE BAY AREA

*Armenian Professional Society of the Bay Area
Scholarships*   *see number 324*

▼ ASIAN CULTURAL COUNCIL

Ford Foundation Fellowships   *see number 335*

▼ CONSORTIUM OF COLLEGE AND UNIVERSITY MEDIA CENTERS

*Consortium of College and University Media
Centers Research Awards*   *see number 383*

▼ PRINCESS GRACE AWARDS

*Dance, Theater, Film, and Playwright
Grants*   *see number 342*

FLEXOGRAPHY

▼ FOUNDATION OF FLEXOGRAPHIC TECHNICAL ASSOCIATION

*Sun Chemical Corporation Graduate
Flexography Fellowship*   • **428**
Non-renewable research fellowship of $10,000. Must be full-time graduate student holding BA or BS and enrolled in qualified graphic arts curriculum with field of study in flexography; or working professional in field of flexography. Deadline: March 31.
Academic/Career Areas: Flexography; Graphics.
Application Requirements: Application, essay, references, transcript. **Deadline:** March 31.
E-mail: srubin@vax.fta.ffta.org
World Wide Web: http://www.fta.ffta.org
Contact: Shelley Rubin, Educational Coordinator
Foundation of Flexographic Technical
Association
900 Marconi Avenue
Ronkonkoma, NY 11779-7212

FOOD SCIENCE/NUTRITION

▼ AMERICAN ASSOCIATION OF CEREAL CHEMISTS FOUNDATION

*American Association of Cereal Chemists
Graduate Fellowships*   *see number 268*

▼ AMERICAN SOCIETY FOR NUTRITIONAL SCIENCES

*American Society for Nurtritional Sciences
Pre-Doctoral Fellowship*   • **429**
One-time award of $5000 to candidates enrolled at the graduate level in an American Institute of Nutrition listed graduate program. Must have an interest in the field of nutrition research.
Academic/Career Areas: Food Science/Nutrition; Health and Medical Sciences.
Award: Prize for use in graduate years; not renewable. *Number:* 4. *Amount:* $5000.
Application Requirements: Application. **Deadline:** December 1.
World Wide Web: http://www.faseb.org/asns
Contact: Dr. Richard G. Allison, Executive Officer
American Society for Nutritional Sciences
9650 Rockville Pike
Bethesda, MD 20814-4596

▼ BLUE CROSS BLUE SHIELD OF MICHIGAN FOUNDATION

*Blue Cross Blue Shield of Michigan Foundation
Student Award Program*   *see number 416*

▼ KAPPA OMICRON NU HONOR SOCIETY

Dorothy I. Mitstifer Fellowship ● 430

One-time award of $2000 awarded to Kappa Omicron Nu chapter advisers for graduate or postgraduate study. Candidates must demonstrate scholarship, research, and leadership potential. Applicants may pursue part-time study. Recipients of fellowship must submit annual progress report.
Academic/Career Areas: Food Science/Nutrition; Home Economics.
Eligibility Requirements: Applicant must have an interest in leadership.
Application Requirements: Application, references. **Deadline:** January 15.
E-mail: dmitstifer@kon.org
Phone: 517-351-8335 **Fax:** 517-351-8336
Contact: Dorothy I. Mitstifer, Executive Director
Kappa Omicron Nu Honor Society
4990 Northwind Drive, Suite 140
East Lansing, MI 48823

Kappa Omicron Nu National Alumni Fellowship ● 431

One award given to graduate home economics student who is a member of Kappa Omicron Nu. Candidates must demonstrate scholarship, research, and leadership potential. Applicants may pursue part-time study. Recipient of award must submit annual progress report. One-time award of $1000.
Academic/Career Areas: Food Science/Nutrition; Home Economics.
Eligibility Requirements: Applicant must have an interest in leadership.
Application Requirements: Application, references. **Deadline:** April 1.
E-mail: dmitstifer@kon.org
Phone: 517-351-8335 **Fax:** 517-351-8336
Contact: Dorothy I. Mitstifer, Executive Director
Kappa Omicron Nu Honor Society
4990 Northwind Drive, Suite 140
East Lansing, MI 48823

Kappa Omicron Nu New Initiatives Grant ● 432

One award given to a graduate home economics student who is a member of Kappa Omicron Nu. Candidate must demonstrate scholarship, research, and leadership potential. Cross-specialization and integrative research should be the research priority. Multiyear proposals are considered. Recipient must submit annual progress report. Renewable award of $3000.
Academic/Career Areas: Food Science/Nutrition; Home Economics.
Award: Grant for use in graduate years; renewable. *Number:* 1. *Amount:* $3000.
Eligibility Requirements: Applicant must be enrolled at a four-year institution and must have an interest in leadership.
Application Requirements: Application, references. **Deadline:** February 15.
E-mail: dmitstifer@kon.org
Phone: 517-351-8335 **Fax:** 517-351-8336
Contact: Dorothy I. Mitstifer, Executive Director
Kappa Omicron Nu Honor Society
4990 Northwind Drive, Suite 140
East Lansing, MI 48823

FOOD SERVICE/HOSPITALITY

▼ FOOD DISTRIBUTION RESEARCH SOCIETY, INC.

Food Distribution Research Society, Inc. Applebaum Master's and PhD Programs Awards ● 433

Two awards for outstanding master's and Ph.D. theses in the area of food distribution or marketing. Must submit short description of career goals and interests. One-time award of $500-$1000.
Academic/Career Areas: Food Service/Hospitality.
Award: Scholarship for use in graduate years; not renewable. *Number:* up to 2. *Amount:* $500–$1000.
Application Requirements: Application. **Deadline:** Continuous.
E-mail: nayga@aesop.rutgers.edu
Phone: 908-932-9158 **Fax:** 908-932-8887
World Wide Web: http://www.fdrs.ag.utk.edu/
Contact: Dr. Rudy Nayga, VP-Education
Food Distribution Research Society, Inc.
Food and Fiber Center
Mississippi State University
Mississippi State, MS 39762

▼ WOMEN GROCERS OF AMERICA

Mary Macey Scholarship *see number 273*

FOREIGN LANGUAGE

▼ AMERICAN JEWISH COMMITTEE

*Harold W. Rosenthal Fellowship in
International Relations*   see number 374

▼ PHI BETA KAPPA SOCIETY

*Mary Isabel Sibley Fellowship for Greek and
French Studies*   see number 332

▼ SOCIETY FARSAROTUL

*Society Farsarotul Financial
Awards*   see number 333

GRAPHICS

▼ FOUNDATION OF FLEXOGRAPHIC TECHNICAL ASSOCIATION

*Sun Chemical Corporation Graduate
Flexography Fellowship*   see number 428

HEALTH ADMINISTRATION

▼ BLUE CROSS BLUE SHIELD OF MICHIGAN FOUNDATION

*Blue Cross Blue Shield of Michigan Foundation
Student Award Program*   see number 416

▼ CAMPUS SAFETY DIVISION

Campus Safety Scholarship   see number 293

▼ CANADIAN FOUNDATION FOR THE STUDY OF INFANT DEATHS

*Dr. Sydney Segal Research
Grants*   see number 275

▼ NATIONAL ENVIRONMENTAL HEALTH ASSOCIATION

*National Environmental Health Association/
AAS Scholarship*   • 434

One-time awards for college juniors, seniors, and graduate students pursuing studies in environmental health sciences and/or public health. Undergraduates must be enrolled in an approved program that is accredited by the Environmental Health Accreditation Council (EHAC).
Academic/Career Areas: Health Administration; Health and Medical Sciences.
Award: Scholarship for use in junior, senior, or graduate years; not renewable. *Number:* 3–4. *Amount:* $500–$2000.
Application Requirements: Application, references, transcript.
Deadline: February 1.
E-mail: neha.org@juno.com
Phone: 303-756-9090 **Fax:** 303-691-9490
World Wide Web: http://www.neha.org/~beckyr
Contact: Veronica White, NEHA Liaison
National Environmental Health Association
720 South Colorado Boulevard
Suite 970 South
Denver, CO 80246-1925

▼ ROSCOE POUND FOUNDATION

*Elaine Osborne Jacobson Award for Women
Working in Health Care Law*   • 435

For female law students who, through academics and career experience, demonstrate commitment to advocacy for health-care needs of women, elderly, the disabled, and children. One-time award of $1000 to $2000.
Academic/Career Areas: Health Administration; Health and Medical Sciences; Legal Services.
Award: Prize for use in graduate years; not renewable. *Number:* 2. *Amount:* $1000–$2000.
Eligibility Requirements: Applicant must be female.
Application Requirements: Application, autobiography, essay, references. **Deadline:** January 23.
E-mail: pound@atlahg.org
Phone: 202-965-3500 **Fax:** 202-965-0355
World Wide Web: http://www.atlanet.org
Contact: Meghan Donohoe, Programs Manager
Roscoe Pound Foundation
1050 31st Street, NW
Washington, DC 20007-4499

HEALTH AND MEDICAL SCIENCES

▼ AMERICAN ACADEMY OF PEDIATRICS

American Academy of Pediatrics Residency Scholarships • 436

One-time award for pediatric residents in a training program who have a definite commitment for another year of residency in a program accredited by the Residency Review Committee for Pediatrics. Submit recommendations.
Academic/Career Areas: Health and Medical Sciences.
Award: Scholarship for use in graduate years; not renewable. *Number:* 30–60. *Amount:* $1000–$5000.
Application Requirements: Application, financial need analysis, references. **Deadline:** February 7.
World Wide Web: http://www.aap.org
Contact: Jackie Burke, Sections Manager
American Academy of Pediatrics
141 Northwest Point Boulevard
PO Box 927
Elk Grove Village, IL 60009

▼ AMERICAN ASSOCIATION FOR THE ADVANCEMENT OF SCIENCE

American Association for the Advancement of Science Mass Media, Science, and Engineering Fellowship see number 421

▼ AMERICAN FEDERATION FOR AGING RESEARCH

Glenn Foundation/American Federation for Aging Research Scholarships for Research in the Biology of Aging • 437

One-time $5500 award for pre-doctoral, Ph.D., and M.D. students to conduct biomedical research in aging for three months. Research must be conducted under the supervision of a faculty mentor in any not-for-profit setting. $4000 is for the student and $1500 is for the mentor. Contact for application.
Academic/Career Areas: Health and Medical Sciences.
Award: Scholarship for use in graduate years; not renewable. *Number:* 25. *Amount:* $5500.
Application Requirements: Application, references, transcript.
Deadline: February 26.
E-mail: amfedaging@aol.com
Phone: 212-752-2327 **Fax:** 212-832-2298

World Wide Web: http://www.afar.org
Contact: Odette van der Willik/ Hattie Herman,
Grants Manager/Administrator
American Federation for Aging Research
1414 Avenue of the Americas, 18th Floor
New York, NY 10019

▼ AMERICAN FOUNDATION FOR PHARMACEUTICAL EDUCATION

American Foundation for Pharmaceutical Education Grant Program for New Investigators • 438

One-time award to provide initial funds for new faculty members to assist in establishing a program of research. Must have earned terminal degree in discipline and hold primary academic faculty appointments in schools of pharmacy for up to five years.
Academic/Career Areas: Health and Medical Sciences.
Award: Scholarship for use in graduate years; not renewable. *Number:* 18.
Eligibility Requirements: Applicant must have employment experience in teaching.
Application Requirements: Application. **Deadline:** June 6.
Phone: 301-738-2160 **Fax:** 301-738-2161
Contact: Mrs. Rachael Probst, Grants Manager
American Foundation for Pharmaceutical Education
1 Church Street, Suite 202
Rockville, MD 20850

Clinical Pharmacy Post-PharmD Fellowship in the Biomedical Sciences • 439

Three awards to enable PharmD-level pharmacists to obtain additional education and training in biomedical and related sciences in order to become clinical scientists and make major contributions to biomedical and pharmaceutical sciences. Preference given to candidates who propose fellowship away from present affiliation. Contact for eligibility and application procedures.
Academic/Career Areas: Health and Medical Sciences.
Eligibility Requirements: Applicant must have employment experience in experience in career field.
Application Requirements: Application. **Deadline:** February 15.
Phone: 301-738-2160 **Fax:** 301-738-2161
Contact: Mrs. Rachael Probst, Grants Manager
American Foundation for Pharmaceutical Education
1 Church Street, Suite 202
Rockville, MD 20850

Merck Research Schol. Program/ Pro. Degree Pharm. • 440

Ten one-time awards of $7000 each to identify and encourage promising students to consider research-oriented careers in the pharmaceutical field. Student must have completed at least two years of college course work, plus one year of professional pharmacy curriculum. Deadline of late January.

Academic/Career Areas: Health and Medical Sciences.
Award: Scholarship for use in graduate years; not renewable. *Number:* 10. *Amount:* $7000.
Application Requirements: Application.
Phone: 301-738-2160 **Fax:** 301-738-2161
Contact: Mrs. Rachael Probst, Grants Manager
American Foundation for Pharmaceutical Education
1 Church Street, Suite 202
Rockville, MD 20850

Rho Chi Scholarship Program • 441

One-time award to encourage outstanding Rho Chi members to pursue a Ph.D. in a college of pharmacy graduate program. Must be in final year of a pharmacy BS or PharmD program and a member of Rho Chi.

Academic/Career Areas: Health and Medical Sciences.
Award: Scholarship for use in graduate years; not renewable. *Number:* 1. *Amount:* $7500.
Application Requirements: Application. **Deadline:** January 15.
Phone: 301-738-2160 **Fax:** 301-738-2161
Contact: Mrs. Rachael Probst, Grants Manager
American Foundation for Pharmaceutical Education
1 Church Street, Suite 202
Rockville, MD 20850

▼ AMERICAN FOUNDATION FOR UROLOGIC DISEASE, INC.

American Foundation for Urologic Disease Fellowship Program • 442

Fellowship program for urologists who have completed their residency within five years of date of application. Program provides for one year of full-time investigation in laboratory research of urologic diseases. It is not intended to fund a urology resident for a year of laboratory research either before or during residency training.

Academic/Career Areas: Health and Medical Sciences.
Award: Scholarship for use in postdoctoral years; not renewable. *Number:* 3–5. *Amount:* $25,000.
Application Requirements: Application. **Deadline:** September 1.
E-mail: lesley@afud.org
Phone: 410-468-1804 **Fax:** 410-468-1808
World Wide Web: http://www.access.digex.net/~afud
Contact: Lesley Finney, Director, Research Program
American Foundation for Urologic Disease, Inc.
1128 North Charles Street
Baltimore, MD 21201

American Foundation for Urologic Disease Health Services Research Scholar Program • 443

One-time award for trained urologist (M.D./DO) within five years of residency who aspires to conduct research in healthcare services related to urology. Must be committed to career in academic urology and be able to demonstrate current interest/accomplishments in issues related to delivery of health services, health economics, and policy. Contact for further information on research areas.

Academic/Career Areas: Health and Medical Sciences.
Award: Scholarship for use in postdoctoral years; not renewable. *Number:* 1–3. *Amount:* $44,000.
Application Requirements: Application. **Deadline:** September 1.
E-mail: lesley@afud.org
Phone: 410-468-1804 **Fax:** 410-468-1808
World Wide Web: http://www.access.digex.net/~afud
Contact: Lesley Finney, Director, Research Program
American Foundation for Urologic Disease, Inc.
1128 North Charles Street
Baltimore, MD 21201

American Foundation for Urologic Disease MD Research Scholar Program • 444

Award for urologist within five years of post-residency. Must be committed to research career and submit evidence of research accomplishments. Two years in program required. Must spend 80% of time on research project to continue funding. Application must state how time will be allocated. Experience should prepare scholar to obtain independent research grant support.

Academic/Career Areas: Health and Medical Sciences.
Award: Scholarship for use in postdoctoral years; not renewable. *Number:* 5–10. *Amount:* $22,000.
Application Requirements: Application. **Deadline:** September 1.
E-mail: lesley@afud.org
Phone: 410-468-1804 **Fax:** 410-468-1808
World Wide Web: http://www.access.digex.net/~afud

American Foundation for Urologic Disease MD Research Scholar Program (continued)

Contact: Lesley Finney, Director, Research Program
American Foundation for Urologic Disease, Inc.
1128 North Charles Street
Baltimore, MD 21201

American Foundation for Urologic Disease PhD Research Scholar Program • 445

Several one-time awards for postdoctoral basic scientists with research interests in urologic or related diseases and disfunctions. A commitment to dedicate two years in the AFUD/Ph.D. program as a full-time researcher is required.
Academic/Career Areas: Health and Medical Sciences.
Award: Scholarship for use in postdoctoral years; not renewable. *Number:* 2–4. *Amount:* $23,000.
Application Requirements: Application. **Deadline:** September 1.
E-mail: lesley@afud.org
Phone: 410-468-1804 **Fax:** 410-468-1808
World Wide Web: http://www.access.digex.net/~afud
Contact: Lesley Finney, Director, Research Program
American Foundation for Urologic Disease, Inc.
1128 North Charles Street
Baltimore, MD 21201

▼ AMERICAN MEDICAL ASSOCIATION EDUCATION AND RESEARCH FOUNDATION

Jerry L. Pettis Memorial Scholarship • 446

For junior or senior year medical student with a demonstrated interest in the communication of science. Submit letter of nomination from dean, letter and curriculum vitae from student, letter from supportive professional, and any other materials to support nomination. One-time award of $2500.
Academic/Career Areas: Health and Medical Sciences.
Award: Scholarship for use in graduate years; not renewable. *Number:* 1. *Amount:* $2500.
Application Requirements: Autobiography, references.
Deadline: January 27.
Phone: 312-464-4543 **Fax:** 312-464-5678
Contact: Rita M. Palulonis, Associate Director
American Medical Association Education and Research Foundation
515 North State Street
Chicago, IL 60610

▼ AMERICAN OTOLOGICAL SOCIETY

American Otological Society Research Training Fellowships • 447

Awarded to foster the academic training of students and resident physicians in sciences related to the investigation of otosclerosis or Meniere's Disease. Must be performed at U.S. or Canadian institution. Submit research proposal and curriculum vitae. Fellowship will support one to two years of full-time research conducted outside of residency training.
Academic/Career Areas: Health and Medical Sciences.
Application Requirements: Application, references, transcript.
Deadline: January 31.
Phone: 404-778-3382
Contact: Dr. Douglas Mattox, Secretary/Treasurer
American Otological Society
Dept. of Otolaryngology-Head & Neck Surgery
The Emory Clinic, 1365 Clifton Road, NE
Atlanta, GA 30322

▼ AMERICAN PHYSIOLOGICAL SOCIETY

American Physiological Society Conference Student Awards see number 347

▼ AMERICAN RESPIRATORY CARE FOUNDATION

Glaxo-Wellcome Literary Award • 448

Award to encourage respiratory care practitioners and physicians to submit for publication original papers involving scientific investigation and evaluation on case reports. Best papers accepted for publication for November and October.
Academic/Career Areas: Health and Medical Sciences; Therapy/Rehabilitation.
Award: Prize for use in graduate years; not renewable. *Number:* up to 6. *Amount:* $500–$2000.
Eligibility Requirements: Applicant must have employment experience in experience in career field.
Application Requirements: Deadline: November 1.
E-mail: demayo@aarc.og
Phone: 972-243-2272 **Fax:** 972-484-2720
Contact: Brenda J. DeMayo, Scholarship Administrator
American Respiratory Care Foundation
11030 Ables Lane
Dallas, TX 75229-4593

▼ AMERICAN SOCIETY FOR NUTRITIONAL SCIENCES

American Society for Nurtritional Sciences Pre-Doctoral Fellowship see number 429

▼ AMERICAN SOCIETY OF MICROBIOLOGY & NATIONAL CENTER FOR INFECTIOUS DISEASES

American Society of Microbiology & National Center for Infectious Diseases Post Doctoral Research Associates Program see number 348

▼ AMERICAN WATER WORKS ASSOCIATION

American Water Works Association/Larson Aquatic Research Support Scholarship see number 288

American Water Works Association/Thomas R. Camp Memorial Scholarship see number 289

▼ BLUE CROSS BLUE SHIELD OF MICHIGAN FOUNDATION

Blue Cross Blue Shield of Michigan Foundation Student Award Program see number 416

▼ BURROUGHS WELLCOME FUND

Wellcome Research Travel Grants for United Kingdom Citizens see number 351

▼ CAMPUS SAFETY DIVISION

Campus Safety Scholarship see number 293

▼ CANADIAN FOUNDATION FOR THE STUDY OF INFANT DEATHS

Dr. Sydney Segal Research Grants see number 275

▼ CENTER FOR INDOOR AIR RESEARCH

Center for Indoor Air Research Postdoctoral Fellowship • 449

Postdoctoral award to sponsor scientific and technical research on the sources and effects of indoor air quality. Applicants must hold a Ph.D., M.D., or equivalent degree at the time of award and have demonstrated ability to conduct independent research.
Academic/Career Areas: Health and Medical Sciences; Natural Resources.
Application Requirements: Application, essay, references, transcript. **Deadline:** October 31.
E-mail: ciarinc@aol.com
Phone: 410-684-3777 **Fax:** 410-684-3729
Contact: Dr. Alice Zeiger, Fellowship Grants Program
Center for Indoor Air Research
1099 Winterson Road, Suite 280
Linthicum, MD 21090

▼ CHEST FOUNDATION

Chest Foundation Clinical Research Fellowship Award • 450

Award for candidates holding M.D. or equivalent degree and entering last year of subspecialty training. Two awards of $25,000 for clinical research project in asthma and two awards of $25,000 for clinical research project in COPD. Deadline: April 30.
Academic/Career Areas: Health and Medical Sciences.
Application Requirements: Application, essay, references.
Deadline: April 30.
E-mail: mkrause@chestnet.org
Phone: 847-498-8308 **Fax:** 847-498-5460
World Wide Web: http://www.chestnet.org
Contact: Mary Katherine Krause, Associate
Vice-President
Chest Foundation
3300 Dundee Road
Northbrook, IL 60062-2348

▼ COOLEY'S ANEMIA FOUNDATION, INC.

Cooley's Anemia Foundation Research Fellowship see number 352

▼ CYSTIC FIBROSIS FOUNDATION

Cystic Fibrosis Foundation Pilot and Feasibility Awards • 451

Grant for developing and testing new hypotheses and/or methods and to support promising new investigators in research areas relevant to cystic fibrosis. Proposed work must be hypothesis driven and reflect innovative approaches to critical questions in cystic fibrosis research. Award is not meant to support continuation of programs begun under other granting mechanisms. Up to $40,000 per year for up to two years may be requested.

Academic/Career Areas: Health and Medical Sciences.
Award: Grant for use in graduate years; renewable. *Amount:* up to $40,000.
Application Requirements: Application. **Deadline:** September 1.
E-mail: kcurley@cff.org
Phone: 301-951-4422 **Fax:** 301-951-6378
World Wide Web: http://www.cff.org
Contact: Kathleen Curley, Office of Grants
 Management
 Cystic Fibrosis Foundation
 6931 Arlington Road
 Bethesda, MD 20814

Cystic Fibrosis Foundation Clinical Research Grants • 452

Renewable awards for support of small or pilot/feasibility clinical research projects directly related to cystic fibrosis treatment and care. Project may add diagnostic or therapeutic methods related to cystic fibrosis or the pathophysiology of cystic fibrosis. Must demonstrate access to cystic fibrosis patients. Potential applicants must submit letter of intent to apply. Up to $80,000 per year for up to three years may be requested for single-center clinical research grants. Up to $150,000 for up to three years for multi-center clinical research.

Academic/Career Areas: Health and Medical Sciences.
Award: Grant for use in graduate years; renewable. *Amount:* up to $150,000.
Eligibility Requirements: Applicant must have employment experience in experience in career field.
Application Requirements: Application. **Deadline:** October 1.
E-mail: kcurley@cff.org
Phone: 301-951-4422 **Fax:** 301-951-6378
World Wide Web: http://www.cff.org

Contact: Kathleen Curley, Office of Grants
 Management
 Cystic Fibrosis Foundation
 6931 Arlington Road
 Bethesda, MD 20814

Cystic Fibrosis Foundation Student Traineeships see number 353

Cystic Fibrosis Foundation Summer Scholarships in Epidemiology • 453

One-time award to increase skills in epidemiology for M.D.'s currently working in cystic fibrosis. Award covers tuition and expenses up to $2000. Course work should include biostatistics and epidemiology, particularly clinical epidemiology and/or clinical trials. Write for further information.

Academic/Career Areas: Health and Medical Sciences.
Award: Scholarship for use in graduate years; not renewable. *Amount:* up to $2000.
Eligibility Requirements: Applicant must have employment experience in experience in career field.
Application Requirements: Application. **Deadline:** April 1.
E-mail: kcurley@cff.org
Phone: 301-951-4422 **Fax:** 301-951-6378
World Wide Web: http://www.cff.org
Contact: Kathleen Curley, Office of Grants
 Management
 Cystic Fibrosis Foundation
 6931 Arlington Road
 Bethesda, MD 20814

Cystic Fibrosis Foundation/National Institutes of Health Funding Award • 454

Renewable award to support excellent cystic fibrosis-related research projects that have been submitted to and approved by the National Institutes of Health, but cannot be supported by available National Institutes of Health funds. Applicant must fall within 40th percentile with a priority score of 200 or better.

Academic/Career Areas: Health and Medical Sciences.
Award: Scholarship for use in graduate years; renewable. *Amount:* $75,000–$125,000.
Application Requirements: Application. **Deadline:** Continuous.
E-mail: kcurley@cff.org
Phone: 301-951-4422 **Fax:** 301-951-6378
World Wide Web: http://www.cff.org

Contact: Kathleen Curley, Office of Grants
Management
Cystic Fibrosis Foundation
6931 Arlington Road
Bethesda, MD 20814

▼ DEAFNESS RESEARCH FOUNDATION

Deafness Research Foundation Grants ● 455

Award for investigators conducting research on any aspect of the ear and its function. Applications from new investigators conducting research in generally unexplored areas are encouraged. Write for further information. One-time award of $15,000.
Academic/Career Areas: Health and Medical Sciences.
Award: Grant for use in graduate years; not renewable. *Number:* 35–45. *Amount:* $15,000.
Application Requirements: Application. **Deadline:** June 1.
E-mail: drfl@village.ios.com
Phone: 212-768-1181 **Fax:** 212-768-1782
Contact: Ms. Rakeela Khan, Grants Administrator
Deafness Research Foundation
15 West 39th Street, 6th Floor
New York, NY 10018-3806

▼ EASTER SEAL RESEARCH INSTITUTE

Elizabeth St. Louis Award   see number 354

▼ FIGHT FOR SIGHT, INC.

Fight for Sight- Grants-in-Aid   see number 295

Fight for Sight-NSPB Postdoctoral Research Fellowships   see number 296

▼ FOUNDATION FOR SCIENCE AND DISABILITY

Foundation for Science and Disability-Student Grant   see number 297

▼ HARRY FRANK GUGGENHEIM FOUNDATION

H. F. Guggenheim Foundation Research Grants   see number 329

▼ HEART AND STROKE FOUNDATION OF CANADA

Heart and Stroke Foundation of Canada Grants in Aid of Research and Development   ● 456

Several grants available to support researchers in projects of experimental nature in cardiovascular or cerebrovascular development. Grants range from one to three years, but only established investigators should request three-year grants. One-time awards of varying amounts.
Academic/Career Areas: Health and Medical Sciences.
Award: Grant for use in graduate years; not renewable.
Application Requirements: Application, applicant must enter a contest, essay, references, self-addressed stamped envelope, transcript. **Deadline:** September 1.
E-mail: jsalo.hsfc@sympatico.ca
Phone: 613-569-4361 Ext. 327 **Fax:** 613-569-3278
World Wide Web: http://www.hsf.ca/research
Contact: Jeanne Salo, Administrative Assistant,
Research Department
Heart and Stroke Foundation of Canada
222 Queen Street, Suite 1402
Ottawa, ON K1P 5V9
Canada

Heart and Stroke Foundation of Canada Nursing Research Fellowships   ● 457

Several "in-training" awards for persons studying some area of cardiovascular or cerebrovascular nursing. For master's degree candidates, the programs must include a thesis or project requirement. Desired applicants are nurses looking to further their education in their field. Renewable awards of varying amounts.
Academic/Career Areas: Health and Medical Sciences; Nursing.
Application Requirements: Application, references, self-addressed stamped envelope, transcript. **Deadline:** March 15.
E-mail: jsalo.hsfc@sympatico.ca
Phone: 613-569-4361 Ext. 327 **Fax:** 613-569-3278
World Wide Web: http://www.hsf.ca/research
Contact: Jeanne Salo, Administrative Assistant,
Research Department
Heart and Stroke Foundation of Canada
222 Queen Street, Suite 1402
Ottawa, ON K1P 5V9
Canada

Heart and Stroke Foundation of Canada Research Fellowships • 458

Several fellowships available to applicants with (or expecting) a Ph.D., M.D., BM, DVM, or equivalent degree. Those with a medical degree may apply for study toward an MSc or Ph.D. degree. Awardee may not be in receipt of another major award or have held a prior faculty appointment. Renewable awards of varying amounts.

Academic/Career Areas: Health and Medical Sciences.

Application Requirements: Application, references, self-addressed stamped envelope, transcript. **Deadline:** October 30.

E-mail: jsalo.hsfc@sympatico.ca

Phone: 613-569-4361 Ext. 327 **Fax:** 613-569-3278

World Wide Web: http://www.hsf.ca/research

Contact: Jeanne Salo, Administrative Assistant,
       Research Department
       Heart and Stroke Foundation of Canada
       222 Queen Street, Suite 1402
       Ottawa, ON K1P 5V9
       Canada

Heart and Stroke Foundation of Canada Research Scholarships • 459

Several scholarships to those who have clearly demonstrated excellence during pre- and postdoctoral training in cardio/cerebrovascular research. Applicant must hold a Ph.D., M.D., or equivalent degree and application must be initiated by the institution. Several five-year awards of varying amounts.

Academic/Career Areas: Health and Medical Sciences.

Award: Scholarship for use in postdoctoral years; not renewable. *Number:* 8–10.

Application Requirements: Application, essay, references, self-addressed stamped envelope, transcript. **Deadline:** September 1.

E-mail: jsalo.hsfc@sympatico.ca

Phone: 613-569-4361 Ext. 327 **Fax:** 613-569-3278

World Wide Web: http://www.hsf.ca/research

Contact: Jeanne Salo, Administrative Assistant,
       Research Department
       Heart and Stroke Foundation of Canada
       222 Queen Street, Suite 1402
       Ottawa, ON K1P 5V9
       Canada

Heart and Stroke Foundation of Canada Research Traineeships • 460

Several awards for candidates to pursue medical school training. Applicants must be under 35 years of age and priority is given to those who have conducted independent research. Renewable awards of varying amounts.

Academic/Career Areas: Health and Medical Sciences.

Eligibility Requirements: Applicant must be age 34 or under.

Application Requirements: Application, essay, references, self-addressed stamped envelope, transcript. **Deadline:** November 1.

E-mail: jsalo.hsfc@sympatico.ca

Phone: 613-569-4361 Ext. 327 **Fax:** 613-569-3278

World Wide Web: http://www.hsf.ca/research

Contact: Jeanne Salo, Administrative Assistant,
       Research Department
       Heart and Stroke Foundation of Canada
       222 Queen Street, Suite 1402
       Ottawa, ON K1P 5V9
       Canada

Heart and Stroke Foundation of Canada Visiting Scientist Program • 461

Several awards to senior individuals whose contribution and visit will be mutually rewarding to the host institution and the scientist. Intended for Canadians studying abroad or in Canada or for foreign visitors to Canada. Several awards of varying amounts for cardiovascular or cerebrovascular research.

Academic/Career Areas: Health and Medical Sciences.

Application Requirements: Application, references, self-addressed stamped envelope. **Deadline:** September 1.

E-mail: jsalo.hsfc@sympatico.ca

Phone: 613-569-4361 Ext. 327 **Fax:** 613-569-3278

World Wide Web: http://www.hsf.ca/research

Contact: Jeanne Salo, Administrative Assistant,
       Research Department
       Heart and Stroke Foundation of Canada
       222 Queen Street, Suite 1402
       Ottawa, ON K1P 5V9
       Canada

▼ HOWARD HUGHES MEDICAL INSTITUTE

Howard Hughes Medical Institute Postdoctoral Research Fellowships for Physicians   *see number 357*

Howard Hughes Medical Institute Predoctoral Fellowships in Biological Sciences see number 358

Howard Hughes Medical Institute Research Training Fellowships for Medical Students   *see number 359*

▼ HUMAN GROWTH FOUNDATION

Human Growth Foundation Small Grants   *see number 361*

▼ HUNTINGTON'S DISEASE SOCIETY OF AMERICA

HDS Research Fellowships and Grants   • 462

One-time postdoctoral award for students from accredited medical schools and universities to conduct basic and clinical research on the cause and treatment of Huntington's Disease. Awards range from $30,000-$35,000. Contact for application requirements.

Academic/Career Areas: Health and Medical Sciences.
Award: Grant for use in postdoctoral years; not renewable. *Number:* 5–10. *Amount:* $30,000–$35,000.
Application Requirements: Application, references. **Deadline:** January 5.
E-mail: curehd@hdsa.ttisms.com
Phone: 212-242-1968 **Fax:** 212-243-2443
Contact: Research Department
Huntington's Disease Society of America
140 West 22nd Street, 6th Floor
New York, NY 10011-2420

▼ INTERNATIONAL ORDER OF THE KING'S DAUGHTERS AND SONS

International Order of the King's Daughters and Sons Health Careers Scholarship   *see number 393*

▼ JANE COFFIN CHILDS MEMORIAL FUND FOR MEDICAL RESEARCH

Jane Coffin Childs Memorial Fund for Medical Research Fellowships   • 463

One-time fellowship for M.D./Ph.D.'s for full-time studies in the medical and related sciences bearing on cancer. Award is for two to three years of research and applicant should have no more than one year of postdoctoral experience. Submit research proposal. Twenty-five one-time awards of $85,500.

Academic/Career Areas: Health and Medical Sciences; Natural Sciences.
Application Requirements: Application, references. **Deadline:** February 1.
Phone: 203-785-4612 **Fax:** 203-785-3301
Contact: Elizabeth Ford, Administrative Director
Jane Coffin Childs Memorial Fund for Medical Research
333 Cedar Street
New Haven, CT 06510

▼ KENTUCKY NATURAL RESOURCES AND ENVIRONMENTAL PROTECTION CABINET

Environmental Protection Scholarships   *see number 269*

▼ LALOR FOUNDATION

Lalor Foundation Post-Doctoral Grants   *see number 362*

▼ LEUKEMIA SOCIETY OF AMERICA, INC.

Leukemia Society Fellow Awards   • 464

Renewable award for postdoctoral students pursuing a career in clinical or fundamental research of leukemia, lymphoma, Hodgkins disease, or myeloma. Applicant should have little or no experience in cancer research, or less than two years of postdoctoral research training.

Academic/Career Areas: Health and Medical Sciences.
Application Requirements: Application. **Deadline:** September 15.
E-mail: lermandb@leukemia.org
Phone: 212-450-8843 **Fax:** 212-856-9686
World Wide Web: http://www.leukemia.org
Contact: Barbara P. Lermand, Director of Research Administration
Leukemia Society of America, Inc.
600 Third Avenue, 4th Floor
New York, NY 10016

Leukemia Society Special Fellow Awards • 465

Renewable award for postdoctoral students with at least two years postdoctoral research training to continue their studies in leukemia, lymphoma, Hodgkins disease or

Leukemia Society Special Fellow Awards (continued)
myeloma research. Non-U.S. citizens may apply. Application deadline: September 15.
Academic/Career Areas: Health and Medical Sciences.
Application Requirements: Application. **Deadline:** September 15.
E-mail: lermandb@leukemia.org
Phone: 212-450-8843 **Fax:** 212-856-9686
World Wide Web: http://www.leukemia.org
Contact: Barbara P. Lermand, Director of Research
Administration
Leukemia Society of America, Inc.
600 Third Avenue, 4th Floor
New York, NY 10016

▼ MARCH OF DIMES BIRTH DEFECTS FOUNDATION—GRANTS ADMINISTRATION
March of Dimes Research Grants • 466
Awards for research scientists with faculty appointments or the equivalent at universities, hospitals, or research institutions. Research must be relevant to the interest of the March of Dimes. Submit letter of intent. Recipients may apply again.
Academic/Career Areas: Health and Medical Sciences.
Award: Grant for use in graduate years; not renewable. *Amount:* $50,000–$70,000.
Eligibility Requirements: Applicant must have employment experience in teaching.
Application Requirements: Application. **Deadline:** March 31.
Phone: 919-997-4564 **Fax:** 919-997-4560
World Wide Web: http://www.modimes.org
Contact: Gail Sullivan, Program Coordinator
March of Dimes Birth Defects Foundation—
Grants Administration
1275 Mamaroneck Avenue
White Plains, NY 10605

▼ MONTREAL NEUROLOGICAL INSTITUTE
Jeanne Timmins Costello Fellowship • 467
Four awards of 25,000 Canadian dollars for Ph.D. scholars to further research and studies in clinical and basic neuroscience at the Montreal Neurological Institute. Must provide sponsor letter with application.
Academic/Career Areas: Health and Medical Sciences.
Application Requirements: Application, autobiography, references. **Deadline:** October 15.

E-mail: fil@mni.lan.mcgill.ca
Phone: 514-398-8998 **Fax:** 514-398-8248
Contact: Fil Lumia
Montreal Neurological Institute
3801 University Street
Room 636
Montreal, PQ H3A 2B4
Canada

Preston Robb Fellowship • 468
One-time award of 25,000 Canadian dollars to support the training of a postdoctoral scholar at the Montreal Neurological Institute. Candidates must have a M.D. degree with clinical studies in neurology or neurosurgery. Must provide sponsor letter with application.
Academic/Career Areas: Health and Medical Sciences.
Application Requirements: Application, autobiography, references. **Deadline:** October 15.
E-mail: fil@mni.lan.mcgill.ca
Phone: 514-398-8998 **Fax:** 514-398-8248
Contact: Fil Lumia
Montreal Neurological Institute
3801 University Street
Room 636
Montreal, PQ H3A 2B4
Canada

▼ MYASTHENIA GRAVIS FOUNDATION OF AMERICA, INC.
Kermit Osserman Fellowship see number 363

▼ NATIONAL ENVIRONMENTAL HEALTH ASSOCIATION
National Environmental Health Association/ AAS Scholarship see number 434

▼ NATIONAL HEADACHE FOUNDATION
National Headache Foundation Research Grant • 469
One-time award to conduct research protocols that are objectively sound and whose results can contribute to the better understanding and treatment of headache and pain. Project must be conducted in U.S. Submit research proposal.
Academic/Career Areas: Health and Medical Sciences.
Award: Grant for use in graduate years; not renewable.
Application Requirements: Application. **Deadline:** December 1.

Phone: 773-388-6399 **Fax:** 773-525-7357
World Wide Web: http://www.headaches.com
Contact: Suzanne Simons, Executive Director
National Headache Foundation
428 West St. James Place, 2nd Floor
Chicago, IL 60614

▼ NATIONAL INSTITUTES OF HEALTH

Fogarty International Center International Research Fellowship   *see number 364*

Fogarty International Center International Training and Research Program   *see number 365*

▼ NATIONAL KIDNEY FOUNDATION

National Kidney Foundation Postdoctoral Research Fellowship • **470**

Renewable training award for those who have completed no more than four and a half years of research training beyond a doctoral degree with a clear commitment to the study of diseases and functions of the kidney. Must be mentored and submit research proposal. Those appointed as Assistant Professors may not apply.
Academic/Career Areas: Health and Medical Sciences.
Application Requirements: Application, references. **Deadline:** September 1.
Phone: 703-522-8544 **Fax:** 703-522-8586
Contact: Dolph Chianchiano, Director, Science Policy
National Kidney Foundation
1911 North Fort Myer Drive, #801
Arlington, VA 22209

National Kidney Foundation Young Investigator Grants • **471**

One-time award for those holding a M.D. or Ph.D. and commencing careers on the faculty of medical schools. Must have completed research fellowship training in nephrology, urology, or closely related fields prior to start of award.
Academic/Career Areas: Health and Medical Sciences.
Award: Grant for use in postdoctoral years; not renewable. *Number:* 10–20. *Amount:* up to $25,000.
Eligibility Requirements: Applicant must have employment experience in teaching.
Application Requirements: Application, references. **Deadline:** September 1.
Phone: 703-522-8544 **Fax:** 703-522-8586

Contact: Dolph Chianchiano, Director, Science Policy
National Kidney Foundation
1911 North Fort Myer Drive, #801
Arlington, VA 22209

▼ OLFACTORY RESEARCH FUND, LTD.

Olfactory Research Fund Research Grants   *see number 368*

▼ ORTHOPAEDIC RESEARCH AND EDUCATION FOUNDATION

American Association of Orthopaedic Surgeons/Orthopaedic Research and Education Foundation Fellowship in Health Service Research • **472**

Grant available to candidates who have completed an accredited North American orthopedic residency and are recommended by their department chair. Two one-year fellowships at up to $70,000 per year.
Academic/Career Areas: Health and Medical Sciences; Therapy/Rehabilitation.
Application Requirements: Application, references. **Deadline:** May 31.
E-mail: mcguire@aaos.org
Phone: 847-384-4348 **Fax:** 847-698-9767
World Wide Web: http://www.oref.org
Contact: Jean McGuire, Director of Grants
Orthopaedic Research and Education
Foundation
6300 North River Road, Suite 700
Rosemont, IL 60018-4261

Orthopaedic Research and Education Foundation Career Development Awards • **473**

Several grants available to candidates who have completed a residency in orthopedic surgery. Must submit letters of support as evidence of candidate's potential to develop as an investigator. Awards up to $75,000 per year for three years.
Academic/Career Areas: Health and Medical Sciences; Therapy/Rehabilitation.
Award: Grant for use in postdoctoral years; renewable. *Number:* 2–3. *Amount:* up to $75,000.
Application Requirements: Application, references. **Deadline:** August 1.
E-mail: mcguire@aaos.org
Phone: 847-384-4348 **Fax:** 847-698-9767

Orthopaedic Research and Education Foundation Career Development Awards (continued)

World Wide Web: http://www.oref.org
Contact: Jean McGuire, Director of Grants
Orthopaedic Research and Education
Foundation
6300 North River Road, Suite 700
Rosemont, IL 60018-4261

Orthopaedic Research and Education Foundation Clinical Research Awards • 474

One award to recognize outstanding clinical research related to musculoskeletal disease or injury. Original manuscripts must be submitted by July 1. One-time award of up to $20,000.
Academic/Career Areas: Health and Medical Sciences; Therapy/Rehabilitation.
Award: Prize for use in graduate years; not renewable. *Number:* 1. *Amount:* up to $20,000.
Application Requirements: Applicant must enter a contest. **Deadline:** July 1.
E-mail: mcguire@aaos.org
Phone: 847-384-4348 **Fax:** 847-698-9767
World Wide Web: http://www.oref.org
Contact: Jean McGuire, Director of Grants
Orthopaedic Research and Education
Foundation
6300 North River Road, Suite 700
Rosemont, IL 60018-4261

Orthopaedic Research and Education Foundation Prospective Clinical Research Proposals • 475

Several grants available to individuals at U.S. and Canadian Medical Training centers for promising clinical research. Grants of $50,000 per year renewable for up to three years.
Academic/Career Areas: Health and Medical Sciences; Therapy/Rehabilitation.
Award: Grant for use in graduate years; renewable. *Number:* 1–2. *Amount:* up to $50,000.
Application Requirements: Application. **Deadline:** August 1.
E-mail: mcguire@aaos.org
Phone: 847-384-4348 **Fax:** 847-698-9767
World Wide Web: http://www.oref.org
Contact: Jean McGuire, Director of Grants
Orthopaedic Research and Education
Foundation
6300 North River Road, Suite 700
Rosemont, IL 60018-4261

Orthopaedic Research and Education Foundation Research Grants • 476

Several grants available to individuals at U.S. and Canadian medical training centers for musculoskeletal research. Grants of $50,000 per year renewable for up to two years.
Academic/Career Areas: Health and Medical Sciences; Therapy/Rehabilitation.
Award: Grant for use in graduate years; renewable. *Number:* 9–12. *Amount:* up to $50,000.
Application Requirements: Application. **Deadline:** August 1.
E-mail: mcguire@aaos.org
Phone: 847-384-4348 **Fax:** 847-698-9767
World Wide Web: http://www.oref.org
Contact: Jean McGuire, Director of Grants
Orthopaedic Research and Education
Foundation
6300 North River Road, Suite 700
Rosemont, IL 60018-4261

▼ PARALYZED VETERANS OF AMERICA—SPINAL CORD RESEARCH FOUNDATION

Fellowships in Spinal Cord Injury Research see number 280

▼ PILOT INTERNATIONAL FOUNDATION

Marie Newton Sepia Memorial Award • 477

One-time award for graduate students planning careers in which they will work with children having brain-related disorders/disabilities. Must be sponsored by a Pilot Club. Minimum 3.5 GPA required. Application deadline March 1.
Academic/Career Areas: Health and Medical Sciences; Nursing; Special Education; Therapy/Rehabilitation.
Award: Scholarship for use in graduate years; not renewable. *Number:* 5–10. *Amount:* $500–$1000.
Application Requirements: Application, essay, financial need analysis, references, self-addressed stamped envelope, transcript. **Deadline:** March 1.
Contact: Awards Director
Pilot International Foundation
244 College Street, Box 5600
Macon, GA 31208-5600

▼ ROSCOE POUND FOUNDATION

Elaine Osborne Jacobson Award for Women Working in Health Care Law see number 435

▼ SIGMA XI, THE SCIENTIFIC RESEARCH SOCIETY

National Academy of Science Grants-in-Aid of Research   see number 281

Sigma Xi Grants-in-Aid of Research   see number 271

▼ SOCIETY FOR THE SCIENTIFIC STUDY OF SEXUALITY

Society for the Scientific Study of Sexuality Student Research Grant   see number 370

▼ TOURETTE SYNDROME ASSOCIATION, INC.

Tourette Syndrome Association Research Grants   • 478

One-time award for research relevant to Tourette Syndrome. Research proposals should be in basic neuroscience or clinical studies related to the etiology, pathophysiology, and treatments of Tourette Syndrome. Several grants of up to $40,000.
Academic/Career Areas: Health and Medical Sciences.
Award: Grant for use in graduate years; not renewable. *Number:* 15–20. *Amount:* $5000–$40,000.
Application Requirements: Application. **Deadline:** December 22.
E-mail: tourette@ix.netcom.com
Phone: 718-224-2999 **Fax:** 718-279-9596
Contact: Sue Levi-Pearl
Tourette Syndrome Association, Inc.
42-40 Bell Boulevard
Bayside, NY 11361-2874

▼ WHITAKER FOUNDATION

Doctoral Fellowship Program in Biomedical Engineering   see number 371

▼ WHITEHALL FOUNDATION, INC.

Whitehall Foundation, Inc. Grants-in-Aid   see number 282

Whitehall Foundation, Inc. Research Grants   see number 283

▼ WILLIAM T. GRANT FOUNDATION

Grant Foundation Faculty Scholars Program   see number 415

Grant Foundation Research Grants   • 479

Renewable research grants for young investigators to study the development of children, adolescents, and youth; and to evaluate social interventions aimed to prevent problem behaviors in children, adolescents, and youth. Submit cover letter, abstract, and full proposal. Write for more information.
Academic/Career Areas: Health and Medical Sciences; Social Sciences.
Award: Grant for use in graduate years; renewable.
Deadline: Continuous.
Phone: 212-752-0071
Contact: Grants Coordinator
William T. Grant Foundation
570 Lexington Avenue, 18th Floor
New York, NY 10022-5403

▼ ZENECA PHARMACEUTICALS GROUP/NATIONAL OSTEOPATHIC FOUNDATION

Zeneca Pharmaceuticals Underserved Healthcare Grants   • 480

Up to two awards open to third-year osteopathic medical students who are committed to serving underserved or minority populations. One-time award of $5000-$10,000.
Academic/Career Areas: Health and Medical Sciences.
Award: Grant for use in graduate years; not renewable. *Number:* 1–2. *Amount:* $5000–$10,000.
Application Requirements: Application, essay, interview, references. **Deadline:** January 31.
E-mail: nof@assnhq.com
Phone: 404-705-9999 **Fax:** 404-252-0774
World Wide Web: http://www.osteopathic.org
Contact: Angela Abney, Staff Associate
Zeneca Pharmaceuticals Group/National
Osteopathic Foundation
5775G Peachtree-Dunwoody Road
Suite 500-G
Atlanta, GA 30342

HEALTH INFORMATION MANAGEMENT/TECHNOLOGY

▼ **BLUE CROSS BLUE SHIELD OF MICHIGAN FOUNDATION**

Blue Cross Blue Shield of Michigan Foundation Student Award Program　　see number 416

▼ **CANADIAN FOUNDATION FOR THE STUDY OF INFANT DEATHS**

Dr. Sydney Segal Research Grants　　see number 275

▼ **EASTER SEAL RESEARCH INSTITUTE**

Elizabeth St. Louis Award　　see number 354

▼ **NATIONAL ASSOCIATION FOR WOMEN IN EDUCATION**

Women's Research Award　　see number 413

HEATING, AIR-CONDITIONING, AND REFRIGERATION MECHANICS

▼ **AMERICAN SOCIETY OF HEATING, REFRIGERATING, AND AIR CONDITIONING ENGINEERS**

ASHRAE Research Grants for Graduate Students　　• 481

One-time award for full-time study in heating, ventilating, air-conditioning, and refrigeration. Participation of applicant and her/his adviser in ASHRAE is given strong consideration in selection of recipients. Submit application which includes description of research project, amount of grant needed, and information on institution and faculty adviser. Transcript required but does not have to be official.
Academic/Career Areas: Heating, Air-Conditioning, and Refrigeration Mechanics; Mechanical Engineering; Trade/Technical Specialties.
Award: Grant for use in graduate years; not renewable. *Number:* 20–25. *Amount:* $7500.

Application Requirements: Application, references, transcript.
Deadline: December 15.
E-mail: benedict@ashrae.org
Phone: 404-636-8400 **Fax:** 404-321-5478
World Wide Web: http://www.ashrae.org
Contact: Lois Benedict, Executive Secretary
　　American Society of Heating, Refrigerating, and Air Conditioning Engineers
　　1791 Tullie Circle, NE
　　Atlanta, GA 30329-1683

▼ **DEMONSTRATION OF ENERGY-EFFICIENT DEVELOPMENTS PROGRAM**

Demonstration of Energy-Efficient Developments Scholarship　　see number 417

HISTORIC PRESERVATION AND CONSERVATION

▼ **ASIAN CULTURAL COUNCIL**

Ford Foundation Fellowships　　see number 335

▼ **CENTER FOR FIELD RESEARCH**

Center for Field Research Grants for Field Research　　see number 294

▼ **JAPAN FOUNDATION**

Japan Foundation Cultural Properties Specialist Fellowship　　see number 310

▼ **SOCIETY OF ARCHITECTURAL HISTORIANS**

Architectural Study Tour Scholarship　　see number 317

Keepers Preservation Education Fund Fellowship　　see number 319

▼ **WINTERTHUR MUSEUM, GARDEN, AND LIBRARY**

NEH Fellowships　　see number 321

Winterthur Research Fellowships see number 322

HISTORY

▼ ALBERT EINSTEIN INSTITUTION

Albert Einstein Institution Fellowships • 482

Renewable fellowship for Ph.D. students for research on strategic uses of nonviolent action. Must submit proposal, transcript, and references by January 1. Write for further information.
Academic/Career Areas: History; Political Science; Social Sciences.
Application Requirements: References, transcript. **Deadline:** January 1.
E-mail: einstein@igc.apc.org
Phone: 617-876-0311 **Fax:** 617-876-0837
Contact: Dr. Ronald M. McCarthy, Program Director
Albert Einstein Institution
50 Church Street
Cambridge, MA 02138

▼ AMERICAN JEWISH COMMITTEE

Harold W. Rosenthal Fellowship in International Relations see number 374

▼ AMERICAN SCHOOLS OF ORIENTAL RESEARCH

Mesopotamian Fellowship • 483

Award for one three- to six-month period of research. Primarily for field research in ancient Mesopotamian civilization carried out in Middle East, but other research projects such as museum or archival research related to Mesopotamian studies may also be considered. One-time award of $5000. Deadline February 1.
Academic/Career Areas: History; Social Sciences.
Application Requirements: Application, references, transcript.
Deadline: February 1.
E-mail: asor@bu.edu
Phone: 617-353-6570 **Fax:** 617-353-6575
World Wide Web: http://www.asor.org/
Contact: Holly Andrews, Administrative Assistant
American Schools of Oriental Research
656 Beacon Street, 5th Floor
Boston, MA 02215-2010

▼ CANADIAN INSTITUTE OF UKRAINIAN STUDIES—PETER JACYK CENTRE FOR UKRAINIAN HISTORICAL RESEARCH

Doctoral Thesis Fellowship in Ukrainian History see number 407

Michael Dorosh Fund Master's Fellowship see number 408

▼ CANADIAN INSTITUTE OF UKRANIAN STUDIES—PETER JACYK CENTRE FOR UKRANIAN HISTORICAL RESEARCH

Helen Darcovich Memorial Endowment Fund Doctoral Fellowship see number 409

▼ CENTER FOR THE STUDY OF THE HISTORY OF NURSING

Lillian Sholtis Brunner Summer Fellowship • 484

One fellowship available to graduate students to support residential study using the Center's collections. Selection based on evidence of preparation and/or productivity in historical research related to nursing. One-time award offered every other year. Application deadline: December 30, 1999.
Academic/Career Areas: History; Nursing.
Award: Scholarship for use in graduate years; not renewable. *Number:* 1. *Amount:* $2500.
Application Requirements: Application. **Deadline:** December 30.
Phone: 215-898-4502
World Wide Web: http://www.upenn.edu/nursing/facres_history.html
Contact: Center for the Study of the History of Nursing
Nursing Education Building
420 Guardian Drive
Philadelphia, PA 19104-6096

▼ CHARLES BABBAGE INSTITUTE

Adelle and Erwin Tomash Fellowship in the History of Information Processing see number 391

▼ DAVID LIBRARY OF THE AMERICAN REVOLUTION

Fellowships for the Study of the American Revolution • 485

One-time fellowship for pre- and postdoctoral scholars for the study of the political, military, diplomatic, and social aspects of American history from 1750-1800. Fellowship takes place at David Library in Pennsylvania. Submit curriculum vitae and project description.

Academic/Career Areas: History; Social Sciences.
Eligibility Requirements: Applicant must be studying in Pennsylvania.
Application Requirements: Application, essay, references.
Deadline: March 1.
E-mail: djfowler@libertynet.org
Phone: 215-493-6776
Contact: David Fowler, Director
David Library of the American Revolution
River Road, Box 748
Washington Crossing, PA 18977

▼ DUMBARTON OAKS

Bliss Prize Fellowship in Byzantine Studies see number 328

▼ FRANKLIN AND ELEANOR ROOSEVELT INSTITUTE

Roosevelt Institute Grant-in-Aid • 486

One-time award given for research at the Franklin D. Roosevelt Library at Hyde Park, New York. Research topic should be designed to expand the knowledge of the Roosevelt period. Deadlines for application: February 15 and September 15. Several grants of up to $2500. Must submit proposal and letters of recommendation. Write for guidelines.

Academic/Career Areas: History; Political Science.
Award: Scholarship for use in graduate years; not renewable. *Number:* 15–25. *Amount:* up to $2500.
Eligibility Requirements: Applicant must be studying in New York.
Application Requirements: Application, references.
E-mail: jhamrah@idsi.net
Phone: 914-229-5321 **Fax:** 914-229-9046
Contact: Julie Hamrah, Assistant to the Executive Director
Franklin and Eleanor Roosevelt Institute
511 Albany Post Road
Hyde Park, NY 12538

▼ GERMAN HISTORICAL INSTITUTE

German Historical Institute Dissertation Scholarships • 487

One-time award for German and American doctoral candidates who have begun work on social science and humanities dissertations. Include curriculum vitae, research proposal, and letter of recommendation from doctoral adviser with application. Research must focus on German history in American archives.

Academic/Career Areas: History; Humanities; Political Science; Social Sciences.
Award: Scholarship for use in graduate years; not renewable. *Number:* 10–12. *Amount:* $1000–$1200.
Application Requirements: Application, essay, references, transcript. **Deadline:** May 31.
Phone: 202-387-3355 **Fax:** 202-483-3430
Contact: Christof Mauch
German Historical Institute
1607 New Hampshire Avenue, NW
Washington, DC 20009

▼ HARRY FRANK GUGGENHEIM FOUNDATION

H. F. Guggenheim Foundation Research Grants see number 329

▼ HARRY S TRUMAN LIBRARY INSTITUTE

Harry S Truman Library Institute Research Grants • 488

Bi-annual, one-time award for graduate students and post-doctoral scholars to use the Library archival facilities for one to three weeks. May only be used for travel and expenses. Application deadlines are April 1 and October 1 and results are announced six weeks later.

Academic/Career Areas: History.
Award: Scholarship for use in graduate years; not renewable. *Amount:* up to $2500.
Application Requirements: Application.
E-mail: lisa.sullivan@truman.nara.gov
Phone: 816-833-0425 **Fax:** 816-833-2715
World Wide Web: http://www.lbjlib.utexas.edu/truman/
Contact: Lisa Sullivan, Office Manager
Harry S Truman Library Institute
US Highway 24 and Delaware Street
Independence, MO 64050

Harry S Truman Library Institute Dissertation Year Fellowships • 489

One-time award for graduate students who have completed their dissertation research and are ready to begin writing. Research should be related to the history of the Truman administration and the public career of Harry S Truman.
Academic/Career Areas: History.
Application Requirements: Application. **Deadline:** February 1.
E-mail: lisa.sullivan@truman.nara.gov
Phone: 816-833-0425 **Fax:** 816-833-2715
World Wide Web: http://www.lbjlib.utexas.edu/truman/
Contact: Lisa Sullivan, Office Manager
Harry S Truman Library Institute
US Highway 24 and Delaware Street
Independence, MO 64050

Harry S Truman Library Institute Scholar's Award • 490

One-time award offered in even-numbered years to an established scholar or a scholar about to embark on his/her career who is engaged in a study of the public career of Harry Truman or some aspect of the Truman administration. Scholar's work must be based on utilization of Truman Library. Award amount is based on applicant's budget but will not exceed half of applicant's academic year salary or comparable figure. Submit informal proposal by December 15 of year preceding the one in which award is available. If selected, submit budget and forms by February 15.
Academic/Career Areas: History.
Award: Scholarship for use in postdoctoral years; not renewable.
Deadline: December 15.
E-mail: lisa.sullivan@truman.nara.gov
Phone: 816-833-0425 **Fax:** 816-833-2715
World Wide Web: http://www.lbjlib.utexas.edu/truman/
Contact: Lisa Sullivan, Office Manager
Harry S Truman Library Institute
US Highway 24 and Delaware Street
Independence, MO 64050

Harry S Truman Library Institute Dissertation Year Fellowships • 491

Award for graduate students who have completed dissertation research on public career of Harry S Truman or Truman era and are ready to begin writing. Two one-time awards of $16,000. Deadline: February 1.
Academic/Career Areas: History; Political Science.

Application Requirements: Application, references. **Deadline:** February 1.
E-mail: library@truman.nara.gov
Phone: 816-833-0425 **Fax:** 816-833-2715
Contact: Harry S Truman Library Institute
US Highway 24 and Delaware Street
Independence, MO 64050-0798

▼ INSTITUTE FOR HUMANE STUDIES

Humane Studies Fellowships see number 384

▼ INSTITUTE OF ELECTRICAL AND ELECTRONICS ENGINEERS CENTER FOR THE HISTORY OF ELECTRICAL ENGINEERING

Institute of Electrical and Electronics Engineers Fellowship in Electrical History see number 422

▼ PHI BETA KAPPA SOCIETY

Mary Isabel Sibley Fellowship for Greek and French Studies see number 332

▼ PI GAMMA MU INTERNATIONAL HONOR SOCIETY IN SOCIETY SCIENCE

Pi Gamma Mu Scholarship see number 392

▼ SHELBY CULLUM DAVIS CENTER FOR HISTORICAL STUDIES, PRINCETON UNIVERSITY

Shelby Cullum Davis Center for Historical Studies Visiting Fellowship • 492

One-time fellowship, at Princeton University, for highly recommended younger scholars who have finished their dissertations or for senior scholars with established reputations. Deadline December 1.
Academic/Career Areas: History.
Eligibility Requirements: Applicant must be studying in New Jersey.
Application Requirements: Application, references. **Deadline:** December 1.
E-mail: kmhoover@princeton.edu
Phone: 609-258-4997 **Fax:** 609-258-5326
Contact: Kari Hoover, Manager
Shelby Cullum Davis Center for Historical Studies, Princeton University
129 Dickinson Hall
Princeton, NJ 08544-1017

▼ SMITHSONIAN INSTITUTION NATIONAL AIR AND SPACE MUSEUM

Guggenheim Fellowship   *see number 300*

▼ STATE HISTORICAL SOCIETY OF WISCONSIN

Alice E. Smith Fellowship   • **493**

Award for female graduate students pursuing a degree in U.S. history. Must submit four copies of a two-page research proposal. Preference given to the study of Wisconsin or the American Midwest. One-time award of $2000.
Academic/Career Areas: History.
Eligibility Requirements: Applicant must be female.
Application Requirements: Essay. **Deadline:** July 15.
Phone: 608-264-6464
Contact: Dr. Michael Stevens, State Historian
State Historical Society of Wisconsin
816 State Street
Madison, WI 53706-1488

Amy Louise Hunter Fellowship   • **494**

Awarded in even-numbered years for research on topics related to the history of women and public policy. Preference given to Wisconsin topics. Must include four copies of two-page research proposal and resume.
Academic/Career Areas: History; Humanities; Social Sciences.
Application Requirements: Essay. **Deadline:** May 1.
Phone: 608-264-6464
Contact: Dr. Michael Stevens, State Historian
State Historical Society of Wisconsin
816 State Street
Madison, WI 53706-1488

J.C. Geilfuss Fellowship   *see number 405*

▼ WINTERTHUR MUSEUM, GARDEN, AND LIBRARY

NEH Fellowships   *see number 321*

Winterthur Research Fellowships   *see number 322*

HOME ECONOMICS

▼ KAPPA OMICRON NU HONOR SOCIETY

Dorothy I. Mitstifer Fellowship   *see number 430*

Kappa Omicron Nu National Alumni Fellowship   *see number 431*

Kappa Omicron Nu New Initiatives Grant   *see number 432*

▼ WINTERTHUR MUSEUM, GARDEN, AND LIBRARY

NEH Fellowships   *see number 321*

Winterthur Research Fellowships   *see number 322*

HORTICULTURE/FLORICULTURE

▼ AMERICAN ORCHID SOCIETY

American Orchid Society/Orchid Research Grant   *see number 346*

▼ GARDEN CLUB OF AMERICA

Garden Club of America Award in Tropical Botany   • **495**

Two grants to promote the preservation of tropical forests by enlarging the body of botanists with field experience. Open to Ph.D. candidates. One-time award of $5500.
Academic/Career Areas: Horticulture/Floriculture.
Award: Scholarship for use in graduate years; not renewable. *Number:* 2. *Amount:* $5500.
Application Requirements: Application, self-addressed stamped envelope. **Deadline:** December 31.
Phone: 202-778-9714 **Fax:** 202-293-9211
World Wide Web: http://www.gcamerica.org
Contact: Ms. Marlar Oo
Garden Club of America
World Wildlife Fund
1250 24th Street, NW
Washington, DC 20037-1175

Interchange Fellowship and Martin McLaren Scholarship • 496

Interchange fellowship available for an American graduate to participate in a work-study program at universities and botanical gardens in the U.K. Funding for a Briton to study for one graduate academic year in the U.S. Two one-time awards. Submit medical form.

Academic/Career Areas: Horticulture/Floriculture.

Award: Scholarship for use in graduate years; not renewable. *Number:* 2.

Application Requirements: Application, autobiography, essay, interview, self-addressed stamped envelope, transcript.

Deadline: November 15.

World Wide Web: http://www.users.interport.net/~gca

Contact: Scholarship Committee
Garden Club of America
14 East 60th Street
New York, NY 10022

▼ **WOMAN'S NATIONAL FARM AND GARDEN ASSOCIATION**

Sarah Bradley Tyson Memorial Fellowships   *see number 272*

HUMANITIES

▼ **ALEXANDER VON HUMBOLDT-STIFTUNG**

Transatlantic Research Cooperation between German and American Scholars in the Human and Social Sciences, Economics, and Law
                                            see number 399

▼ **AMERICAN JEWISH COMMITTEE**

Harold W. Rosenthal Fellowship in International Relations   *see number 374*

▼ **ARCHAEOLOGICAL INSTITUTE OF AMERICA AND THE AMERICAN FRIENDS OF APHRODISIAS**

Archaeological Institute of America/Kenan T. Erim Award   *see number 323*

▼ **CANADIAN INSTITUTE OF UKRAINIAN STUDIES—PETER JACYK CENTRE FOR UKRAINIAN HISTORICAL RESEARCH**

Doctoral Thesis Fellowship in Ukrainian History   *see number 407*

Michael Dorosh Fund Master's Fellowship   *see number 408*

▼ **CANADIAN INSTITUTE OF UKRANIAN STUDIES—PETER JACYK CENTRE FOR UKRANIAN HISTORICAL RESEARCH**

Helen Darcovich Memorial Endowment Fund Doctoral Fellowship   *see number 409*

▼ **CENTER FOR FIELD RESEARCH**

Center for Field Research Grants for Field Research   *see number 294*

▼ **CENTER FOR HELLENIC STUDIES**

Center for Hellenic Studies Fellowships   *see number 327*

▼ **CHARLES BABBAGE INSTITUTE**

Adelle and Erwin Tomash Fellowship in the History of Information Processing *see number 391*

▼ **DUMBARTON OAKS**

Bliss Prize Fellowship in Byzantine Studies   *see number 328*

▼ **GERMAN ACADEMIC EXCHANGE SERVICE (DEUTSCHER AKADEMISCHER AUSTAUSCHDIENST)**

DAAD-ALCS Collaborative Research Grants • 497

Award for German scholars who wish to carry out joint research projects in the social sciences and humanities with U.S. researchers. German and American scholars apply as co-applicants.

DAAD-ALCS Collaborative Research Grants (continued)

Academic/Career Areas: Humanities; Social Sciences.
Award: Scholarship for use in postdoctoral years; not renewable.
Application Requirements: Application. **Deadline:** September 1.
E-mail: daadny@daad.org
Phone: 212-758-3223 **Fax:** 212-755-5780
World Wide Web: http://www.daad.org
Contact: Dr. Rolf Hoffman, Director
German Academic Exchange Service
(Deutscher Akademischer
Austauschdienst)
950 Third Avenue, 19th Floor
New York, NY 10022

▼ GERMAN HISTORICAL INSTITUTE

*German Historical Institute Dissertation
Scholarships*   see number 487

▼ HAGLEY MUSEUM AND LIBRARY

*Hagley Museum and Library
Grants-in-Aid*   see number 308

*Henry Belin du Pont Dissertation
Fellowship*   see number 309

▼ HARRY FRANK GUGGENHEIM FOUNDATION

*H. F. Guggenheim Foundation Research
Grants*   see number 329

▼ HERBERT HOOVER PRESIDENTIAL LIBRARY ASSOCIATION

*Herbert Hoover Presidential Library
Association Travel Grants*   • 498
One-time award for travel to West Branch, Iowa to conduct research at the Herbert Hoover Presidential Library. Graduate students of the social sciences or humanities may apply. Submit application and references. Awards range from $500 to $1200.
Academic/Career Areas: Humanities; Social Sciences.
Award: Grant for use in graduate years; not renewable.
Amount: $500–$1200.
Eligibility Requirements: Applicant must be studying in Iowa.
Application Requirements: Application, references. **Deadline:** March 1.

E-mail: hhpla@aol.com
Phone: 319-643-5327 **Fax:** 319-643-2391
Contact: Patricia Hand, Office Manager
Herbert Hoover Presidential Library
Association
PO Box 696
West Branch, IA 52358-0696

▼ INSTITUTE FOR GLOBAL STUDIES IN CULTURE, POWER, AND HISTORY

*Postdoctoral Fellowships in African-American
Culture*   • 499
Fellow will be affiliated with the Institute for Global Studies in Culture, Power, and History in Maryland. Open to scholars in all disciplines working on Afro-American culture. Submit proposal, course suggestions.
Academic/Career Areas: Humanities; Social Sciences.
Eligibility Requirements: Applicant must be studying in Maryland.
Application Requirements: Application, autobiography, references. **Deadline:** January 16.
E-mail: iscph@jhuvms.hcf.jhu.edu
World Wide Web: http://www.jhu.edu/~igscph
Contact: Institute for Global Studies in Culture,
Power, and History
404 Macaulay Hall
3400 North Charles Street
Baltimore, MD 21218-2684

▼ INSTITUTE FOR HUMANE STUDIES

Humane Studies Fellowships   see number 384

▼ INTERNATIONAL RESEARCH AND EXCHANGES BOARD

*International Research and Exchanges Board
Short-term Travel Grants*   • 500
Several grants available to graduate students for scholarly projects focusing on Central and Eastern Europe, Eurasia, and Mongolia. Ph.D. or equivalent professional degree required at time of application. Applicants in the humanities and social sciences only. Deadlines are February 1 and June 1. Several awards not to exceed $3000 each.
Academic/Career Areas: Humanities; Social Sciences.
Award: Scholarship for use in graduate years; not renewable. *Amount:* up to $3000.
Application Requirements: Application.
E-mail: irex@irex.org

Phone: 202-628-8188 **Fax:** 202-628-8189
World Wide Web: http://www.irex.org
Contact: Program Officer
International Research and Exchanges
Board
1616 H Street, NW
Washington, DC 20006

▼ IRISH-AMERICAN CULTURAL INSTITUTE

Irish Research Funds   *see number 330*

▼ JAPAN FOUNDATION

Japan Foundation Doctoral Fellowship   • **501**

Award for doctoral candidates in the humanities and social sciences, as well as in other disciplines, who are conducting comparative research projects and need the opportunity to conduct research in Japan. Fifteen one-time awards. Must submit language evaluation.
Academic/Career Areas: Humanities; Social Sciences.
Eligibility Requirements: Applicant must have an interest in Japanese language.
Application Requirements: Application, essay, references, transcript. **Deadline:** November 1.
E-mail: chris_watanabe@jfny.org
Phone: 212-489-0299 **Fax:** 212-489-0409
World Wide Web: http://www.jfny.org
Contact: Christopher Watanabe, Program Assistant
Japan Foundation
152 West 57th Street, 39th Floor
New York, NY 10019

Japan Foundation Research Fellowship   • **502**

Awards for scholars, researchers, and professionals who wish to conduct research in Japan for periods ranging from two to twelve months. Fifteen one-time awards. Research must be related to the social sciences or humanities.
Academic/Career Areas: Humanities; Social Sciences.
Eligibility Requirements: Applicant must have employment experience in experience in career field and must have an interest in Japanese language.
Application Requirements: Application, essay, references.
Deadline: November 1.
E-mail: chris_watanabe@jfny.org
Phone: 212-489-0299 **Fax:** 212-489-0409
World Wide Web: http://www.jfny.org

Contact: Christopher Watanabe, Program Assistant
Japan Foundation
152 West 57th Street, 39th Floor
New York, NY 10019

▼ LYNDON BAINES JOHNSON FOUNDATION

Lyndon Baines Johnson Foundation
Grants-in-Aid Research   • **503**

Candidates for assistance should have thoughtful and well written proposals that state clearly and precisely how the holdings of the Lyndon Baines Johnson Library will contribute to historical research. Deadlines: July 31 and January 31.
Academic/Career Areas: Humanities; Social Sciences.
Award: Grant for use in graduate years; not renewable.
Amount: $500–$2000.
Eligibility Requirements: Applicant must be studying in Texas.
Application Requirements: Application.
Phone: 512-478-7829 Ext. 296 **Fax:** 512-478-9104
Contact: Lawrence Reed, Assistant Director
Lyndon Baines Johnson Foundation
2313 Red River Street
Austin, TX 78705

▼ MRS. GILES WHITING FOUNDATION

Whiting Fellowships in the Humanities   • **504**

Offered at seven participating universities: Bryn Mawr College, University of Chicago, Columbia, Harvard, Princeton, Stanford, and Yale. For Ph.D. student in humanities in last year of dissertation writing. Recipients selected by university. Submit applications to universities, not to Foundation. Sixty awards of varying amounts.
Academic/Career Areas: Humanities.
Eligibility Requirements: Applicant must be studying in California, Connecticut, Illinois, Massachusetts, New Jersey, New York, or Pennsylvania.
Application Requirements: Application. **Deadline:** Continuous.
Phone: 212-336-2138
Contact: Kellye Rosenheim, Assistant Director
Mrs. Giles Whiting Foundation
1133 Avenue of Americas, 22nd Floor
New York, NY 10036-6710

▼ NATIONAL ACADEMY OF EDUCATION

Spencer Postdoctoral Fellowship
Program   *see number 411*

▼ NATIONAL ASSOCIATION FOR WOMEN IN EDUCATION

Women's Research Award see number 413

▼ PHI BETA KAPPA SOCIETY

Mary Isabel Sibley Fellowship for Greek and French Studies see number 332

▼ SOCIAL SCIENCE RESEARCH COUNCIL

Abe Fellowship Program see number 404

Japan Fellowship for Dissertation Workshop • 505

Award for full-time advanced graduate students who are enrolled at any U.S. institutions. Applicants may be at any stage in the dissertation process except the very last write-up stage leading toward submission and must have an approved dissertation prospectus. A narrative description of dissertation topic is required. Workshop will take place in early January in Monterey, California.
Academic/Career Areas: Humanities; Social Sciences.
Application Requirements: Application, references. **Deadline:** November 15.
World Wide Web: http://www.ssrc.org
Contact: Social Science Research Council
810 Seventh Avenue
New York, NY 10019

▼ SOCIAL SCIENCE RESEARCH COUNCIL-MACARTHUR FOUNDATION

Postdoctoral Fellowships on Peace and Security in a Changing World see number 369

▼ SOCIETY FARSAROTUL

Society Farsarotul Financial Awards see number 333

▼ STATE HISTORICAL SOCIETY OF WISCONSIN

Amy Louise Hunter Fellowship see number 494

▼ WOODROW WILSON NATIONAL FELLOWSHIP FOUNDATION

Woodrow Wilson National Fellowship Foundation Women's Studies Dissertation Grant • 506

Women's studies research grants for Ph.D. candidates writing their dissertations on topics concerning women. Must submit research prospectus, bibliography, and timetable. One-time award of $1500.
Academic/Career Areas: Humanities; Social Sciences.
Award: Grant for use in graduate years; not renewable.
Number: 15. *Amount:* $1500.
Application Requirements: Application, references, transcript.
Deadline: October 15.
Phone: 609-452-7007 **Fax:** 609-452-0066
World Wide Web: http://www.woodrow.org
Contact: Judith Pinch, Vice President
Woodrow Wilson National Fellowship
Foundation
PO Box 2437
Princeton, NJ 08543-2437

INTERIOR DESIGN

▼ AMERICAN SOCIETY OF INTERIOR DESIGNERS EDUCATIONAL FOUNDATION

Mabelle Wilhelmina Boldt Memorial Scholarship • 507

Award open to designers who have practiced for at least five years and are enrolled in or have applied for admission to a graduate-level program. Send self-addressed stamped envelope for more information. One scholarship of $2000.
Academic/Career Areas: Interior Design.
Award: Scholarship for use in graduate years; not renewable. *Number:* 1. *Amount:* $2000.
Eligibility Requirements: Applicant must have employment experience in experience in career field.
Application Requirements: Application, essay, references, self-addressed stamped envelope, transcript. **Deadline:** March 4.

Contact: Jenna Ashley, Associate Director of Student
Services
American Society of Interior Designers
Educational Foundation
608 Massachusetts Avenue, NE
Washington, DC 20002-6006

▼ WINTERTHUR MUSEUM, GARDEN, AND LIBRARY

NEH Fellowships **see number 321**

Winterthur Research Fellowships **see number 322**

INTERNATIONAL MIGRATION

▼ SOCIAL SCIENCE RESEARCH COUNCIL

Social Science Research Center International Migration Research Planning Grant • 508

Awarded to two teams of two or more scholars from at least two different disciplines. Applicants must hold Ph.D. or equivalent in a social science or applied professional field. International scholars who will be affiliated with a U.S. academic or research institution during the time of award may apply. One-time award. Contact Web site for most recent information.
Academic/Career Areas: International Migration; Social Sciences.
Award: Grant for use in postdoctoral years; not renewable. *Number:* up to 8.
Application Requirements: Application. **Deadline:** January 10.
World Wide Web: http://www.ssrc.org
Contact: Social Science Research Council
810 Seventh Avenue
New York, NY 10019

JOURNALISM

▼ ARMENIAN PROFESSIONAL SOCIETY OF THE BAY AREA

Armenian Professional Society of the Bay Area Scholarships **see number 324**

▼ INTER AMERICAN PRESS ASSOCIATION SCHOLARSHIP FUND

Inter American Press Association Scholarship Fund for Latin American Reporters • 509

Two scholarships available for Latin American newspaper reporters, fluent in English or French, to study in Canada or the U.S. Must submit three samples of published articles. Must be between the ages of 21 and 35.
Academic/Career Areas: Journalism.
Award: Scholarship for use in graduate years; not renewable. *Number:* 2. *Amount:* $10,200–$12,200.
Eligibility Requirements: Applicant must be Latin American/Caribbean; ages 21-35 and have employment experience in journalism.
Application Requirements: Application, autobiography, essay, references, test scores, transcript. **Deadline:** December 21.
Phone: 305-376-3522 **Fax:** 305-376-8950
Contact: Ms. Zulay Dominguez Chirinos, Assistant Secretary
Inter American Press Association Scholarship Fund
2911 Northwest 39th Street
Miami, FL 33142

▼ MARINE BIOLOGICAL LABORATORY, WOODS HOLE

Marine Biological Laboratory Science Writing Fellowships Program • 510

One-time fellowship for one to eight weeks to conduct field or laboratory research at the Marine Biological Laboratory. Applicants must be professional science writers with at least two years experience. Preference given to print/broadcast journalists with staff positions.
Academic/Career Areas: Journalism; TV/Radio Broadcasting.
Eligibility Requirements: Applicant must be studying in Massachusetts and have employment experience in experience in career field or journalism.
Application Requirements: Application, essay. **Deadline:** March 9.
E-mail: pclapp@mbl.edu
Phone: 508-289-7423 **Fax:** 508-457-1924
World Wide Web: http://www.mbl.edu
Contact: Pamela Clapp, Director of Communications
Marine Biological Laboratory, Woods Hole
7 MBL Street
Woods Hole, MA 02543-1015

▼ NATIONAL ASSOCIATION OF
BROADCASTERS

*National Association of Broadcasters Grants
for Research in Broadcasting*   *see number 385*

▼ SOCIAL SCIENCE RESEARCH
COUNCIL-MACARTHUR
FOUNDATION

*Postdoctoral Fellowships on Peace and Security
in a Changing World*   *see number 369*

LANDSCAPE ARCHITECTURE

▼ HAGLEY MUSEUM AND LIBRARY

*Hagley Museum and Library
Grants-in-Aid*   *see number 308*

*Henry Belin du Pont Dissertation
Fellowship*   *see number 309*

▼ JAPAN FOUNDATION

*Japan Foundation Cultural Properties
Specialist Fellowship*   *see number 310*

▼ NATIONAL GALLERY OF ART

*Center for Advanced Study in the Visual Arts
Senior Fellowship Program*   *see number 311*

▼ NATIONAL GALLERY OF ART,
CENTER FOR ADVANCED STUDY IN
THE VISUAL ARTS

*Robert H. and Clarice Smith
Fellowship*   *see number 312*

▼ SKIDMORE, OWINGS, AND MERRILL
FOUNDATION

*Urban Design Traveling Fellowship
Program*   *see number 316*

▼ WINTERTHUR MUSEUM, GARDEN,
AND LIBRARY

NEH Fellowships   *see number 321*

Winterthur Research Fellowships   *see number 322*

▼ WOMAN'S NATIONAL FARM AND
GARDEN ASSOCIATION

*Sarah Bradley Tyson Memorial
Fellowships*   *see number 272*

LEGAL SERVICES

▼ ALEXANDER VON
HUMBOLDT-STIFTUNG

*Transatlantic Research Cooperation between
German and American Scholars in the Human
and Social Sciences, Economics, and Law*
    see number 399

▼ AMERICAN BAR FOUNDATION

*American Bar Foundation Doctoral Dissertation
Fellowships in Law and Social Science*   ● 511
Renewable awards for Ph.D. candidates writing disserta-
tions involving sociolegal studies. Must submit curriculum
vitae, dissertation prospectus, transcript, and references
by February 1.
Academic/Career Areas: Legal Services; Social Sciences.
Application Requirements: References, transcript. **Deadline:**
February 1.
E-mail: anne@abfn.org
Phone: 312-988-6500 **Fax:** 312-988-6579
Contact: Anne Tatalovich, Assistant Director
    American Bar Foundation
    750 North Lake Shore Drive
    Chicago, IL 60611

▼ AMERICAN GEOPHYSICAL UNION

*American Geophysical Union Horton Research
Grant*   *see number 284*

▼ CANADIAN INSTITUTE OF
UKRAINIAN STUDIES—PETER
JACYK CENTRE FOR UKRAINIAN
HISTORICAL RESEARCH
*Doctoral Thesis Fellowship in Ukrainian
History* see number 407

*Michael Dorosh Fund Master's
Fellowship* see number 408

▼ CANADIAN INSTITUTE OF
UKRANIAN STUDIES—PETER JACYK
CENTRE FOR UKRANIAN
HISTORICAL RESEARCH
*Helen Darcovich Memorial Endowment Fund
Doctoral Fellowship* see number 409

▼ INSTITUTE FOR HUMANE STUDIES
Humane Studies Fellowships see number 384

▼ ROSCOE POUND FOUNDATION
*Elaine Osborne Jacobson Award for Women
Working in Health Care Law* see number 435

▼ SOCIAL SCIENCE RESEARCH
COUNCIL-MACARTHUR
FOUNDATION
*Postdoctoral Fellowships on Peace and Security
in a Changing World* see number 369

▼ UNITED STATES DEPARTMENT OF
HOUSING AND URBAN
DEVELOPMENT, OFFICE OF POLICY
DEVELOPMENT AND RESEARCH
*Doctoral Dissertation Research Grant
(HUD)* see number 334

LIBRARY SCIENCES

▼ AMERICAN SOCIETY FOR
INFORMATION SCIENCE
*Institute for Scientific Information Doctoral
Dissertation Scholarship* see number 386

*Pratt-Severn Student Research
Award* see number 387

*Special Interest Group/STI BIOSIS Student
Award* see number 388

*Special Interest Group/STI Chemical Abstracts
Service Student Award* see number 389

UMI Doctoral Dissertation Award see number 390

▼ BETA PHI MU INTERNATIONAL
LIBRARY AND INFORMATION
STUDIES HONOR SOCIETY
Sarah Rebecca Reed Scholarship • 512
Award for a graduate student pursuing a master's in library science at an American Library Association-accredited library school. Write for further information. One-time award of $1500. Application period November 1 through March 15.
Academic/Career Areas: Library Sciences.
Award: Scholarship for use in graduate years; not renewable. *Number:* 1. *Amount:* $1500.
Application Requirements: Application, references, transcript.
E-mail: beta_phi_mu@lis.fsu.edu
Phone: 904-644-3907 **Fax:** 904-644-6253
Contact: Executive Director
Beta Phi Mu International Library and
Information Studies Honor Society
228 Louis Shores Building,
Florida State University
Tallahassee, FL 32306-2048

▼ CANADIAN INSTITUTE OF
UKRAINIAN STUDIES—PETER
JACYK CENTRE FOR UKRAINIAN
HISTORICAL RESEARCH
*Doctoral Thesis Fellowship in Ukrainian
History* see number 407

*Michael Dorosh Fund Master's
Fellowship*   *see number 408*

▼ CANADIAN INSTITUTE OF UKRANIAN STUDIES—PETER JACYK CENTRE FOR UKRANIAN HISTORICAL RESEARCH

*Helen Darcovich Memorial Endowment Fund
Doctoral Fellowship*   *see number 409*

▼ CANADIAN LIBRARY ASSOCIATION

*Canadian Library Association DaFoe
Scholarships*   • 513

One scholarship open to a college graduate entering an accredited Canadian library school. Application form, transcripts, reference, and proof of admission required. One-time award of 1750 Canadian dollars.
Academic/Career Areas: Library Sciences.
Award: Scholarship for use in graduate years; not renewable. *Number:* 1.
Application Requirements: Application, financial need analysis, references, transcript. **Deadline:** May 1.
Phone: 613-232-9625 Ext. 318 **Fax:** 613-563-9895
World Wide Web: http://www.cla.amlibs.ca
Contact: Brenda Shields, Scholarship and Awards
       Committee
       Canadian Library Association
       200 Elgin Street, Suite 602
       Ottawa, ON K2P 1L5
       Canada

▼ CHINESE AMERICAN LIBRARIANS ASSOCIATION

*Seetoo/Chinese American Librarians
Association Conference Travel
Scholarship*   • 514

One-time $500 award for graduate student of Chinese heritage to attend the American Librarians Association conference and the Chinese American Librarians Association program. Currently enrolled library/information science students encouraged to apply.
Academic/Career Areas: Library Sciences.
Award: Scholarship for use in graduate years; not renewable. *Number:* 1. *Amount:* $500.
Eligibility Requirements: Applicant must be Chinese.

Application Requirements: Application, essay, references, transcript. **Deadline:** February 16.
E-mail: yma@uriacc.uri.edu
Phone: 401-874-2819 **Fax:** 401-874-4964
Contact: Dr. Yan Ma, Assistant Professor
       Chinese American Librarians Association
       University of Rhode Island
       Kingston, RI 02881

Sheila Suen Lai Scholarship   • 515

One-time award of $500 for full-time-student of Chinese heritage currently enrolled at an American Librarians Association-accredited library school. Include transcript, essay, and references with application.
Academic/Career Areas: Library Sciences.
Award: Scholarship for use in graduate years; not renewable. *Number:* 1. *Amount:* $500.
Eligibility Requirements: Applicant must be Chinese.
Application Requirements: Application, essay, references, transcript. **Deadline:** February 16.
E-mail: yma@uriacc.uri.edu
Phone: 401-874-2819 **Fax:** 401-874-4964
Contact: Dr. Yan Ma, Assistant Professor
       Chinese American Librarians Association
       University of Rhode Island
       Kingston, RI 02881

▼ CONSORTIUM OF COLLEGE AND UNIVERSITY MEDIA CENTERS

*Consortium of College and University Media
Centers Research Awards*   *see number 383*

▼ DOCUMENTATION ABSTRACTS, INC.

*Information Science Abstracts Research
Grants*   • 516

One-time $1500 award for information science professionals who hold a graduate degree in library or information science. Applicants may not be associated with Information Science Abstracts. Grant to be used to conduct research project regarding the study of primary or secondary literature of information science. Submit project proposal and research description.
Academic/Career Areas: Library Sciences.
Award: Grant for use in postdoctoral years; not renewable. *Amount:* $1500.
Application Requirements: Application. **Deadline:** August 31.
E-mail: careid@mail.med.cornell.edu

Phone: 212-746-6069
World Wide Web: http://www.cox.smu.edu/dai
Contact: Carolyn Anne Reid, Research Grant
　　　　　Coordinator
　　　　　Documentation Abstracts, Inc.
　　　　　Carolyn Anne Reid, Cornell Medical Library
　　　　　1300 York Avenue
　　　　　New York, NY 10021-4896

▼ INTERNATIONAL RESEARCH & EXCHANGES BOARD

International Research and Exchange Board Special Projects in Library and Information Science • 517

Grants to support librarians, archivists, and information specialists pursuing projects relating to Eurasia. The objective of these grants is to increase access and improve working conditions for American scholars using libraries, archivers, and other resources in Eurasia. Must submit proposal.
Academic/Career Areas: Library Sciences.
Award: Grant for use in graduate years; not renewable. *Number:* 6–10. *Amount:* up to $10,000.
Eligibility Requirements: Applicant must have employment experience in experience in career field.
Application Requirements: Application. **Deadline:** March 31.
E-mail: bberrean@irex.orrg
Phone: 202-628-8188 **Fax:** 202-628-8189
World Wide Web: http://www.irex.org
Contact: Beth Berrean, Program Associate
　　　　　International Research & Exchanges Board
　　　　　1616 H Street, NW
　　　　　Washington, DC 20006

▼ LIBRARY AND INFORMATION TECHNOLOGY ASSOCIATION

Library and Information Technology Association/GEAC Scholarship • 518

Scholarship for those who plan to follow a career in library automation. Candidate must have applied for admission to a formal degree program of library education with emphasis on library automation leading to a master's degree. Leadership, work experience, and academic excellence are considered. Must submit personal statement. Renewable award of $2500.
Academic/Career Areas: Library Sciences.
Award: Scholarship for use in graduate years; renewable. *Number:* 1. *Amount:* $2500.

Eligibility Requirements: Applicant must have employment experience in experience in career field and must have an interest in leadership.
Application Requirements: Application, references, transcript.
Deadline: April 1.
E-mail: vedmonds@ala.org
Phone: 312-280-4269 **Fax:** 312-280-3257
World Wide Web: http://www.lita.org
Contact: Valerie Edmonds, Secretary
　　　　　Library and Information Technology
　　　　　　Association
　　　　　50 East Huron Street
　　　　　Chicago, IL 60611-2795

▼ SPECIAL LIBRARIES ASSOCIATION

Plenum Scholarship • 519

Scholarship available to Special Libraries Association members who are doctoral candidates. Dissertation topic approval required. Must have worked in a special library. Submit five copies of the application. Essay required. Deadline is October 31. One-time award of $1000.
Academic/Career Areas: Library Sciences.
Award: Scholarship for use in postdoctoral years; not renewable. *Number:* 1. *Amount:* $1000.
Eligibility Requirements: Applicant must be member of Special Libraries Association and have employment experience in experience in career field.
Application Requirements: Application, essay, financial need analysis, interview, references, transcript. **Deadline:** October 31.
E-mail: taunya@sla.org
Phone: 202-234-4700 Ext. 641 **Fax:** 202-265-9317
World Wide Web: http://www.sla.org
Contact: Taunya Ferguson, Membership Assistant
　　　　　Special Libraries Association
　　　　　1700 18th Street, NW
　　　　　Washington, DC 20009

Special Libraries Association Scholarship • 520

Three scholarships available to graduating college seniors and master's candidates enrolled in a program for library science. May be used for tuition, fees, research, and other related costs. Members of SLA preferred. One-time awards of $6000 each.
Academic/Career Areas: Library Sciences.
Award: Scholarship for use in senior or graduate years; not renewable. *Number:* 3. *Amount:* $6000.
Eligibility Requirements: Applicant must be enrolled at a four-year institution.

Special Libraries Association Scholarship (continued)

Application Requirements: Application, essay, financial need analysis, interview, references, test scores, transcript.
Deadline: October 31.
E-mail: taunya@sla.org
Phone: 202-234-4700 Ext. 641 **Fax:** 202-265-9317
World Wide Web: http://www.sla.org
Contact: Taunya Ferguson, Membership Assistant
Special Libraries Association
1700 18th Street, NW
Washington, DC 20009

▼ YOUNG ADULT LIBRARY SERVICES ASSOCIATION

Econo Clad Award for a Young Adult Reading or Literature Program • 521

One-time award to honor a member of YALSA who has developed an outstanding reading or literature program for young adults. Must work directly with young adults. Award provides expenses to attend the ALA Annual Conference in California.
Academic/Career Areas: Library Sciences.
Award: Prize for use in graduate years; not renewable.
Number: 1. *Amount:* $1000.
Eligibility Requirements: Applicant must have employment experience in experience in career field.
Application Requirements: Application, applicant must enter a contest. **Deadline:** December 1.
E-mail: lwaddle@ala.org
Phone: 312-280-4391 **Fax:** 312-664-7459
Contact: Linda Waddle, Deputy Executive Director
Young Adult Library Services Association
50 East Huron Street
Chicago, IL 60611

LITERATURE/ENGLISH/WRITING

▼ ARMENIAN PROFESSIONAL SOCIETY OF THE BAY AREA

Armenian Professional Society of the Bay Area Scholarships see number 324

▼ INSTITUTE FOR HUMANE STUDIES

Humane Studies Fellowships see number 384

▼ MEMORIAL FOUNDATION FOR JEWISH CULTURE

International Fellowships in Jewish Culture Program see number 340

▼ PHI BETA KAPPA SOCIETY

Mary Isabel Sibley Fellowship for Greek and French Studies see number 332

▼ WINTERTHUR MUSEUM, GARDEN, AND LIBRARY

NEH Fellowships see number 321

Winterthur Research Fellowships see number 322

MECHANICAL ENGINEERING

▼ AMERICAN SOCIETY OF HEATING, REFRIGERATING, AND AIR CONDITIONING ENGINEERS

ASHRAE Research Grants for Graduate Students see number 481

▼ ASSOCIATED WESTERN UNIVERSITIES, INC.

Associated Western Universities-DOE Post-Graduate Fellowship see number 290

Associated Western Universities/DOE Faculty Fellowships see number 291

Associated Western Universities/DOE Laboratory Graduate Research Fellowships see number 292

▼ BLUE CROSS BLUE SHIELD OF MICHIGAN FOUNDATION

Blue Cross Blue Shield of Michigan Foundation Student Award Program see number 416

▼ DEMONSTRATION OF ENERGY-EFFICIENT DEVELOPMENTS PROGRAM

Demonstration of Energy-Efficient Developments Scholarship see number 417

▼ FOUNDATION FOR SCIENCE AND DISABILITY

Foundation for Science and Disability-Student Grant see number 297

▼ INTERNATIONAL DESALINATION ASSOCIATION

International Desalination Association Scholarship see number 298

▼ SKIDMORE, OWINGS, AND MERRILL FOUNDATION

Mechanical/Electrical Traveling Fellowship Program see number 314

▼ VERTICAL FLIGHT FOUNDATION

Vertical Flight Foundation Scholarship see number 345

▼ WOMEN'S AUXILIARY TO THE AMERICAN INSTITUTE OF MINING, METALLURGICAL AND PETROLEUM ENGINEERS

Women's Auxiliary to the American Institute of Mining, Metallurgical and Petroleum Engineers Scholarship Loan Fund see number 398

METEOROLOGY/ATMOSPHERIC SCIENCE

▼ ASSOCIATED WESTERN UNIVERSITIES, INC.

Associated Western Universities-DOE Post-Graduate Fellowship see number 290

Associated Western Universities/DOE Faculty Fellowships see number 291

Associated Western Universities/DOE Laboratory Graduate Research Fellowships see number 292

▼ CENTER FOR FIELD RESEARCH

Center for Field Research Grants for Field Research see number 294

▼ NATIONAL CENTER FOR ATMOSPHERIC RESEARCH

National Center for Atmospheric Research Postdoctoral Research Fellowship • 522

One-time award for scientists just receiving Ph.D. and scientists with no more than four years postdoctoral experience. Fellowship is for two years. Submit curriculum vitae, abstract of doctoral thesis, list of publications, four reference letters, and statement of objectives in atmospheric science with application.

Academic/Career Areas: Meteorology/Atmospheric Science.
Eligibility Requirements: Applicant must be studying in Colorado.
Application Requirements: Application, autobiography, essay, references, transcript. **Deadline:** January 5.
E-mail: barbm@ucar.edu
Phone: 303-497-1601 **Fax:** 303-497-1646
World Wide Web: http://www.ncar.ucar.edu/
Contact: Barbara Hansford, Administrator
National Center for Atmospheric Research
PO Box 3000
Boulder, CO 80307-3000

▼ SIGMA XI, THE SCIENTIFIC RESEARCH SOCIETY

National Academy of Science Grants-in-Aid of Research see number 281

Sigma Xi Grants-in-Aid of Research see number 271

▼ WOODS HOLE OCEANOGRAPHIC INSTITUTION

Woods Hole Oceanographic Institution Postdoctoral Fellowships see number 372

MUSEUM STUDIES

▼ ASIAN CULTURAL COUNCIL
Ford Foundation Fellowships   see number 335

▼ HAGLEY MUSEUM AND LIBRARY
*Hagley Museum and Library
Grants-in-Aid*   see number 308

*Henry Belin du Pont Dissertation
Fellowship*   see number 309

▼ WINTERTHUR MUSEUM, GARDEN, AND LIBRARY
NEH Fellowships   see number 321

Winterthur Research Fellowships see number 322

NATURAL RESOURCES

▼ AMERICAN GEOPHYSICAL UNION
*American Geophysical Union Horton Research
Grant*   see number 284

▼ AMERICAN WATER WORKS ASSOCIATION
*American Water Works Association/Abel
Wolman Fellowship*   see number 286

*American Water Works Association/Holly A.
Cornell Scholarship*   see number 287

*American Water Works Association/Larson
Aquatic Research Support
Scholarship*   see number 288

*American Water Works Association/Thomas R.
Camp Memorial Scholarship*   see number 289

▼ CENTER FOR FIELD RESEARCH
*Center for Field Research Grants for Field
Research*   see number 294

▼ CENTER FOR INDOOR AIR RESEARCH
*Center for Indoor Air Research Postdoctoral
Fellowship*   see number 449

▼ DEMONSTRATION OF ENERGY-EFFICIENT DEVELOPMENTS PROGRAM
*Demonstration of Energy-Efficient
Developments Scholarship*   see number 417

▼ INTERNATIONAL SOCIETY OF ARBORICULTURE
Shade Tree Research Grants   ● 523

Award for graduate students to conduct research on the biological, ecological, and economical effects of shade trees. Write for specific information. Grant can only be used for expenses associated with conducting approved research projects in arboriculture (e.g. equipment purchases, supplies, etc.), not for expenses of attending graduate school (e.g. tuition, books, lab fees, etc.). One-time award of up to $5000.

Academic/Career Areas: Natural Resources.
Award: Grant for use in graduate years; not renewable.
Number: up to 10. *Amount:* up to $5000.
Application Requirements: Application. **Deadline:** November 1.
World Wide Web: http://www.ag.uiuc.edu/~isa/
Contact: International Society of Arboriculture
Department of Botany and Microbiology
Ohio Wesleyan University
Delaware, OH 43015

▼ INTERNATIONAL WOMEN'S FISHING ASSOCIATION SCHOLARSHIP TRUST
*International Women's Fishing Association
Graduate Scholarships in the Marine
Sciences*   see number 276

▼ KENTUCKY NATURAL RESOURCES AND ENVIRONMENTAL PROTECTION CABINET

*Environmental Protection
Scholarships*   see number 269

▼ NORTH AMERICAN BLUEBIRD SOCIETY

*North American Bluebird Society Research
Grant*   see number 367

▼ RESOURCES FOR THE FUTURE

*Gilbert F. White Postdoctoral
Fellowships*   see number 402

*Joseph L. Fisher Dissertation
Awards*   see number 403

▼ SIGMA XI, THE SCIENTIFIC RESEARCH SOCIETY

*National Academy of Science Grants-in-Aid of
Research*   see number 281

▼ SIGURD OLSON ENVIRONMENTAL INSTITUTE

*Sigurd T. Olson Common Loon Research
Awards*   • 524

One-time awards for graduate students to research the biology, ecology, management, and education about the common loon and its habitat. Research is restricted to the Lake Superior region of the U.S.
Academic/Career Areas: Natural Resources.
Award: Grant for use in graduate years; not renewable.
Number: 1–2. *Amount:* $1000–$2000.
Eligibility Requirements: Applicant must be enrolled at a four-year institution and studying in Michigan, Minnesota, or Wisconsin.
Application Requirements: Application. **Deadline:** January 15.
E-mail: tgostomski@wheeler.northland.edu
Phone: 715-682-1223 **Fax:** 715-682-1218
World Wide Web: http://www.northland.edu/soei

Contact: Ted Gostomski, Loon Watch Assistant
Sigurd Olson Environmental Institute
Northland College
Ashland, WI 54806-9989

▼ WOMAN'S NATIONAL FARM AND GARDEN ASSOCIATION

*Sarah Bradley Tyson Memorial
Fellowships*   see number 272

NATURAL SCIENCES

▼ AMERICAN OIL CHEMISTS' SOCIETY

*American Oil Chemists' Society Honored
Student Awards*   see number 379

▼ INTERNATIONAL DESALINATION ASSOCIATION

*International Desalination Association
Scholarship*   see number 298

▼ JANE COFFIN CHILDS MEMORIAL FUND FOR MEDICAL RESEARCH

*Jane Coffin Childs Memorial Fund for Medical
Research Fellowships*   see number 463

NUCLEAR SCIENCE

▼ ASSOCIATED WESTERN UNIVERSITIES, INC.

*Associated Western Universities-DOE
Post-Graduate Fellowship*   see number 290

*Associated Western Universities/DOE Faculty
Fellowships*   see number 291

*Associated Western Universities/DOE
Laboratory Graduate Research
Fellowships*   see number 292

▼ BLUE CROSS BLUE SHIELD OF MICHIGAN FOUNDATION

Blue Cross Blue Shield of Michigan Foundation Student Award Program   *see number 416*

NURSING

▼ BETHESDA LUTHERAN HOMES AND SERVICES, INC.

Nursing Scholastic Achievement Scholarship for Lutheran College Students   • 525

One-time award for college nursing students with minimum 3.0 GPA who are Lutheran and have completed the sophomore year of a four-year nursing program or one year of a two-year nursing program. Must be interested in working with people with mental retardation. Awards of up to $1000.

Academic/Career Areas: Nursing.
Award: Scholarship for use in junior, senior, or graduate years; not renewable. *Number:* 1–10. *Amount:* $50–$1000.
Eligibility Requirements: Applicant must be Lutheran; enrolled at a two-year or four-year institution and have employment experience in helping handicapped.
Application Requirements: Application, autobiography, essay, references, transcript. **Deadline:** March 15.
E-mail: blhsncrc@execpc.com
Phone: 920-261-3050 Ext. 525 **Fax:** 920-261-8441
World Wide Web: http://www.bethesdainfo.org
Contact: Kevin W. Keller, Coordinator, Outreach
      Programs and Services
      Bethesda Lutheran Homes and Services,
      Inc.
      National Christian Resource Center
      700 Hoffmann Drive
      Watertown, WI 53094-6294

▼ BLUE CROSS BLUE SHIELD OF MICHIGAN FOUNDATION

Blue Cross Blue Shield of Michigan Foundation Student Award Program   *see number 416*

▼ CAMPUS SAFETY DIVISION

Campus Safety Scholarship   *see number 293*

▼ CANADIAN FOUNDATION FOR THE STUDY OF INFANT DEATHS

Dr. Sydney Segal Research Grants   *see number 275*

▼ CENTER FOR THE STUDY OF THE HISTORY OF NURSING

Lillian Sholtis Brunner Summer Fellowship   *see number 484*

▼ EASTER SEAL RESEARCH INSTITUTE

Elizabeth St. Louis Award   *see number 354*

▼ GLAXO WELLCOME ONCOLOGY

Oncology Nursing Foundation/Glaxo Wellcome Oncology Master's Scholarship   • 526

Two awards for registered nurses with demonstrated interest in oncology nursing. Must be currently enrolled in a graduate nursing program at an NLN-accredited school. Candidate may be a full- or part-time student. Must not have received any previous aid from Foundation. Application fee: $5. One-time award of $3000.

Academic/Career Areas: Nursing.
Award: Scholarship for use in graduate years; not renewable. *Number:* 2. *Amount:* $3000.
Application Requirements: Application, transcript. **Fee:** $5.
Deadline: February 1.
Phone: 412-921-7373 Ext. 231 **Fax:** 412-921-6565
World Wide Web: http://www.ons.org
Contact: Celia A. Hindes, CFRE, Development
      Associate
      Glaxo Wellcome Oncology
      501 Holiday Drive
      Pittsburgh, PA 15220

▼ HEART AND STROKE FOUNDATION OF CANADA

Heart and Stroke Foundation of Canada Nursing Research Fellowships   *see number 457*

▼ INTERNATIONAL ORDER OF THE KING'S DAUGHTERS AND SONS

International Order of the King's Daughters and Sons Health Careers Scholarship   *see number 393*

▼ NATIONAL ASSOCIATION OF PEDIATRIC NURSE ASSOCIATES AND PRACTITIONERS

National Association of Pediatric Nurse Associates and Practitioners McNeil Scholarships   • 527

Award for students enrolled in a pediatric nurse practitioner program. Must be registered nurse with work experience in pediatrics. Must demonstrate financial need and state rationale for seeking pediatric nurse practitioner education. Deadlines are May 30 and September 30.
Academic/Career Areas: Nursing.
Award: Scholarship for use in graduate years; not renewable. *Number:* 2. *Amount:* $2000.
Eligibility Requirements: Applicant must be enrolled at a four-year institution and have employment experience in experience in career field.
Application Requirements: Application, financial need analysis.
Phone: 609-667-1773 **Fax:** 609-667-7187
World Wide Web: http://www.napnap.org
Contact: Renee Wolf, Executive Secretary
National Association of Pediatric Nurse
Associates and Practitioners
1101 Kings Highway North, Suite 206
Cherry Hill, NJ 08034-1912

▼ NURSING ECONOMIC$ FOUNDATION

Nursing Economic$ Foundation Scholarships   • 528

Awards for registered nurses who are graduate students pursuing nursing degrees with an emphasis on nursing administration or management. Submit curriculum vitae. One-time award of $5000.
Academic/Career Areas: Nursing.
Award: Scholarship for use in graduate years; not renewable. *Number:* 1–4. *Amount:* $5000.
Application Requirements: Application, test scores, transcript.
Deadline: May 1.
E-mail: ajjinc@mail.ajj.com

Phone: 609-256-2300 **Fax:** 609-589-7463
Contact: Karen Jannetti Hester, Executive Director
Nursing Economic$ Foundation
East Holly Avenue, Box 56
Pitman, NJ 08071-0056

▼ ONCOLOGY NURSING FOUNDATION/ONCOLOGY NURSING SOCIETY

Oncology Nursing Foundation Doctoral Scholarships   • 529

Three scholarships available to registered nurses who have demonstrated interest and commitment to oncology nursing and who currently hold a license to practice as a registered nurse. Must be enrolled or applying to a doctoral nursing or related program. May not have previously received a doctoral scholarship from the Foundation. Application fee: $5. One-time award of $3000.
Academic/Career Areas: Nursing.
Award: Scholarship for use in graduate years; not renewable. *Number:* 3. *Amount:* $3000.
Eligibility Requirements: Applicant must have employment experience in experience in career field.
Application Requirements: Application, references, transcript.
Fee: $5. **Deadline:** February 1.
Phone: 412-921-8597 **Fax:** 412-921-6565
World Wide Web: http://www.ons.org
Contact: Oncology Nursing Foundation/Oncology
Nursing Society
501 Holiday Drive
Pittsburgh, PA 15220

Oncology Nursing Foundation Master's Scholarship   • 530

Nine awards for registered nurses with demonstrated interest in oncology. Must be currently enrolled in a graduate nursing program at an NLN-accredited school and currently hold a license to practice as a registered nurse. May be a full-time or part-time student. Must not have previously received an MA scholarship. Application fee: $5. One-time award of $3000.
Academic/Career Areas: Nursing.
Award: Scholarship for use in graduate years; not renewable. *Number:* 9. *Amount:* $3000.
Eligibility Requirements: Applicant must have employment experience in experience in career field.
Application Requirements: Application, transcript. **Fee:** $5.
Deadline: February 1.
Phone: 412-921-8597 **Fax:** 412-921-6565

Oncology Nursing Foundation Master's Scholarship (continued)

World Wide Web: http://www.ons.org
Contact: Oncology Nursing Foundation/Oncology
Nursing Society
501 Holiday Drive
Pittsburgh, PA 15220

Oncology Nursing Foundation/Ann Olson Memorial Doctoral Scholarship • 531

One award for registered nurse with demonstrated interest in oncology nursing who is currently enrolled in or applying to doctoral nursing degree or related program. One-time award of $3000.
Academic/Career Areas: Nursing.
Award: Scholarship for use in graduate years; not renewable. *Number:* 1. *Amount:* $3000.
Application Requirements: Application, references, transcript. **Deadline:** February 1.
Phone: 412-921-8597 **Fax:** 412-921-6565
World Wide Web: http://www.ons.org
Contact: Oncology Nursing Foundation/Oncology
Nursing Society
501 Holiday Drive
Pittsburgh, PA 15220

Oncology Nursing Foundation/Nursing Certification Corporation Master's Scholarship • 532

Two awards for registered nurses with demonstrated interest in oncology nursing. Must be currently enrolled in a graduate nursing program at an NLN-accredited school and must currently hold a license to practice as a registered nurse. May be a full-time or part-time student. Must not have received any MA scholarship previously from Foundation. Application fee: $5. One-time award of $3000.
Academic/Career Areas: Nursing.
Award: Scholarship for use in graduate years; not renewable. *Number:* 2. *Amount:* $3000.
Eligibility Requirements: Applicant must have employment experience in experience in career field.
Application Requirements: Application, transcript. **Fee:** $5.
Deadline: February 1.
Phone: 412-921-8597 **Fax:** 412-921-6565
World Wide Web: http://www.ons.org
Contact: Oncology Nursing Foundation/Oncology
Nursing Society
501 Holiday Drive
Pittsburgh, PA 15220

Oncology Nursing Foundation/Pharmacia and Upjohn, Inc. Master's Scholarship • 533

One-time award for registered nurse with demonstrated interest in oncology nursing who is currently enrolled in graduate nursing degree program that has application to oncology nursing. Must attend NLN-accredited school and may be full- or part-time student. One award of $3000.
Academic/Career Areas: Nursing.
Award: Scholarship for use in graduate years; not renewable. *Number:* 1. *Amount:* $3000.
Application Requirements: Application, transcript. **Deadline:** February 1.
Phone: 412-921-8597 **Fax:** 412-921-6565
World Wide Web: http://www.ons.org
Contact: Oncology Nursing Foundation/Oncology
Nursing Society
501 Holiday Drive
Pittsburgh, PA 15220

Oncology Nursing Foundation/Thomas Jordan Doctoral Scholarship • 534

One award to improve oncology nursing by assisting registered nurses in fulfilling their education. Must be currently enrolled in or applying to a doctoral nursing degree program. Application fee: $5. One-time award of $3000. One award available per level of education.
Academic/Career Areas: Nursing.
Award: Scholarship for use in graduate years; not renewable. *Number:* 1. *Amount:* $3000.
Application Requirements: Application, references, transcript. **Fee:** $5. **Deadline:** February 1.
Phone: 412-921-8597 **Fax:** 412-921-6565
World Wide Web: http://www.ons.org
Contact: Oncology Nursing Foundation/Oncology
Nursing Society
501 Holiday Drive
Pittsburgh, PA 15220

▼ PILOT INTERNATIONAL FOUNDATION

Marie Newton Sepia Memorial Award *see number 477*

▼ UNITED OSTOMY ASSOCIATION

Archie Vinitsky ET Scholarship • 535

One-time award for registered nurses desiring a career in enterostomal therapy nursing and have been accepted

into an accredited enterostomal nursing program. Must be a dues-paying member of a United Ostomy Association chapter at time of application. Deadlines are October 15 and March 30.
Academic/Career Areas: Nursing.
Award: Scholarship for use in graduate years; not renewable. *Number:* 2–6. *Amount:* $250–$500.
Eligibility Requirements: Applicant must be member of United Ostomy Association and have employment experience in experience in career field.
Application Requirements: Application, references.
Phone: 714-660-8624 **Fax:** 714-660-9262
Contact: Jean Smith, Director of Program Services
United Ostomy Association
19772 MacArthur Boulevard, #200
Irvine, CA 92612

PEACE AND CONFLICT STUDIES

▼ HARRY FRANK GUGGENHEIM FOUNDATION

H. F. Guggenheim Foundation Research Grants see number 329

PERFORMING ARTS

▼ ARMENIAN PROFESSIONAL SOCIETY OF THE BAY AREA

Armenian Professional Society of the Bay Area Scholarships see number 324

▼ ASIAN CULTURAL COUNCIL
Ford Foundation Fellowships see number 335

▼ KURT WEILL FOUNDATION FOR MUSIC

Kurt Weill Foundation for Music Grants Program • 536
One-time awards for uses that must perpetuate, either through performance or research, the legacies of Kurt Weill and Lotte Lenya. Deadline is November 1. Write for more information.

Academic/Career Areas: Performing Arts.
Award: Grant for use in graduate years; not renewable.
Eligibility Requirements: Applicant must have an interest in music/singing.
Application Requirements: Application. **Deadline:** November 1.
World Wide Web: http://www.kwf.org
Contact: Joanna C. Lee, Associate Director for
Business Affairs
Kurt Weill Foundation for Music
7 East 20th Street
New York, NY 10003

▼ PRINCESS GRACE AWARDS

Dance, Theater, Film, and Playwright Grants see number 342

PHOTOJOURNALISM

▼ CONSORTIUM OF COLLEGE AND UNIVERSITY MEDIA CENTERS

Consortium of College and University Media Centers Research Awards see number 383

PHYSICAL SCIENCES AND MATH

▼ AMERICAN ASSOCIATION FOR THE ADVANCEMENT OF SCIENCE

American Association for the Advancement of Science Mass Media, Science, and Engineering Fellowship see number 421

▼ AMERICAN SOCIETY FOR ENGINEERING EDUCATION

Army Research Laboratory Postdoctoral Fellowship Program see number 420

▼ AMERICAN SOCIETY FOR PHOTOGRAMMETRY AND REMOTE SENSING

Earth Observation Satellite Company Award for Application of Digital Landsat TM Data　　see number 285

▼ ASSOCIATED WESTERN UNIVERSITIES, INC.

Associated Western Universities-DOE Post-Graduate Fellowship　　see number 290

Associated Western Universities/DOE Faculty Fellowships　　see number 291

Associated Western Universities/DOE Laboratory Graduate Research Fellowships　　see number 292

▼ ASSOCIATION FOR WOMEN GEOSCIENTISTS

Chrysalis Scholarship　　see number 394

▼ ASSOCIATION FOR WOMEN IN MATHEMATICS

Association for Women in Mathematics Workshop for Graduate Students and Postdoctoral Mathematicians　　● 537

Award for female graduate students and recent Ph.D.'s in math to attend the annual workshop in Florida. Graduate students must have begun work on thesis problem and present it at workshop. Postdoctorates present talks on research. Deadlines: March 1 and September 1.
Academic/Career Areas: Physical Sciences and Math.
Award: Grant for use in graduate years; not renewable. *Number:* 20–40. *Amount:* $800–$1000.
Eligibility Requirements: Applicant must be female.
Application Requirements: Application.
Contact: Association for Women in Mathematics
4114 Computer and Space Sciences Building
University of Maryland
College Park, MD 20742-2461

Travel Grants for Women in Mathematics ● 538
One-time award for women who recently received Ph.D. in mathematics to provide travel expenses to attend research conferences in their field. Submit description of recent research, curriculum vitae, and budget. Deadlines: February 1, May 1, and October 1.
Academic/Career Areas: Physical Sciences and Math.
Award: Grant for use in postdoctoral years; not renewable. *Number:* 3–6. *Amount:* $1000–$2000.
Eligibility Requirements: Applicant must be female.
Contact: Association for Women in Mathematics
4114 Computer and Space Sciences Building
University of Maryland
College Park, MD 20742-2461

▼ ASSOCIATION FOR WOMEN IN SCIENCE EDUCATIONAL FOUNDATION

Ruth Satter Memorial Award　　see number 350

▼ CAMPUS SAFETY DIVISION

Campus Safety Scholarship　　see number 293

▼ CENTER FOR FIELD RESEARCH

Center for Field Research Grants for Field Research　　see number 294

▼ FOUNDATION FOR SCIENCE AND DISABILITY

Foundation for Science and Disability-Student Grant　　see number 297

▼ HARRY FRANK GUGGENHEIM FOUNDATION

H. F. Guggenheim Foundation Research Grants　　see number 329

▼ HUDSON RIVER NATIONAL ESTUARINE RESEARCH RESERVE— NEW YORK STATE DEPARTMENT OF ENVIRONMENTAL CONSERVATION AND THE HUDSON RIVER FOUNDATION

Tibor T. Polgar Fellowship　　see number 360

▼ MYASTHENIA GRAVIS FOUNDATION OF AMERICA, INC.

Kermit Osserman Fellowship see number 363

▼ SIGMA XI, THE SCIENTIFIC RESEARCH SOCIETY

National Academy of Science Grants-in-Aid of Research see number 281

Sigma Xi Grants-in-Aid of Research see number 271

▼ SOCIAL SCIENCE RESEARCH COUNCIL-MACARTHUR FOUNDATION

Postdoctoral Fellowships on Peace and Security in a Changing World see number 369

▼ SOCIETY OF EXPLORATION GEOPHYSICISTS FOUNDATION (SEG)

Society of Exploration Geophysicists Foundation Scholarship see number 397

▼ WOODS HOLE OCEANOGRAPHIC INSTITUTION

Woods Hole Oceanographic Institution Postdoctoral Fellowships see number 372

POLITICAL SCIENCE

▼ ALBERT EINSTEIN INSTITUTION

Albert Einstein Institution Fellowships see number 482

▼ AMERICAN JEWISH COMMITTEE

Harold W. Rosenthal Fellowship in International Relations see number 374

▼ ASSOCIATION TO UNITE THE DEMOCRACIES

Mayme and Herbert Frank Educational Fund see number 325

▼ FRANKLIN AND ELEANOR ROOSEVELT INSTITUTE

Roosevelt Institute Grant-in-Aid see number 486

▼ GERMAN HISTORICAL INSTITUTE

German Historical Institute Dissertation Scholarships see number 487

▼ HARRY FRANK GUGGENHEIM FOUNDATION

H. F. Guggenheim Foundation Research Grants see number 329

▼ HARRY S TRUMAN LIBRARY INSTITUTE

Harry S Truman Library Institute Dissertation Year Fellowships see number 491

▼ INSTITUTE FOR HUMANE STUDIES

Humane Studies Fellowships see number 384

▼ PI GAMMA MU INTERNATIONAL HONOR SOCIETY IN SOCIETY SCIENCE

Pi Gamma Mu Scholarship see number 392

▼ RESOURCES FOR THE FUTURE

Gilbert F. White Postdoctoral Fellowships see number 402

Joseph L. Fisher Dissertation Awards see number 403

▼ SOCIAL SCIENCE RESEARCH COUNCIL

Abe Fellowship Program see number 404

Social Science Research Council International Peace and Security Research Workshop Competition • 539

For small groups of junior faculty and other junior scholars to meet for discussions about peace and security. Workshop must be initiated by individual recipients of grants from the MacArthur Program on Peace and International Cooperation. One-time award of up to $7500.
Academic/Career Areas: Political Science; Social Sciences.
Award: Scholarship for use in graduate years; not renewable. *Amount:* up to $7500.
Application Requirements: Application. **Deadline:** April 1.
World Wide Web: http://www.ssrc.org
Contact: Social Science Research Council
810 Seventh Avenue
New York, NY 10019

▼ **UNITED STATES DEPARTMENT OF HOUSING AND URBAN DEVELOPMENT, OFFICE OF POLICY DEVELOPMENT AND RESEARCH**

Doctoral Dissertation Research Grant (HUD) see number 334

REAL ESTATE

▼ **REAL ESTATE EDUCATORS ASSOCIATION**

Harwood Memorial Real Estate Scholarship • 540

Cash scholarship given to students pursuing a career in any facet of real estate. One-time merit-based award of $250-$500 for students who have completed at least one year of study. Must have Real Estate Educators Association member on campus.
Academic/Career Areas: Real Estate.
Award: Scholarship for use in sophomore, junior, senior, or graduate years; not renewable. *Number:* 3. *Amount:* $250–$500.
Eligibility Requirements: Applicant must be enrolled at a two-year or four-year institution.
Application Requirements: Application, references, self-addressed stamped envelope, transcript. **Deadline:** December 31.
E-mail: reea@washingtongroupinc.com

Phone: 703-352-6688 **Fax:** 703-352-6767
World Wide Web: http://www.reea.org
Contact: Real Estate Educators Association
10565 Lee Highway #104
Fairfax, VA 22030

RELIGION/THEOLOGY

▼ **COMMUNITY CHURCH OF NEW YORK**

John Haynes Holmes Memorial Fund • 541

One-time award for graduate religion students to prepare for the Unitarian ministry. Based on merit and financial need. Include transcript, test scores, essay, references, and photo with application.
Academic/Career Areas: Religion/Theology.
Award: Scholarship for use in graduate years; not renewable. *Number:* 7–9. *Amount:* $750–$2000.
Eligibility Requirements: Applicant must be Other Specific Denomination.
Application Requirements: Application, essay, financial need analysis, photo, references, test scores, transcript.
Deadline: April 15.
Phone: 212-683-4988
Contact: Bruce Southworth, Senior Minister
Community Church of New York
40 East 35th Street
New York, NY 10016

▼ **MEMORIAL FOUNDATION FOR JEWISH CULTURE**

International Fellowships in Jewish Culture Program see number 340

Memorial Foundation for Jewish Culture International Doctoral Scholarship • 542

Purpose of scholarship is to train qualified individuals for careers in Jewish scholarship and research and to help Jewish educational, religious, and communal workers train for leadership positions. Award for graduate study only.
Academic/Career Areas: Religion/Theology.
Award: Scholarship for use in graduate years; not renewable. *Amount:* $2000–$7500.
Application Requirements: Application, references, transcript.
Deadline: October 31.
Phone: 212-679-4074

Contact: Lorraine Blass, Associate Director
Memorial Foundation for Jewish Culture
15 East 26th Street, Room 1703
New York, NY 10010

Memorial Foundation for Jewish Culture
Scholarships for Post-Rabbinical Students • **543**

One-time award for post-rabbinical students for use in furthering their studies. This award is open to non-U.S. citizens and is not restricted to use in the U.S. Write for application. Deadline is October 31.
Academic/Career Areas: Religion/Theology.
Award: Scholarship for use in graduate years; not renewable. *Amount:* $1000–$3000.
Eligibility Requirements: Applicant must be Jewish.
Application Requirements: Application, references. **Deadline:** October 31.
Phone: 212-679-4074
Contact: Lorraine Blass, Associate Director
Memorial Foundation for Jewish Culture
15 East 26th Street, Room 1703
New York, NY 10010

▼ **PHI BETA KAPPA SOCIETY**

Mary Isabel Sibley Fellowship for Greek and French Studies   *see number 332*

▼ **UNITED METHODIST CHURCH**

Georgia Harkness Scholarships   • **544**

One-time award for female preparing for ordained ministry as an elder in the United Methodist Church. Must be 35 or older and enrolled in an accredited school of theology and working toward a basic seminary degree.
Academic/Career Areas: Religion/Theology.
Award: Scholarship for use in graduate years; not renewable.
Eligibility Requirements: Applicant must be Methodist; age 35 or over and female.
Application Requirements: Application, essay, references, transcript. **Deadline:** March 1.
Contact: P. Zimmerman, Scholarship Director
United Methodist Church
PO Box 871
Nashville, TN 37020-0871

SCIENCE, TECHNOLOGY & SOCIETY

▼ **CAMPUS SAFETY DIVISION**

Campus Safety Scholarship   *see number 293*

▼ **CHARLES BABBAGE INSTITUTE**

Adelle and Erwin Tomash Fellowship in the History of Information Processing see number 391

▼ **OLFACTORY RESEARCH FUND, LTD.**

Olfactory Research Fund Research Grants   *see number 368*

SOCIAL SCIENCES

▼ **ALBERT EINSTEIN INSTITUTION**

Albert Einstein Institution Fellowships   *see number 482*

▼ **ALEXANDER VON HUMBOLDT-STIFTUNG**

Transatlantic Research Cooperation between German and American Scholars in the Human and Social Sciences, Economics, and Law
          see number 399

▼ **AMERICAN BAR FOUNDATION**

American Bar Foundation Doctoral Dissertation Fellowships in Law and Social Science   *see number 511*

▼ **AMERICAN GEOPHYSICAL UNION**

American Geophysical Union Horton Research Grant   *see number 284*

▼ **AMERICAN JEWISH COMMITTEE**

Harold W. Rosenthal Fellowship in International Relations   *see number 374*

▼ AMERICAN SCHOOLS OF ORIENTAL RESEARCH

Mesopotamian Fellowship   see number 483

▼ ARCHAEOLOGICAL INSTITUTE OF AMERICA AND THE AMERICAN FRIENDS OF APHRODISIAS

Archaeological Institute of America/Kenan T. Erim Award   see number 323

▼ ARMENIAN PROFESSIONAL SOCIETY OF THE BAY AREA

Armenian Professional Society of the Bay Area Scholarships   see number 324

▼ ASSOCIATION FOR WOMEN IN SCIENCE EDUCATIONAL FOUNDATION

Ruth Satter Memorial Award   see number 350

▼ BLUE CROSS BLUE SHIELD OF MICHIGAN FOUNDATION

Blue Cross Blue Shield of Michigan Foundation Student Award Program   see number 416

▼ CANADIAN INSTITUTE OF UKRAINIAN STUDIES—PETER JACYK CENTRE FOR UKRAINIAN HISTORICAL RESEARCH

Doctoral Thesis Fellowship in Ukrainian History   see number 407

Michael Dorosh Fund Master's Fellowship   see number 408

▼ CANADIAN INSTITUTE OF UKRANIAN STUDIES—PETER JACYK CENTRE FOR UKRANIAN HISTORICAL RESEARCH

Helen Darcovich Memorial Endowment Fund Doctoral Fellowship   see number 409

Neporany Research Teaching Fellowship   see number 326

▼ CENTER FOR FIELD RESEARCH

Center for Field Research Grants for Field Research   see number 294

▼ CENTER FOR HELLENIC STUDIES

Center for Hellenic Studies Fellowships   see number 327

▼ DAVID LIBRARY OF THE AMERICAN REVOLUTION

Fellowships for the Study of the American Revolution   see number 485

▼ EDUCATIONAL TESTING SERVICE

Educational Testing Service Postdoctoral Fellowship Program   see number 375

▼ GERMAN ACADEMIC EXCHANGE SERVICE (DEUTSCHER AKADEMISCHER AUSTAUSCHDIENST)

DAAD-ALCS Collaborative Research Grants   see number 497

▼ GERMAN HISTORICAL INSTITUTE

German Historical Institute Dissertation Scholarships   see number 487

▼ HARRY FRANK GUGGENHEIM FOUNDATION

H. F. Guggenheim Foundation Research Grants   see number 329

▼ HERBERT HOOVER PRESIDENTIAL LIBRARY ASSOCIATION

Herbert Hoover Presidential Library Association Travel Grants   see number 498

▼ INSTITUTE FOR GLOBAL STUDIES IN CULTURE, POWER, AND HISTORY

Postdoctoral Fellowships in African-American Culture   *see number 499*

▼ INSTITUTE FOR HUMANE STUDIES

Humane Studies Fellowships   *see number 384*

▼ INTERNATIONAL RESEARCH AND EXCHANGES BOARD

International Research and Exchanges Board Short-term Travel Grants   *see number 500*

▼ IRISH-AMERICAN CULTURAL INSTITUTE

Irish Research Funds   *see number 330*

▼ JAPAN FOUNDATION

Japan Foundation Doctoral Fellowship   *see number 501*

Japan Foundation Research Fellowship   *see number 502*

▼ L.S.B. LEAKEY FOUNDATION

L.S.B. Leakey Foundation General Research Grants   *see number 277*

L.S.B. Leakey Foundation Paleoanthropology Award   • 545

Renewable grant for long-term, multidisciplinary research program which seeks to recover physical and/or cultural remains of early humans and their hominid ancestors. Usually awarded to senior scientists. Submit full research proposal, scientific field report and projection.
Academic/Career Areas: Social Sciences.
Award: Grant for use in graduate years; renewable. *Number:* 1. *Amount:* $20,000.
Application Requirements: Application, financial need analysis, references. **Deadline:** October 15.
World Wide Web: http://www.leakeyfoundation.org

Contact: Dr. Karla Savage, Program and Grants Officer
L.S.B. Leakey Foundation
PO Box 29346
Presidio Building #1002A, O'Reilly Avenue
San Francisco, CA 94129

Leakey Foundation Fellowship for Great Ape Research and Conservation   *see number 278*

Leakey Foundation Study of Foraging Peoples Fellowship   *see number 279*

▼ LAMBDA ALPHA NATIONAL COLLEGIATE HONORS SOCIETY FOR ANTHROPOLOGY

Lambda Alpha National Collegiate Honor Society for Anthropology Scholarship Award   • 546

Award to give academic recognition to students and to encourage them to pursue a career in anthropology. Must submit statement of future plans. Deadline: March 1.
Academic/Career Areas: Social Sciences.
Award: Scholarship for use in graduate years; not renewable. *Number:* 1. *Amount:* $4000.
Application Requirements: Application, autobiography, essay, references. **Deadline:** March 1.
E-mail: 01bkswartz@bsuuc.bsu.edu
Phone: 765-285-1575 **Fax:** 765-285-2163
World Wide Web: http://www.geocities.com/collegepark/3022
Contact: B.K. Swartz, Jr., National Executive Secretary
Lambda Alpha National Collegiate Honors Society for Anthropology
Dept. of Anthropology, Ball State University
Muncie, IN 47306-1099

▼ LYNDON BAINES JOHNSON FOUNDATION

Lyndon Baines Johnson Foundation Grants-in-Aid Research   *see number 503*

▼ NATIONAL ACADEMY OF EDUCATION

Spencer Postdoctoral Fellowship Program   *see number 411*

▼ NATIONAL ASSOCIATION FOR WOMEN IN EDUCATION

Women's Research Award   *see number 413*

▼ NATIONAL INSTITUTES OF HEALTH

Fogarty International Center International Research Fellowship   *see number 364*

Fogarty International Center International Training and Research Program   *see number 365*

▼ PARAPSYCHOLOGY FOUNDATION

D. Scott Rogo Award for Parapsychological Literature   • **547**

One-time award given to an author working on a manuscript pertaining to the science of parapsychology. Submit brief synopsis of the proposed contents of the manuscript. One $3000 award.
Academic/Career Areas: Social Sciences.
Award: Prize for use in graduate years; not renewable. *Number:* 1. *Amount:* $3000.
Eligibility Requirements: Applicant must have an interest in writing.
Application Requirements: Application. **Deadline:** April 15.
Phone: 212-628-1550 **Fax:** 212-628-1559
World Wide Web: http://www.parapsychology.org
Contact: Lisette Coly, Vice President
Parapsychology Foundation
228 East 71st Street
New York, NY 10021

▼ PHI BETA KAPPA SOCIETY

Mary Isabel Sibley Fellowship for Greek and French Studies   *see number 332*

▼ PI GAMMA MU INTERNATIONAL HONOR SOCIETY IN SOCIETY SCIENCE

Pi Gamma Mu Scholarship   *see number 392*

▼ POPULATION COUNCIL

Population Council Fellowships in Population Study   *see number 400*

Population Council Postdoctoral Fellowships in the Social Sciences   *see number 401*

▼ RESOURCES FOR THE FUTURE

Gilbert F. White Postdoctoral Fellowships   *see number 402*

Joseph L. Fisher Dissertation Awards   *see number 403*

▼ SIGMA XI, THE SCIENTIFIC RESEARCH SOCIETY

Sigma Xi Grants-in-Aid of Research   *see number 271*

▼ SOCIAL SCIENCE RESEARCH COUNCIL

Abe Fellowship Program   *see number 404*

International Migration Postdoctoral Fellowships   • **548**

Must hold Ph.D. or its equivalent in one of the social sciences to foster innovative research that will advance theoretical understandings of immigration to the U.S., the processes of settlement, and the outcomes for both immigrants and America. One-time award of up to $20,000. Contact Web site for the most recent information.
Academic/Career Areas: Social Sciences.
Application Requirements: Application. **Deadline:** February 1.
World Wide Web: http://www.ssrc.org
Contact: Social Science Research Council
810 Seventh Avenue
New York, NY 10019

Japan Fellowship for Dissertation Workshop   *see number 505*

Social Science Research Center International Migration Research Planning Grant   *see number 508*

Social Science Research Council International Peace and Security Research Workshop Competition   *see number 539*

Social Science Research Council Sexuality Research Fellowship Program-Dissertation Fellowships • 549

Award provided to students for twelve continuous months to cover direct research costs, matriculation fees, and living expenses. Students should have completed all requirements for the Ph.D., except dissertation, and be matriculating in a full-time program leading to a Ph.D. in social or behavioral science. Must submit joint application with research adviser.
Academic/Career Areas: Social Sciences.
Application Requirements: Application. **Deadline:** December 13.
World Wide Web: http://www.ssrc.org
Contact: Social Science Research Council
810 Seventh Avenue
New York, NY 10019

Social Science Research Council Sexuality Research Fellowship Program-Postdoctoral Fellowships • 550

Award given to support up to twenty-four continuous months of research costs and living expenses for Ph.D. holders or equivalent in a social or behavioral science. Postdoctoral candidates who have conducted research on sexuality for more than eight years will not be considered. Only joint applications from the applicant and a research adviser will be considered.
Academic/Career Areas: Social Sciences.
Application Requirements: Application. **Deadline:** December 13.
World Wide Web: http://www.ssrc.org
Contact: Social Science Research Council
810 Seventh Avenue
New York, NY 10019

Social Science Research Council Sexuality Research Fellowship Program-Research Advisor/Associate • 551

Award of $3000 for this co-applicant, who should hold a Ph.D. and demonstrate a commitment to the training of the candidate. Must present evidence of commitment to human sexuality research through research work and/or past mentoring. Only joint applications from the research adviser/associate and fellowship candidate will be accepted. Additional $3000 for fellow's host institution.
Academic/Career Areas: Social Sciences.
Application Requirements: Application. **Deadline:** December 5.
World Wide Web: http://www.ssrc.org

Contact: Social Science Research Council
810 Seventh Avenue
New York, NY 10019

▼ SOCIAL SCIENCE RESEARCH COUNCIL-MACARTHUR FOUNDATION

Postdoctoral Fellowships on Peace and Security in a Changing World **see number 369**

▼ SOCIETY FOR THE PSYCHOLOGICAL STUDY OF SOCIAL ISSUES

Gordon Allport Intergroup Relations Prize • 552

One-time award for papers published during the current year or unpublished manuscripts. The paper's topic should be intergroup relations. Originality will be given special weight. Graduate students are encouraged to submit papers.
Academic/Career Areas: Social Sciences.
Award: Prize for use in graduate years; not renewable. *Amount:* $1000.
Eligibility Requirements: Applicant must have an interest in writing.
Application Requirements: Applicant must enter a contest.
Deadline: December 31.
E-mail: spssi@umich.edu
Phone: 313-662-9130 **Fax:** 313-662-5607
World Wide Web: http://www.umich.edu/~sociss/
Contact: Michelle Angus, Administrative Assistant
Society for the Psychological Study of Social Issues
PO Box 1248
Ann Arbor, MI 48106-1248

Louise Kidder Early Career Award • 553

One-time award for social science researchers who have made substantial contributions to their field early in their careers. Must be nominated. Submit cover letter, curriculum vitae, and three letters of support.
Academic/Career Areas: Social Sciences.
Award: Prize for use in graduate years; not renewable. *Amount:* $500.
Application Requirements: Applicant must enter a contest, references. **Deadline:** May 1.
E-mail: spssi@umich.edu
Phone: 734-662-9130 **Fax:** 734-662-5607

Louise Kidder Early Career Award (continued)

World Wide Web: http://www.umich.edu/~sociss/
Contact: Michelle Angus, Administrative Assistant
Society for the Psychological Study of Social
Issues
PO Box 1248
Ann Arbor, MI 48106-1248

▼ SOCIETY FOR THE SCIENTIFIC STUDY OF SEXUALITY

*Society for the Scientific Study of Sexuality
Student Research Grant*   see number 370

▼ STATE HISTORICAL SOCIETY OF WISCONSIN

Amy Louise Hunter Fellowship   see number 494

▼ UNITED STATES DEPARTMENT OF HOUSING AND URBAN DEVELOPMENT, OFFICE OF POLICY DEVELOPMENT AND RESEARCH

*Doctoral Dissertation Research Grant
(HUD)*   see number 334

▼ WILLIAM T. GRANT FOUNDATION

*Grant Foundation Research
Grants*   see number 479

▼ WOODROW WILSON NATIONAL FELLOWSHIP FOUNDATION

*Woodrow Wilson National Fellowship
Foundation Women's Studies Dissertation
Grant*   see number 506

SOCIAL SERVICES

▼ COUNCIL OF JEWISH FEDERATIONS

*Federation Executive Recruitment and
Education Program*   see number 410

▼ NATIONAL ASSOCIATION FOR WOMEN IN EDUCATION

Women's Research Award   see number 413

▼ PI GAMMA MU INTERNATIONAL HONOR SOCIETY IN SOCIETY SCIENCE

Pi Gamma Mu Scholarship   see number 392

▼ UNITED STATES DEPARTMENT OF HOUSING AND URBAN DEVELOPMENT, OFFICE OF POLICY DEVELOPMENT AND RESEARCH

*Doctoral Dissertation Research Grant
(HUD)*   see number 334

SPECIAL EDUCATION

▼ ASSOCIATION FOR THE STUDY OF HIGHER EDUCATION

*Association for the Study of Higher Education
Dissertation of the Year Award*   see number 406

▼ EASTER SEAL RESEARCH INSTITUTE

Elizabeth St. Louis Award   see number 354

▼ PILOT INTERNATIONAL FOUNDATION

*Marie Newton Sepia Memorial
Award*   see number 477

THERAPY/REHABILITATION

▼ AMERICAN RESPIRATORY CARE FOUNDATION

Glaxo-Wellcome Literary Award   see number 448

▼ AUDITORY-VERBAL INTERNATIONAL, INC.

Doreen Pollack Award   • 554

Award for graduate or postgraduate students in therapy to receive training in auditory-verbal therapy and its philosophy. Write for further information. One-time award of $1000.

Academic/Career Areas: Therapy/Rehabilitation.
Award: Scholarship for use in graduate years; not renewable. *Number:* 1. *Amount:* $1000.
Application Requirements: Application. **Deadline:** April 1.
E-mail: aviinc@juno.com
Phone: 703-739-1049 **Fax:** 703-739-0395
Contact: Renee Levinson, Executive Director
     Auditory-Verbal International, Inc.
     2121 Eisenhower Avenue, Suite 402
     Alexandria, VA 22314

▼ BLUE CROSS BLUE SHIELD OF MICHIGAN FOUNDATION

Blue Cross Blue Shield of Michigan Foundation Student Award Program   see number 416

▼ EASTER SEAL RESEARCH INSTITUTE

Elizabeth St. Louis Award   see number 354

▼ INTERNATIONAL ORDER OF THE KING'S DAUGHTERS AND SONS

International Order of the King's Daughters and Sons Health Careers Scholarship   see number 393

▼ OLFACTORY RESEARCH FUND, LTD.

Olfactory Research Fund Research Grants   see number 368

▼ ORTHOPAEDIC RESEARCH AND EDUCATION FOUNDATION

American Association of Orthopaedic Surgeons/Orthopaedic Research and Education Foundation Fellowship in Health Service Research   see number 472

Orthopaedic Research and Education Foundation Career Development Awards   see number 473

Orthopaedic Research and Education Foundation Clinical Research Awards   see number 474

Orthopaedic Research and Education Foundation Prospective Clinical Research Proposals   see number 475

Orthopaedic Research and Education Foundation Research Grants   see number 476

▼ PARALYZED VETERANS OF AMERICA—SPINAL CORD RESEARCH FOUNDATION

Fellowships in Spinal Cord Injury Research   see number 280

▼ PILOT INTERNATIONAL FOUNDATION

Marie Newton Sepia Memorial Award   see number 477

TRADE/TECHNICAL SPECIALTIES

▼ AMERICAN ELECTROPLATERS AND SURFACE FINISHERS SOCIETY

American Electroplaters and Surface Finishers Society Scholarships   see number 378

▼ AMERICAN JEWISH COMMITTEE

Harold W. Rosenthal Fellowship in International Relations   see number 374

▼ AMERICAN SOCIETY OF HEATING, REFRIGERATING, AND AIR CONDITIONING ENGINEERS

ASHRAE Research Grants for Graduate Students   *see number 481*

▼ NATIONAL ACADEMIC ADVISING ASSOCIATION

National Academic Advising Association Research Grants   *see number 396*

▼ SPECIALTY EQUIPMENT MARKET ASSOCIATION

Specialty Equipment Market Association Memorial Scholarship Fund   *see number 426*

TRAVEL/TOURISM

▼ AMERICAN SOCIETY OF TRAVEL AGENTS SCHOLARSHIP FOUNDATION

A.L. Simmons Scholarship Fund   • 555

One-time award for graduate students pursuing master's or doctoral degrees with emphasis on travel/tourism. Must have minimum 2.5 GPA, as well as a previously submitted paper on travel/tourism. Write for application by sending a self-addressed stamped business-size envelope.

Academic/Career Areas: Travel/Tourism.

Award: Scholarship for use in graduate years; not renewable. *Number:* 2. *Amount:* $2000.

Eligibility Requirements: Applicant must be enrolled at a four-year institution and must have an interest in writing.

Application Requirements: Application, essay, references, self-addressed stamped envelope, transcript. **Deadline:** July 28.

World Wide Web: http://www.astanet.com

Contact: Scholarship Manager
American Society of Travel Agents
Scholarship Foundation
1101 King Street
Suite 200
Alexandria, VA 22314-2187

Avis Rent-A-Car Scholarship   • 556

One-time, $2000 award for student currently enrolled in MS, MBA, or equivalent accredited graduate-level degree program. Must have minimum four years full-time travel agency experience and be an owner/officer/employee of an agency. Send self-addressed stamped business-size envelope for application. Minimum 3.0 GPA required. Submit essay.

Academic/Career Areas: Travel/Tourism.

Award: Scholarship for use in graduate years; not renewable. *Number:* 1. *Amount:* $2000.

Eligibility Requirements: Applicant must be enrolled at a four-year institution and have employment experience in experience in career field.

Application Requirements: Application, essay, references, self-addressed stamped envelope, transcript. **Deadline:** July 28.

World Wide Web: http://www.astanet.com

Contact: Scholarship Manager
American Society of Travel Agents
Scholarship Foundation
1101 King Street
Suite 200
Alexandria, VA 22314-2187

David Hallissey Memorial Scholarship   • 557

One-time award for graduate students or professors of travel/tourism planning research in travel/tourism. Submit 500-word abstract on intended topic of research and include methodology and objectives. Minimum 2.5 GPA. Write for application by sending self-addressed stamped business-size envelope.

Academic/Career Areas: Travel/Tourism.

Award: Scholarship for use in graduate years; not renewable. *Number:* 1. *Amount:* $2000.

Application Requirements: Application, essay, references, self-addressed stamped envelope, transcript. **Deadline:** July 28.

World Wide Web: http://www.astanet.com

Contact: Scholarship Manager
American Society of Travel Agents
Scholarship Foundation
1101 King Street
Suite 200
Alexandria, VA 22314-2187

▼ TRAVEL AND TOURISM RESEARCH ASSOCIATION

Travel and Tourism Research Association Student Research Award • 558

One-time prizes for master's and undergraduate students who submit recently written research papers on travel and tourism completed between March 1, 1997, and March 1, 1998. Submit the abstract and paper of a completed, original research survey. Five awards given; first prize is $1000; registration and travel allowance for conference; and plaque.

Academic/Career Areas: Travel/Tourism.
Award: Prize for use in freshman, sophomore, junior, senior, or graduate years; not renewable. *Number:* 5.
Application Requirements: Deadline: March 1.
E-mail: dornuf@mgtserv.com
Phone: 606-226-4344 **Fax:** 606-226-4355
Contact: Cynde Dornuf, Awards Committee
Travel and Tourism Research Association
546 East Main Street
Lexington, KY 40508

Travel and Tourism Research Association William B. Keeling Dissertation Award • 559

One-time award for doctoral student who submits the best doctoral dissertation on a subject directly related to the travel and tourism field. Only dissertations completed between January 1, 1996, and January 1, 1999 may be entered. Award presented every three years; the next one will be presented in 1999.

Academic/Career Areas: Travel/Tourism.
Award: Prize for use in graduate years; not renewable. *Number:* 1.
Application Requirements: Deadline: March 1.

E-mail: dornuf@mgtserv.com
Phone: 606-226-4344 **Fax:** 606-226-4355
Contact: Cynde Dornuf, Awards Committee
Travel and Tourism Research Association
546 East Main Street
Lexington, KY 40508

▼ WINTERTHUR MUSEUM, GARDEN, AND LIBRARY

NEH Fellowships see number 321

Winterthur Research Fellowships see number 322

TV/RADIO BROADCASTING

▼ CONSORTIUM OF COLLEGE AND UNIVERSITY MEDIA CENTERS

Consortium of College and University Media Centers Research Awards see number 383

▼ MARINE BIOLOGICAL LABORATORY, WOODS HOLE

Marine Biological Laboratory Science Writing Fellowships Program see number 510

▼ NATIONAL ASSOCIATION OF BROADCASTERS

National Association of Broadcasters Grants for Research in Broadcasting see number 385

NONACADEMIC/NONCAREER CRITERIA–GRADUATE

▲

ASSOCIATION AFFILIATION

▼ DAUGHTERS OF PENELOPE

Daughters of Penelope Graduate Student Award   • 560

Award for women accepted or enrolled in graduate program for minimum 9 units per academic year. Must verify acceptance. Applicant must have immediate family member who has been member of Daughters of Penelope or Order of Ahepa for two years, or herself have been member of Daughters of Penelope or Maids of Athena for two years. Must verify membership. One-time award of $1000, based on academic merit. Deadline: June 20.
Award: Scholarship for use in graduate years; not renewable. *Number:* 1. *Amount:* $1000.
Eligibility Requirements: Applicant must be female and member of Daughters of Penelope/Maids of Athena/Order of Ahepa.
Application Requirements: Application, essay, photo, references, test scores, transcript. **Deadline:** June 20.
Contact: Daughters of Penelope
1909 Q Street, NW, Suite 500
Washington, DC 20009

Sonja Stefandis Graduate Student Award   • 561

Award for women accepted or enrolled in graduate program for minimum 9 units per academic year. Must verify acceptance. Applicant must have immediate family member who has been member of Daughters of Penelope or Order of Ahepa for two years, or herself have been a member of Daughters of Penelope or Maids of Athena for two years. Must verify membership. One-time award of $1000, based on academic merit. Deadline: June 20.
Award: Scholarship for use in graduate years; not renewable. *Amount:* $1000.
Eligibility Requirements: Applicant must be female and member of Daughters of Penelope/Maids of Athena/Order of Ahepa.
Application Requirements: Application, essay, photo, references, test scores, transcript. **Deadline:** June 20.

Contact: Daughters of Penelope
1909 Q Street, NW, Suite 500
Washington, DC 20009

IMPAIRMENT

▼ GALLAUDET UNIVERSITY ALUMNI ASSOCIATION

Gallaudet University Alumni Association Graduate Fellowship Funds   • 562

One-time award for deaf or hard-of-hearing doctoral-level students. Submit application, transcript, financial aid form, references, and audiogram. Write for more information and to request application form.
Award: Scholarship for use in postdoctoral years; not renewable. *Number:* 15–20. *Amount:* $500–$5000.
Eligibility Requirements: Applicant must be enrolled at a four-year institution. Applicant must be hearing impaired.
Application Requirements: Application, financial need analysis, references, transcript. **Deadline:** April 20.
E-mail: dcmcgregor@gallua.gallaudet.edu
Phone: 202-651-5060 **Fax:** 202-651-5062
World Wide Web: http://www.gallaudet.edu/~alumweb
Contact: Daphne Cox McGregor, Assistant Director
Gallaudet University Alumni Association
800 Florida Avenue, NE
Washington, DC 20002-3695

▼ MICHIGAN COMMISSION FOR THE BLIND

Roy Johnson Trust Graduate School Grants   • 563

Award for graduate school tuition expenses for legally blind college students attending an accredited college or university in the state of Michigan. Non-U.S. citizens must have bachelor's degree from U.S. college or university.

Must submit eye report, proof of acceptance into graduate school, copy of Form 1040. Deadline: May 31.
Award: Grant for use in graduate years; not renewable. *Number:* 4–15. *Amount:* $250–$2000.
Eligibility Requirements: Applicant must be studying in Michigan. Applicant must be visually impaired.
Application Requirements: Application, transcript. **Deadline:** May 31.
Phone: 517-373-0579 **Fax:** 517-335-5140
Contact: James S. Buscetta, Administrator
Michigan Commission for the Blind
PO Box 30652
Lansing, MI 48909

NATIONAL OR ETHNIC BACKGROUND

▼ ALEXANDER VON HUMBOLDT FOUNDATION

Feodor-Lynen Research Fellowship for German Scholars • 564

Renewable award for highly qualified German scholars no older than 38 years of age to conduct research of their choice at non-German home institution. Must have doctoral degree or other high academic qualification. Fellowship stipend: DM 3,200-DM 4,000.
Eligibility Requirements: Applicant must be German and age 38 or under.
Application Requirements: Application. **Deadline:** Continuous.
Contact: Director
Alexander von Humboldt Foundation
1055 Thomas Jefferson Street, NW, #2030
Washington, DC 20007

▼ AMERICAN-SCANDINAVIAN FOUNDATION

Awards for Advanced Study or Research in the USA • 565

Awards for graduate and post-graduate research in the U.S. available to citizens of Denmark, Finland, Iceland, Norway, and Sweden. Preference given to dissertation-level research. Several one-time grants of up to $20,000.
Award: Scholarship for use in graduate years; not renewable. *Number:* 60–80. *Amount:* $1000–$20,000.

Eligibility Requirements: Applicant must be Danish, Finnish, Icelandic, Norwegian, or Swedish.
Application Requirements: Application, references, transcript.
Deadline: Continuous.
E-mail: emckey@amscan.org
Phone: 212-879-9779 **Fax:** 212-249-3444
World Wide Web: http://www.amscan.org
Contact: Ellen McKey, Director of Fellowships and Grants
American-Scandinavian Foundation
725 Park Avenue
New York, NY 10021

▼ LI FOUNDATION, INC.

Li Foundation Fellowships • 566

Fellowship assists deserving Chinese students and scholars who are sponsored by selected institutions for one to two years of study and training in the U.S. Grant provides $17,500 annually to cover cost of living, professional expenses, return transportation to China and $700 to attend a professional meeting.
Eligibility Requirements: Applicant must be Chinese and Asian.
Application Requirements: Application, applicant must enter a contest, autobiography, test scores, transcript. **Deadline:** March 15.
Contact: Administrative Officer
Li Foundation, Inc.
513 Parnassus Avenue, South, 1210
San Francisco, CA 94143

▼ MAKARIOS SCHOLARSHIP FUND INC.

Cyprus Children's Fund Scholarship Endowment • 567

Ten one-time awards of $1000 for college undergraduate or graduate students aged 18 to 30 pursuing any field of study. Must be of Greek origin. Must submit application and other materials by May 5.
Award: Scholarship for use in freshman, sophomore, junior, senior, or graduate years; not renewable. *Number:* 10. *Amount:* $1000.
Eligibility Requirements: Applicant must be Greek and ages 18-30.
Application Requirements: Application, autobiography, photo, references, test scores, transcript. **Deadline:** May 5.
Phone: 212-696-4590 **Fax:** 212-447-1988

Cyprus Children's Fund Scholarship Endowment (continued)

Contact: Kyriaki Christodoulou, Executive Director
Makarios Scholarship Fund Inc.
13 East 40th Street
New York, NY 10016

Makarios Scholarship Fund Inc. Scholarships • 568

Ten one-time awards of $1000 for college undergraduate or graduate student aged 18 to 30 pursuing any field of study. Must be of Cypriot heritage and maintain residence on the island of Cyprus. Must submit application and other materials by May 5.
Award: Scholarship for use in freshman, sophomore, junior, senior, or graduate years; not renewable. *Number:* 10. *Amount:* $1000.
Eligibility Requirements: Applicant must be Cypriot and ages 18-30.
Application Requirements: Application, autobiography, financial need analysis, photo, references, test scores, transcript. **Deadline:** May 5.
Phone: 212-696-4590 **Fax:** 212-447-1988
Contact: Kyriaki Christodoulou, Executive Director
Makarios Scholarship Fund Inc.
13 East 40th Street
New York, NY 10016

▼ SHASTRI INDO-CANADIAN INSTITUTE

Faculty Research Fellowships for Indian Scholars • 569

Faculty research fellowships help support research by Indian scholars who are committed to the promotion of Canadian studies at their own institution in India. Recipients must contribute to the pedagogical material on Canada in India through scholarly publications. One-time award for four to five weeks of study.
Eligibility Requirements: Applicant must be Indian.
Application Requirements: Application. **Deadline:** October 15.
E-mail: sici@acs.ucalgary.ca
Phone: 403-220-7467
Contact: Shastri Indo-Canadian Institute
2500 University Drive, NW
1402 Education Tower
Calgary, AB T2N 1N4
Canada

Shastri Faculty Enrichment Fellowship for Indian Scholars • 570

Faculty enrichment fellowships available to Indian university professors to assist them in developing and teaching new courses on Canada or expanding new courses. Fellows must complete a final report and attend a week-long summer institute. Four- to five-week awards of varying amounts.
Eligibility Requirements: Applicant must be Indian.
Application Requirements: Application. **Deadline:** October 15.
E-mail: sici@acs.ucalgary.ca
Phone: 403-220-7467
Contact: Shastri Indo-Canadian Institute
2500 University Drive, NW
1402 Education Tower
Calgary, AB T2N 1N4
Canada

Shastri Women & Development Awards for Indians • 571

Up to three awards available to do research in Canada. Indian scholars may apply for faculty, doctoral, and preliminary research fellowships or a visiting lectureship. Up to three one-time awards of varying amounts.
Award: Scholarship for use in postdoctoral years; not renewable. *Number:* up to 3.
Eligibility Requirements: Applicant must be Indian.
Application Requirements: Application. **Deadline:** October 15.
E-mail: sici@acs.ucalgary.ca
Phone: 403-220-7467
Contact: Shastri Indo-Canadian Institute
2500 University Drive, NW
1402 Education Tower
Calgary, AB T2N 1N4
Canada

▼ ST. ANDREW'S SOCIETY OF WASHINGTON, DC

Donald Malcolm MacArthur Scholarship • 572

One-time award for college juniors, seniors, or graduate students of Scottish descent to pursue studies in the U.S. or Scotland. Available to residents of specified states in the U.S. and the U.K. Send self-addressed stamped envelope for application.
Award: Scholarship for use in junior, senior, or graduate years; not renewable. *Number:* 1. *Amount:* $2500.
Eligibility Requirements: Applicant must be Scottish; enrolled at a four-year institution and resident of

Delaware, District of Columbia, Maryland, New Jersey, North Carolina, Pennsylvania, Virginia, or West Virginia. **Application Requirements:** Application, essay, financial need analysis, references, self-addressed stamped envelope. **Deadline:** March 15.
E-mail: mcleodjim@aol.com
Phone: 301-229-6140 **Fax:** 301-656-5130
Contact: James S. McLeod, Chairman
St. Andrew's Society of Washington, DC
7012 Arandale Road
Bethesda, MD 20817-4702

James and Mary Dawson Scholarship • 573

One-time award for college juniors, seniors, and graduate students who are Scottish natives and citizens of the U.K. to study in the U.S. Submit essay, references, and financial aid form with application. Send self-addressed, stamped envelope for application.
Award: Scholarship for use in junior, senior, or graduate years; not renewable. *Number:* 1–3. *Amount:* $1000–$5000.
Eligibility Requirements: Applicant must be Scottish and enrolled at a four-year institution.
Application Requirements: Application, essay, financial need analysis, references, self-addressed stamped envelope.
Deadline: March 15.
E-mail: mcleodjim@aol.com
Phone: 301-229-6140 **Fax:** 301-656-5130
Contact: James S. McLeod, Chairman
St. Andrew's Society of Washington, DC
7012 Arandale Road
Bethesda, MD 20817-4702

▼ STUDENTENWERK HAMBURG AMT FUR AUSBILDUNGSFOERDERUNG

Bafoeg for Study Abroad • 574

One-time award for students at German institution who have permanent residency in Germany to travel to the U.S. to conduct research at U.S. institution. Courses must be eligible for credit at German institution.
Award: Scholarship for use in junior, senior, or graduate years; not renewable.
Eligibility Requirements: Applicant must be German.
Application Requirements: Application, test scores, transcript.
Deadline: Continuous.
Contact: Studentenwerk Hamburg Amt fur
Ausbildungsfoerderung
Von-Melle-Park 2
20146 Hamburg
Germany

▼ SWISS BENEVOLENT SOCIETY OF NEW YORK

Medicus Student Exchange • 575

One-time award to students of Swiss nationality or parentage. U.S. residents study in Switzerland and Swiss residents study in the U.S. Awards to undergraduates are based on merit and need; those to graduates based only on merit. Open to U.S. residents of New York, New Jersey, Connecticut, Pennsylvania, and Delaware. Must be proficient in a foreign language.
Award: Scholarship for use in junior, senior, or graduate years; not renewable. *Number:* 1–5. *Amount:* $2000–$10,000.
Eligibility Requirements: Applicant must be Swiss; enrolled at a four-year institution; resident of Connecticut, Delaware, New Jersey, New York, or Pennsylvania and must have an interest in foreign language.
Application Requirements: Application, financial need analysis, references, test scores, transcript. **Deadline:** January 31.
Contact: Ann Marie Gilman, Scholarship Director
Swiss Benevolent Society of New York
608 Fifth Avenue, #309
New York, NY 10020

RELIGIOUS AFFILIATION

▼ MUSTARD SEED FOUNDATION AND THE COALITION FOR CHRISTIAN COLLEGES AND UNIVERSITIES

Harvey Fellows Program • 576

Award for Christian graduate students who plan to enter culturally influential vocations in which there is currently little Christian leadership. Must enroll in a top-five-ranked program. Competitive and extensive application required. Submit a work sample from major area of study.
Eligibility Requirements: Applicant must be Christian.
Application Requirements: Application, essay, references, test scores, transcript. **Deadline:** November 30.
E-mail: harvey@msfdn.org
Phone: 703-524-5650 **Fax:** 703-524-5643

Harvey Fellows Program (continued)

Contact: Susan Powell, Harvey Fellows Program
Director
Mustard Seed Foundation and The
Coalition for Christian Colleges and
Universities
3330 North Washington Boulevard, #100
Arlington, VA 22201

STATE OF RESIDENCE

▼ MICHIGAN COMMISSION FOR THE BLIND

Roy Johnson Trust Graduate School
Grants   *see number 563*

▼ MICHIGAN SOCIETY OF FELLOWS

Michigan Society of Fellows Postdoctoral
Fellowships   • 577
Fellowship for Ph.D. holders at the beginning of their
careers. Appointments are for three years as assistant
professors or research scientists at the University of
Michigan and as postdoctoral scholars at the Michigan
Society of Fellows. Recipients expected to be in residence
in Ann Arbor. One-time award of $32,500. Application
fee of $30.
Eligibility Requirements: Applicant must be studying in
Michigan.
Application Requirements: Application, essay, references.
Fee: $30. **Deadline:** October 13.
E-mail: society.of.fellows@umich.edu
Phone: 313-763-1259 **Fax:** 734-763-2447
Contact: Luan McCarty Briefer, Administrative
Assistant
Michigan Society of Fellows
3030 Rackham Building
Ann Arbor, MI 48109-1070

▼ NEW YORK CITY DEPARTMENT OF CITYWIDE ADMINISTRATIVE SERVICES

Urban Fellows Program   • 578
A nine-month program which combines full-time employment in New York City government with a comprehensive
seminar. Must be recent college graduate, or out of col-
lege a maximum of two years. Finalists will be invited to
interview in New York City. Twenty-five one-time intern-
ships at $18,000 each. Must submit a resume.
Eligibility Requirements: Applicant must be studying in
New York.
Application Requirements: Application, essay, interview,
references, transcript. **Deadline:** January 20.
Phone: 212-487-5698 **Fax:** 212-487-5706
Contact: Ms. Nancy Lehman, Director, Fellowship
Programs
New York City Department of Citywide
Administrative Services
One Centre Street, 24th Floor
New York, NY 10007

▼ SMITHSONIAN INSTITUTION NATIONAL AIR AND SPACE MUSEUM

A. Verville Fellowship   • 579
Fellowship to facilitate analysis of major trends, developments, and accomplishments in the history of aviation or
space studies. Must have demonstrated research and writ-
ing skills. Twelve-month residence at National Air and
Space Museum. Fellow receives $30,000 stipend, plus
$1000 research fund and travel expenses. Senior fellow-
ship not normally awarded to undergraduates.
Eligibility Requirements: Applicant must be studying in
District of Columbia and must have an interest in
writing.
Application Requirements: Application, references. **Deadline:**
January 15.
Phone: 202-357-2515 **Fax:** 202-786-2447
Contact: Ms. Anita Mason, Fellowship Coordinator
Smithsonian Institution National Air and
Space Museum
Aeronautics Department
MRC 312
Washington, DC 20560

▼ ST. ANDREW'S SOCIETY OF WASHINGTON, DC

Donald Malcolm MacArthur
Scholarship   *see number 572*

▼ SWISS BENEVOLENT SOCIETY OF NEW YORK

Medicus Student Exchange   *see number 575*

▼ VERMONT STUDENT ASSISTANCE CORPORATION

Vermont Incentive Grants • 580

Renewable grants for Vermont residents based on financial need. Must meet needs test. Must be college undergraduate or graduate student enrolled full-time at an approved postsecondary institution. Only available to U.S. citizens or permanent residents.

Award: Grant for use in freshman, sophomore, junior, senior, or graduate years; renewable. *Amount:* $500–$5200.

Eligibility Requirements: Applicant must be resident of Vermont.

Application Requirements: Application, financial need analysis. **Deadline:** March 1.

Phone: 802-655-9602 **Fax:** 802-654-3765

World Wide Web: http://www.vsac.org

Contact: Grant Program
Vermont Student Assistance Corporation
PO Box 2000
Winooski, VT 05404-2000

▼ WOMEN'S RESEARCH AND EDUCATION INSTITUTE

Congressional Fellowships on Women and Public Policy • 581

Congressional fellows spend one academic year working in offices of members of Congress or on congressional committee staffs. Must be currently enrolled in graduate or professional degree program. Focus is on analysis of gender differences and effect on federal laws and legislating.

Eligibility Requirements: Applicant must be studying in District of Columbia.

Application Requirements: Application, essay, references, self-addressed stamped envelope, transcript. **Deadline:** February 15.

E-mail: wrei@ix.netcom.com

Phone: 202-628-0444 **Fax:** 202-628-0458

Contact: Fellowship Program Director
Women's Research and Education Institute
1750 New York Avenue, NW, Suite 350
Washington, DC 20006-5301

TALENT

▼ AMERICAN NUMISMATIC SOCIETY

American Numismatic Society Graduate Fellowships • 582

Fellowship for alumni of Society's Graduate Seminar who are writing a dissertation in the coming academic year in which the use of numismatic evidence plays a significant part. Society's Council may waive the Seminar requirement in exceptional circumstances.

Eligibility Requirements: Applicant must have an interest in numismatics.

Application Requirements: Application, references, transcript.

Deadline: March 1.

E-mail: info@amnumsoc.org

Phone: 212-234-3130 **Fax:** 212-234-3381

World Wide Web: http://www.amnumsoc2.org

Contact: Mr. William Metcalf, Chief Curator
American Numismatic Society
Broadway at 155th Street
New York, NY 10032

▼ ASSOCIATION OF UNIVERSITIES AND COLLEGES OF CANADA

Programme Canadian de Bourses de la Francophone • 583

Renewable award for non-Canadian students from developing countries in the Francophonie. Open to students of all disciplines likely to contribute to the students' country. Must be fluent in French.

Award: Scholarship for use in freshman, sophomore, junior, senior, or graduate years; renewable.

Eligibility Requirements: Applicant must be enrolled at a four-year institution and must have an interest in French language.

Application Requirements: Application, essay, references, transcript. **Deadline:** December 15.

World Wide Web: http://www.aucc.ca

Contact: Jeanne Gallagher
Association of Universities and Colleges of Canada
350 Albert Street, Suite 600
Ottawa, ON K1R 1B1
Canada

▼ SMITHSONIAN INSTITUTION NATIONAL AIR AND SPACE MUSEUM

A. Verville Fellowship   see number 579

▼ SWISS BENEVOLENT SOCIETY OF NEW YORK

Medicus Student Exchange   see number 575

MISCELLANEOUS CRITERIA—GRADUATE

▲

▼ ALBERTA HERITAGE SCHOLARSHIP FUND

Alberta Ukrainian Centennial Commemorative Scholarships • 584

Award to provide academic opportunities for student from Ukraine to study in Alberta and for student from Alberta to study in Ukraine. Scholarships are for graduate level study and will be awarded every second year. Deadline: February 1.

Award: Scholarship for use in graduate years; not renewable. *Number:* 2.

Application Requirements: Application. **Deadline:** February 1.

E-mail: stuart.dunn@aecd.gov.ab.ca

Phone: 403-427-8640 **Fax:** 403-422-4516

Contact: Director
Alberta Heritage Scholarship Fund
9940 106th Street, 9th Floor
Edmonton, AB T5J 4R4
Canada

▼ AMERICAN ASSOCIATION OF UNIVERSITY WOMEN EDUCATIONAL FOUNDATION

American Association of University Women Educational Foundation Community Action Grants • 585

One-time award for women to create activities that address the contemporary needs of girls and women and have direct community impact. $15 application fee for members of the American Association of University Women; $25 fee for non-members. Application deadlines are February 4 and September 4.

Award: Grant for use in graduate years; not renewable. *Amount:* $500–$5000.

Eligibility Requirements: Applicant must be female.

Application Requirements: Application.

E-mail: ertf@mail.aauw.org

Phone: 202-728-7609 **Fax:** 202-872-1425

Contact: Bob Swinehart, Program Manager
American Association of University Women
Educational Foundation
1111 16th Street, NW
Washington, DC 20036-4873

▼ HEART AND STROKE FOUNDATION OF BRITISH COLUMBIA AND YUKON

Heart and Stroke Foundation of British Columbia and Yukon Program/ Project Grant • 586

Award to provide support for three or more investigators to undertake collaborative, multidisciplinary research. Each component grant-in-aid must be based in British Columbia. Grant is renewable and normally awarded for four years. Letter of Intent must be submitted by May 15; full application form, by Sept. 30.

Award: Grant for use in postdoctoral years; renewable.

Application Requirements: Application.

E-mail: kjany@heartstroke.istar.ca

Phone: 604-737-3401 **Fax:** 604-736-8732

World Wide Web: http://www.hsf.ca/research

Contact: Kathy Jany, Research Officer
Heart and Stroke Foundation of British
Columbia and Yukon
1212 West Broadway
Vancouver, BC V6H 3V2
Canada

▼ HUDSON RIVER FOUNDATION

Hudson River Foundation Graduate Fellowships • 587

One year of support for graduate research on Hudson River-specific study. Also includes support for research expenses. Up to five one-time awards: $9000 master's award and $12,000 Ph.D. award.

Application Requirements: Application, references. **Deadline:** March 4.

E-mail: dennis@hudsonriver.org

Phone: 212-924-8290

Hudson River Foundation Graduate Fellowships (continued)

World Wide Web: http://www.hudsonriver.org
Contact: Science Director
Hudson River Foundation
40 West 20th Street, 9th Floor
New York, NY 10011

Tibor T. Polgar Fellowships • 588

Several fellowships available to graduate or undergraduate students to conduct research on the Hudson River. Applicants must submit five copies of the application including a letter of interest and a letter of support from an adviser. Eight one-time awards of $3500 each.
Application Requirements: Application, essay, references.
Deadline: March 4.
E-mail: dennis@hudsonriver.org
Phone: 212-924-8290
World Wide Web: http://www.hudsonriver.org
Contact: Science Director
Hudson River Foundation
40 West 20th Street, 9th Floor
New York, NY 10011

▼ MARGARET MCNAMARA MEMORIAL FUND

Margaret McNamara Memorial Fund Fellowships • 589

One-time awards for female students from developing countries enrolled in accredited graduate programs relating to women and children. Must be attending an accredited institution in the U.S. Candidates must plan to return to their countries within two years. Must be over 25 years of age.
Eligibility Requirements: Applicant must be age 25 or over and female.
Application Requirements: Application, essay, photo, references, transcript. **Deadline:** February 1.
E-mail: wservices1@worldbank.org
Phone: 202-473-8751 **Fax:** 202-676-0419
Contact: Chair, MMMF Selection Committee
Margaret McNamara Memorial Fund
1818 H Street, NW, Room G-1000
Washington, DC 20433

▼ MERRILL LYNCH FORUM

Innovation Grants Competition • 590

Award for Ph.D. candidates in the sciences, liberal arts and engineering, who successfully defend their dissertation during the 17 months prior to the June 1 application deadline. Applicants should persuasively and creatively describe means to translate their academic research into commercially viable business enterprise. Contact for applications and entry information.
Award: Grant for use in postdoctoral years; not renewable.
Application Requirements: Application. **Deadline:** June 1.
Phone: 212-449-1000
World Wide Web: http://www.ml.com/innovation
Contact: Merrill Lynch Forum
World Financial Center
North Tower, 250 Vesey Street
New York, NY 10281

▼ PILOT INTERNATIONAL FOUNDATION

Ruby Newhall Memorial Scholarship Program • 591

One-time award for foreign students studying in the U.S. or Canada who plan to return to their home country. Must have completed at least one semester of undergraduate work. Must be sponsored by a local Pilot Club.
Award: Scholarship for use in sophomore, junior, senior, or graduate years; not renewable. *Number:* 5–20. *Amount:* $500–$1500.
Eligibility Requirements: Applicant must be enrolled at a two-year or four-year institution.
Application Requirements: Application, financial need analysis, references, self-addressed stamped envelope, transcript. **Deadline:** March 1.
Contact: Awards Director
Pilot International Foundation
244 College Street, Box 5600
Macon, GA 31208-5600

▼ SHASTRI INDO-CANADIAN INSTITUTE

Shastri Social Sciences & Humanities Fellowships • 592

Three fellowships available for Indian scholars to undertake research and related activities in Canada for four months.

Recipients are expected to help strengthen research expertise on development issues at Canadian universities. Three one-time awards of varying amounts. Must be a citizen of India.
Application Requirements: Application. **Deadline:** October 15.
E-mail: sici@acs.ucalgary.ca
Phone: 403-220-7467

Contact: Shastri Indo-Canadian Institute
2500 University Drive, NW
1402 Education Tower
Calgary, AB T2N 1N4
Canada

UNDERGRADUATE INDEXES

Award Name Index–Undergraduate

SPONSOR INDEX–UNDERGRADUATE

▲

ACADEMIC/CAREER AREAS INDEX– UNDERGRADUATE

▲

Meteorology/Atmospheric Science
Associated Western Universities Student Research
  Fellowships • 18
Garden Club of America-"GCA Awards in
  Environmental Studies" • 5
National Academy of Science Grants-in-Aid of
  Research (G/UG) • 13
Sigma Xi Grants-in-Aid of Research (G/UG) • 8

Museum Studies
Endowment for Biblical Research and American
  Schools of Oriental Research Summer Research
  Grants and Travel Scholarships (G/UG) • 30

Natural Resources
Associated Western Universities Student Research
  Fellowships • 18
Bluebird Student Research Grant (G/UG) • 64
Canada-Taiwan Student Exchange Program • 34
Demonstration of Energy-Efficient Developments
  Scholarship (G/UG) • 89
Dorothy Vandercook Peace Scholarship • 137
Environmental Protection Scholarships (G/UG) • 6
Garden Club of America-"GCA Awards in
  Environmental Studies" • 5
Louis Agassiz Fuertes Award (G/UG) • 14
Margaret Morse Nice Award (G/UG) • 15
Masonic Range Science Scholarship • 1
National Academy of Science Grants-in-Aid of
  Research (G/UG) • 13
Paul A. Stewart Awards (G/UG) • 16

Nuclear Science
Associated Western Universities Student Research
  Fellowships • 18
Paul Cole Scholarship (G/UG) • 121

Nursing
Campus Safety Scholarship (G/UG) • 19
International Order of the King's Daughters and
  Sons Health Careers Scholarship (G/UG) • 82
Lindbergh Grants Program (G/UG) • 4
Miriam Neveren Summer Studentship • 61
Nursing Scholastic Achievement Scholarship for
  Lutheran College Students (G/UG) • 139
Oncology Nursing Foundation Roberta Pierce
  Scofield Bachelor's Scholarships (G/UG) • 140
Oncology Nursing Foundation/Josh Gottheil
  Memorial Bone Marrow Transplant Career
  Development Awards (G/UG) • 141
Oncology Nursing Foundation/Oncology Nursing
  Certification Corporation Bachelor's Scholarships
  • 142
Oncology Nursing Foundation/Oncology Nursing
  Society/Cancer Public Education Projects (G/
  UG) • 143
Oncology Nursing Foundation/Pearl Moore Career
  Development Awards (G/UG) • 138

Peace and Conflict Studies
Dorothy Vandercook Peace Scholarship • 137

Performing Arts
Armenian Professional Society of the Bay Area
  Scholarships (G/UG) • 31
Canada Council Music Touring Grants (G/UG)
  • 144
Canada-Taiwan Student Exchange Program • 34
Contemporary Record Society National Competition
  for Performing Arts (G/UG) • 145
Curtis Institute of Music Scholarships (G/UG) • 146
Dance, Theater, Film, and Playwright Grants (G/UG)
  • 45
Gina Bachauer International Piano Competition
  Award (G/UG) • 147
Glenn Miller Instrumental Scholarship • 148
International Competition for Symphonic
  Composition (G/UG) • 156
Jack Pullan Memorial Scholarship • 149
Kosciuszko Foundation Chopin Piano Competition
  (G/UG) • 151
New Jersey State Opera Vocal Competition (G/UG)
  • 155
Ralph Brewster Vocal Scholarship • 150
Thelonious Monk International Jazz Competition
  (G/UG) • 157
University of Maryland International Leonard Rose
  Cello Competition and Festival (G/UG) • 152
University of Maryland International Marian
  Anderson Vocal Arts Competition and Festival
  (G/UG) • 153
University of Maryland International William Kapell
  Piano Competition and Festival (G/UG) • 154

Photojournalism
Donald E. Keyhoe Journalism Award (G/UG) • 128
International Foodservice Editorial Council
  Scholarship Award (G/UG) • 75
Photojournalism Competitions • 76

Physical Sciences and Math
American Association for the Advancement of
  Science Mass Media, Science, and Engineering
  Fellowship (G/UG) • 95
American Association of Cereal Chemists
  Undergraduate Scholarships • 3
American Society of Crime Laboratory Directors
  Scholarship Award (G/UG) • 59
Associated Western Universities Student Research
  Fellowships • 18
BFGoodrich Collegiate Inventors Program (G/UG)
  • 22
Campus Safety Scholarship (G/UG) • 19
Chemical Heritage Foundation Travel Grants
  (G/UG) • 20

Earth Observation Satellite Company Award for Application of Digital Landsat TM Data (G/UG) • 17

Garden Club of America-"GCA Awards in Environmental Studies" • 5

Masonic Range Science Scholarship • 1

Master Brewers Association-America's Scholarships • 7

McDermott Scholarship • 23

Microscopy Society of America Presidential Student Awards (G/UG) • 63

National Academy of Science Grants-in-Aid of Research (G/UG) • 13

Sigma Xi Grants-in-Aid of Research (G/UG) • 8

Society of Exploration Geophysicists Foundation Scholarship (G/UG) • 83

SPE Foundation Scholarships • 68

SPIE Educational Scholarships and Grants in Optical Engineering (G/UG) • 21

Tibor T. Polgar Fellowship (G/UG) • 62

Political Science

Albert Corey Prize in American-Canadian Relations (G/UG) • 123

Dorothy Vandercook Peace Scholarship • 137

Humane Studies Fellowships (G/UG) • 74

Kennedy Research Grants (G/UG) • 26

Real Estate

Harwood Memorial Real Estate Scholarship (G/UG) • 158

Religion/Theology

Jesse Lee Prize (G/UG) • 124

Memorial Foundation for Jewish Culture International Scholarship Program for Community Service (G/UG) • 86

Opal Dancey Memorial Foundation (G/UG) • 159

Science, Technology & Society

Campus Safety Scholarship (G/UG) • 19

Social Sciences

Albert Corey Prize in American-Canadian Relations (G/UG) • 123

Armenian Professional Society of the Bay Area Scholarships (G/UG) • 31

Dorothy Vandercook Peace Scholarship • 137

Eileen J. Garrett Scholarship for Parapsychological Research (G/UG) • 162

Endowment for Biblical Research and American Schools of Oriental Research Summer Research Grants and Travel Scholarships (G/UG) • 30

Humane Studies Fellowships (G/UG) • 74

Kennedy Research Grants (G/UG) • 26

Lambda Alpha National Collegiate Honor Society of Anthropology National Dean's List Award • 160

Sigma Xi Grants-in-Aid of Research (G/UG) • 8

Soviet Jewry Community Service Scholarship Program (G/UG) • 161

Social Services

Memorial Foundation for Jewish Culture International Scholarship Program for Community Service (G/UG) • 86

Mental Retardation Scholastic Achievement Scholarship for Lutheran College Students • 81

Soviet Jewry Community Service Scholarship Program (G/UG) • 161

Special Education

Mental Retardation Scholastic Achievement Scholarship for Lutheran College Students • 81

Miriam Neveren Summer Studentship • 61

Sports-related

Mental Retardation Scholastic Achievement Scholarship for Lutheran College Students • 81

Therapy/Rehabilitation

International Order of the King's Daughters and Sons Health Careers Scholarship (G/UG) • 82

Mental Retardation Scholastic Achievement Scholarship for Lutheran College Students • 81

Miriam Neveren Summer Studentship • 61

William W. Burgin Educational Recognition Awards • 163

Trade/Technical Specialties

Alwin B. Newton Scholarship Fund • 88

American Dental Hygienists' Association Institute-Baccalaureate Scholarship • 80

American Electroplaters and Surface Finishers Society Scholarships (G/UG) • 69

Bud Glover Memorial Scholarship (G/UG) • 47

Castleberry Instruments Scholarship • 48

Eunice Miles Scholarship (G/UG) • 164

Fel-Pro Automotive Technicians Scholarship Program • 92

International Executive Housekeepers Educational Foundation (G/UG) • 111

International Women's Helicopter Pilots Whirly-Girls/Doris Mullen Memorial Scholarship & Memorial Flight Training Scholarship (G/UG) • 57

Morris Hanauer and Irene Mack Scholarships (G/UG) • 165

Myrtle and Earl Walker Scholarship Fund • 102

National Association of Women in Construction Undergraduate Scholarships (G/UG) • 27

National Association of Women in Contruction Founder's Scholarship Award • 28

National Scholarship Trust Fund of the Graphic Arts • 42

Northern Airborne Technology Scholarship • 53

Paul and Blanche Wulfsberg Scholarship (G/UG) • 54

Association Affiliation Index—
Undergraduate

▲

Corporate Affiliation Index– Undergraduate

▲

EMPLOYMENT EXPERIENCE INDEX– UNDERGRADUATE

▲

Impairment Index—Undergraduate

▲

Hearing Impaired
Alexander Graham Bell Scholarship Award (G/UG)
  • 200
International Art Show for Disabled Artists (G/UG)
  • 203
Optimist International Communication Contest for
  the Deaf and Hard of Hearing (G/UG) • 202

Learning Disabled
International Art Show for Disabled Artists (G/UG)
  • 203

Physically Disabled
International Art Show for Disabled Artists (G/UG)
  • 203
National Amputation Foundation Scholarships • 201

Visually Impaired
International Art Show for Disabled Artists (G/UG)
  • 203

MILITARY SERVICE INDEX—UNDERGRADUATE

▲

NATIONAL OR ETHNIC BACKGROUND INDEX– UNDERGRADUATE

▲

RELIGIOUS AFFILIATION INDEX– UNDERGRADUATE

▲

Christian
Opal Dancey Memorial Foundation (G/UG) • 159
Jewish
Memorial Foundation for Jewish Culture International Scholarship Program for Community Service (G/UG) • 86
Soviet Jewry Community Service Scholarship Program (G/UG) • 161

Lutheran
Mental Retardation Scholastic Achievement Scholarship for Lutheran College Students • 81
Nursing Scholastic Achievement Scholarship for Lutheran College Students (G/UG) • 139
Other Specific Denomination
Sikh Education Aid Fund (G/UG) • 213

State of Residence Index—Undergraduate
▲

Talent Index—Undergraduate

▲

Animal/Agricultural Competition
Dog Writers' Educational Trust Scholarship (G/UG)
• 11

Art
Dance, Theater, Film, and Playwright Grants (G/UG)
• 45
Elizabeth Greenshields Award/Grant (G/UG) • 37
Fine Arts Work Center Fellowships (G/UG) • 38
International Art Show for Disabled Artists (G/UG)
• 203
Light Work Artist-in-Residence Program (G/UG)
• 246
National Scholarship Trust Fund of the Graphic Arts
• 42
National Sculpture Competition for Young Sculptors
(G/UG) • 43
National Sculpture Society Alex J. Ettl Grant (G/UG)
• 44
National Sculpture Society Scholarship (G/UG)
• 250
Scholastic Art and Writing Awards-Art Section • 35

Automotive
Specialty Equipment Market Association Memorial
Scholarship Fund (G/UG) • 106

Bowling
Alberta E. Crow Star of Tomorrow Scholarship • 259
Chuck Hall Star of Tomorrow Scholarship (G/UG)
• 231

Foreign Language
Medicus Student Exchange (G/UG) • 217

French Language
Programme Canadian de Bourses de la Francophone
(G/UG) • 236

Leadership
Alexander Graham Bell Scholarship Award (G/UG)
• 200
Alwin B. Newton Scholarship Fund • 88
American Association of Cereal Chemists
Undergraduate Scholarships • 3
American Institute for Foreign Study International
Scholarships • 233
Glamour's Top Ten College Competition • 244
International Foodservice Editorial Council
Scholarship Award (G/UG) • 75

National Association for Campus Activities
Educational Foundation Scholarships for Student
Leaders • 248

Music/Singing
Adeline Rosenberg Memorial Prize (G/UG) • 242
American Guild of Organists Regional Competitions
for Young Organists (G/UG) • 232
BMI Student Composer Awards (G/UG) • 237
Contemporary Record Society National Competition
for Performing Arts (G/UG) • 145
Contemporary Record Society National Festival for
the Performing Arts (G/UG) • 238
Curtis Institute of Music Scholarships (G/UG) • 146
Delius Composition Contest (G/UG) • 240
Gina Bachauer International Piano Competition
Award (G/UG) • 147
Glenn Miller Instrumental Scholarship • 148
Inter-American Music Award Competition (G/UG)
• 255
International Competition for Symphonic
Composition (G/UG) • 156
Jack Pullan Memorial Scholarship • 149
Kosciuszko Foundation Chopin Piano Competition
(G/UG) • 151
National Competition for Composers Recording
(G/UG) • 239
New Jersey State Opera Vocal Competition (G/UG)
• 155
Omaha Symphony Guild New Music Competition
(G/UG) • 251
Ralph Brewster Vocal Scholarship • 150
Thelonious Monk International Jazz Competition
(G/UG) • 157
University of Maryland International Leonard Rose
Cello Competition and Festival (G/UG) • 152
University of Maryland International Marian
Anderson Vocal Arts Competition and Festival
(G/UG) • 153
University of Maryland International William Kapell
Piano Competition and Festival (G/UG) • 154

Photography/Photogrammetry/Filmmaking
Dance, Theater, Film, and Playwright Grants (G/UG)
• 45
International Foodservice Editorial Council
Scholarship Award (G/UG) • 75

GRADUATE INDEXES

AWARD NAME INDEX—GRADUATE

▲

SPONSOR INDEX—GRADUATE

▲

Academic/Career Areas Index–Graduate

▲

Katharine and Bryant Mather Fellowship • 302
Keepers Preservation Education Fund Fellowship
    • 319
Mechanical/Electrical Traveling Fellowship Program
    • 314
NEH Fellowships • 321
Robert H. and Clarice Smith Fellowship • 312
Rosann S. Berry Annual Meeting Fellowship • 320
Structural Engineering Traveling Fellow. Program
    • 315
Urban Design Traveling Fellowship Program • 316
W. R. Grace Fellowship • 303
Winterthur Research Fellowships • 322

Area/Ethnic Studies
American Jewish Archives Fellowships • 331
Archaeological Institute of America/Kenan T. Erim
    Award • 323
Armenian Professional Society of the Bay Area
    Scholarships (G/UG) • 324
Bliss Prize Fellowship in Byzantine Studies • 328
Center for Field Research Grants for Field Research
    • 294
Center for Hellenic Studies Fellowships • 327
Doctoral Dissertation Research Grant (HUD) • 334
Dr. Sydney Segal Research Grants • 275
H. F. Guggenheim Foundation Research Grants
    • 329
Irish Research Funds • 330
Japan Foundation Cultural Properties Specialist
    Fellowship • 310
Mary Isabel Sibley Fellowship for Greek and French
    Studies • 332
Mayme and Herbert Frank Educational Fund • 325
Neporany Research Teaching Fellowship • 326
Society Farsarotul Financial Awards (G/UG) • 333

Art History
Architectural Study Tour Scholarship • 317
Bliss Prize Fellowship in Byzantine Studies • 328
Center for Advanced Study in the Visual Arts Senior
    Fellowship Program • 311
Center for Field Research Grants for Field Research
    • 294
Edilia and Francois-Auguste de Montequin
    Fellowship in Iberian and Latin American
    Architecture • 318
Ford Foundation Fellowships • 335
Hagley Museum and Library Grants-in-Aid • 308
Henry Belin du Pont Dissertation Fellowship • 309
J. Paul Getty Postdoctoral Fellowships in the History
    of Art and the Humanities • 336
Keepers Preservation Education Fund Fellowship
    • 319
Kress Travel Fellowships • 337
Mary Isabel Sibley Fellowship for Greek and French
    Studies • 332

NEH Fellowships • 321
Robert H. and Clarice Smith Fellowship • 312
Rosann S. Berry Annual Meeting Fellowship • 320
Winterthur Research Fellowships • 322

Arts
Archaeological Institute of America/Kenan T. Erim
    Award • 323
Bliss Prize Fellowship in Byzantine Studies • 328
Dance, Theater, Film, and Playwright Grants (G/UG)
    • 342
Fellowships for Advanced Training in Fine Arts
    Conservation • 343
Ford Foundation Fellowships • 335
Hagley Museum and Library Grants-in-Aid • 308
Henry and Chiyo Kuwahara Creative Arts Scholarship
    (G/UG) • 338
Henry Belin du Pont Dissertation Fellowship • 309
International Fellowships in Jewish Culture Program
    • 340
Mary Isabel Sibley Fellowship for Greek and French
    Studies • 332
NEH Fellowships • 321
Pollock-Krasner Grants • 341
Posey Foundation Graduate Art Scholarship • 339
Winterthur Research Fellowships • 322

Aviation/Aerospace
Guggenheim Fellowship • 300
Vertical Flight Foundation Scholarship (G/UG)
    • 345
William E. Jackson Award • 344

Biology
American Geophysical Union Horton Research Grant
    • 284
American Orchid Society/Orchid Research Grant
    • 346
American Physiological Society Conference Student
    Awards • 347
American Society of Microbiology & National Center
    for Infectious Diseases Post Doctoral Research
    Associates Program • 348
American Water Works Association/Abel Wolman
    Fellowship • 286
American Water Works Association/Holly A. Cornell
    Scholarship • 287
American Water Works Association/Larson Aquatic
    Research Support Scholarship • 288
American Water Works Association/Thomas R. Camp
    Memorial Scholarship • 289
Campus Safety Scholarship (G/UG) • 293
Center for Field Research Grants for Field Research
    • 294
Cooley's Anemia Foundation Research Fellowship
    • 352
Cystic Fibrosis Foundation Student Traineeships
    (G/UG) • 353

Business/Consumer Services

Campus Activities

Chemical Engineering

Civil Engineering

Communications

Consortium of College and University Media Centers Research Awards • 383

Harold W. Rosenthal Fellowship in International Relations • 374

Humane Studies Fellowships (G/UG) • 384

Mary Macey Scholarship (G/UG) • 273

National Association of Broadcasters Grants for Research in Broadcasting • 385

William E. Jackson Award • 344

Computer Science/Data Processing

Adelle and Erwin Tomash Fellowship in the History of Information Processing • 391

Associated Western Universities-DOE Post-Graduate Fellowship • 290

Associated Western Universities/DOE Faculty Fellowships • 291

Associated Western Universities/DOE Laboratory Graduate Research Fellowships • 292

Educational Testing Service Postdoctoral Fellowship Program • 375

Foundation for Science and Disability-Student Grant • 297

Institute for Scientific Information Doctoral Dissertation Scholarship • 386

Pratt-Severn Student Research Award • 387

Special Interest Group/STI BIOSIS Student Award • 388

Special Interest Group/STI Chemical Abstracts Service Student Award • 389

UMI Doctoral Dissertation Award • 390

Criminal Justice/Criminology

H. F. Guggenheim Foundation Research Grants • 329

Pi Gamma Mu Scholarship • 392

Dental Health/Services

International Order of the King's Daughters and Sons Health Careers Scholarship (G/UG) • 393

Earth Science

American Geophysical Union Horton Research Grant • 284

Associated Western Universities-DOE Post-Graduate Fellowship • 290

Associated Western Universities/DOE Faculty Fellowships • 291

Associated Western Universities/DOE Laboratory Graduate Research Fellowships • 292

Center for Field Research Grants for Field Research • 294

Chrysalis Scholarship • 394

Environmental Protection Scholarships (G/UG) • 269

Geological Society of America Student Research Grants • 395

National Academic Advising Association Research Grants • 396

National Academy of Science Grants-in-Aid of Research (G/UG) • 281

Ruth Satter Memorial Award • 350

Sigma Xi Grants-in-Aid of Research (G/UG) • 271

Society of Exploration Geophysicists Foundation Scholarship (G/UG) • 397

Tibor T. Polgar Fellowship (G/UG) • 360

Women's Auxiliary to the American Institute of Mining, Metallurgical and Petroleum Engineers Scholarship Loan Fund (G/UG) • 398

Woods Hole Oceanographic Institution Postdoctoral Fellowships • 372

Economics

Abe Fellowship Program • 404

American Geophysical Union Horton Research Grant • 284

Doctoral Dissertation Research Grant (HUD) • 334

Gilbert F. White Postdoctoral Fellowships • 402

Humane Studies Fellowships (G/UG) • 384

J.C. Geilfuss Fellowship • 405

Joseph L. Fisher Dissertation Awards • 403

Mary Macey Scholarship (G/UG) • 273

National Association of Purchasing Management Doctoral Grants • 376

Pi Gamma Mu Scholarship • 392

Population Council Fellowships in Population Study • 400

Population Council Postdoctoral Fellowships in the Social Sciences • 401

Transatlantic Research Cooperation between German and American Scholars in the Human and Social Sciences, Economics, and Law • 399

Education

Armenian Professional Society of the Bay Area Scholarships (G/UG) • 324

Association for the Study of Higher Education Dissertation of the Year Award • 406

Consortium of College and University Media Centers Research Awards • 383

Doctoral Thesis Fellowship in Ukrainian History • 407

Educational Testing Service Postdoctoral Fellowship Program • 375

Federation Executive Recruitment and Education Program • 410

Grant Foundation Faculty Scholars Program • 415

Helen Darcovich Memorial Endowment Fund Doctoral Fellowship • 409

Hollingworth Award Competition • 412

Michael Dorosh Fund Master's Fellowship • 408

Phi Delta Kappa International Graduate Fellowships in Educational Leadership • 414

Spencer Postdoctoral Fellowship Program • 411

Food Science/Nutrition
American Association of Cereal Chemists Graduate Fellowships • 268
American Society for Nurtritional Sciences Pre-Doctoral Fellowship • 429
Blue Cross Blue Shield of Michigan Foundation Student Award Program • 416
Dorothy I. Mitstifer Fellowship • 430
Kappa Omicron Nu National Alumni Fellowship • 431
Kappa Omicron Nu New Initiatives Grant • 432

Food Service/Hospitality
Food Distribution Research Society, Inc. Applebaum Master's and PhD Programs Awards • 433
Mary Macey Scholarship (G/UG) • 273

Foreign Language
Harold W. Rosenthal Fellowship in International Relations • 374
Mary Isabel Sibley Fellowship for Greek and French Studies • 332
Society Farsarotul Financial Awards (G/UG) • 333

Graphics
Sun Chemical Corporation Graduate Flexography Fellowship • 428

Health Administration
Blue Cross Blue Shield of Michigan Foundation Student Award Program • 416
Campus Safety Scholarship (G/UG) • 293
Dr. Sydney Segal Research Grants • 275
Elaine Osborne Jacobson Award for Women Working in Health Care Law • 435
National Environmental Health Association/AAS Scholarship (G/UG) • 434

Health and Medical Sciences
American Academy of Pediatrics Residency Scholarships • 436
American Association for the Advancement of Science Mass Media, Science, and Engineering Fellowship (G/UG) • 421
American Association of Orthopaedic Surgeons/ Orthopaedic Research and Education Foundation Fellowship in Health Service Research • 472
American Foundation for Pharmaceutical Education Grant Program for New Investigators • 438
American Foundation for Urologic Disease Fellowship Program • 442
American Foundation for Urologic Disease Health Services Research Scholar Program • 443
American Foundation for Urologic Disease MD Research Scholar Program • 444
American Foundation for Urologic Disease PhD Research Scholar Program • 445
American Otological Society Research Training Fellowships • 447

American Physiological Society Conference Student Awards • 347
American Society for Nurtritional Sciences Pre-Doctoral Fellowship • 429
American Society of Microbiology & National Center for Infectious Diseases Post Doctoral Research Associates Program • 348
American Water Works Association/Larson Aquatic Research Support Scholarship • 288
American Water Works Association/Thomas R. Camp Memorial Scholarship • 289
Blue Cross Blue Shield of Michigan Foundation Student Award Program • 416
Campus Safety Scholarship (G/UG) • 293
Center for Indoor Air Research Postdoctoral Fellowship • 449
Chest Foundation Clinical Research Fellowship Award • 450
Clinical Pharmacy Post-PharmD Fellowship in the Biomedical Sciences • 439
Cooley's Anemia Foundation Research Fellowship • 352
Cystic Fibrosis Fndn. Pilot and Feasibility Awards • 451
Cystic Fibrosis Foundation Clinical Research Grants • 452
Cystic Fibrosis Foundation Student Traineeships (G/UG) • 353
Cystic Fibrosis Foundation Summer Scholarships in Epidemiology • 453
Cystic Fibrosis Foundation/National Institutes of Health Funding Award • 454
Deafness Research Foundation Grants • 455
Doctoral Fellowship Program in Biomedical Engineering • 371
Dr. Sydney Segal Research Grants • 275
Elaine Osborne Jacobson Award for Women Working in Health Care Law • 435
Elizabeth St. Louis Award • 354
Environmental Protection Scholarships (G/UG) • 269
Fellowships in Spinal Cord Injury Research • 280
Fight for Sight- Grants-in-Aid • 295
Fight for Sight-NSPB Postdoctoral Research Fellowships • 296
Fogarty International Center International Research Fellowship • 364
Fogarty International Center International Training and Research Program • 365
Foundation for Science and Disability-Student Grant • 297
Glaxo-Wellcome Literary Award • 448
Glenn Foundation/American Federation for Aging Research Scholarships for Research in the Biology of Aging • 437

Health Information Management/Technology

Heating, Air-Conditioning, and Refrigeration Mechanics

Historic Preservation and Conservation

History

Harold W. Rosenthal Fellowship in International Relations • 374

Harry S Truman Library Institute Research Grants • 488

Harry S Truman Library Institute Dissertation Year Fellowships • 489

Harry S Truman Library Institute Scholar's Award • 490

Harry S Truman Library Institute Dissertation Year Fellowships • 491

Helen Darcovich Memorial Endowment Fund Doctoral Fellowship • 409

Humane Studies Fellowships (G/UG) • 384

Institute of Electrical and Electronics Engineers Fellowship in Electrical History • 422

J.C. Geilfuss Fellowship • 405

Lillian Sholtis Brunner Summer Fellowship • 484

Mary Isabel Sibley Fellowship for Greek and French Studies • 332

Mesopotamian Fellowship • 483

Michael Dorosh Fund Master's Fellowship • 408

NEH Fellowships • 321

Pi Gamma Mu Scholarship • 392

Roosevelt Institute Grant-in-Aid • 486

Shelby Cullum Davis Center for Historical Studies Visiting Fellowship • 492

Winterthur Research Fellowships • 322

Home Economics

Dorothy I. Mitstifer Fellowship • 430

Kappa Omicron Nu National Alumni Fellowship • 431

Kappa Omicron Nu New Initiatives Grant • 432

NEH Fellowships • 321

Winterthur Research Fellowships • 322

Horticulture/Floriculture

American Orchid Society/Orchid Research Grant • 346

Garden Club of America Award in Tropical Botany • 495

Interchange Fellowship and Martin McLaren Scholarship • 496

Sarah Bradley Tyson Memorial Fellowships • 272

Humanities

Abe Fellowship Program • 404

Adelle and Erwin Tomash Fellowship in the History of Information Processing • 391

Amy Louise Hunter Fellowship • 494

Archaeological Institute of America/Kenan T. Erim Award • 323

Bliss Prize Fellowship in Byzantine Studies • 328

Center for Field Research Grants for Field Research • 294

Center for Hellenic Studies Fellowships • 327

DAAD-ALCS Collaborative Research Grants • 497

Doctoral Thesis Fellowship in Ukrainian History • 407

German Historical Institute Dissertation Scholarships • 487

H. F. Guggenheim Foundation Research Grants • 329

Hagley Museum and Library Grants-in-Aid • 308

Harold W. Rosenthal Fellowship in International Relations • 374

Helen Darcovich Memorial Endowment Fund Doctoral Fellowship • 409

Henry Belin du Pont Dissertation Fellowship • 309

Herbert Hoover Presidential Library Association Travel Grants • 498

Humane Studies Fellowships (G/UG) • 384

International Research and Exchanges Board Short-term Travel Grants • 500

Irish Research Funds • 330

Japan Fellowship for Dissertation Workshop • 505

Japan Foundation Doctoral Fellowship • 501

Japan Foundation Research Fellowship • 502

Lyndon Baines Johnson Foundation Grants-in-Aid Research • 503

Mary Isabel Sibley Fellowship for Greek and French Studies • 332

Michael Dorosh Fund Master's Fellowship • 408

Postdoctoral Fellowships in African-American Culture • 499

Postdoctoral Fellowships on Peace and Security in a Changing World • 369

Society Farsarotul Financial Awards (G/UG) • 333

Spencer Postdoctoral Fellowship Program • 411

Transatlantic Research Cooperation between German and American Scholars in the Human and Social Sciences, Economics, and Law • 399

Whiting Fellowships in the Humanities • 504

Women's Research Award • 413

Woodrow Wilson National Fellowship Foundation Women's Studies Dissertation Grant • 506

Interior Design

Mabelle Wilhelmina Boldt Memorial Scholarship • 507

NEH Fellowships • 321

Winterthur Research Fellowships • 322

International Migration

Social Science Research Center International Migration Research Planning Grant • 508

Journalism

Armenian Professional Society of the Bay Area Scholarships (G/UG) • 324

Inter American Press Association Scholarship Fund for Latin American Reporters • 509

Marine Biological Laboratory Science Writing Fellowships Program • 510

National Association of Broadcasters Grants for Research in Broadcasting • 385

Postdoctoral Fellowships on Peace and Security in a Changing World • 369

Landscape Architecture

Center for Advanced Study in the Visual Arts Senior Fellowship Program • 311

Hagley Museum and Library Grants-in-Aid • 308

Henry Belin du Pont Dissertation Fellowship • 309

Japan Foundation Cultural Properties Specialist Fellowship • 310

NEH Fellowships • 321

Robert H. and Clarice Smith Fellowship • 312

Sarah Bradley Tyson Memorial Fellowships • 272

Urban Design Traveling Fellowship Program • 316

Winterthur Research Fellowships • 322

Legal Services

American Bar Foundation Doctoral Dissertation Fellowships in Law and Social Science • 511

American Geophysical Union Horton Research Grant • 284

Doctoral Dissertation Research Grant (HUD) • 334

Doctoral Thesis Fellowship in Ukrainian History • 407

Elaine Osborne Jacobson Award for Women Working in Health Care Law • 435

Helen Darcovich Memorial Endowment Fund Doctoral Fellowship • 409

Humane Studies Fellowships (G/UG) • 384

Michael Dorosh Fund Master's Fellowship • 408

Postdoctoral Fellowships on Peace and Security in a Changing World • 369

Transatlantic Research Cooperation between German and American Scholars in the Human and Social Sciences, Economics, and Law • 399

Library Sciences

Canadian Library Association DaFoe Scholarships • 513

Consortium of College and University Media Centers Research Awards • 383

Doctoral Thesis Fellowship in Ukrainian History • 407

Econo Clad Award for a Young Adult Reading or Literature Program • 521

Helen Darcovich Memorial Endowment Fund Doctoral Fellowship • 409

Information Science Abstracts Research Grants • 516

Institute for Scientific Information Doctoral Dissertation Scholarship • 386

International Research and Exchange Board Special Projects in Library and Information Science • 517

Library and Information Technology Association/ GEAC Scholarship • 518

Michael Dorosh Fund Master's Fellowship • 408

Plenum Scholarship • 519

Pratt-Severn Student Research Award • 387

Sarah Rebecca Reed Scholarship • 512

Seetoo/Chinese American Librarians Association Conference Travel Scholarship • 514

Sheila Suen Lai Scholarship • 515

Special Interest Group/STI BIOSIS Student Award • 388

Special Interest Group/STI Chemical Abstracts Service Student Award • 389

Special Libraries Association Scholarship (G/UG) • 520

UMI Doctoral Dissertation Award • 390

Literature/English/Writing

Armenian Professional Society of the Bay Area Scholarships (G/UG) • 324

Humane Studies Fellowships (G/UG) • 384

International Fellowships in Jewish Culture Program • 340

Mary Isabel Sibley Fellowship for Greek and French Studies • 332

NEH Fellowships • 321

Winterthur Research Fellowships • 322

Mechanical Engineering

ASHRAE Research Grants for Graduate Students • 481

Associated Western Universities-DOE Post-Graduate Fellowship • 290

Associated Western Universities/DOE Faculty Fellowships • 291

Associated Western Universities/DOE Laboratory Graduate Research Fellowships • 292

Blue Cross Blue Shield of Michigan Foundation Student Award Program • 416

Demonstration of Energy-Efficient Developments Scholarship (G/UG) • 417

Foundation for Science and Disability-Student Grant • 297

International Desalination Association Scholarship • 298

Mechanical/Electrical Traveling Fellowship Program • 314

Vertical Flight Foundation Scholarship (G/UG) • 345

Women's Auxiliary to the American Institute of Mining, Metallurgical and Petroleum Engineers Scholarship Loan Fund (G/UG) • 398

Meteorology/Atmospheric Science

Associated Western Universities-DOE Post-Graduate Fellowship • 290

Associated Western Universities/DOE Faculty Fellowships • 291

Associated Western Universities/DOE Laboratory Graduate Research Fellowships • 292

Center for Field Research Grants for Field Research • 294

National Academy of Science Grants-in-Aid of Research (G/UG) • 281

National Center for Atmospheric Research Postdoctoral Research Fellowship • 522

Sigma Xi Grants-in-Aid of Research (G/UG) • 271

Woods Hole Oceanographic Institution Postdoctoral Fellowships • 372

Museum Studies

Ford Foundation Fellowships • 335

Hagley Museum and Library Grants-in-Aid • 308

Henry Belin du Pont Dissertation Fellowship • 309

NEH Fellowships • 321

Winterthur Research Fellowships • 322

Natural Resources

American Geophysical Union Horton Research Grant • 284

American Water Works Association/Abel Wolman Fellowship • 286

American Water Works Association/Holly A. Cornell Scholarship • 287

American Water Works Association/Larson Aquatic Research Support Scholarship • 288

American Water Works Association/Thomas R. Camp Memorial Scholarship • 289

Center for Field Research Grants for Field Research • 294

Center for Indoor Air Research Postdoctoral Fellowship • 449

Demonstration of Energy-Efficient Developments Scholarship (G/UG) • 417

Environmental Protection Scholarships (G/UG) • 269

Gilbert F. White Postdoctoral Fellowships • 402

International Women's Fishing Association Graduate Scholarships in the Marine Sciences • 276

Joseph L. Fisher Dissertation Awards • 403

National Academy of Science Grants-in-Aid of Research (G/UG) • 281

North American Bluebird Society Research Grant • 367

Sarah Bradley Tyson Memorial Fellowships • 272

Shade Tree Research Grants • 523

Sigurd T. Olson Common Loon Research Awards • 524

Natural Sciences

American Oil Chemists' Society Honored Student Awards • 379

International Desalination Association Scholarship • 298

Jane Coffin Childs Memorial Fund for Medical Research Fellowships • 463

Nuclear Science

Associated Western Universities-DOE Post-Graduate Fellowship • 290

Associated Western Universities/DOE Faculty Fellowships • 291

Associated Western Universities/DOE Laboratory Graduate Research Fellowships • 292

Blue Cross Blue Shield of Michigan Foundation Student Award Program • 416

Nursing

Archie Vinitsky ET Scholarship • 535

Blue Cross Blue Shield of Michigan Foundation Student Award Program • 416

Campus Safety Scholarship (G/UG) • 293

Dr. Sydney Segal Research Grants • 275

Elizabeth St. Louis Award • 354

Heart and Stroke Foundation of Canada Nursing Research Fellowships • 457

International Order of the King's Daughters and Sons Health Careers Scholarship (G/UG) • 393

Lillian Sholtis Brunner Summer Fellowship • 484

Marie Newton Sepia Memorial Award • 477

National Association of Pediatric Nurse Associates and Practitioners McNeil Scholarships • 527

Nursing Economic$ Foundation Scholarships • 528

Nursing Scholastic Achievement Scholarship for Lutheran College Students (G/UG) • 525

Oncology Nursing Foundation Doctoral Scholarships • 529

Oncology Nursing Foundation Master's Scholarship • 530

Oncology Nursing Foundation/Ann Olson Memorial Doctoral Scholarship • 531

Oncology Nursing Foundation/Glaxo Wellcome Oncology Master's Scholarship • 526

Oncology Nursing Foundation/Nursing Certification Corporation Master's Scholarship • 532

Oncology Nursing Foundation/Pharmacia and Upjohn, Inc. Master's Scholarship • 533

Oncology Nursing Foundation/Thomas Jordan Doctoral Scholarship • 534

Peace and Conflict Studies

H. F. Guggenheim Foundation Research Grants • 329

Performing Arts

Armenian Professional Society of the Bay Area Scholarships (G/UG) • 324

Dance, Theater, Film, and Playwright Grants (G/UG) • 342

Ford Foundation Fellowships • 335

Kurt Weill Foundation for Music Grants Program • 536

Photojournalism

Consortium of College and University Media Centers Research Awards • 383

Fogarty International Center International Training and Research Program • 365

German Historical Institute Dissertation Scholarships • 487

Gilbert F. White Postdoctoral Fellowships • 402

Gordon Allport Intergroup Relations Prize • 552

Grant Foundation Research Grants • 479

H. F. Guggenheim Foundation Research Grants • 329

Harold W. Rosenthal Fellowship in International Relations • 374

Helen Darcovich Memorial Endowment Fund Doctoral Fellowship • 409

Herbert Hoover Presidential Library Association Travel Grants • 498

Humane Studies Fellowships (G/UG) • 384

International Migration Postdoctoral Fellowships • 548

International Research and Exchanges Board Short-term Travel Grants • 500

Irish Research Funds • 330

Japan Fellowship for Dissertation Workshop • 505

Japan Foundation Doctoral Fellowship • 501

Japan Foundation Research Fellowship • 502

Joseph L. Fisher Dissertation Awards • 403

L.S.B. Leakey Foundation General Research Grants • 277

L.S.B. Leakey Foundation Paleoanthropology Award • 545

Lambda Alpha National Collegiate Honor Society for Anthropology Scholarship Award • 546

Leakey Foundation Fellowship for Great Ape Research and Conservation • 278

Leakey Foundation Study of Foraging Peoples Fellowship • 279

Louise Kidder Early Career Award • 553

Lyndon Baines Johnson Foundation Grants-in-Aid Research • 503

Mary Isabel Sibley Fellowship for Greek and French Studies • 332

Mesopotamian Fellowship • 483

Michael Dorosh Fund Master's Fellowship • 408

Neporany Research Teaching Fellowship • 326

Pi Gamma Mu Scholarship • 392

Population Council Fellowships in Population Study • 400

Population Council Postdoctoral Fellowships in the Social Sciences • 401

Postdoctoral Fellowships in African-American Culture • 499

Postdoctoral Fellowships on Peace and Security in a Changing World • 369

Ruth Satter Memorial Award • 350

Sigma Xi Grants-in-Aid of Research (G/UG) • 271

Social Science Research Center International Migration Research Planning Grant • 508

Social Science Research Council International Peace and Security Research Workshop Competition • 539

Social Science Research Council Sexuality Research Fellowship Program-Dissertation Fellowships • 549

Social Science Research Council Sexuality Research Fellowship Program-Postdoctoral Fellowships • 550

Social Science Research Council Sexuality Research Fellowship Program-Research Advisor/Associate • 551

Society for the Scientific Study of Sexuality Student Research Grant • 370

Spencer Postdoctoral Fellowship Program • 411

Transatlantic Research Cooperation between German and American Scholars in the Human and Social Sciences, Economics, and Law • 399

Women's Research Award • 413

Woodrow Wilson National Fellowship Foundation Women's Studies Dissertation Grant • 506

Social Services

Doctoral Dissertation Research Grant (HUD) • 334

Federation Executive Recruitment and Education Program • 410

Pi Gamma Mu Scholarship • 392

Women's Research Award • 413

Special Education

Association for the Study of Higher Education Dissertation of the Year Award • 406

Elizabeth St. Louis Award • 354

Marie Newton Sepia Memorial Award • 477

Therapy/Rehabilitation

American Association of Orthopaedic Surgeons/ Orthopaedic Research and Education Foundation Fellowship in Health Service Research • 472

Blue Cross Blue Shield of Michigan Foundation Student Award Program • 416

Doreen Pollack Award • 554

Elizabeth St. Louis Award • 354

Fellowships in Spinal Cord Injury Research • 280

Glaxo-Wellcome Literary Award • 448

International Order of the King's Daughters and Sons Health Careers Scholarship (G/UG) • 393

Marie Newton Sepia Memorial Award • 477

Olfactory Research Fund Research Grants • 368

Orthopaedic Research and Education Foundation Career Development Awards • 473

Orthopaedic Research and Education Foundation Clinical Research Awards • 474

Orthopaedic Research and Education Foundation Prospective Clinical Research Proposals • 475

Orthopaedic Research and Education Foundation Research Grants • 476

Trade/Technical Specialties

Travel/Tourism

TV/Radio Broadcasting

Association Affiliation Index—Graduate

▲

Appaloosa Horse Club/Appaloosa Youth Association
Lew & JoAnn Eklund Educational Scholarship
(G/UG) • 274

Daughters of Penelope/Maids of Athena/Order of Ahepa
Daughters of Penelope Graduate Student Award
• 560
Sonja Stefandis Graduate Student Award • 561

Entomological Society of America
John Henry Comstock Graduate Student Award
• 356

Institute of Industrial Engineers
E.J. Sierleja Memorial Fellowship • 423
Institute of Industrial Engineers-Dwight D. Gardner
Scholarship (G/UG) • 424

Japanese-American Citizens League
Henry and Chiyo Kuwahara Creative Arts Scholarship
(G/UG) • 338

Other Student Academic Clubs
Dorothy I. Mitstifer Fellowship • 430
Kappa Omicron Nu National Alumni Fellowship
• 431
Kappa Omicron Nu New Initiatives Grant • 432
Phi Delta Kappa International Graduate Fellowships
in Educational Leadership • 414
Rho Chi Scholarship Program • 441
Tau Beta Pi Fellowships for Graduate Study in
Engineering • 427

Special Libraries Association
Plenum Scholarship • 519

United Ostomy Association
Archie Vinitsky ET Scholarship • 535

EMPLOYMENT EXPERIENCE INDEX—GRADUATE

▲

Community Service
Federation Executive Recruitment and Education
Program • 410

Experience in Career Field
Archie Vinitsky ET Scholarship • 535
Avis Rent-A-Car Scholarship • 556
Clinical Pharmacy Post-PharmD Fellowship in the
Biomedical Sciences • 439
Cystic Fibrosis Foundation Clinical Research Grants
• 452
Cystic Fibrosis Foundation Summer Scholarships in
Epidemiology • 453
Econo Clad Award for a Young Adult Reading or
Literature Program • 521
Glaxo-Wellcome Literary Award • 448
Howard Hughes Medical Institute Postdoctoral
Research Fellowships for Physicians • 357
International Research and Exchange Board Special
Projects in Library and Information Science • 517
Japan Foundation Cultural Properties Specialist
Fellowship • 310
Japan Foundation Research Fellowship • 502
Jennifer Robinson Scholarship • 349
Library and Information Technology Association/
GEAC Scholarship • 518
Mabelle Wilhelmina Boldt Memorial Scholarship
• 507
Marine Biological Laboratory Science Writing
Fellowships Program • 510
National Association of Pediatric Nurse Associates
and Practitioners McNeil Scholarships • 527

Oncology Nursing Foundation Doctoral Scholarships
• 529
Oncology Nursing Foundation Master's Scholarship
• 530
Oncology Nursing Foundation/Nursing Certification
Corporation Master's Scholarship • 532
Plenum Scholarship • 519
Pollock-Krasner Grants • 341
Wellcome Research Travel Grants for United
Kingdom Citizens • 351

Helping Handicapped
Nursing Scholastic Achievement Scholarship for
Lutheran College Students (G/UG) • 525

Journalism
Inter American Press Association Scholarship Fund
for Latin American Reporters • 509
Marine Biological Laboratory Science Writing
Fellowships Program • 510

Teaching
American Foundation for Pharmaceutical Education
Grant Program for New Investigators • 438
Associated Western Universities/DOE Faculty
Fellowships • 291
Grant Foundation Faculty Scholars Program • 415
March of Dimes Research Grants • 466
National Kidney Foundation Young Investigator
Grants • 471

IMPAIRMENT·INDEX—GRADUATE

▲

Hearing Impaired
Foundation for Science and Disability-Student Grant
 • 297
Gallaudet University Alumni Association Graduate
 Fellowship Funds • 562

Physically Disabled
Foundation for Science and Disability-Student Grant
 • 297

Visually Impaired
Foundation for Science and Disability-Student Grant
 • 297
Roy Johnson Trust Graduate School Grants • 563

NATIONAL OR ETHNIC BACKGROUND INDEX–
GRADUATE

▲

Arumanian/Ulacedo-Romanian
Society Farsarotul Financial Awards (G/UG) • 333

Chinese
Li Foundation Fellowships • 566
Seetoo/Chinese American Librarians Association
   Conference Travel Scholarship • 514
Sheila Suen Lai Scholarship • 515

Cypriot
Makarios Scholarship Fund Inc. Scholarships
   (G/UG) • 568

Danish
Awards for Advanced Study or Research in the USA
   • 565

English
Wellcome Research Travel Grants for United
   Kingdom Citizens • 351

Finnish
Awards for Advanced Study or Research in the USA
   • 565

German
Bafoeg for Study Abroad (G/UG) • 574
Feodor-Lynen Research Fellowship for German
   Scholars • 564

Greek
Cyprus Children's Fund Scholarship Endowment
   (G/UG) • 567

Icelandic
Awards for Advanced Study or Research in the USA
   • 565

Indian
Faculty Research Fellowships for Indian Scholars
   • 569
Shastri Faculty Enrichment Fellowship for Indian
   Scholars • 570
Shastri Women & Development Awards for Indians
   • 571

Irish
Wellcome Research Travel Grants for United
   Kingdom Citizens • 351

Latin American/Caribbean
Inter American Press Association Scholarship Fund
   for Latin American Reporters • 509

Norwegian
Awards for Advanced Study or Research in the USA
   • 565

Scottish
Donald Malcolm MacArthur Scholarship (G/UG)
   • 572
James and Mary Dawson Scholarship (G/UG) • 573

Swedish
Awards for Advanced Study or Research in the USA
   • 565

Swiss
Medicus Student Exchange (G/UG) • 575

Religious Affiliation Index–Graduate

▲

Connecticut
Medicus Student Exchange (G/UG) • 575

Delaware
Donald Malcolm MacArthur Scholarship (G/UG)
• 572
Medicus Student Exchange (G/UG) • 575

District of Columbia
Donald Malcolm MacArthur Scholarship (G/UG)
• 572

Maryland
Donald Malcolm MacArthur Scholarship (G/UG)
• 572

New Jersey
Donald Malcolm MacArthur Scholarship (G/UG)
• 572
Medicus Student Exchange (G/UG) • 575

New York
Medicus Student Exchange (G/UG) • 575

North Carolina
Donald Malcolm MacArthur Scholarship (G/UG)
• 572

Pennsylvania
Donald Malcolm MacArthur Scholarship (G/UG)
• 572
Medicus Student Exchange (G/UG) • 575

Vermont
Vermont Incentive Grants (G/UG) • 580

Virginia
Donald Malcolm MacArthur Scholarship (G/UG)
• 572

West Virginia
Donald Malcolm MacArthur Scholarship (G/UG)
• 572

TALENT INDEX—GRADUATE

▲

Art
Dance, Theater, Film, and Playwright Grants (G/UG)
• 342
Automotive
Specialty Equipment Market Association Memorial
    Scholarship Fund (G/UG) • 426
Foreign Language
Medicus Student Exchange (G/UG) • 575
French Language
Mary Isabel Sibley Fellowship for Greek and French
    Studies • 332
Programme Canadian de Bourses de la Francophone
    (G/UG) • 583
Greek Language
Mary Isabel Sibley Fellowship for Greek and French
    Studies • 332
Japanese Language
Japan Foundation Doctoral Fellowship • 501
Japan Foundation Research Fellowship • 502
Leadership
American Association of Cereal Chemists Graduate
    Fellowships • 268
Dorothy I. Mitstifer Fellowship • 430
Federation Executive Recruitment and Education
    Program • 410

Kappa Omicron Nu National Alumni Fellowship
    • 431
Kappa Omicron Nu New Initiatives Grant • 432
Library and Information Technology Association/
    GEAC Scholarship • 518
Music/Singing
Kurt Weill Foundation for Music Grants Program
    • 536
Numismatics
American Numismatic Society Graduate Fellowships
    • 582
Photography/Photogrammetry/Filmmaking
Dance, Theater, Film, and Playwright Grants (G/UG)
    • 342
Writing
A.L. Simmons Scholarship Fund • 555
A.Verville Fellowship • 579
D. Scott Rogo Award for Parapsychological Literature
    • 547
Dance, Theater, Film, and Playwright Grants (G/UG)
    • 342
Gordon Allport Intergroup Relations Prize • 552
Pratt-Severn Student Research Award • 387

GETTING INTO COLLEGE ISN'T AS HARD AS YOU THINK—AS LONG AS YOU THINK PETERSON'S!

Get on line at petersons.com for a jump start on your college search.

- Search our college database
- Get financial aid tips
- Browse our bookstore

And when you're ready to apply, you're ready for ApplyToCollege.com!

ApplyToCollege.com is our **free** online college application service that lets you apply to *more colleges than anyone else on the Internet!*

Why ApplyToCollege.com?
- Fill out one application for nearly 1,000 colleges!
- Talk with admissions deans!
- Keep track of your applications!
- IT'S FREE!

Peterson's is on your side with everything you need to get ready for college. And it's all just a mouse click away!

PETERSON'S
Princeton, New Jersey
www.petersons.com
609-243-9111

Wait! There's more!➔

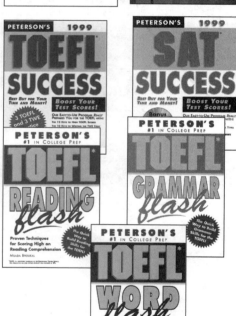